Better Homes and Gardens®

healthy family
COOKBOOK

Better Homes and Gardens® Books
Des Moines, Iowa

BETTER HOMES AND GARDENS® BOOKS
An Imprint of Meredith® Books

HEALTHY FAMILY COOKBOOK
Editor: Mary Williams
Contributing Editor: Marlene Brown
Associate Art Director: Tom Wegner
Test Kitchen Product Supervisor: Marilyn Cornelius
Food Stylists: Lynn Blanchard, Jennifer Peterson, Janet Pittman
Photographers: Mike Dieter, Scott Little
Electronic Production Coordinator: Paula Forest
Production Manager: Douglas Johnston

Vice President and Editorial Director: Elizabeth P. Rice
Executive Editor: Kay M. Sanders
Art Director: Ernest Shelton
Managing Editor: Christopher Cavanaugh
Test Kitchen Director: Sharon Stilwell

President, Book Group: Joseph J. Ward
Vice President, Retail Marketing: Jamie L. Martin
Vice President, Direct Marketing: Timothy Jarrell

On the cover: Roasted Pepper Pasta with Basil Pesto (see recipe, page 181)

Meredith Corporation
Chairman of the Executive Committee: E.T. Meredith III
Chairman of the Board and Chief Executive Officer: Jack D. Rehm
President and Chief Operating Officer: William T. Kerr

WE CARE!

All of us at Better Homes and Gardens® Books are dedicated to providing you with the
information and ideas you need to create delicious food. We welcome your questions,
comments, or suggestions. Please write to us at: Better Homes and Gardens® Books,
Cookbook Editorial Department, LN 112, 1716 Locust Street, Des Moines, IA 50309-3023.

Our seal assures you that every recipe in *Healthy Family Cookbook*
has been tested in the Better Homes and Gardens® Test Kitchen.
This means that each recipe is practical and reliable, and meets our
highest standards of taste appeal. We guarantee your satisfaction
with this book for as long as you own it.

INTRODUCTION

Cooking family-pleasing meals night after night challenges the best of cooks. And, for those who aim to serve healthy and great-tasting dishes, the task becomes even more difficult. But, with the aid of the HEALTHY FAMILY COOKBOOK, high-flavor, low-fat cooking is easy. In this collection, you will find more than 365 recipes, from appetizers to desserts, that were developed specifically for families like yours. These recipes were trimmed of fat, calories, and sodium with no sacrifice in flavor. Once your family samples the enticing appetizers, mouth-watering main dishes, colorful side dishes, and sweetly satisfying desserts, they'll be convinced that light eating is delectable eating. And you'll have the pleasure of offering delicious dishes that help the ones you love live healthier and longer.

CONTENTS

Lighten Up For a Lifetime

If you're interested in healthier cooking for your family and in lightening up on fat, cholesterol, and sodium, you've come to the right cookbook! Though we all know that eating lighter is the best route to lifelong good health and well-being, it's often a challenge to persuade loved ones that it can be delicious, too. So, we packed this chapter with information to help get you and your family on the road to lighter eating.

It's true that all of the recipes in this book were specially designed to be light, but they also had to be great tasting, convenient to prepare, and as appealing as your old favorites. Discover the secrets for making recipes lighter without eliminating their taste appeal.

TECHNIQUES TO GET YOU INTO THE LIGHT COOKING HABIT

Adjusting to a lifestyle of light eating is really a simple matter of using some smart cooking techniques and substituting some low-fat ingredients for the high-fat ones. You can apply these techniques to many of your own favorite recipes so that you still can enjoy them, but in a lighter style.

Cooking Smart

● When sautéing or stir-frying, you need a lot less fat than you think. Use a nonstick skillet or wok, then a small amount of margarine or, better yet, an aerosol cooking spray. If you prefer to use oil, olive oil is a good low-cholesterol choice.

● Opt for grilling or broiling tender cuts of meat rather than sautéing or pan-frying.

● For fish or seafood, try broiling, grilling, poaching, steaming, or baking it "dry," without the fat.

● Fat often serves the purpose of preventing foods from drying out, particularly during baking or broiling/grilling. Start by brushing a small amount of oil or margarine over the food; then, during the baking or grilling process, use a low-fat salad dressing or marinade, mustard, chutney, fruit preserves, or salsa to keep the food moist.

● Often a recipe begins with sautéing or browning vegetables or meat, then adding liquid or vegetables to braise the food. Start by using just a teaspoon or two of fat or nonstick spray coating for browning in a nonstick skillet, then add a couple of teaspoons of water and cover, cooking the food over low heat, stirring occasionally, till softened.

● Be sure to drain off any excess fat from sautéing or browning before adding remaining ingredients.

● Trim meat of all visible fat before cooking; remove skin and fat from poultry. Use tuna packed in water, not oil.

● To cook vegetables quickly and preserve their texture and vitamins, opt for steaming or microwaving.

● If you have more time to cook your vegetables, try roasting them to bring out their natural sweetness. Prepare more than you need as a side dish; the extras can be tossed into a salad or pasta dish the next day.

● Cook fruits and vegetables in their skins whenever possible to preserve fiber and nutrients.

● To cut down on salt, never add salt during the cooking process. Wait until you serve the dish, and salt it at the table with a low-sodium product, if needed.

● Rinse and drain canned shrimp and canned vegetables before adding them to a recipe; you'll remove much of their salt.

● Take advantage of low-sodium chicken broth for stir-frying, sautéing, braising, or poaching meat or fish.

● Be sure to measure ingredients carefully, especially the high-fat ones such as oil and butter.

Ingredient Substitutions

- Rather than making meat the focus of every meal, use smaller portions (2 to 4 ounces per serving) and add pasta, rice, beans, or vegetables to "flesh out" your entrées.

- Nowadays, for many of your favorite condiments, there is a low-fat or fat-free product that you can substitute. Try fat-free or low-fat mayonnaise, sour cream, yogurt, milk, cottage cheese, salad dressings, pasta sauces, and fruit spreads.

- If you are a fan of sausage, bacon, or ham, try the turkey-based version for fewer calories and less saturated fat. When a recipe calls for bacon, lean smoked ham is a substitute, and you still will get a rich, smoky flavor.

- When choosing meat cuts, select those that look lean, without a lot of fat marbling. A good rule of thumb is to look for cuts with the word "loin" or "round" in the name. Figure on 3 to 4 ounces of cooked meat per serving. (Six to 8 ounces is all we need each day.)

- Substitute ground turkey breast or chicken breast for ground beef or pork in casseroles, meat loaf, and chili recipes.

- If you like the convenience of purchasing cooked meats from your deli, opt for rotisserie-style chicken and extra-lean deli-sliced turkey or roast beef.

- Cheeses, both hard and soft varieties, come in lower-fat and fat-free varieties. As a rule of thumb, aim for no more than 5 fat grams per ounce. Many of these products also are low in sodium.

- To add fiber to recipes, substitute whole-wheat flour for up to half of the all-purpose flour called for in a recipe.

- When buying breads, crackers, or grain products, read the labels. The first ingredient should read whole-wheat or other whole-grain flour (wheat flour is not good enough).

- For extra fiber, experiment with a variety of grains, such as couscous, barley, brown rice, oatmeal, rye, wild rice, and bulgur, as well as whole-wheat pasta, corn tortillas, and rye crackers.

- Include both fresh and dried fruits in dishes other than desserts. Add them to dips, purée them for entrée sauces, or add them to salads, cold pasta dishes, side dishes, casseroles, or meat stuffings.

- To incorporate more dark green, leafy vegetables, add lettuces such as spinach and kale to sandwiches, salads, and vegetable side dishes and stir-fries.

- Shredded cabbage, especially red cabbage, is a high-fiber addition to salads, stir-fries, sandwich fillings, soups, and even meat loaf.

- Befriend those deep yellow and dark green fruits and vegetables that are rich in vitamin A, such as apricots, cantaloupe, carrots, peaches, sweet potatoes, winter squashes, spinach, broccoli, and Swiss chard.
- Low-fat or nonfat yogurt can replace high-fat ingredients such as sour cream and mayonnaise in soups, sauces, dips, and the like.
- Evaporated skim milk, low-fat or nonfat milk, or buttermilk work well in place of whole milk in rich sauces and soups and in baked items.
- Substitute two egg whites or ¼ cup fat-free egg product for one whole egg in recipes.
- Look for fat-free refried beans and bean soups.
- Purchase canned fruits packed in their own juices or frozen, loose-pack fruits that have no added sugar or syrup.
- Read cereal labels carefully; even low-fat granola calories add up quickly, because the serving sizes listed typically are smaller than what you normally would consume in a serving. Opt for high-fiber cereals with few additions of nuts, fruit, or "clusters" of high-sugar or high-fat ingredients.
- Low-fat cottage cheese is a good substitute for ricotta cheese.
- Use just small amounts of high-fat foods to flavor dishes; be stingy with such ingredients as avocados, coconut, cheese, and nuts.

Fat-Free Flavor-Makers

One reason we enjoy high-fat foods so much is because fat adds flavor. When the fat is reduced, however, you have a wonderful opportunity to use spices, herbs, and condiments that have intriguing new tastes to offer. If you haven't tried some of these before, you'll be pleasantly surprised at the effect they can have on your taste buds. Keep a good assortment of the following on hand to flavor-up your fat-reduced recipes.

- Lemon, lime, and orange juices
- Low-sodium soy sauce and teriyaki sauce
- Low-sugar fruit spreads
- Red and green onions or shallots

- Salsas—all types are low in sodium and fat
- Chutneys—mango, peach, and others
- Fresh cilantro, parsley, or watercress
- Fresh or dried herbs, from basil to thyme
- Dried herb mixtures, such as curry powder, fines herbes, Cajun seasoning, or Beau Monde seasoning
- Bottled hot pepper sauces
- Salt-free herb seasonings in a variety of flavors
- Lemon-pepper and garlic-pepper seasonings
- Low-fat or nonfat salad dressings
- Mild flavored vinegars such as balsamic, rice, or raspberry
- Fresh garlic
- Fresh grated gingerroot and horseradish
- Fresh grated citrus peel (lemon, lime, orange, and grapefruit)
- Mustards in many types, from mild to hot
- Fresh or canned chilies, from mild to hair-raising

READING THOSE NEW FOOD LABELS

As consumers, we need to take advantage of the fact that more information is available on packaging than ever before. Recent legislation has helped streamline the type of ingredient information and nutritional data that food packaging must contain.

The best part is that virtually all processed food products will have nutritional information on their labels. Fresh fruits and vegetables, fresh meats, fish, poultry, and items from the deli case are not required to carry nutritional labeling, although some purveyors voluntarily will offer nutrient information. Ask your grocer if a nutritional breakdown is available on these items.

Look for labels that are headlined "Nutrition Facts," which indicates that the new labeling requirements have been met. Here are some of the new features you'll find on a typical food label.

• Only foods that meet government standards will be able to make label claims of "fat-free," "light," "low-fat," and "cholesterol free." For example, only those foods that are at least 97 percent free of fat will be able to use the fat-free claim on the label. This

Nutrition Facts
Cornflakes
Serving Size: 1⅓ cups (30 g) with ½ cup 2% milk

Amount Per Serving

Calories 177	Calories From Fat 18

	% Daily Value*
Total Fat 2 g	4%
Saturated Fat 1 g	7%
Cholesterol 9 mg	3%
Sodium 368 mg	15%
Total Carbohydrate 32 g	11%
Dietary Fiber 1 g	2%
Sugars 2 g	
Protein 7 g	

Vitamin A	47%	•	Vitamin C	28%
Calcium	13%	•	Iron	13%

*Percent Daily Values are based on a 2,000 calorie diet. Your daily values may be higher or lower depending on your calorie needs:

		Calories	2,000	2,500
Total Fat	Less than		65 g	80 g
Sat Fat	Less than		20 g	25 g
Cholesterol	Less than		300 mg	300 mg
Sodium	Less than		2,400 mg	2,400 mg
Total Carbohydrate			300 g	375 g
Fiber			25 g	30 g

Calories per gram:
Fat 9 • Carbohydrates 4 • Protein 4

will apply to meat and poultry products as well as nonmeat products.

• Standard serving sizes will be used to determine a food's calorie, fat, and nutrient count. Regulations stipulate that serving sizes must reflect amounts consumed by an average person over 4 years old.

• The FDA will allow health claims to be made in only four areas: those linking fat and cancer, calcium and

osteoporosis, fat and cardiovascular disease, and sodium and hypertension.

• For sugar, a claim of "no sugars added" will be made only on products to which no sugar of any kind (including fructose, concentrated fruit juice, and the like) has been added during processing. Also, grams of sugar per serving will appear on the nutrient breakdown.

• In the past, some products carried the term "cholesterol free" even though they contained saturated fat that has been shown to raise blood cholesterol levels. Soon, a cholesterol-free product will not be able to use this type of claim if it contains a specific amount of saturated fat.

The fat information you'll find on the new package labels will include the amount of total fat and saturated fat contained in a serving of food. It will be listed both in grams and as a "% Daily Value" on the label. The daily value percentage will tell you how much fat one serving of the food would contribute to a daily diet of 2,000 calories.

You can use these figures to determine how much fat and saturated fat the food will contribute to your diet. For example, if the label says a food has 6 grams of fat and the daily value is 10 percent, it means that 6 grams of fat is one-tenth (10 percent) of the total daily fat recommended for a person consuming 2,000 calories per day.

Also listed on the nutritional label will be calories from fat—the number of calories supplied by the fat in one serving of the food. (This number is computed by multiplying the grams of fat by 9 calories per gram.)

Here's a dictionary of the fat claims you'll find on labels and what they mean.

- **Fat Free**—contains less than 0.5 grams of fat per serving (it cannot have an added ingredient that is fat or oil).
- **Low Fat**—No more than 3 grams of fat per serving and per 100 grams of food.
- **Fat Free and Percent Fat Free**—these terms may be used only to describe the foods that meet FDA definition of "low fat" as previously described.
- **Reduced Fat**—no more than half of the fat of a similar food used as a comparison; for example, "Reduced fat, 50 percent less fat than our regular oatmeal cookie. Fat content has been reduced from 10 grams to 5 grams." The FDA says these claims must exceed 3 grams of fat per serving.
- **Low in Saturated Fat**—can be used to describe a food that has no more than 1 gram of saturated fat per serving and no more than 15 percent of calories from saturated fat.
- **Reduced Saturated Fat**—no more than 50 percent of the saturated fat than the comparison food.
- **Less Saturated Fat**—offers a reduction of 25 percent or more.

USING THE FOOD PYRAMID TO KEEP IN BALANCE

When you're planning a menu, it's a good idea to become familiar with your family's actual food needs each day. Don't worry—it's not as difficult as it sounds! An easy way to do this is to refer to the Food Guide Pyramid, designed by the U.S. Department of Agriculture (see below). It's a great tool for gaining a healthy perspective on how your food choices need to be balanced over the course of a day.

The pyramid displays each food group with the recommended daily number of servings, beginning with the Breads and Cereals group at its base. You need the most servings from this group. The fruit and vegetable group is on the next tier of the pyramid, and it's second in the number of servings needed. Meats, other proteins, and dairy products have been given less importance in terms of the amounts you need, because your body requires fewer portions of these foods. Fats and sugars, found at the top of the pyramid, can be used in very small amounts to maintain good health.

In short, the pyramid sums up the basic principles of the U.S. Dietary Guidelines.

- Eat a variety of foods.
- Maintain a healthy weight.
- Choose a diet low in fat, saturated fat, and cholesterol.
- Choose a diet with plenty of vegetables, fruits, and grain products.
- Use sugars only in moderation.
- Use salt and sodium only in moderation.

FOOD GUIDE PYRAMID
A Guide to Daily Food Choices

Simple tools such as the Food Guide Pyramid, the Dietary Guidelines, and the new food labels can be extremely helpful in daily food planning. Here are some tips to use when you are shopping for food.

• When buying groceries, visualize the food pyramid, and remember to include at least a minimum number of servings from each of the five food groups daily.

• Read labels to find foods that are a good source of, or are high in, certain vitamins, minerals, and fiber.

• For fresh fruits and vegetables, look for voluntary nutrient listings posted in the grocer's produce section.

• Check out the serving size and calories per serving on the label to help achieve your ideal calorie intake for the day.

• Take note of the daily value percentages on the label for fat, saturated fat, and cholesterol; aim to keep your daily intake below 100 percent.

• Check the label for the amount of sugars (listed in grams) in one serving of the food.

• Note the sodium values on the label, especially if you have a health problem, such as high blood pressure.

HOW TO LIGHTEN UP A RECIPE

Once you've reviewed the tools we used to lighten up the fat, cholesterol, and sodium in our recipes, you'll be on your way to de-fatting your favorites. The best part is, when you become accustomed to eating this way, you probably won't be tempted to cook the "old" way again!

Read through this chapter several times to familiarize yourself with the ingredients that are high in fat, cholesterol, and sodium. Obviously, some recipes cannot be revamped without losing their special character; save those for special occasions. You'll be surprised at how many of your favorite foods can be adjusted—often for the better—to a new, lighter version.

Use our recommended fat-free flavoring ingredients and the Food Guide Pyramid to direct you in de-fatting recipes. Check food labels on your ingredients for fat, cholesterol, and sodium content. And remember these three guidelines:

1. Change to a lighter cooking technique (see our hints on page 7).

2. Reduce the high-fat, high-sugar, and high-sodium ingredients, or eliminate them entirely.

3. Find a low-fat substitute for a high-fat ingredient.

Here are three examples of classic recipes and their updated counterparts from this book.

Eggs Benedict
(Classic version)

8 **slices Canadian-style bacon**
4 **eggs**
½ **cup margarine or butter**
3 **beaten egg yolks**
1 **tablespoon water**
1 **tablespoon lemon juice**
   Dash salt
   Dash white pepper
2 **English muffins, split and toasted, or 4 rusks**

In a 12-inch skillet lightly brown Canadian-style bacon over medium heat for 3 minutes on each side. Cover and keep warm. Lightly grease a medium saucepan or skillet. Add water to half-fill the pan; bring to boiling. Reduce the heat to simmering. Break 1 egg into a small dish. Carefully slide egg into simmering water, holding the lip of the dish as close to the water as possible. Repeat with remaining eggs, allowing each egg an equal amount of space. Simmer eggs, uncovered, about 5 minutes or till yolk is just set. Remove with a slotted spoon. Place eggs in a large pan of warm water to keep them warm while preparing the Hollandaise Sauce.

Cut margarine or butter into thirds and bring it to room temperature. In the top of a double boiler, combine egg yolks, water, lemon juice, salt, and pepper. Add one piece of the margarine or butter. Place over boiling water (upper pan should not touch water). Cook, stirring rapidly, till margarine melts and sauce begins to thicken. Add the remaining margarine or butter, a piece at a time, stirring constantly. Cook and stir till sauce thickens (1 to 2 minutes). Remove from heat at once.

If desired, butter the muffin halves. To serve, top each English muffin half or rusk with 2 slices of bacon and an egg; spoon Hollandaise Sauce over eggs. Makes 4 servings.

Nutritional facts per serving: 477 calories, 36 g total fat (8 g saturated fat), 400 mg cholesterol, 1,220 mg sodium, 15 g carbohydrate, 0 g fiber, 22 g protein. **Daily values:** 61% vitamin A, 19% vitamin C, 8% calcium, 15% iron.

To lighten this classic recipe, we created a new version of the Hollandaise Sauce that uses a nonfat mayonnaise dressing and nonfat milk. We eliminated the Canadian bacon, instead opting for spinach and tomato slices. We added herbs, including dill and paprika, and some Dijon mustard to punch up the flavor and lend character to the de-fatted sauce. As

long as you don't boil the sauce, there's no need for a double boiler, either.

Along with the recommendations of the Dietary Guidelines, this new version cuts down on the protein and adds a vegetable serving, which also increases the fiber content. The eggs and butter in the original sauce also were eliminated.

Benedict-Style Eggs Florentine
(Updated version)

 4 **medium eggs**
 ½ **cup nonfat mayonnaise dressing**
 ¼ **cup skim milk**
 1 **teaspoon lemon juice**
 1 **teaspoon Dijon-style mustard**
 ¼ **teaspoon dried dillweed**
 ¼ **teaspoon paprika**
 2 **English muffins, split and toasted**
 4 **slices tomato**
 ½ **of a 10-ounce package frozen leaf spinach, cooked and drained**
 Fresh dill, optional

Fill a large skillet half-full of water. Bring to boiling; reduce heat to simmering. Break one egg into a small dish or measuring cup; slide the egg into simmering water. Repeat with remaining eggs, keeping eggs separate. Simmer eggs, uncovered, about 5 minutes or just till yolks are set.

Meanwhile, for sauce, in a small saucepan combine mayonnaise dressing, milk, lemon juice, mustard, dill, and paprika. Whisk over medium-low heat just till mixture is heated through; do not boil. Remove from heat.

For each serving, arrange one muffin half on a serving plate; top with a slice of tomato. Add ¼ of the cooked spinach; top with 1 tablespoon sauce. With a slotted spoon, transfer one of the poached eggs to cover spinach and sauce. Spoon an additional 2 tablespoons of the sauce mixture over egg. Garnish with fresh dill, if desired. Serve immediately. Makes 4 servings.

Nutritional facts per serving: 190 calories, 6 g total fat (2 g saturated fat), 213 mg cholesterol, 649 mg sodium, 24 g carbohydrate, 1 g fiber, 10 g protein. **Daily values:** 40% vitamin A, 17% vitamin C, 12% calcium, 14% iron.

Desserts are another food category where fat and cholesterol are notorious companions in many classic recipes. Is there hope for the chocolate lover? Here we'll take a classic recipe for brownies and show you how we lightened it for guilt-free enjoyment and turned it into a sundae to boot!

Brownie Sundaes
(Classic version)

½ **cup margarine or butter**
2 **ounces unsweetened chocolate**
1 **cup sugar**
2 **eggs**
1 **teaspoon vanilla**
¾ **cup all-purpose flour**
½ **cup chopped nuts**
1 **quart any flavor ice-cream**
½ **cup fudge ice cream topping**
½ **cup chopped nuts**

In a medium saucepan melt margarine and chocolate over low heat. Remove from heat. Stir in sugar, eggs, and vanilla. Beat lightly by hand just till combined. Stir in flour and ½ cup nuts. Spread batter into an 8x8x2-inch baking pan. Bake in a 350° oven for 30 minutes. Cool on a wire rack. To serve,

cut into 12 rectangles. Place a brownie in a dessert dish; split vertically. Top with a scoop of ice cream. Top each with ice-cream topping and nuts. Makes 12 servings.

Nutritional facts per serving: 390 calories, 24 g total fat (7 g saturated fat), 55 mg cholesterol, 146 mg sodium, 43 g carbohydrate, 1 g fiber, 6 g protein.
Daily values: 16% vitamin A, 1% vitamin C, 7% calcium, 8% iron.

In our updated version, we used unsweetened cocoa powder instead of unsweetened chocolate to reduce the fat. We cut the margarine in half, reduced the sugar, and added water to moisten the batter. We also used 2 egg whites in place of the 2 whole eggs to eliminate the cholesterol, and beat the egg whites until light to give the brownies volume. We switched the high-fat ice cream to frozen yogurt and skipped the nuts.

Frozen Yogurt Brownie Sundaes
(Updated version)

Nonstick spray coating
1 **cup all-purpose flour**
¼ **cup unsweetened cocoa powder**
1 **teaspoon baking powder**
¼ **teaspoon baking soda**
¼ **cup margarine**
⅔ **cup sugar**
½ **teaspoon vanilla**
⅔ **cup cold water**
2 **egg whites**
1 **quart any flavor frozen yogurt**
½ **cup chocolate syrup**

Spray 12 muffin cups with nonstick spray coating. In a medium mixing bowl stir together flour, cocoa powder, baking powder, and baking soda; set aside. In a large mixing bowl beat margarine on medium speed for 30 seconds. Add the ⅔ cup sugar and vanilla; beat on medium speed till well combined. Add dry ingredients and cold water alternately, beating on low speed after each addition. Thoroughly wash beaters. In a small bowl beat egg whites till stiff peaks form (tips stand straight). Fold egg whites into flour mixture. Spoon dough into prepared muffin cups, filling ¾ full. Bake in a 375° oven for 13 to 15 minutes or till brownies spring back when lightly touched. Cool 2 minutes in pan; turn out onto a wire rack to cool. To serve, place a brownie in a dessert dish; split vertically. Top with a scoop of frozen yogurt. Spoon 2 teaspoons chocolate syrup over each. Makes 12 servings.

Nutritional facts per serving: 224 calories, 5 g total fat (1 g saturated fat), 0 mg cholesterol, 118 mg sodium, 41 g carbohydrate, 0 g fiber, 5 g protein.
Daily values: 4% vitamin A, 0% vitamin C, 10% calcium, 6% iron.

Eggnog is one of our most popular holiday beverages, yet it's fraught with high-fat ingredients. But some clever substitutions save the day—and the character and flavor—of traditional eggnog.

Eggnog
(Classic version)

6 beaten eggs
2¼ to 2½ cups milk
⅓ cup sugar
1 teaspoon vanilla
1 cup whipping cream
2 tablespoons sugar
Ground nutmeg

In a large heavy saucepan mix eggs, milk, and ⅓ cup sugar. Cook and stir over medium heat till mixture coats a metal spoon. Remove from heat. Cool quickly by placing pan in a sink or

bowl of ice water and stirring for 1 to 2 minutes. Stir in vanilla. Chill for 4 to 24 hours.

At serving time, in a bowl whip cream and 2 tablespoons sugar till soft peaks form. Transfer chilled egg mixture to a punch bowl. Fold in whipped cream mixture. Serve at once. Sprinkle each serving with nutmeg. Makes about 10 (4-ounce) servings.

Nutritional facts per serving: 191 calories, 13 g total fat (7 g saturated fat), 166 mg cholesterol, 74 mg sodium, 13 g carbohydrate, 0 g fiber, 6 g protein.
Daily values: 19% vitamin A, 1% vitamin C, 8% calcium, 3% iron.

We cut the number of eggs in half and also included the option of using a frozen egg substitute. The whole milk easily could be changed to skim or low-fat milk. We went up on the sugar just a bit and doubled the vanilla to bring out the traditional flavor. We achieved a big fat and calorie savings by switching from heavy whipping cream to frozen nondairy whipped topping. It's still appropriate as a make-ahead beverage; you just add the whipped topping to each mug at serving time.

Fluffy Light Eggnog
(Updated version)

6 cups skim or low-fat milk
3 eggs or ¾ cup refrigerated or frozen egg product, thawed
Dash salt
½ cup sugar
2 teaspoons vanilla
¾ cup frozen light whipped dessert topping, thawed
Ground nutmeg

In a large saucepan heat milk till hot (do not boil). Remove saucepan from heat. In a large heatproof bowl beat together eggs and salt using a wire whisk; gradually add sugar. Slowly stir in hot milk, beating constantly. Return mixture to saucepan; cook and stir over medium-low heat till mixture thinly coats a metal spoon, about 12 to 17 minutes. (Do not boil.) Remove from heat; stir in vanilla. Set pan in a bowl of ice cubes; let stand about 5 minutes, stirring occasionally, to cool. Chill mixture till serving time. To serve, pour into mugs; top each serving with 1 tablespoon of the nondairy topping and a sprinkling of nutmeg. Makes 12 (½-cup) servings.

Nutritional facts per serving: 94 calories, 2 g total fat (0 g saturated fat), 55 mg cholesterol, 69 mg sodium, 14 g carbohydrate, 0 g fiber, 4 g protein.
Daily values: 7% vitamin A, 1% vitamin C, 8% calcium, 1% iron.

USING OUR NUTRITIONAL ANALYSIS

You'll notice that each of our lightened recipes is followed by a helpful nutritional analysis. It gives you the number of calories per serving, the amount of protein, carbohydrates, and fat the food contains, along with the sodium and fiber content.

Fat gram information is broken down into three categories. You can find information on the total number of fat grams, along with the amount of saturated fat grams and milligrams of cholesterol contained in the total amount of fat. If you have special dietary considerations, this information should be helpful. Be sure to consult your doctor about your own or your family's special dietary requirements, as well.

Remember that the nutrients contained in a particular food or recipe should be considered as part of a full day's calories, fat, and other nutrients.

INGREDIENT EQUIVALENTS AND SUBSTITUTIONS

Refer to this list in order to make some smart substitutions in these recipes and your own favorites. It's a handy guide that will steer you away from the high-fat ingredients and over to the low-fat or nonfat ones.

Smart Fat Substitutes

1 whole egg = 2 egg whites or ¼ cup frozen egg substitute, thawed

1 cup whole milk = 1 cup skim or low-fat milk

1 cup buttermilk = 1 cup low-fat buttermilk

1 cup cottage cheese = 1 cup low-fat cottage cheese

1 cup mayonnaise or salad dressing = 1 cup low-fat or nonfat mayonnaise or salad dressing

1 cup dairy sour cream = 1 cup nonfat or low-fat dairy sour cream or low-fat or nonfat yogurt

1 ounce unsweetened baking chocolate = 3 tablespoons unsweetened cocoa powder

Ingredient Equivalents

Use these ingredient equivalents to take the guesswork out of measuring.

Ingredient	Equivalent
Fruit	
1 cup sliced apple	1 medium apple
½ cup mashed banana	1 medium banana
2 cups sliced banana	3 medium bananas
3 tablespoons lemon juice	1 medium lemon
2 teaspoons shredded lemon peel	1 medium lemon
2 tablespoons lime juice	1 medium lime
1½ teaspoons shredded lime peel	1 medium lime
Vegetables	
1 pound (2½ cups) dry black, kidney, or garbanzo beans	6⅔ cups cooked
1 pound (2⅓ cups) navy beans	6 cups cooked
8 ounces fresh broccoli	3 cups cut up
1 pound cabbage (1 small head)	5 cups shredded
1 pound carrots (6–8 medium)	3 cups shredded or 2¼ cups chopped
1 bulb garlic	14 cloves
1 pound (1 head) lettuce	6 cups torn
1 medium onion	½ cup chopped
1 pound potatoes (3 medium)	2 cups cubed cooked or 1¾ cups mashed
1 pound fresh spinach	1½ cups cooked
1 pound tomatoes	1½ cups peeled and chopped
1 pound (3 medium) zucchini	3½ cups sliced or chopped or 4 cups shredded

Ingredient	Equivalent
Crumbs/Cereals	
¾ cup soft or ¼ cup fine dry bread crumbs	1 slice
1 cup finely crushed cracker crumbs	14 graham cracker squares, 28 saltines, 15 gingersnaps, or 22 vanilla wafers
1 cup uncooked macaroni	2½ cups cooked
3 cups uncooked noodles	3 cups cooked
8 ounces uncooked spaghetti	4 cups cooked
1 cup uncooked long grain rice	3 cups cooked
1 cup quick-cooking rice	2 cups cooked
¼ cup unpopped popcorn	5 cups popped corn
Meat/Eggs	
4 whole eggs or 8 egg yolks	1 cup eggs or 8 egg whites
4 ounces shredded cheese	1 cup shredded
1 pound boneless raw meat	2 cups cooked and chopped
1 pound cooked meat	3 cups chopped

Quick Ingredient Substitutions

If you don't have:	Substitute:
1 tablespoon cornstarch (used for thickening)	2 tablespoon all-purpose flour
1 teaspoon baking powder	¼ teaspoon baking soda + ½ cup buttermilk or sour milk (to replace part of liquid called for)
1 cup buttermilk	1 tablespoon lemon juice or vinegar + whole milk to make 1 cup (let stand 5 minutes) or 1 cup plain yogurt
1 cup nonfat milk	⅓ cup nonfat dry milk + ¾ cup water
2 cups tomato sauce	¾ cup tomato paste + 1 cup water
1 cup tomato juice	½ cup tomato sauce + ½ cup water
1 tablespoon lemon juice	1 tablespoon lime juice or white vinegar
1 clove garlic	⅛ teaspoon garlic powder or minced dried garlic
1 tablespoon chopped fresh herbs	1 teaspoon crushed dried herb
1 small onion	1 teaspoon onion powder or 1 tablespoon minced dried onion, rehydrated
1 teaspoon dry mustard	1 tablespoon prepared mustard
1 teaspoon finely shredded lemon peel	½ teaspoon lemon extract
1 cup honey	1¼ cups granulated sugar

Appealing Appetizers & Snacks

Bite-size meatballs, tiny pastries, creamy dips, and refreshing beverages make flavorful preludes to any meal. The tantalizing morsels on the following pages offer healthful alternatives to the fat-laden, high-sodium foods that often serve as appetizers and snacks. Looking for a low-fat dip? Try Roasted Garlic Spread with Chives—it's sure to be a hit with family members of all ages. Company coming? Spinach and Blue Cheese Puffs are elegant enough for any occasion, and you can make them ahead of time and just pop them in the oven when your guests arrive. Need an after-school snack for the kids? Cut up fresh fruit for them to dip in Orange Cream Dunk. Whatever the occasion, you'll find the perfect appetizer or snack.

Low-fat
Low-calorie

MARYLAND CRAB CAKES WITH HORSERADISH SAUCE

This bite-size version of an East Coast classic makes a terrific start to any party. (See photo, right.)

1 6-ounce package frozen
    cooked crab, thawed,
    drained, and flaked
½ cup fine dry bread crumbs
2 tablespoons finely chopped
    green onion
2 tablespoons finely chopped
    green sweet pepper
2 tablespoons fat-free
    mayonnaise dressing or
    salad dressing
½ teaspoon dry mustard
½ teaspoon finely shredded
    lemon or lime peel
1 egg white

1. Combine crabmeat, bread crumbs, green onion, green sweet pepper, mayonnaise dressing, mustard, lemon peel, egg white, and ⅛ teaspoon *pepper,* mixing well. (If mixture seems dry, stir in 1 tablespoon *milk.*) Gently shape into 18 small patties. Spray a shallow baking pan with *nonstick spray coating.* Place patties in pan.

2. Bake in a 350° oven about 15 minutes or till the patties are a light golden brown. Pass Horseradish Sauce with hot crab cakes. Makes 9 appetizer servings.

Horseradish Sauce: Stir together ¼ cup *plain nonfat yogurt,* 2 tablespoons *fat-free mayonnaise dressing or salad dressing,* 2 tablespoons finely chopped *green onion,* 1½ teaspoons *prepared horseradish,* and 1 teaspoon snipped *parsley.*

Nutritional facts per serving: 43 calories, 1 g total fat (0 g saturated fat), 19 mg cholesterol, 178 mg sodium, 4 g carbohydrate, 0 g fiber, 5 g protein. **Daily values:** 0% vitamin A, 7% vitamin C, 3% calcium, 2% iron.

Low-calorie
Low-sodium

SHRIMP-STUFFED MUSHROOMS

Serve these delectable appetizers with a bowlful of fresh-from-the-garden cherry tomatoes.

  Nonstick spray coating
24 medium mushrooms
2 teaspoons olive oil or
    vegetable oil
¼ cup chopped onion
1 clove garlic, minced
⅓ cup chopped tiny shrimp
⅓ cup snipped fresh parsley
⅔ cup soft whole wheat bread
    crumbs
2 tablespoons dry red wine or
    sherry
1 teaspoon dried basil, crushed
¼ teaspoon pepper

1. Line a 13x9x2-inch baking pan with foil; spray with nonstick coating. Rinse mushrooms; pat dry. Remove stems, hollowing out centers of mushrooms. Chop stems, reserving ⅔ cup (discard remaining stems). Arrange mushroom caps stem side up in prepared pan.

2. In a medium skillet, heat oil. Cook chopped mushrooms, onion, and garlic in hot oil for 3 minutes. Stir in shrimp and parsley; heat through. Remove from heat; stir in bread crumbs, wine, basil, and pepper. Spoon shrimp mixture into each mushroom cap. Cover pan with foil. Bake in a 350° oven for 10 minutes; remove foil. Bake 10 minutes more or till mushrooms are heated through. Immediately remove with slotted spoon or spatula. Serve hot. Makes 24 appetizers.

Nutritional facts per appetizer: 14 calories, 1 g total fat (0 g saturated fat), 5 mg cholesterol, 13 mg sodium, 1 g carbohydrate, 0 g fiber, 1 g protein. **Daily values:** 0% vitamin A, 2% vitamin C, 0% calcium, 2% iron.

Low-calorie
Low-sodium

TURKEY MEATBALLS WITH TOMATO SAUCE

Another time, try these mini meatballs with ground chicken.

1 **slightly beaten egg white**
¼ **cup fine dry bread crumbs**
2 **tablespoons plain nonfat**
   yogurt
2 **tablespoons snipped fresh**
   basil or 2 teaspoons dried
   basil, crushed
12 **ounces ground raw turkey**
1 **16-ounce can low-sodium**
   tomatoes
3 **tablespoons low-sodium**
   tomato paste
½ **teaspoon sugar**

1. Spray a shallow baking pan with *nonstick spray coating;* set aside. In a medium bowl combine beaten egg white, bread crumbs, yogurt, *half* of the basil, and ¼ teaspoon *pepper.* Add ground turkey; mix well. Shape into thirty-six 1-inch meatballs. Place in prepared pan. Bake in a 400° oven about 20 minutes or till no pink remains.

2. Meanwhile, for sauce, in a blender container or food processor bowl, combine *undrained* tomatoes, tomato paste, remaining basil, sugar, and ⅛ teaspoon *salt.* Cover and blend or process just till mixed and tomatoes are still slightly chunky. Transfer mixture to a medium saucepan. Bring to boiling. Reduce heat; simmer, uncovered, for 10 to 15 minutes or till desired consistency. Serve meatballs on wooden picks with tomato sauce for dipping. Makes 12 appetizer servings.

Nutritional facts per serving: 58 calories, 2 g total fat (1 g saturated fat), 11 mg cholesterol, 64 mg sodium, 4 g carbohydrate, 1 g fiber, 5 g protein. **Daily values:** 3% vitamin A, 12% vitamin C, 1% calcium, 4% iron.

Low-calorie
Low-sodium

CRUSTLESS CARROT QUICHES

Use your food processor to make quick work of shredding the carrots, or purchase them already shredded.

¼ **cup sliced green onion**
1 **clove garlic, minced**
1 **tablespoon margarine**
1½ **cups shredded carrot**
3 **slightly beaten eggs or ¾ cup**
   refrigerated or frozen egg
   product, thawed
1½ **cups shredded reduced-fat**
   Monterey Jack or cheddar
   cheese (6 ounces)
3 **tablespoons yellow cornmeal**
½ **teaspoon dried basil, crushed**
¼ **teaspoon ground nutmeg**

1. In a medium skillet cook green onion and garlic in margarine till onion is tender but not brown. Add carrot and cook about 2 minutes more or till crisp-tender. Remove from heat. In a large bowl beat together eggs, cheese, cornmeal, basil, and nutmeg. Stir in carrot mixture. Spray twenty-four 1¾-inch muffin cups with *nonstick spray coating.* Spoon about *1 tablespoon* of the egg mix into each muffin cup.

2. Bake in a 325° oven for 15 to 18 minutes or till set. Let stand 2 minutes. Remove from pans. (Or, pour all the batter into a 9-inch round pie plate or quiche dish sprayed with nonstick coating. Bake for 20 to 25 minutes or till set. Let stand 10 minutes. Cut into 12 thin wedges; cut each wedge in half crosswise.) Serve hot. Makes 24 appetizers.

Nutritional facts per appetizer: 41 calories, 2 g total fat (1 g saturated fat), 32 mg cholesterol, 62 mg sodium, 2 g carbohydrate, 0 g fiber, 3 g protein. **Daily values:** 17% vitamin A, 0% vitamin C, 4% calcium, 1% iron.

Low-fat

Low-calorie

Low-sodium

DRIED TOMATO WONTON CUPS

Dried tomato halves, in both red and yellow varieties, can be found in the specialty produce section of larger supermarkets.

12 dried tomato halves (dry pack)

½ cup boiling water

2 tablespoons balsamic or red wine vinegar

Nonstick spray coating

12 wonton skins

1 cup chopped fresh tomatoes

¼ cup sliced green onion

1 tablespoon snipped parsley

1 tablespoon snipped fresh basil or 1 teaspoon dried basil, crushed

2 teaspoons snipped fresh thyme or ½ teaspoon dried thyme, crushed

1 clove garlic, minced

2 tablespoons shredded part-skim mozzarella cheese

1. In a small mixing bowl combine dried tomatoes, water, and vinegar. Let stand 15 to 20 minutes to soften tomatoes. Meanwhile, spray twelve 2½-inch muffin cups with nonstick coating. Place one wonton skin in each cup, fitting center of skins into bottoms of cups. Bake in a 400° oven about 8 minutes or till lightly browned.

2. Drain tomatoes; discard liquid. Finely chop dried tomatoes; return to bowl. Stir in fresh tomatoes, green onion, parsley, basil, thyme, and garlic till combined. Spoon about *1 tablespoon* of the mixture into each warm wonton cup. Sprinkle shredded cheese over filling. Bake in a 400° oven for 4 to 5 minutes or till cheese melts and filling is warm. Serve warm. Makes 12 appetizers.

Nutritional facts per appetizer: 37 calories, 1 g total fat (0 g saturated fat), 2 mg cholesterol, 56 mg sodium, 7 g carbohydrate, 0 g fiber, 2 g protein. **Daily values:** 13% vitamin A, 10% vitamin C, 1% calcium, 3% iron.

Place a wonton skin in each muffin cup. With your fingers, gently press the wonton skin into the center of the cup and out to the edges so it fits snuggly.

SPINACH AND BLUE CHEESE PUFFS

Low-calorie

The spinach filling also can be used as a spread on crackers or pita bread triangles. (See photo, left.)

3 tablespoons margarine
½ cup water
½ cup all-purpose flour
1 teaspoon finely shredded
    lemon peel
⅛ teaspoon salt
⅛ teaspoon dried dillweed
2 eggs
1 10-ounce package frozen
    chopped spinach, thawed
    and well drained
¼ cup low-fat blue cheese salad
    dressing
1 tablespoon grated Parmesan
    or Romano cheese
¼ teaspoon pepper

1. For cream puffs, in a medium saucepan combine margarine and water. Bring to boiling. Add flour, lemon peel, salt, and dillweed all at once, stirring vigorously. Cook and stir till mixture forms a ball that doesn't separate. Remove from heat. Cool 10 minutes. Add eggs, one at a time, beating with a wooden spoon after each egg till the mixture is smooth. Drop batter by rounded teaspoonfuls, 2 inches apart, onto a greased baking sheet. Bake in a 400° oven for 25 to 30 minutes or till golden brown. Cool on a wire rack. Split puffs and remove any soft dough from inside.

2. For filling, squeeze excess liquid from spinach. Stir together drained spinach, salad dressing, cheese, and pepper. Mix well. (If preparing ahead, cover and chill spinach mixture. Store cooled cream puffs in a tightly covered container for up to 12 hours; puffs are best served the same day.) Spoon about *2 teaspoons* of filling into cream puffs; add tops. Place on a baking sheet. Bake in a 350° oven for 15 to 20 minutes or till heated through. Serve hot. Makes 20.

Nutritional facts per puff: 39 calories, 3 g total fat (1 g saturated fat), 22 mg cholesterol, 89 mg sodium, 3 g carbohydrate, 0 g fiber, 1 g protein. **Daily values:** 10% vitamin A, 2% vitamin C, 2% calcium, 2% iron.

Low-fat
Low-calorie
Low-sodium

OVEN-FRIED POTATO SKINS

For a colorful variation, try purple or yellow potatoes or sweet potatoes.

2 large baking potatoes
    (about 1 pound total)
2 teaspoons cooking oil
2 teaspoons grated Parmesan or
    Romano cheese
½ teaspoon paprika
½ teaspoon dried Italian
    seasoning, crushed
¼ teaspoon salt
¼ teaspoon garlic powder
⅓ cup fat-free or light dairy
    sour cream or salsa

1. One day or several hours ahead, prick potatoes with a fork. Bake in a 425° oven for 40 to 50 minutes or till tender; cool. Wrap and store in refrigerator. At serving time, halve baked potatoes lengthwise. Scoop out the insides, leaving ¼-inch-thick shells. Lightly brush both sides of potato skins with oil. Cut each half lengthwise into 4 pieces. Place cut side up on a large baking sheet.

2. In a small bowl stir together cheese, paprika, Italian seasoning, salt, and garlic powder. Sprinkle evenly over skins. Bake in a 425° oven for 10 to 15 minutes or till crisp. Pass hot skins with sour cream or salsa. Makes 16 appetizers.

Nutritional facts per appetizer: 40 calories, 1 g total fat (0 g saturated fat), 0 mg cholesterol, 44 mg sodium, 7 g carbohydrate, 0 g fiber, 1 g protein. **Daily values:** 1% vitamin A, 7% vitamin C, 1% calcium, 1% iron.

Low-calorie
Low-sodium

ROASTED GARLIC SPREAD WITH CHIVES

You'll be surprised at the mild, sweet flavor of roasted garlic. It's perfect for this creamy spread.

1 whole bulb garlic
¼ teaspoon olive oil or vegetable oil
½ of an 8-ounce container (½ cup) light cream cheese product
½ cup fat-free or light dairy sour cream
2 tablespoons diced pimiento, drained
1 tablespoon snipped fresh chives or 1 teaspoon dried snipped chives
½ teaspoon dried thyme, crushed
½ teaspoon dried basil, crushed
½ teaspoon Worcestershire sauce
⅛ teaspoon salt
⅛ teaspoon pepper
Carrot and celery sticks, melba toast rounds, or Pita Crisps (See tip, page 27)

1. Remove papery husk from garlic bulb, leaving garlic whole. Slice ¼ inch off the top of garlic bulb to expose cloves. Brush cut side of garlic with oil. Wrap in aluminum foil; place in a small baking dish. Bake in a 350° oven for 60 to 65 minutes or till garlic is tender when pierced with a knife. Unwrap garlic; cool 10 minutes.

2. Remove soft garlic pulp from cloves; transfer to a blender container or food processor bowl. Add cream cheese, sour cream, pimiento, chives, thyme, basil, Worcestershire sauce, salt, and pepper. Cover and blend or process till mixture is smooth. Serve immediately or cover and chill. (Let chilled spread stand 15 to 20 minutes at room temperature before serving.) Serve with carrot or celery sticks or spread on melba toast rounds or pita bread triangles. Makes about 1 cup.

Nutritional facts per tablespoon: 31 calories, 2 g total fat (1 g saturated fat), 5 mg cholesterol, 52 mg sodium, 2 g carbohydrate, 0 g fiber, 1 g protein. **Daily values:** 3% vitamin A, 4% vitamin C, 1% calcium, 0% iron.

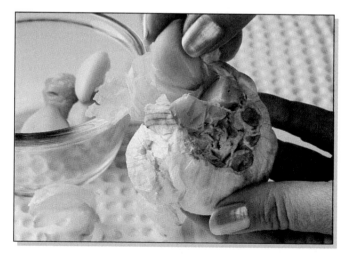

Gently pull the cloves of garlic away from each other as you slip them out of their papery skins.

Low-fat
Low-calorie

BLACK BEAN DIP

You also can prepare this dip with canned, rinsed, and drained garbanzo beans, pinto beans, or navy beans.

1 15-ounce can black beans,
    rinsed and drained
2 tablespoons chopped onion
2 tablespoons snipped fresh
    cilantro or parsley
1 tablespoon lemon juice
2 cloves garlic, minced
¼ teaspoon ground cumin
¼ teaspoon pepper
¼ cup plain nonfat yogurt
    Pita Crisps (see tip at right)
    or Tortilla Crisps (see
    recipe, page 28)

1. Measure ½ *cup* of the black beans; set aside. In a blender container or food processor bowl combine the remaining beans, the onion, cilantro or parsley, lemon juice, garlic, cumin, and pepper. Cover and process or blend till mixture is smooth.

2. Stir in reserved black beans and yogurt. Serve with Pita Crisps or Tortilla Crisps. Makes about 1 cup.

Nutritional facts per tablespoon: 83 calories, 1 g total fat (0 g saturated fat), 0 mg cholesterol, 160 mg sodium, 11 g carbohydrate, 1 g fiber, 6 g protein. **Daily values:** 34% vitamin A, 21% vitamin C, 12% calcium, 20% iron.

Pita Crisps

Try these great-tasting, low-fat chips as an alternative to the greasy ones that once invaded your snack tray. Cut pita bread rounds in half horizontally; cut each half into 6 or 8 wedges. Place pita wedges in a single layer on an ungreased baking sheet. Bake, uncovered, in a 350° oven for 10 to 12 minutes or till crisp.

Low-calorie
Low-sodium

ORANGE CREAM DUNK FOR FRESH FRUIT

Vary this dip by using a low-calorie fruit spread, such as apricot, raspberry, or boysenberry, in place of the orange marmalade.

1 8-ounce package light cream
    cheese (Neufchâtel)
⅓ cup low-calorie orange
    marmalade spread
1 teaspoon finely shredded
    orange peel
1 to 2 tablespoons skim milk
    (optional)
    Apple slices, pear slices,
    orange sections, banana
    slices, or whole strawberries

1. In a blender container or food processor bowl combine cream cheese product, marmalade, and orange peel. Cover and blend or process till smooth, stopping and scraping sides as necessary.

2. Transfer to a serving bowl. If necessary, stir in milk to desired consistency. Serve with fresh fruit. Makes 1¼ cups.

Nutritional facts per tablespoon: 36 calories, 3 g total fat (2 g saturated fat), 9 mg cholesterol, 45 mg sodium, 2 g carbohydrate, 0 g fiber, 1 g protein. **Daily values:** 3% vitamin A, 0% vitamin C, 0% calcium, 0% iron.

CREAMY AVOCADO DIP WITH TORTILLA CRISPS

Low-calorie

For a spicy version, substitute 1 tablespoon finely chopped, seeded jalapeño chili pepper for the mild pepper. (See photo, right.)

2 ripe avocados
⅓ cup fat-free mayonnaise
    dressing or salad dressing
3 tablespoons lime juice
½ cup diced tomato
3 tablespoons chopped green
    onion
1 tablespoon finely chopped
    mild green chili pepper
2 tablespoons snipped cilantro
½ teaspoon dried thyme,
    crushed
¼ teaspoon garlic powder
¼ teaspoon pepper
    Tortilla Crisps

1. Peel and pit avocados. In a medium bowl mash avocado pulp with a fork. Add mayonnaise dressing or salad dressing, lime juice, tomato, green onion, chili pepper, cilantro, thyme, garlic powder, and pepper; stir till well combined.

2. Cover and chill till serving. Makes 16 appetizer servings (2¼ cups dip).

Tortilla Crisps: Spray eight 6-inch corn or flour *tortillas* with *nonstick spray coating*. Stack tortillas. With a sharp knife cut stack into eight triangles; separate triangles and place on baking sheets. Bake in a 425° oven about 8 minutes or till brown and crisp. Makes about 3 cups.

Nutritional facts per serving: 78 calories, 4 g total fat (1 g saturated fat), 0 mg cholesterol, 86 mg sodium, 11 g carbohydrate, 1 g fiber, 1 g protein. **Daily values:** 3% vitamin A, 11% vitamin C, 2% calcium, 3% iron.

Low-fat

Low-calorie

Low-sodium

ARTICHOKE-CHILI PEPPER DIP

Serve this warm dip as the prelude to a special-occasion dinner or as a snack for a casual get-together.

1 9-ounce package frozen
    artichoke hearts, thawed
    and finely chopped
½ cup plain nonfat yogurt
½ cup fat-free mayonnaise
    dressing or salad dressing
¼ cup grated Parmesan or
    Romano cheese
2 tablespoons canned, diced
    green chili peppers, drained
1 teaspoon dried Italian
    seasoning, crushed
    Pita Crisps (see tip, page 27)
    or carrot or celery sticks

1. In a medium bowl stir together artichoke hearts, yogurt, mayonnaise dressing or salad dressing, Parmesan cheese, chili peppers, and Italian seasoning.

2. Spray a 9-inch pie plate or an 8-inch round quiche dish with *nonstick spray coating*. Turn mixture into pie plate. Bake in a 350° oven about 20 minutes or till heated through. Serve warm with Pita Crisps or carrot or celery sticks. Makes about 2¼ cups.

Nutritional facts per tablespoon: 13 calories, 0 g total fat (0 g saturated fat), 1 mg cholesterol, 69 mg sodium, 2 g carbohydrate, 0 g fiber, 1 g protein. **Daily values:** 0% vitamin A, 2% vitamin C, 1% calcium, 1% iron.

Low-fat
Low-calorie
Low-sodium

CINNAMON BAGEL CHIPS

These crisp and crunchy snacks make great treats for kids as well as grown-ups.

3 unsplit plain, cinnamon-raisin, egg, sesame, or poppy seed bagels
2 teaspoons cooking oil
2 tablespoons sugar
1 teaspoon ground cinnamon
¼ teaspoon ground nutmeg

1. Slice bagels from top to bottom into ⅛-inch-thick slices. Arrange bagel slices on an ungreased baking sheet. Brush bagel slices very lightly with oil. Bake in a 325° oven for 20 to 25 minutes or till toasted.

2. In a 1-gallon clear plastic bag, combine sugar, cinnamon, and nutmeg. Add hot bagel slices; seal bag. Toss chips until coated with spice mixture. Shake off excess coating. Cool; store in an airtight container. Makes about 3 dozen chips.

Nutritional facts per chip: 21 calories, 0 g total fat (0 g saturated fat), 0 mg cholesterol, 32 mg sodium, 4 g carbohydrate, 0 g fiber, 1 g protein. **Daily values:** 0% vitamin A, 0% vitamin C, 0% calcium, 1% iron.

Low-fat
Low-calorie
Low-sodium

APPLE SUNRISE

Make ice cubes from apple or cranberry juice to float in a glass of this refreshing drink.

1 cup apple juice or cider, chilled
1 cup low-calorie cranberry juice cocktail, chilled
½ cup chilled club soda
Ice cubes
2 orange slices (optional)

1. In a 1-quart measuring cup, stir together apple juice or cider, cranberry juice cocktail, and club soda.

2. Fill two tall glasses with ice cubes; pour mixture over ice. If desired, cut a slit in each orange slice and twist one over the rim of each glass. Makes 2 (10-ounce) servings.

Nutrition facts per serving: 85 calories, 0 g total fat (0 g saturated fat), 0 mg cholesterol, 26 mg sodium, 21 g carbohydrate, 0 g fiber, 0 g protein. **Daily Value:** 0% vitamin A, 1% vitamin C, 0% calcium, and 4% iron.

Low-fat
Low-sodium
High-fiber

CITRUS-MELON FRAPPÉ

Next time, in place of the orange juice, try one of the new juice blends, such as orange-banana-pineapple juice.

1½ cups orange, grapefruit, or pineapple juice, chilled
1 cup cantaloupe or honeydew melon chunks
½ of a 6-ounce can (⅓ cup) frozen lemonade or limeade concentrate
2 tablespoons sugar
1½ cups ice cubes

1. In a blender container or food processor bowl combine juice, melon chunks, lemonade or limeade concentrate, and sugar. Cover and blend or process for 10 seconds.

2. Gradually add ice cubes, blending or processing till frothy. Pour into 4 or 5 tall glasses. Makes 4 (8-ounce) servings.

Nutritional facts per serving: 256 calories, 0 g total fat (0 g saturated fat), 0 mg cholesterol, 9 mg sodium, 66 g carbohydrate, 3 g fiber, 1 g protein. **Daily values:** 14% vitamin A, 127% vitamin C, 1% calcium, 4% iron.

Low-fat

Low-calorie

Low-sodium

FROSTY FRUIT SMOOTHIE

Another kid-pleasing snack that's especially rich in vitamin C.

1 medium banana, peeled, and
cut into chunks

1 cup orange, pineapple, grape,
or apple juice or low-
calorie cranberry juice
cocktail; chilled

½ cup skim milk

1 teaspoon vanilla extract

3 ice cubes

1. In a blender container combine the banana chunks, juice, milk, vanilla, and ice cubes. Cover and blend till frothy.

2. Pour into two glasses; serve immediately. Makes 2 (10-ounce) servings.

Nutritional facts per serving: 137 calories, 1 g total fat (0 g saturated fat), 1 mg cholesterol, 34 mg sodium, 30 g carbohydrate, 2 g fiber, 4 g protein. **Daily values:** 6% vitamin A, 112% vitamin C, 7% calcium, 3% iron.

Low-fat

Low-calorie

ORANGE YOGURT DRINK

Yogurt, skim milk, and fat-free sour cream make this beverage taste positively dreamy.

2½ cups skim milk

2 8-ounce containers vanilla,
lemon, or orange low-fat
yogurt

½ cup fat-free or light dairy
sour cream

¼ cup frozen orange or apple
juice concentrate, thawed

1. With a wire whip or rotary beater combine milk, yogurt, sour cream, and juice concentrate; beat till smooth.

2. Chill or serve immediately. Store leftovers in the refrigerator. Makes 8 (5-ounce) servings.

Nutritional facts per serving: 116 calories, 1 g total fat (1 g saturated fat), 5 mg cholesterol, 90 mg sodium, 19 g carbohydrate, 0 g fiber, 7 g protein. **Daily values:** 6% vitamin A, 23% vitamin C, 17% calcium, 0% iron.

Cheers!

Toasting friends and family with low- and no-alcohol beers not only makes good sense, but is easier than ever. Just check out the beverage aisle at your liquor or grocery store to discover the growing number of beer alternatives. Here's a rundown of what's readily available.

Alcohol-free beer: Only malt beverages with no alcohol whatsoever may display this term. This product typically is made without fermentation and instead gets its beer taste from natural flavorings.

Nonalcoholic beer: Although the label suggests that these are free of alcohol, by law they must contain less than 0.5 percent alcohol. Don't look for

the word beer on the label. They are called malt beverage, cereal beverage, or near beer.

Light beer: This term is not defined by law but generally refers to beer with about half the calories of regular beer. This does not mean half the alcohol content. Different brands vary in the amount of alcohol they contain.

Low-fat

Low-calorie

Low-sodium

ICED ESPRESSO

Serve this refreshing coffee drink after a light lunch or dinner in place of dessert. (See photo, left.)

½ cup ground espresso coffee or
  French roast coffee
1 teaspoon finely shredded
  orange peel
4 cups water
1½ cups skim milk
3 tablespoons sugar
  Ice cubes
  Orange peel strips (optional)
1 teaspoon grated semisweet
  chocolate (optional)

1. Prepare coffee with shredded orange peel and water in a drip coffeemaker or percolator according to manufacturer's directions. Pour coffee into a heatproof pitcher; stir in sugar and milk. Chill till serving time.

2. To serve, fill 6 glasses with ice cubes; pour coffee mixture over ice. Garnish with orange peel strips and grated chocolate, if desired. Makes 6 (6-ounce) servings.

Nutritional facts per serving: 54 calories, 0 g total fat (0 g saturated fat), 1 mg cholesterol, 35 mg sodium, 11 g carbohydrate, 0 g fiber, 2 g protein. **Daily values:** 3% vitamin A, 1% vitamin C, 6% calcium, 0% iron.

Low-fat

Low-calorie

HOT CHOCOLATE BEVERAGE MIX

Wrapped in a pretty glass container, this mix makes a great holiday gift (along with instructions for serving, of course).

2⅔ cups nonfat dry milk powder
½ cup sugar
⅓ cup unsweetened cocoa
  powder
½ teaspoon ground cinnamon
¼ teaspoon ground nutmeg

In a large bowl stir together milk powder, sugar, cocoa powder, cinnamon, and nutmeg. Store in an airtight container. Makes enough mix for 12 servings.

Hot Chocolate: In a mug place ¼ cup of the mix; stir in ¾ cup *boiling water* and ½ teaspoon *vanilla.*

Nutritional facts per serving: 97 calories, 0 g total fat (0 g saturated fat), 3 mg cholesterol, 88 mg sodium, 17 g carbohydrate, 0 g fiber, 6 g protein. **Daily values:** 10% vitamin A, 1% vitamin C, 18% calcium, 2% iron.

Hot Mocha: In a mug place ¼ cup of the mix; stir in ¾ cup *boiling water,* ½ teaspoon *vanilla,* and ½ to 1 teaspoon *instant coffee crystals.*

Nutritional facts per serving: 97 calories, 0 g total fat (0 g saturated fat), 3 mg cholesterol, 88 mg sodium, 17 g carbohydrate, 0 g fiber, 6 g protein. **Daily values:** 10% vitamin A, 1% vitamin C, 18% calcium, 2% iron.

Low-fat

Low-calorie

Low-sodium

FLUFFY LIGHT EGGNOG

Who says eggnog has to be fattening? Nonfat milk and frozen nondairy topping make this version seem too rich to be light!

6 cups skim or low-fat milk

3 eggs or ¾ cup refrigerated or
    frozen egg product, thawed

Dash salt

½ cup sugar

2 teaspoons vanilla

¾ cup frozen light whipped
    dessert topping, thawed

Ground nutmeg

1. In a large saucepan heat milk till hot (*do not* boil). Remove saucepan from heat. In a large heatproof bowl beat together eggs and salt using a wire whisk; gradually add sugar. Slowly stir in hot milk, beating constantly. Return mixture to saucepan; cook and stir with the wire whisk over medium-low heat for 12 to 17 minutes or till mixture thinly coats a metal spoon (*do not* boil). Remove from heat; stir in vanilla.

2. Set the saucepan in a bowl of ice cubes; let stand for 5 minutes, stirring occasionally. Chill till serving time. To serve, pour into mugs. Top each serving with 1 tablespoon of the whipped topping and a sprinkling of nutmeg. Makes 12 (½-cup) servings.

Nutritional facts per serving: 94 calories, 2 g total fat (0 g saturated fat), 55 mg cholesterol, 69 mg sodium, 14 g carbohydrate, 0 g fiber, 4 g protein. **Daily values:** 7% vitamin A, 1% vitamin C, 8% calcium, 1% iron.

Low-fat

Low-calorie

Low-sodium

SAVVY SANGRIA

For an alcohol-free version, substitute nonalcoholic wine for the white wine.

2 fresh peaches, peeled and
    sliced, or 2 cups frozen
    unsweetened peach slices,
    thawed

1 cup sliced strawberries or
    frozen unsweetened whole
    strawberries, thawed

1 orange, halved and thinly
    sliced

1 lemon or lime, sliced

1 1-liter bottle carbonated
    water (club soda), chilled

2 cups dry white wine, chilled

½ cup orange juice, chilled

½ cup low-calorie cranberry
    juice cocktail, chilled

1. In a large punch bowl place peach slices, strawberries, orange slices, and lemon or lime slices. Pour carbonated water over fruit; add wine, orange juice, and cranberry juice cocktail. Stir gently to combine.

2. To serve, ladle some of the fruit into glasses; ladle wine mixture over fruit. Makes 14 (6-ounce) servings.

Nutritional facts per serving: 43 calories, 0 g total fat (0 g saturated fat), 0 mg cholesterol, 17 mg sodium, 5 g carbohydrate, 1 g fiber, 0 g protein. **Daily values:** 1% vitamin A, 21% vitamin C, 0% calcium, 1% iron.

Fantastic Fish & Seafood

Fish and seafood have long been thought of as low-fat, low-calorie entrées. But the old concept of bland broiled fish as diet food has been replaced. Today, exciting new flavors can be incorporated to please even the pickiest connoisseurs. Fresh fish is more readily available than ever before, and because it is quick to cook, it fits right into the busiest of lifestyles. Some of our prize catches in this chapter are oven-fried Crispy Orange Roughy with Dilled Yogurt Sauce and the Oriental-inspired Sherried Shrimp with Snow Peas. For family suppers, Seafood Burgers, made with tuna and crabmeat, are a tasty alternative to hamburgers. And in a light twist on a classic, try Scallops Scampi-Style served on a bed of spinach fettuccine. If you're not already tempted, turn the page and take a fresh look at fish.

Low-fat

Low-calorie

Low-sodium

FENNEL AND FISH AU GRATIN

Become a fennel fan! It's bulb shaped with feathery, dill-like leaves and a mild anise flavor. Try this tasty dish. (See photo, right.)

1 pound fresh or frozen fish
  fillets, such as salmon or
  orange roughy
2 fennel bulbs
3 carrots, julienned (1½ cups)
1¼ cups skim milk
3 tablespoons all-purpose flour
2 tablespoons dry white wine
  (optional)
⅛ teaspoon salt
⅛ teaspoon pepper
2 tablespoons grated Parmesan
  cheese
1 tablespoon fine dry bread
  crumbs
2 teaspoons margarine or
  butter, melted

1. Thaw fish, if frozen. Rinse fish and pat dry with paper towels. Cut fish into 4 serving-size portions; set aside. Remove upper stalks from fennel, including feathery leaves; reserve leaves and discard stalks. Discard any wilted outer layers on fennel bulbs; cut off a thin slice from each base. Wash fennel and pat dry. Quarter each fennel bulb lengthwise and discard core; julienne each quarter lengthwise. Chop enough of the reserved fennel leaves to make ¼ cup.

2. In a large saucepan simmer julienned fennel and carrots, covered, in a small amount of boiling water for 8 to 10 minutes or till tender; drain. Transfer vegetables to a 2-quart square or rectangular baking dish. Rinse saucepan.

3. Meanwhile, in a large skillet cook fish in a small amount of simmering water till fish flakes easily with a fork (allow 4 to 6 minutes per ½-inch thickness of fish); drain. Arrange fish atop vegetables in baking dish.

4. For sauce, in the large saucepan combine milk and flour. Cook and stir over medium heat till thickened and bubbly; stir in the ¼ cup chopped fennel leaves, wine (if desired), salt, and pepper. Pour sauce over fish and vegetables. Combine Parmesan cheese, bread crumbs, and margarine; sprinkle over the sauce. Bake, uncovered, in a 350° oven for 10 minutes or till heated through. Makes 4 servings.

Nutrition facts per serving: 199 calories, 4 g total fat (1 g saturated fat), 49 mg cholesterol, 308 mg sodium, 16 g carbohydrate, 1 g fiber, 24 g protein. **Daily values:** 96% vitamin A, 12% vitamin C, 15% calcium, 6% iron.

Storing Fish

Fish is very perishable, so it's best to cook it the same day that you buy it. When that isn't possible, store fish in the coldest part of the refrigerator for up to 2 days. Keep it properly wrapped in moisture- and vaporproof material.

Frozen fish should be stored in its original packaging and kept solidly frozen in your freezer at 0° or lower. For best quality, keep frozen fish in the freezer no longer than 3 months.

Low-fat

Low-calorie

Low-sodium

SWEET PEPPER-STUFFED FLOUNDER ROLLS

For an elegant dinner, serve these wine-sauced fish rolls with Brown Rice Pilaf (see recipe, page 198) and steamed asparagus.

4 4-ounce fresh or frozen
   flounder or sole fillets
   (¼ to ½ inch thick)
2 small red, yellow, or green
   sweet peppers, julienned
   (1½ cups)
4 green onions, halved
   lengthwise and cut into
   3-inch slices
2 teaspoons margarine
⅓ cup dry white wine or chicken
   broth
¼ teaspoon dried fines herbes,
   crushed
2 teaspoons cornstarch
1 tablespoon cold water

1. Thaw fish, if frozen. Cook sweet peppers and onions, covered, in a small amount of boiling water for 3 minutes; drain. Rinse fish and pat dry with paper towels. Dot each fillet with ½ *teaspoon* of the margarine. Place ¼ of the pepper mixture across the center of each fillet. Roll up fillets from short sides (if necessary, fasten securely with wooden picks). Place fish rolls, seam sides down, in a shallow baking dish. Stir together wine, fines herbes, ⅛ teaspoon *salt* (omit if using chicken broth), and ⅛ teaspoon *pepper;* drizzle over fish.

2. Cover and bake in a 350° oven for 25 to 30 minutes or till fish flakes easily with a fork. Transfer fish to serving platter; cover and keep warm. Measure the pan juices; add enough *water* to equal ¾ cup liquid. In a small saucepan, combine cornstarch and the 1 tablespoon cold water; stir in pan juices. Cook and stir over medium heat till mixture is thickened and bubbly. Cook and stir for 2 minutes more. Spoon sauce over fish rolls. Makes 4 servings.

Nutrition facts per serving: 150 calories, 3 g total fat (1 g saturated fat), 60 mg cholesterol, 184 mg sodium, 4 g carbohydrate, 0 g fiber, 22 g protein. **Daily values:** 33% vitamin A, 108% vitamin C, 2% calcium, 4% iron.

Low-fat

Low-calorie

Low-sodium

SOUTHERN-STYLE SNAPPER

1 pound fresh or frozen red
   snapper or other firm fish
   fillets (½ to ¾ inch thick)
   Nonstick spray coating
3 tablespoons lemon juice
1 tablespoon snipped fresh
   parsley
¼ teaspoon paprika
¼ teaspoon pepper
⅛ teaspoon salt
½ pound kale, mustard, or
   collard greens
1 cup sliced red onion

1. Thaw fish, if frozen. Rinse fish; pat dry with paper towels. Cut into 4 serving-size portions. Spray a shallow baking dish with nonstick coating; arrange fish in dish. Tuck under any thin edges for an even thickness. In a small bowl combine lemon juice, parsley, paprika, pepper, and salt. Spoon mixture over fish; set aside.

2. Remove stems from greens. Wash greens thoroughly in cold water and drain well; tear into pieces. In a Dutch oven cook greens and onion, covered, in a small amount of boiling water for 9 to 12 minutes or till tender.

3. Meanwhile, bake fish in a 450° oven till fish flakes easily with a fork (allow 4 to 6 minutes per ½-inch thickness of fish). Using a slotted spoon, transfer greens and onions to a serving platter; arrange fish fillets over greens and onions. Serves 4.

Nutrition facts per serving: 156 calories, 2 g total fat (0 g saturated fat), 42 mg cholesterol, 132 mg sodium, 9 g carbohydrate, 3 g fiber, 25 g protein. **Daily values:** 43% vitamin A, 53% vitamin C, 7% calcium, 6% iron.

Low-fat

Low-calorie

Low-sodium

SOLE WITH FETA AND TOMATOES

Small amounts of feta cheese, with its sharp, distinctive flavor, can make salads, main dishes, and pizzas more interesting.

1¼ **pounds fresh or frozen sole or other fish fillets (½ to ¾ inch thick)**

1 **16-ounce can low-sodium tomatoes, cut up**

8 **green onions, sliced (1 cup)**

2 **tablespoons lemon juice**

1 **teaspoon dried Italian seasoning, crushed**

¼ **teaspoon pepper**
  Nonstick spray coating

2 **tablespoons crumbled feta cheese or 2 tablespoons sliced pitted ripe olives**

1. Thaw fish, if frozen. Rinse and pat dry with paper towels. Cut into 4 serving-size portions.

2. For sauce, in a large skillet combine *undrained* tomatoes, green onions, lemon juice, Italian seasoning, and pepper. Bring to boiling; reduce heat. Simmer, uncovered, for 8 to 10 minutes or till nearly all the liquid has evaporated.

3. Spray a shallow 2-quart baking dish with nonstick coating. Arrange fish fillets in the dish; tuck under any thin edges for an even thickness. Spoon tomato sauce over fish. Cover; bake in a 350° oven for 20 to 25 minutes or till fish flakes easily with a fork. Before serving, sprinkle with feta cheese or olives. Makes 4 servings.

Nutrition facts per serving: 164 calories, 4 g total fat (2 g saturated fat), 74 mg cholesterol, 207 mg sodium, 7 g carbohydrate, 1 g fiber, 26 g protein. **Daily values:** 14% vitamin. A, 42% vitamin C, 8% calcium, 9% iron.

Turn under any thin edges of the fillets. This makes the fillets about the same thickness so the thinner ends won't get done before the thicker edges.

CRISPY ORANGE ROUGHY WITH DILLED YOGURT SAUCE

If you're fond of crispy fried fish, this flavorful alternative will make you a light-eating convert. (See photo, left.)

1 pound fresh or frozen orange roughy or other fish fillets (½ to ¾ inch thick)
¼ cup cornmeal
½ teaspoon dried thyme, crushed
¼ teaspoon lemon-pepper seasoning
1 egg white
2 tablespoons water
¼ cup fine dry bread crumbs
2 tablespoons toasted wheat germ
1 tablespoon snipped fresh parsley
½ teaspoon paprika
Nonstick spray coating
1 8-ounce carton plain fat-free yogurt
¼ cup lemon fat-free yogurt
1 teaspoon dried dillweed
Few dashes bottled hot pepper sauce
Lemon wedges (optional)

1. Thaw fish, if frozen. Rinse fish and pat dry with paper towels. Cut fish into 4 serving-size portions; set aside.

2. In a shallow dish combine cornmeal, thyme, and lemon-pepper seasoning; set aside. In another shallow bowl beat egg white and water till frothy. In a third shallow bowl combine bread crumbs, wheat germ, parsley, and paprika. Dip fish fillets into cornmeal mixture, shaking off any excess. Dip into egg white, then coat with bread crumb mixture. Spray a shallow baking pan with nonstick coating. Place fillets in baking pan, tucking under any thin edges for an even thickness.

3. Bake in a 450° oven till fish flakes easily with a fork (allow 4 to 6 minutes per ½-inch thickness of fish). Meanwhile, for sauce, in a small bowl stir together plain and lemon yogurt, dillweed, and hot pepper sauce. Serve sauce with fish; if desired, garnish with lemon wedges. Makes 4 servings.

Nutrition facts per serving: 221 calories, 3 g total fat (0 g saturated fat), 62 mg cholesterol, 271 mg sodium, 20 g carbohydrate, 1 g fiber, 29 g protein. **Daily values:** 3% vitamin A, 2% vitamin C, 14% calcium, 10% iron.

Thawing Fish

When planning a meal using frozen fish, remember to allow time for it to thaw. To thaw frozen fish properly, place the unopened package in a container in the refrigerator, allowing overnight thawing for a 1-pound package. If necessary, you can place the wrapped package of fish under cold running water to hasten the process.

Thawing fish at room temperature or in warm water is not recommended, since the fish won't thaw evenly and may spoil.

Fillets and steaks can be cooked from the frozen state, without thawing. If you use this technique, add a few extra minutes to the cooking time.

Low-fat

Low-calorie

Low-sodium

SHRIMP-STUFFED SNAPPER

Easy-to-mix stuffing makes baked fish a classy dish.

1 2- to 2½-pound fresh or
    frozen dressed red snapper,
    pike, or perch (head and
    tail removed)
1½ cups soft white or whole
    wheat bread crumbs
4 ounces cooked shrimp,
    coarsely chopped (1 cup)
½ cup shredded carrots or
    zucchini
1 green onion, thinly sliced
1 teaspoon light soy sauce
1 teaspoon orange or lemon
    juice
¼ teaspoon ground ginger

1. Thaw fish, if frozen. Rinse fish and pat dry with paper towels. Place fish in a greased 3-quart rectangular baking dish; set aside.

2. For stuffing, in a medium bowl combine bread crumbs, shrimp, carrots or zucchini, green onion, soy sauce, orange juice, and ginger. Spoon stuffing into fish cavity and pat lightly to flatten. (If necessary to hold all the stuffing, enlarge the cavity by cutting a larger slit toward tail end with a sharp knife.)

3. Bake in a 350° oven, loosely covered with foil, for 25 minutes. Uncover and bake 5 to 15 minutes more or till fish flakes easily with a fork. Transfer fish to a serving platter. Makes 4 or 5 servings.

Nutrition facts per serving: 295 calories, 4 g total fat (1 g saturated fat), 139 mg cholesterol, 286 mg sodium, 8 g carbohydrate, 0 g fiber, 54 g protein. **Daily values:** 41% vitamin A, 5% vitamin C, 8% calcium, 12% iron.

Low-fat

Low-calorie

TUNA DIVAN

Fat-free yogurt, skim milk, water-pack tuna, and low-fat cheese transform this old favorite into a deliciously healthy recipe.

1 pound fresh broccoli, cut into
    spears, or 1¼ pounds fresh
    asparagus spears
1 tablespoon margarine
1 cup skim milk
½ cup plain fat-free yogurt
2 tablespoons all-purpose flour
    Dash ground nutmeg
1 teaspoon lemon juice
1 6¼-ounce can chunk-style
    tuna (water pack), drained
    and flaked
4 slices reduced-fat Swiss- or
    Monterey Jack-flavored
    process cheese product
    Dash paprika

1. If using asparagus, trim spears, breaking off woody bases where spears snap easily; scrape off scales. In a large saucepan cook broccoli or asparagus, covered, in a small amount of boiling water for 3 minutes; drain. Arrange cooked vegetable in a 2-quart rectangular baking dish; set aside.

2. For sauce, in a medium saucepan melt margarine; stir in skim milk. In a small bowl combine yogurt and flour. Add to saucepan. Cook and stir over medium heat till mixture is thickened and bubbly. Stir in nutmeg and ⅛ teaspoon *pepper*. Cook and stir 2 minutes more. Stir in lemon juice. Arrange tuna over cooked vegetable; pour sauce over tuna and vegetable.

3. Bake in a 350° oven for 20 minutes. Meanwhile, cut cheese slices diagonally into quarters. Arrange cheese quarters on hot casserole. Sprinkle with paprika. Bake 5 to 10 minutes more or till casserole is heated through and cheese melts. Serves 4.

Nutrition facts per serving: 203 calories, 6 g total fat (2 g saturated fat), 25 mg cholesterol, 514 mg sodium, 14 g carbohydrate, 3 g fiber, 22 g protein. **Daily Value:** 22% vitamin. A, 116% vitamin C, 25% calcium, 10% iron.

Low-fat

Low-calorie

Low-sodium

STEAMED TROUT WITH WATERCRESS SAUCE

This same, light, creamy watercress sauce is great over poached salmon or steamed vegetables such as asparagus or cauliflower.

4 8- to 10-ounce fresh or
    frozen dressed trout or
    other fish (with heads and
    tails)
1 tablespoon lemon juice
¼ teaspoon lemon-pepper
    seasoning
    Nonstick spray coating
2 large shallots, finely chopped
¾ cup reduced-sodium chicken
    broth
¼ cup light dairy sour cream
1 tablespoon all-purpose flour
½ cup chopped fresh watercress
    or spinach leaves
2 teaspoons snipped fresh dill
    or ½ teaspoon dried
    dillweed
⅛ teaspoon pepper
1 lemon, quartered (optional)
    Fresh watercress sprigs
    (optional)

1. Thaw fish, if frozen. Rinse and pat dry with paper towels. Score fish by making 4 diagonal cuts on the top sides, slicing almost to the bone. Brush fish with lemon juice and sprinkle with lemon-pepper seasoning; set aside.

2. Spray a rack that fits a wok or Dutch oven with nonstick spray coating. Place steamer rack over water in a wok or Dutch oven. Bring water to boiling over high heat. Arrange fish on the rack so the pieces do not touch. Cover and steam about 15 minutes or till fish flakes easily with a fork.

3. Meanwhile, for sauce, spray a medium saucepan with nonstick coating. Cook shallots for 2 minutes or till tender. In a small mixing bowl stir together broth, sour cream, and flour; add all at once to saucepan. Cook and stir over medium heat till mixture is thickened and bubbly. Cook and stir for 1 minute more. Stir in the ½ cup watercress or spinach, dill, and pepper. Transfer fish to a serving platter; serve with watercress sauce. If desired, garnish with lemon wedges and watercress sprigs. Makes 4 servings.

Nutrition facts per serving: 198 calories, 6 g total fat (1 g saturated fat), 75 mg cholesterol, 135 mg sodium, 7 g carbohydrate, 0 g fiber, 28 g protein. **Daily values:** 18% vitamin A, 26% vitamin C, 9% calcium, 19% iron.

Using a sharp knife, make four diagonal cuts on the top side of each fish. Cut almost to the bone. The slits allow the lemon juice and lemon-pepper seasoning to flavor the flesh.

Low-fat

Low-calorie

Low-sodium

COLD POACHED SALMON WITH ASPARAGUS

Prepare this make-ahead dish as a spring or summer cold entrée (see photo, right), or use small servings for an elegant first course.

1 pound fresh or frozen skinless salmon or other fish fillets (½ to ¾ inch thick)

½ teaspoon garlic-pepper seasoning or seasoned pepper

1½ cups water

1 pound asparagus spears

1 small onion, sliced

½ cup dry white wine or reduced-sodium chicken broth

¼ cup fat-free mayonnaise or salad dressing

2 tablespoons skim milk or water

1 teaspoon finely shredded lime peel or lemon peel

1 tablespoon lime juice or lemon juice

Watercress sprigs and/or lettuce leaves (optional)

1. Thaw fish, if frozen. Rinse and pat dry with paper towels. Cut into 4 serving-size portions. Rub fish fillets with garlic-pepper seasoning; set aside.

2. Bring water to boiling in a large skillet. Wash asparagus; snap off and discard woody bases. Scrape off scales. Cook asparagus in boiling water, covered, for 4 to 8 minutes or till crisp-tender. Remove asparagus from cooking liquid, reserving liquid in skillet. Rinse asparagus in cold water; cool.

3. Add onion and wine or broth to skillet; return to boiling. Add salmon; reduce heat. Simmer, covered, till fish flakes easily with a fork (allow 4 to 6 minutes per ½-inch thickness of fish). Remove fish from pan; cool. Discard cooking liquid, including onion. Transfer fish and asparagus to separate storage containers and chill for up to 24 hours.

4. For dressing, in a small bowl stir together mayonnaise or salad dressing, milk or water, lime peel or lemon peel, and lime juice or lemon juice. If desired, line 4 plates with watercress and/or lettuce. Arrange fish and asparagus atop greens. Spoon some of the dressing over fish. Pass remaining dressing. Makes 4 servings.

Nutrition facts per serving: 162 calories, 4 g total fat (1 g saturated fat), 20 mg cholesterol, 271 mg sodium, 8 g carbohydrate, 2 g fiber, 18 g protein. **Daily values:** 8% vitamin A, 34% vitamin C, 3% calcium, 9% iron.

Fish and Seafood Buymanship

You don't need to be a marine specialist to make smart fish and seafood choices. Here are a few tips to keep in mind at the fresh fish counter.

Whole Fish: Eyes should be clear, bright, and not sunken. The gills should be bright red or pink, the skin should be shiny and elastic, and the scales should be tightly in place.

Fish Fillets and Steaks: Make sure the fish in the counter is displayed on a bed of ice. It should have a mild smell, not a fishy odor. Avoid fish that is dry around the edges.

Scallops: Select firm, sweet-smelling scallops in thin cloudy liquid. Don't buy scallops if they are in a thick liquid or have a strong sulfur odor.

Shrimp: Pick fresh shrimp that are moist and firm with translucent flesh and a fresh aroma. Avoid shrimp with an ammonialike smell.

Low-fat
Low-calorie
Low-sodium

HERBED BAKED FLOUNDER

Instead of sautéing the vegetables in oil, they are simmered in reduced-sodium chicken broth till tender.

1 pound fresh or frozen
    flounder, sole, or red
    snapper fillets
1 tablespoon lemon juice
½ cup chopped celery
½ cup chopped carrots
½ cup chopped onion
½ teaspoon dried basil, crushed
½ teaspoon dried thyme,
    crushed
¼ teaspoon dried rosemary,
    crushed
¼ cup reduced-sodium chicken
    broth
1 large tomato, seeded and
    chopped

1. Thaw fish, if frozen. Rinse and pat dry with paper towels. Cut fish into 4 serving-size portions. Arrange fish in a shallow baking dish, tucking under any thin edges for an even thickness. Drizzle with lemon juice.

2. In a medium skillet simmer celery, carrots, onion, and dried herbs in hot chicken broth, covered, for 5 to 8 minutes or till vegetables are tender. Remove from heat; stir in tomato, ⅛ teaspoon *salt*, and ⅛ teaspoon *pepper*. Spoon mixture evenly over fish fillets.

3. Bake, uncovered, in a 350° oven for 20 to 25 minutes or till fish flakes easily with a fork. Makes 4 servings.

Nutrition facts per serving: 141 calories, 2 g total fat (0 g saturated fat), 60 mg cholesterol, 208 mg sodium, 8 g carbohydrate, 2 g fiber, 23 g protein. **Daily values:** 76% vitamin A, 18% vitamin C, 4% calcium, 6% iron.

Low-fat
Low-calorie
Low-sodium

CIDER-BAKED FISH WITH RICE

1 pound fresh or frozen orange
    roughy or other white fish
    fillets (½ inch thick)
1 onion, thinly sliced
1 small red baking apple, thinly
    sliced
¼ teaspoon pepper
⅛ teaspoon salt
1½ cups apple cider or juice
2 cups hot cooked wild rice,
    brown rice, and/or long
    grain rice
¼ cup water
2 tablespoons all-purpose flour
2 tablespoons snipped fresh
    parsley

1. Thaw fish, if frozen. Rinse; pat dry with paper towels. Cut into 4 serving-size portions. Spray a shallow 2-quart baking dish with *nonstick spray coating*. Arrange fish fillets in pan, tucking under any thin edges for even thickness. Place onion and apple slices on top of fish; sprinkle with pepper and salt. Pour apple cider into dish.

2. Bake, uncovered, in a 350° oven for 15 to 20 minutes or till fish flakes easily with a fork. Spoon cooked rice onto a serving platter. Arrange fish and onion and apple slices atop rice; cover and keep warm. Reserve pan drippings.

3. For sauce, transfer pan drippings to a small saucepan. In a bowl stir water into the flour; add to pan. Cook and stir till mixture is thickened and bubbly. Stir in parsley; cook and stir 2 minutes more. Spoon sauce over fish and rice. Makes 4 servings.

Nutrition facts per serving: 285 calories, 2 g total fat (0 g saturated fat), 60 mg cholesterol, 168 mg sodium, 41 g carbohydrate, 3 g fiber, 25 g protein. **Daily values:** 2% vitamin A, 10% vitamin C, 3% calcium, 10% iron.

Low-fat

Low-calorie

Low-sodium

CATFISH EN PAPILLOTE

Baking fish in parchment is an elegant way to cook light. The paper allows the fish to cook in its own steam.

4 fresh or frozen skinless catfish or sole fillets (¾ to 1 pound)

Parchment paper or clean brown paper

2 tablespoons fat-free mayonnaise or salad dressing

1 2-ounce jar diced pimiento, drained

1 tablespoon lemon juice

1 tablespoon snipped fresh chives or 1 teaspoon dried chives

1 tablespoon snipped fresh parsley

1 teaspoon anchovy paste

¼ teaspoon pepper

1. Thaw fish, if frozen. Rinse fish and pat dry with paper towels. Cut 4 pieces of parchment paper or clean brown paper into heart shapes that are 12 inches wide and 9 inches high. In a small bowl stir together mayonnaise or salad dressing, pimiento, lemon juice, chives, parsley, anchovy paste, and pepper.

2. To assemble each packet, place one of the fish fillets in the center of one side of a parchment heart, tucking under any thin edges for an even thickness. Spoon ¼ of the mayonnaise mixture over each fish fillet. Fold the other side of each parchment heart over the fillet. Starting at the top and continuing to the bottom, seal tightly by turning up edges of the heart and folding in twice. At the bottom, twist the tip of the heart to seal.

3. Place packets in a shallow baking pan. Bake in a 450° oven about 10 minutes or till slightly puffed. Transfer to plates. To serve, cut an X in the top of each packet and pull back the paper. Makes 4 servings.

Nutrition facts per serving: 91 calories, 1 g total fat (0 g saturated fat), 66 mg cholesterol, 250 mg sodium, 3 g carbohydrate, 0 g fiber, 16 g protein. **Daily values:** 5% vitamin A, 28% vitamin C, 1% calcium, 4% iron.

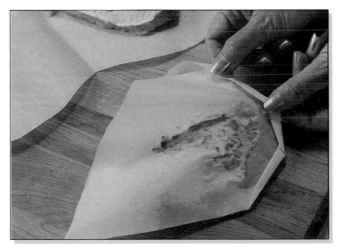

To make the parchment paper packets, fold the remaining half of the heart over the fish. Fold in the edges of the paper heart twice to make a tight seal, then twist the tip of the heart to complete the seal.

Low-fat

Low-calorie

RED SNAPPER WITH GINGER SAUCE

Fresh gingerroot imparts a tantalizing zing to this Oriental-style sauce. (See photo, right.)

1 pound fresh or frozen red snapper or other firm fish fillets (¾ inch thick)

¼ cup light soy sauce

3 tablespoons dry white or red wine or water

2 tablespoons sliced green onion

1 tablespoon grated gingerroot

1 clove garlic, quartered
  Nonstick spray coating

2 cups red or green sweet pepper strips and/or sliced zucchini

  Thin, long green onion strips (optional)

1. Thaw fish, if frozen. Rinse fish and pat dry with paper towels. Cut fish into 4 serving-size portions. Preheat broiler.

2. For sauce, in a blender container or food processor bowl combine the soy sauce, wine or water, sliced green onion, gingerroot, and garlic. Cover, and blend or process till pureed; set aside.

3. Spray the unheated rack of a broiler pan with nonstick coating. Place fish and sweet pepper strips or zucchini slices on rack. Broil 4 inches from the heat for 6 to 9 minutes or till fish flakes easily with a fork and vegetables are tender, brushing fish and vegetables with some of the sauce halfway through cooking. Place remaining sauce in a small saucepan and bring just to boiling. Transfer fish and vegetables to a serving platter; spoon remaining ginger sauce over fish. If desired, garnish with green onion strips. Makes 4 servings.

Nutrition facts per serving: 148 calories, 2 g total fat (0 g saturated fat), 42 mg cholesterol, 607 mg sodium, 4 g carbohydrate, 0 g fiber, 25 g protein. **Daily values:** 28% vitamin A, 105% vitamin C, 3% calcium, 5% iron.

Low-fat

Low-calorie

Low-sodium

BRAISED BASS WITH LEEKS AND MUSHROOMS

Top-of-the-stove cooking produces a quick, delicious, and a healthy, low-calorie dish.

1 pound fresh or frozen sea
   bass or other fish fillets
   ($\frac{1}{2}$ to $\frac{3}{4}$ inch thick)
1 cup dried shiitake or oyster
   mushrooms
1 cup boiling water
3 leeks
1 cup reduced-sodium chicken
   broth
1 tablespoon grated gingerroot
1 tablespoon finely shredded
   lemon peel
$\frac{1}{8}$ teaspoon pepper
1 tablespoon cornstarch
1 tablespoon water

1. Thaw fish, if frozen. Rinse fish and pat dry with paper towels. Cut into 4 serving-size portions. Place mushrooms in a bowl; add boiling water. Cover and let stand for 30 minutes. Drain mushrooms; trim off stems and discard. Slice mushrooms. Clean leeks by separating the leaves under running water. Slice leeks, using only the tender white parts (you should have about 1 cup).

2. In a large skillet combine mushrooms, leeks, chicken broth, gingerroot, lemon peel, and pepper. Bring mixture to boiling. Add fish to skillet. Cover; reduce heat and simmer over medium-low heat till fish flakes easily with a fork (allow 4 to 6 minutes per $\frac{1}{2}$-inch thickness of fish). Carefully transfer fish fillets to a serving platter; cover and keep warm.

3. In a small bowl combine cornstarch and water; stir into mushroom mixture in skillet. Cook and stir till thickened and bubbly; cook and stir 2 minutes more. Pass mushroom mixture with the fish. Makes 4 servings.

Nutrition facts per serving: 187 calories, 3 g total fat (1 g saturated fat), 47 mg cholesterol, 113 mg sodium, 17 g carbohydrate, 2 g fiber, 23 g protein. **Daily values:** 6% vitamin A, 27% vitamin C, 6% calcium, 18% iron.

Remove and discard the stems from the rehydrated mushrooms. Then cut the mushroom caps into thin slices.

Low-fat

Low-calorie

Low-sodium

CITRUS-SAUCED FISH

Orange sections are a pretty, nutritious addition to main dishes such as this one.
Just wait to stir them in until the last 2 minutes of cooking so the sections retain their shape.

1 pound fresh or frozen salmon,
    red snapper, or other fish
    fillets (¾ inch thick)
⅔ cup orange juice
1 teaspoon finely shredded
    lemon peel
2 tablespoons lemon juice or
    lime juice
1 green onion, chopped
1 clove garlic, minced
2 teaspoons cornstarch
1 orange, peeled and sectioned
2 tablespoons snipped fresh
    parsley
2 cups hot cooked rice

1. Thaw fish, if frozen. Rinse fish and pat dry with paper towels. Cut fish into 4 serving-size portions. In a medium skillet stir together orange juice, lemon peel, lemon juice or lime juice, onion, garlic, and ⅛ teaspoon *pepper.* Heat to boiling; add fish. Cover and simmer till fish flakes easily with a fork (allow 4 to 6 minutes per ½-inch thickness of fish). Transfer fish to a serving platter, cover and keep warm. Reserve juices in skillet.

2. For sauce, in a small bowl stir cornstarch into ¼ cup *water;* stir into reserved juices in skillet. Cook and stir till thickened and bubbly. Cook and stir 2 minutes more. Stir in orange sections and parsley; heat through. To serve, spoon sauce and fruit sections over fish; serve with hot cooked rice. Makes 4 servings.

Nutrition facts per serving: 241 calories, 4 g total fat (1 g saturated fat), 20 mg cholesterol, 71 mg sodium, 31 g carbohydrate, 1 g fiber, 19 g protein. **Daily values:** 5% vitamin A, 60% vitamin C, 2% calcium, 13% iron.

Low-fat

Low-calorie

Low-sodium

HERBED HALIBUT

Try this fish served over a bed of steamed, julienned carrots and zucchini tossed with a bit of olive oil and grated Parmesan cheese.

4 fresh or frozen halibut,
    salmon, or swordfish steaks,
    cut ¾ to 1 inch thick
    (1¼ to 1½ pounds total)
⅓ cup chopped onion
½ teaspoon dried basil, crushed
½ teaspoon dried chervil,
    crushed, or dried dillweed
1 clove garlic, minced
⅛ teaspoon pepper
2 teaspoons cooking oil
¼ cup snipped fresh parsley
⅓ cup plain fat-free yogurt
    Lemon wedges and parsley
    sprigs (optional)

1. Thaw fish, if frozen. Rinse fish and pat dry with paper towels. In a small saucepan cook onion, basil, chervil or dillweed, garlic, and pepper in hot oil till onion is tender but not brown. Stir in parsley.

2. Spray a rack with *nonstick spray coating;* place on a shallow baking pan. Arrange fish steaks on rack. Bake, uncovered, in a 400° oven for 10 minutes. Remove from oven. Spread fish with yogurt; sprinkle with onion-herb mixture. Bake 5 to 10 minutes more or till fish flakes easily with a fork. If desired, garnish with lemon wedges and parsley sprigs. Makes 4 servings.

Nutrition facts per serving: 195 calories, 6 g total fat (1 g saturated fat), 46 mg cholesterol, 93 mg sodium, 4 g carbohydrate, 0 g fiber, 31 g protein. **Daily values:** 8% vitamin A, 10% vitamin C, 9% calcium, 10% iron.

Low-calorie
Low-sodium

GRILLED CATFISH WITH HORSERADISH SAUCE

Spunky horseradish sauce adds spirit to the fish (see photo, left) and also is great with lean roast beef.

1 pound fresh or frozen skinless
    catfish or other firm fish
    fillets (¾ to 1 inch thick)
1 tablespoon all-purpose flour
¾ cup skim milk
1 tablespoon snipped chives
    or 1 teaspoon dried
    snipped chives
2 teaspoons prepared
    horseradish
1 teaspoon lemon juice
⅛ teaspoon salt
1 teaspoon olive or
    vegetable oil
½ teaspoon salt-free seasoning
    blend
⅛ teaspoon pepper (optional)
    Fresh chives (optional)

1. Thaw fish, if frozen. Rinse fish and pat dry with paper towels. Cut fish into 4 serving-size portions; set aside.

2. For horseradish sauce, place flour in a small saucepan. Stir in milk till smooth. Cook and stir till thickened and bubbly. Cook 1 minute more; remove from heat. Stir in snipped chives, horseradish, lemon juice, and salt. Cover and set aside.

3. Brush fish with oil; sprinkle with seasoning blend and, if desired, pepper. Place fish in a greased grill basket on the grill over medium coals. Grill till fish flakes easily with a fork (allow 4 to 6 minutes per ½-inch thickness of fish), turning once. (Or to broil, spray the unheated rack of a broiler pan with *nonstick spray coating*. Place fish on the rack. Broil 4 inches from the heat till fish flakes easily with a fork, allowing 4 to 6 minutes per ½-inch thickness of fish).

4. To serve, dollop horseradish sauce atop fish. If desired, garnish with fresh chives. Makes 4 servings.

Nutrition facts per serving: 208 calories, 10 g total fat (2 g saturated fat), 73 mg cholesterol, 210 mg sodium, 4 g carbohydrate, 0 g fiber, 23 g protein. **Daily values:** 4% vitamin A, 4% vitamin C, 5% calcium, 7% iron.

Farm-Raised Fish

It's not as strange as it sounds, thanks to aquaculture—raising fish and shellfish in a controlled environment. The fish and shellfish hatch, feed, and stay disease-free in pens, ponds, or tanks until they show up at the fish counter. And that's good news because it means greater availability of high-quality seafood at lower prices.

Catfish, salmon, and trout lead the market so far, followed by hybrid striped bass, redfish, mussels, clams, oysters, crawfish, shrimp, sturgeon, and tilapia (a mild-flavored white fish). These farm-raised fish are generally milder tasting than their wild counterparts since they eat a consistent and controlled diet.

Low-fat

Low-calorie

Low-sodium

SWEET AND SOUR MAHIMAHI

You can make this marinade the night before and chill it in a covered jar.

1 **pound fresh or frozen mahimahi, swordfish, or tuna steaks (about ¾ inch thick)**

3 **tablespoons rice wine or dry white wine**

2 **tablespoons dry sherry**

1 **tablespoon honey**

2 **teaspoons light soy sauce**

1½ **teaspoons grated gingerroot**

2 **cloves garlic, minced**

⅛ **teaspoon pepper**

Nonstick spray coating

Hot cooked rice or egg noodles (optional)

1. Thaw fish, if frozen. Rinse fish and pat dry with paper towels. Cut into 4 serving-size portions. Place fish in a shallow nonmetal dish. In a small bowl stir together wine, sherry, honey, soy sauce, gingerroot, garlic, and pepper. Pour over fish; cover and marinate at room temperature for 30 minutes. Drain, reserving marinade.

2. Preheat broiler. Spray the unheated rack of a broiler pan with nonstick spray coating. Arrange fish on broiler pan; brush with reserved marinade. Broil 4 to 5 inches from heat till fish flakes easily with a fork (allow 4 to 6 minutes per ½-inch thickness of fish), brushing occasionally with marinade. If desired, serve fish with hot cooked rice or egg noodles. Makes 4 servings.

Nutrition facts per serving: 134 calories, 1 g total fat (0 g saturated fat), 83 mg cholesterol, 205 mg sodium, 6 g carbohydrate, 0 g fiber, 21 g protein. **Daily values:** 0% vitamin A, 0% vitamin C, 0% calcium, 9% iron.

Low-calorie
Low-sodium

CAJUN-STYLE BROILED SWORDFISH

If you're short on preparation time, use a premixed, bottled, Cajun-style seasoning in place of this seasoning mixture.

4 fresh or frozen swordfish or
  shark steaks, cut ¾ to 1
  inch thick (1 to 1¼ pounds)
1 teaspoon paprika
½ teaspoon dried thyme,
  crushed
¼ teaspoon garlic powder
¼ teaspoon black pepper
¼ teaspoon dried oregano,
  crushed
⅛ teaspoon salt
⅛ teaspoon ground red pepper
¼ cup lemon or orange juice
  Nonstick spray coating

1. Thaw fish, if frozen. Rinse fish and pat dry with paper towels. For seasoning mixture, in a shallow dish stir together paprika, thyme, garlic powder, black pepper, oregano, salt, and ground red pepper. Place lemon juice or orange juice in a shallow bowl. Dip steaks in juice, then coat lightly with seasoning mixture.

2. Preheat broiler. Spray the unheated rack of a broiler pan with nonstick spray coating. Arrange seasoned fish on broiler rack. Broil 4 inches from heat till fish flakes easily with a fork (allow 4 to 6 minutes per ½-inch thickness), turning once. Makes 4 servings.

Nutrition facts per serving: 145 calories, 5 g total fat (1 g saturated fat), 45 mg cholesterol, 169 mg sodium, 2 g carbohydrate, 0 g fiber, 23 g protein. **Daily values:** 7% vitamin A, 14% vitamin C, 0% calcium, 8% iron.

Low-fat
Low-calorie
Low-sodium

CANTONESE GRILLED SHARK

For a spicier marinade, add a few dashes of bottled hot pepper sauce or a minced fresh serrano or jalapeño pepper.

1¼ to 1½ pounds fresh or frozen
  shark, swordfish, or tuna
  steaks (about 1 inch thick)
¼ cup finely chopped green
  onion
3 tablespoons light soy sauce
3 tablespoons dry sherry or
  water
2 tablespoons snipped fresh
  cilantro or parsley
2 cloves garlic, minced
1 teaspoon sesame seed, toasted
  Lime slices or lemon slices
  (optional)

1. Thaw fish, if frozen. Rinse fish and pat dry with paper towels. Cut fish into 4 serving-size portions. In a small bowl stir together green onion, soy sauce, sherry or water, cilantro or parsley, garlic, and sesame seed. Place fish in a shallow nonmetal dish; spoon soy mixture over fish. Cover and marinate in the refrigerator for up to 2 hours. Drain, reserving marinade.

2. Spray a grill rack with *nonstick spray coating.* Grill fish directly over medium coals, uncovered, for 8 to 12 minutes or till fish flakes easily with a fork; turn fish and brush with marinade once during grilling. (Or to broil, spray the unheated rack of a broiler pan with nonstick coating and arrange fish steaks atop. Broil 4 inches from heat for 8 to 12 minutes, turning and brushing with marinade once.) If desired, garnish with lime slices or lemon slices. Makes 4 servings.

Nutrition facts per serving: 194 calories, 6 g total fat (2 g saturated fat), 56 mg cholesterol, 596 mg sodium, 2 g carbohydrate, 0 g fiber, 29 g protein. **Daily values:** 5% vitamin A, 4% vitamin C, 1% calcium, 10% iron.

Low-fat

Low-calorie

Low-sodium

MAHIMAHI WITH YELLOW PEPPER SAUCE

Roasting peppers enhances their naturally sweet flavor and is the key to this recipe. (See photo, right.)

1 pound skinless mahimahi
   fillets or other firm fish
   fillets (¾ to 1 inch thick)
2 yellow or red sweet peppers
½ cup plain fat-free yogurt
1 tablespoon fresh parsley
   leaves
1½ teaspoons snipped fresh basil
   or ½ teaspoon dried basil,
   crushed
½ teaspoon finely shredded
   lemon peel
⅛ teaspoon pepper
   Nonstick spray coating
1 tablespoon lemon juice
   Skim milk
   Sliced tomatoes (optional)
   Lime or lemon slices
   (optional)

1. Thaw fish, if frozen. Rinse fish and pat dry with paper towels. Cut fish into 4 serving-size portions.

2. Quarter sweet peppers; remove stems, seeds, and membranes. Place pepper pieces, cut sides down, on a foil-lined baking sheet. Bake in a 425° oven for 20 to 25 minutes or till skins are blistered and dark. Transfer peppers to a clean paper bag; close bag and let stand about 15 minutes to steam so the skin peels away more easily. With a small sharp knife, peel skin from peppers in strips. Discard skin. Cut 6 narrow strips of roasted pepper; halve strips and reserve for garnish.

3. For sauce, place remaining roasted sweet pepper in a blender container or food processor bowl. Cover, and blend or process till nearly smooth, stopping and scraping sides of container as necessary. Add yogurt, parsley, basil, lemon peel, and pepper; blend or process till combined. Transfer to a small saucepan; cover and set aside.

4. Spray the unheated rack of a broiler pan with nonstick coating. Arrange fish on broiler pan; brush with lemon juice. Broil 4 inches from heat till fish flakes easily with a fork (allow 4 to 6 minutes per ½-inch thickness of fish), turning once. Heat and stir sauce over medium-low heat till warmed through (do not boil). Stir up to 2 tablespoons milk into sauce till it reaches the desired consistency.

5. If desired, serve fish atop hot cooked rice. Spoon sauce over fish. Garnish with reserved sweet pepper strips and, if desired, sliced tomatoes and lime or lemon slices. Makes 4 servings.

Nutrition facts per serving: 127 calories, 1 g total fat (0 g saturated fat), 84 mg cholesterol, 125 mg sodium, 6 g carbohydrate, 0 g fiber, 23 g protein. **Daily .values:** 3% vitamin A, 51% vitamin C, 6% calcium, 10% iron.

Low-fat

Low-sodium

High-fiber

ZESTY JALAPEÑO FISH FILLETS

Jalapeño pepper jelly contributes a little heat and a touch of sweetness to an easy sauce mixture.

3 medium carrots, julienned
     (1½ cups)
1 medium zucchini, julienned
     (1½ cups)
1 pound skinless fish fillets,
     such as red snapper,
     flounder, sole, haddock, or
     orange roughy
½ teaspoon instant chicken
     bouillon granules
1½ cups boiling water
1 cup couscous
⅓ cup jalapeño pepper jelly
1 tablespoon white wine vinegar
     or vinegar
1 tablespoon snipped fresh
     cilantro or parsley

1. In a saucepan cook carrots, covered, in a small amount of boiling water for 2 minutes; add the zucchini and cook 2 minutes more or till vegetables are crisp-tender. Drain, cover, and keep warm.

2. Rinse fish and pat dry with paper towels. Cut into 4 serving-size portions. Spray the unheated rack of a broiler pan with *nonstick spray coating.* Place fish on the rack. Season with *salt* and *pepper.* Measure the thickness of the fish. Broil fish 4 inches from the heat just till it flakes easily with a fork (allow 4 to 6 minutes per ½-inch thickness of fish).

3. Meanwhile, for couscous, dissolve the chicken bouillon granules in 1½ cups boiling water. Stir in couscous. Cover and let stand for 3 to 5 minutes or till the liquid is absorbed.

4. In a small saucepan stir together jelly and vinegar. Heat and stir over low heat till jelly is melted.

5. To serve, use a fork to fluff the couscous; stir in the cilantro or parsley. Spoon the couscous onto dinner plates. Top with a fish portion and vegetables. Drizzle with the warm jelly mixture. Makes 4 servings.

Nutrition facts per serving: 375 calories, 2 g total fat (0 g saturated fat), 60 mg cholesterol, 358 mg sodium, 60 g carbohydrate, 10 g fiber, 28 g protein. **Daily values:** 130% vitamin A, 5% vitamin C, 4% calcium, 9% iron.

Low-fat

Low-calorie

Low-sodium

SEAFOOD BURGERS

You can substitute one 7½-ounce can low-sodium salmon—drained, flaked, and skin and bones removed—for the tuna.

½ cup finely chopped red sweet
  pepper
½ cup thinly sliced green onions
¼ cup skim milk
1 tablespoon all-purpose flour
¼ teaspoon dried dillweed
1 6½-ounce can low-sodium
  chunk light tuna, drained
  and flaked
1 6½-ounce can crabmeat,
  drained, flaked, and
  cartilage removed
1 egg white
¾ cup fine dry bread crumbs
4 hamburger buns, split and
  toasted

1. In a small saucepan bring ¼ cup *water* to boiling. Add sweet pepper and green onions. Cover and cook for 5 minutes or till vegetables are tender; do not drain. In a small bowl stir together milk and flour; add to vegetable mixture. Stir in dillweed and a dash *pepper*. Cook and stir till thickened and bubbly. Cool slightly (about 5 minutes). Stir in tuna, crabmeat, egg white, and *½ cup* of the bread crumbs. With your hands, shape mixture into four ½-inch-thick patties (mixture will be slightly wet). Coat patties with remaining bread crumbs.

2. Spray a 12-inch skillet with *nonstick spray coating*. Cook patties over medium heat for 5 minutes; turn patties over and cook for 3 to 4 minutes more or till golden and heated through. Serve on toasted buns. If desired, top burgers with fat-free mayonnaise or salad dressing, tomato slices, and/or lettuce. Makes 4 servings.

Nutrition facts per serving: 298 calories, 5 g total fat (1 g saturated fat), 58 mg cholesterol, 479 mg sodium, 36 g carbohydrate, 1 g fiber, 26 g protein. **Daily values:** 12% vitamin A, 36% vitamin C, 6% calcium, 14% iron.

Low-fat

Low-calorie

Low-sodium

SALMON HASH WITH POTATOES AND PEPPERS

This easy one-dish dinner brings color, taste and a change of pace to the table.

1 pound (3 medium) potatoes
1 medium red sweet pepper
1 medium green sweet pepper
½ cup reduced-sodium chicken
  broth
½ cup chopped onion
1 teaspoon dried basil, crushed
¼ teaspoon dried thyme,
  crushed
1 7½-ounce can low-sodium
  salmon, drained, flaked,
  and skin and bones
  removed
½ cup drained, canned whole-
  kernel corn

1. If desired, peel potatoes; dice potatoes. In a large skillet bring 1 cup *water* to boiling. Add potatoes; cover and cook for 20 to 25 minutes or till tender. Drain; return potatoes to skillet.

2. Meanwhile, chop red and green sweet peppers. To the skillet, add sweet peppers, chicken broth, onion, basil, thyme, ⅛ teaspoon *salt*, and ⅛ teaspoon *pepper*. Cover and simmer for 5 minutes or till sweet peppers are tender. Stir in salmon and corn. Cover and cook 2 to 3 minutes more or till heated through. If desired, garnish with snipped fresh parsley. Makes 4 servings.

Nutrition facts per serving: 228 calories, 3 g total fat (0 g saturated fat), 0 mg cholesterol, 204 mg sodium, 34 g carbohydrate, 2 g fiber, 15 g protein. **Daily values:** 16% vitamin A, 108% vitamin C, 12% calcium, 19% iron.

Low-fat

Low-calorie

Low-sodium

SEAFOOD JAMBALAYA

Cajun cooking comes to life here (see photo, left). Use purchased Cajun seasoning or mix up your own using the recipe below.

½ pound fresh or frozen firm
    fish fillets or steaks, such as
    halibut, swordfish, or tuna
½ pound fresh or frozen shrimp
    in shells
1 28-ounce can low-sodium
    tomatoes, cut up
1½ cups chopped yellow, green,
    and/or red sweet pepper
1½ cups reduced-sodium chicken
    broth
1 cup chopped onion
1 cup chopped celery
1 teaspoon Cajun seasoning
2 cloves garlic, minced
1 bay leaf
¼ teaspoon ground cloves
⅔ cup long grain rice
¼ cup snipped fresh parsley

1. Thaw fish and shrimp, if frozen. Rinse fish and pat dry with paper towels. Cut into 1-inch pieces. Peel and devein shrimp; set aside.

2. In a large saucepan combine *undrained* tomatoes, sweet pepper, chicken broth, onion, celery, Cajun seasoning, garlic, bay leaf, and cloves. Bring to boiling; reduce heat. Simmer, covered, for 10 minutes.

3. Add rice; return to boiling. Reduce heat. Simmer, covered, for 15 minutes. Add fish and shrimp; cook 5 minutes more or till shrimp turn opaque and fish flakes easily with a fork, stirring occasionally. Stir in parsley; remove bay leaf. Ladle mixture into bowls. Makes 6 to 8 servings.

Nutrition facts per serving: 200 calories, 2 g total fat (0 g saturated fat), 56 mg cholesterol, 167 mg sodium, 29 g carbohydrate, 3 g fiber, 17 g protein. **Daily values:** 32% vitamin A, 115% vitamin C, 8% calcium, 22% iron.

Homemade Cajun Seasoning: In a small mixing bowl combine 1 teaspoon *white pepper*, 1 teaspoon *garlic powder*, 1 teaspoon *onion powder*, 1 teaspoon *ground red pepper*, 1 teaspoon *paprika*, and 1 teaspoon *black pepper*. Store in an airtight container in a cool, dry place. Makes 2 tablespoons.

Fast and Fabulous Fish

When you're looking for a healthy, fast meal, there's no need to go out for dinner. You can serve broiled fish in minutes.

To broil fish fillets or steaks, spray the cold rack of a broiler pan with nonstick spray coating. Place the fresh or thawed frozen fillets or steaks on the rack. For fillets, tuck under any thin edges. Broil 4 inches from the heat for 4 to 6 minutes per ½-inch thickness or just till fish begins to flake easily. (If the fish is 1 inch or more thick, turn it over halfway through broiling.)

Add flavor and variety to the fish with any one of these low-calorie, nonfat accompaniments.

- Stir together nonfat plain yogurt; chopped, seeded cucumber; and a little dillweed.
- Use your favorite nonfat salad dressing as a marinade or dipping sauce for the fish.
- Squeeze fresh lemon juice over the fish and sprinkle with snipped fresh chives, dillweed, or parsley.

Low-fat

Low-calorie

Low-sodium

SPICY CRAWFISH BOIL

Serve this in true Louisiana style: Set a newspaper-covered table with large napkins and a big bowl for the discarded shells.

**4 pounds live crawfish or
1¼ pounds fresh or frozen
shrimp in shells**

**3 tablespoons salt (only if using
crawfish)**

3 lemons, quartered

2 stalks celery, chopped

2 small onions, quartered

**2 teaspoons salt-free seasoning
blend**

1 teaspoon dried basil, crushed

1 teaspoon celery seed

**1 teaspoon dried thyme or
marjoram, crushed**

1 teaspoon pepper

½ teaspoon dry mustard

2 bay leaves

½ teaspoon ground allspice

**½ teaspoon bottled hot pepper
sauce**

¼ teaspoon whole cloves

Fresh lemon wedges

Cocktail Sauce

1. If using crawfish, rinse the live crawfish under cold running water. In a 12- to 16-quart kettle combine 8 quarts *cold water* and the salt. Add crawfish and soak for 15 minutes; drain. Rinse well; drain again. If using shrimp, thaw it, if frozen; do not soak. Rinse under cold running water; drain. Shell and devein shrimp.

2. Place lemons, celery, onions, seasoning blend, basil, celery seed, thyme, pepper, dry mustard, bay leaves, allspice, hot pepper sauce, and cloves on a large piece of 100% cotton cheesecloth several layers thick. Bring up corners of cheesecloth and tie closed with cotton string. For crawfish, place cheesecloth bundle in a 12- to 16-quart kettle with 8 quarts *water* and bring to boiling. For shrimp, place cheesecloth bundle in a Dutch oven with 4 quarts *water* and bring to boiling. Boil mixture, covered, for 10 minutes. Add crawfish or shrimp; return to boiling. Reduce heat and cover. Simmer crawfish about 5 minutes or till shells turn bright red; simmer shrimp about 3 minutes or till shrimp turn pink. Drain; serve on a large serving platter. Serve with fresh lemon wedges and Cocktail Sauce. Serves 6.

Nutrition facts per serving: 111 calories, 3 g total fat (1 g saturated fat), 145 mg cholesterol, 273 mg sodium, 4 g carbohydrate, 1 g fiber, 16 g protein. **Daily values:** 12% vitamin A, 17% vitamin C, 4% calcium, 22% iron.

Cocktail Sauce: In a 1-quart saucepan cook 1 tablespoon finely chopped *onion* and 1 clove minced *garlic* in 1 tablespoon *margarine* till tender. Stir in ⅔ cup *water*, ½ of a 6-ounce can (⅓ cup) low-sodium *tomato paste*, 1 tablespoon *prepared horseradish*, 2 teaspoons *lemon juice*, ½ teaspoon *dry mustard*, ⅛ teaspoon *salt*, and a dash to ⅛ teaspoon *ground red pepper*. Bring to boiling. Reduce heat. Simmer, uncovered, for 5 to 10 minutes or till it reaches the desired consistency. Serve warm or chilled. Store any remaining sauce in a tightly covered container in the refrigerator for up to 1 week. Makes about ¾ cup.

When eating cooked crawfish, remove the meat from the shell by gently twisting the tail away from the body. Unwrap sections of the shell to expose the meat.

SHRIMP AND CRAB MORNAY

Low-fat

½ pound fresh or frozen shelled
   shrimp
1 6-ounce package frozen
   crabmeat
2 cups fresh pea pods
1 cup dry white wine
1 cup reduced-sodium chicken
   broth
¼ teaspoon lemon-pepper
   seasoning
½ cup sliced green onions
⅔ cup skim milk
1 tablespoon cornstarch
1 cup shredded reduced-fat
   process Swiss cheese
Hot cooked pasta

1. Thaw shrimp, if frozen, and crab. Remove strings from pea pods; cut pods crosswise in thirds and set aside. In a large skillet combine wine, broth, and lemon-pepper seasoning; bring to boiling. Add shrimp and green onions. Return to boiling. Cover; simmer for 1 to 3 minutes or till shrimp turn opaque. With a slotted spoon, remove shrimp; set aside.

2. Boil liquid, uncovered, for 5 to 10 minutes or till reduced to ½ cup. In a small bowl stir together milk and cornstarch. Add to the ½ cup liquid. Add pea pods and crab. Cook and stir till bubbly. Stir in cheese till melted. Remove from heat. Stir in shrimp. Toss with hot cooked pasta. Makes 4 servings.

Nutrition facts per serving: 308 calories, 5 g total fat (2 g saturated fat), 145 mg cholesterol, 679 mg sodium, 23 g carbohydrate, 2 g fiber, 30 g protein. **Daily values:** 11% vitamin A, 56% vitamin C, 25% calcium, 26% iron.

Low-fat

Low-calorie

SHERRIED SHRIMP WITH SNOW PEAS

1 pound fresh or frozen shrimp
   in shells
1 medium red, yellow, or green
   sweet pepper
2 tablespoons dry sherry
2 tablespoons light soy sauce
1 teaspoon toasted sesame seed
⅛ teaspoon crushed red pepper
½ cup reduced-sodium chicken
   broth
2 green onions, bias-sliced into
   ½-inch pieces
1 cup bias-sliced celery
2 cups fresh snow peas,
   trimmed
2 cloves garlic, minced
Hot cooked rice

1. Thaw shrimp, if frozen. Rinse shrimp and drain. Peel and devein shrimp; set aside. (To devein shrimp, use a sharp knife to make a shallow slit along the back from head to tail. Use the tip of a knife to remove the vein, or rinse it out under cold running water.) Julienne sweet pepper; set aside. In a small bowl combine sherry, soy sauce, sesame seed, and crushed red pepper; set aside.

2. Spray an unheated wok or large skillet with _nonstick spray coating_. Heat _2 tablespoons_ of the broth in the wok. Add sweet pepper and green onions; cook for 1½ minutes. With a slotted spoon, remove vegetables from wok. Add more broth, if necessary; add celery, and cook and stir for 3 minutes. Remove celery from wok. Add more broth, if necessary; add snow peas and garlic; cook and stir for 1 to 2 minutes. Remove vegetables from wok. Add more broth, if necessary; stir-fry shrimp for 2 minutes or till shrimp turn opaque. Add sherry-soy sauce mixture to wok. Return all vegetables to wok; toss all ingredients to coat with sauce. Cover; cook 1 to 2 minutes more or till heated through. Serve over hot cooked rice. Makes 4 servings.

Nutrition facts per serving: 230 calories, 2 g total fat (0 g saturated fat), 142 mg cholesterol, 528 mg sodium, 31 g carbohydrate, 3 g fiber, 21 g protein. **Daily values:** 22% vitamin A, 104% vitamin C, 7% calcium, 32% iron.

Low-fat

Low-calorie

Low-sodium

POACHED SHRIMP WITH GREEN CHILI RICE

Look for the tomatillos used in this dish (photo, right) in the produce section of a supermarket or a Mexican grocery store.

1 pound fresh or frozen shrimp
    in shells

8 tomatillos, husked and cut up

1 medium onion, cut up

1 jalapeño, serrano, or banana
    pepper, seeded and cut up

1 tablespoon chopped mild
    green chili pepper (canned
    or fresh)

1 tablespoon cilantro or parsley
    leaves

1 clove garlic, quartered

½ teaspoon dried oregano,
    crushed

½ teaspoon sugar

¼ teaspoon salt-free seasoning
    blend

2 cups hot cooked rice

1 cup water

1 cup dry white wine or
    reduced-sodium chicken
    broth

2 lemon or lime slices

¼ teaspoon peppercorns
    Fresh cilantro or parsley
    sprigs (optional)

1. Thaw shrimp, if frozen. Peel and devein shrimp; set aside.

2. For green chili rice, in a blender container or food processor bowl combine tomatillos; onion; jalapeño, serrano, or banana pepper; mild green chili pepper; cilantro or parsley; garlic; oregano; sugar; and seasoning blend. Cover, and blend or process till smooth, stopping and scraping sides of container as necessary. Transfer mixture to a medium saucepan; heat through. Stir in hot cooked rice; cover and keep warm.

3. In a Dutch oven or large saucepan combine water, wine or broth, lemon or lime slices, and peppercorns. Bring to boiling; add shrimp. Simmer for 3 to 5 minutes or till shrimp turn opaque; drain. Spoon green chili rice onto serving platter; top with shrimp. If desired, garnish with cilantro or parsley sprigs. Makes 4 servings.

Nutrition facts per serving: 247 calories, 2 g total fat (0 g saturated fat), 131 mg cholesterol, 177 mg sodium, 31 g carbohydrate, 1 g fiber, 17 g protein. **Daily values:** 6% vitamin A, 34% vitamin C, 5% calcium, 22% iron.

Give Tomatillos a Try

Popular in Mexican and Tex-Mex cooking, tomatillos (toe muh TEE yos) are not related to tomatoes, even though the names sound similar. This small, olive green fruit is covered with a thin, papery brown husk, which is removed before using. Its texture is like that of a firm tomato with lots of seeds and the flavor is rather acidic with hints of lemon and apple.

Fresh tomatillos are available year-round. Look for firm tomatillos with tight-fitting, dry husks. Avoid shriveled and bruised ones. Canned, husked tomatillos also are available.

Low-fat

Low-calorie

Low-sodium

High-fiber

OVEN-BAKED CRAB CAKES

You can roast your own peppers for this special relish—see page 56 for directions.

1 beaten egg

1 beaten egg white

1 cup soft bread crumbs

2 tablespoons mayonnaise

2 teaspoons dried dillweed

2 tablespoons sliced green
   onion (optional)

2 teaspoons Dijon-style mustard

1 teaspoon seafood seasoning

¼ teaspoon pepper

12 ounces fresh lump crabmeat
   or frozen crabmeat, thawed
   Red Pepper Relish

1. In a medium mixing bowl combine egg, egg white, bread crumbs, mayonnaise, dillweed, green onion (if desired), mustard, seafood seasoning, and pepper. Stir in crabmeat. Shape mixture into five ½-inch-thick patties. Place in a greased shallow baking pan.

2. Bake, uncovered, in a 450° oven for 10 minutes, turning once. Serve with Red Pepper Relish. Makes 5 servings.

Red Pepper Relish: In a small mixing bowl combine half of a 7-ounce jar *roasted red sweet peppers,* drained and chopped; 1 tablespoon drained and chopped *oil-packed dried tomatoes;* and ½ teaspoon *seafood seasoning.* Makes ½ cup.

Nutrition facts per crab cake with 2 tablespoons relish: 157 calories, 8 g total fat (1 g saturated fat), 113 mg cholesterol, 338 mg sodium, 5 g carbohydrate, 0 g fiber, 17 g protein. **Daily values:** 2% vitamin A, 3% vitamin C, 7% calcium, 7% iron.

Low-fat

Low-calorie

Low-sodium

SCALLOPS SCAMPI-STYLE

Sea scallops can be quite large. For this recipe, halve or quarter them. (See photo, left.)

1 9-ounce package refrigerated
   spinach fettuccine or plain
   fettuccine

12 ounces fresh or frozen bay or
   sea scallops

¾ cup reduced-sodium chicken
   broth

½ cup dry white wine

½ teaspoon dried oregano,
   crushed

½ teaspoon dried rosemary,
   crushed

¼ teaspoon cracked black
   pepper

3 cloves garlic, minced

4 teaspoons cornstarch

3 tablespoons snipped parsley

1. Cook pasta according to package directions; drain. Keep warm.

2. Thaw scallops, if frozen. Halve or quarter any large scallops. In a large saucepan combine chicken broth, ¼ cup of the wine, oregano, rosemary, cracked pepper, and garlic. Heat to boiling. Add scallops; return to boiling. Reduce heat; cover and simmer for 1 to 2 minutes or till scallops are opaque. Drain, reserving cooking liquid. Return liquid to saucepan.

3. In a small bowl combine the remaining wine and cornstarch. Add to cooking liquid; cook and stir till thickened and bubbly. Cook and stir for 2 minutes more. Stir in scallops and parsley; heat through. Serve scallop mixture over the hot cooked pasta. Makes 4 servings.

Nutrition facts per serving: 272 calories, 2 g total fat (0 g saturated fat), 72 mg cholesterol, 223 mg sodium, 40 g carbohydrate, 0 g fiber, 19 g protein. **Daily values:** 3% vitamin A, 17% vitamin C, 8% calcium, 18% iron.

Low-fat

Low-calorie

Low-sodium

CRAB LEGS IN VERMOUTH

Use the full-flavored cooking liquid to create a quick and tasty dipping sauce.

2 pounds fresh or frozen split
    crab legs
1 cup dry vermouth or dry
    white wine
1 cup clam juice
2 tablespoons lemon juice
2 parsley sprigs
2 cloves garlic, minced
1 tablespoon cornstarch
2 tablespoons cold water
    Lemon wedges (optional)

1. Thaw crab legs, if frozen. In a large saucepan or Dutch oven combine vermouth, clam juice, lemon juice, parsley, and garlic. Bring to boiling; reduce heat. Cover and simmer for 10 minutes. Add crab; simmer for 2 to 3 minutes or till crab is heated through. Transfer crab to a serving platter and keep warm; reserve cooking liquid.

2. For dipping sauce, strain cooking liquid; measure 1 cup. In a small saucepan stir together cornstarch and cold water. Add the 1 cup cooking liquid. Cook and stir till thickened and bubbly. Cook and stir 2 minutes more. Serve crab legs with dipping sauce and, if desired, lemon wedges. Makes 4 servings.

Nutrition facts per serving: 113 calories, 1 g total fat (0 g saturated fat), 71 mg cholesterol, 264 mg sodium, 3 g carbohydrate, 0 g fiber, 15 g protein. **Daily values:** 3% vitamin A, 15% vitamin C, 6% calcium, 37% iron.

Low-calorie

Low-sodium

CRAB-STUFFED SUMMER SQUASH

1 6-ounce package frozen
    crabmeat
4 medium zucchini or yellow
    summer squash
8 dried tomatoes (dry pack)
2 teaspoons olive or cooking oil
¼ cup chopped onion
¼ cup chopped red, yellow, or
    green sweet pepper
1 clove garlic, minced
2 tablespoons all-purpose flour
1 teaspoon dried basil, crushed
½ teaspoon dried dillweed
¾ cup skim milk
½ cup shredded part-skim
    mozzarella cheese
1 teaspoon finely shredded
    lemon peel
1 tablespoon lemon juice
    Few dashes bottled hot
    pepper sauce

1. Thaw and flake crabmeat; set aside. Halve squash lengthwise. Trim a thin slice from the bottom of each squash half. Turn squash cut side up. Scoop out pulp leaving ¼-inch-thick shells. Chop enough pulp to equal 1 cup; set aside. Cook squash shells in enough boiling water to cover for 5 minutes. With a slotted spoon, remove from pan, reserving liquid in pan. Drain shells upside down on paper towels; set aside. Add tomatoes to reserved cooking liquid; let stand for 15 minutes. Drain tomatoes and finely chop.

2. Heat oil in a medium skillet. Cook reserved squash pulp, onion, sweet pepper, and garlic in the hot oil for 5 minutes. Stir in flour, basil, dillweed, and ⅛ teaspoon *pepper*. Add milk all at once. Cook and stir till thickened and bubbly; remove from heat. Stir in cheese till melted. Add crabmeat, tomatoes, lemon peel, lemon juice, and hot pepper sauce.

3. Arrange squash shells, cut sides up, in a 3-quart rectangular baking dish. Spoon crab mixture into squash shells. Cover dish with foil. Bake in a 350° oven for 20 to 25 minutes or till heated through. Makes 4 servings.

Nutrition facts per serving: 175 calories, 6 g total fat (2 g saturated fat), 53 mg cholesterol, 243 mg sodium, 15 g carbohydrate, 2 g fiber, 16 g protein. **Daily values:** 40% vitamin A, 44% vitamin C, 19% calcium, 9% iron.

Low-fat

Low-sodium

GREEK-STYLE SKEWERED CALAMARI

The firm white meat of squid is mild and marries well with the flavor of the herbed marinade.

1 pound fresh or frozen clean
    squid or 1½ pounds
    unclean squid
½ cup dry white or rosé wine
    or clam juice
2 tablespoons lemon juice
1 tablespoon snipped fresh
    parsley
1 teaspoon dried thyme or
    oregano, crushed
¼ teaspoon pepper
⅛ teaspoon salt
2 cloves garlic, minced
8 cherry tomatoes
2 tablespoons olive oil or
    cooking oil
8 thin slices French bread

1. Thaw squid, if frozen, and clean, if necessary. Quarter squid bodies lengthwise and leave tentacles whole. In a shallow glass dish stir together wine or clam juice, lemon juice, parsley, thyme or oregano, pepper, salt, and *1 clove* of the garlic. Place squid in marinade. Cover and marinate in the refrigerator for 30 to 60 minutes. Drain, reserving marinade. In a small saucepan heat marinade to boiling; remove from heat and set aside.

2. Thread squid onto 8 metal skewers, placing a cherry tomato on the end of each skewer. Brush liberally with reserved marinade. In a small skillet cook remaining garlic in olive oil over medium heat for 1 minute. Brush garlic mixture atop French bread slices.

3. Grill squid skewers and bread, uncovered, over medium-hot coals about 5 minutes or till squid is tender and bread is lightly browned; turn squid once and baste it several times with marinade. Serve squid and tomatoes with the bread. Makes 4 servings.

Nutrition facts per serving: 335 calories, 10 g total fat (2 g saturated fat), 264 mg cholesterol, 426 mg sodium, 33 g carbohydrate, 1 g fiber, 23 g protein. **Daily values:** 4% vitamin A, 29% vitamin C, 7% calcium, 17% iron.

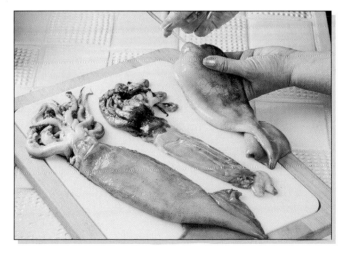

To clean squid, firmly grasp the head. Then pull the head, tentacles, and entrails out of the body. Discard any entrails that remain in the body. Pull out and discard the clear cartilage pen that serves as a backbone. With your fingers, peel the skin off the outside of the body. Rinse body and pat dry.

Low-fat

Low-calorie

Low-sodium

SAFFRON LOBSTER WITH COUSCOUS

Make the investment in a small amount of saffron for this delectable dish of lobster in a creamy wine sauce. (See photo, right.)

4 4-ounce frozen lobster tails*

2 lemon slices

4 peppercorns

1 bay leaf

½ cup reduced-sodium chicken
    broth

4 shallots, peeled and chopped
    (⅓ cup)

2 cloves garlic, minced

1½ cups chopped tomatoes

1½ teaspoons snipped fresh
    thyme or ½ teaspoon dried
    thyme, crushed

¼ teaspoon lemon-pepper
    seasoning

   Dash powdered saffron or
    ⅛ teaspoon thread saffron

2 tablespoons cornstarch

1 cup skim milk

¼ cup dry white wine or
    reduced-sodium chicken
    broth

2 cups hot cooked couscous
    or rice

   Fresh thyme sprigs (optional)

1. Thaw lobster tails. In a 3-quart saucepan combine 6 cups *water*, lemon slices, peppercorns, and bay leaf; bring to boiling. Add lobster tails; return to boiling. Simmer, uncovered, for 4 to 8 minutes or till shells turn bright red and meat is opaque. Drain, discarding cooking liquid. Cool lobster; remove meat from shells. Chop meat; set aside.

2. In a large skillet, heat chicken broth. Add shallots and garlic; cook, uncovered, over medium heat for 3 minutes or till shallots and garlic are tender.

3. Stir in tomatoes, thyme, lemon-pepper seasoning, and saffron. Simmer, uncovered, for 5 minutes. In a small bowl stir cornstarch into milk; add to skillet. Cook and stir till mixture is thickened and bubbly; cook 2 minutes more. Stir in chopped lobster, and wine or broth. Cook 1 minute more to heat through. Serve mixture over hot cooked couscous or rice. If desired, garnish with fresh thyme sprigs. Makes 4 servings.

*Note: You can use 1½ cups fully cooked lobster meat in place of the lobster tails. Omit the simmering directions and the 6 cups water, lemon slices, peppercorns, and bay leaf. Begin with Step 2 of the recipe method.

Nutrition facts per serving: 237 calories, 1 g total fat (0 g saturated fat), 40 mg cholesterol, 325 mg sodium, 37 g carbohydrate, 1 g fiber, 17 g protein. **Daily values:** 27% vitamin A, 33% vitamin C, 11% calcium, 14% iron.

Saffron—The World's Most Expensive Spice

From a special variety of crocus comes saffron threads—dried, reddish orange, threadlike filaments called stigmas. Used as a spice, saffron threads impart a bright yellow color, bittersweet flavor, and exotic aroma to classic dishes. Because the delicate filaments must be carefully picked by hand, saffron is the world's most expensive spice. There are only three filaments per flower, and it takes at least 225,000 filaments to make a pound of saffron. Saffron is sold as a powder and in tiny strands called threads.

Low-calorie
Low-sodium

STEAMED MUSSELS WITH ORANGE SAUCE

Mussel shells may be blue, black, or tinged with green. Look for tightly closed shells that are moist, intact, and not chipped.

2 pounds mussels
1 cup dry white wine or reduced-sodium chicken broth
1 shallot, peeled and chopped
1 clove garlic, minced
½ cup orange juice
2 tablespoons margarine
1 tablespoon snipped parsley
1 tablespoon snipped fresh tarragon or 1 teaspoon dried tarragon, crushed
¼ teaspoon finely shredded orange peel

1. To clean mussels, scrub shells with a stiff brush under cold water. Rinse mussels and remove beards. In a 4-quart Dutch oven bring wine or broth to boiling; add shallot and garlic, and cook for 3 minutes or till tender. Add mussels; cover and return to boiling. Reduce heat. Simmer for 3 to 5 minutes or till mussels open; stir and remove from heat. Discard simmering liquid and any mussels that have not opened.

2. Meanwhile, for orange sauce, in a small saucepan heat orange juice and margarine till margarine is melted. Stir in parsley, tarragon, orange peel, and ¼ teaspoon *pepper;* heat through. Divide orange sauce between 4 small bowls. Serve mussels with sauce. Makes 4 servings.

Nutrition facts per serving: 202 calories, 9 g total fat (2 g saturated fat), 40 mg cholesterol, 330 mg sodium, 10 g carbohydrate, 0 g fiber, 17 g protein. **Daily values:** 17% vitamin A, 45% vitamin C, 3% calcium, 33% iron.

Low-fat
Low-calorie
Low-sodium

STEAMED CLAMS MARENGO

Serve this flavorful dish with hot cooked pasta or rice (to sop up the extra sauce) and a large tossed green salad.

2 pounds clams in shells, rinsed
1 14½-ounce can low-sodium tomatoes, cut up
1 cup sliced mushrooms
½ cup sliced celery
½ cup chopped onion
½ cup hot-style tomato juice
2 tablespoons snipped fresh parsley
1 tablespoon lemon juice
½ teaspoon dried thyme, crushed
¼ teaspoon ground sage
⅛ teaspoon pepper

1. Scrub live clams under cold running water. In a large Dutch oven combine 4 quarts *cold water* and 3 tablespoons *salt.* Add clams; soak for 15 minutes. Drain and rinse. Discard water; repeat soaking process two more times. Set clams aside.

2. Meanwhile, for sauce, in medium saucepan combine *undrained* tomatoes, mushrooms, celery, onion, tomato juice, parsley, lemon juice, thyme, sage, and pepper. Bring to boiling. Reduce heat and simmer, uncovered, for 15 minutes or till it reaches desired consistency, stirring occasionally.

3. To steam clams, fill Dutch oven with ½ inch *water.* Bring to boiling. Place clams in a steamer basket set in the Dutch oven. Steam, covered, for 5 to 7 minutes or till shells open and clams are thoroughly cooked. Discard any clams that do not open. Serve with sauce. Makes 4 servings.

Nutrition facts per serving: 153 calories, 2 g total fat (0 g saturated fat), 48 mg cholesterol, 231 mg sodium, 14 g carbohydrate, 2 g fiber, 20 g protein. **Daily values:** 21% vitamin A, 74% vitamin C, 9% calcium, 142% iron.

MOUTH-WATERING MEATS

If enjoying steaks, chops, and roasts while keeping fat and calories in check sounds too good to be true, then you will be pleasantly surprised with this collection of succulent meat dishes. For family-style dining, serve up Tomato-Stuffed Flank Steak with Sauce or Country Pot Roast with Baby Vegetables. On a more adventurous night, try Hot and Sour Beef with Broccoli or Ginger Pork with Mango Sauce. Take a look at these and the other amazingly light recipes as you welcome meat back to the table.

Low-fat
Low-calorie
Low-sodium

GRILLED SIRLOIN WITH SMOKY PEPPER SAUCE

Chipotle chili peppers are actually smoked jalapeños; they have a smoky, slightly sweet, spicy flavor. (See photo, left.)

12 dried tomato halves (not oil
    pack)
1 to 3 dried chipotle chili
    peppers
1 cup boiling water
1 cup dry red or white wine,
    or 1 cup water plus
    ½ teaspoon beef bouillon
    granules
½ cup chopped onion
1 tablespoon brown sugar
1 tablespoon lime or lemon
    juice
2 cloves garlic, quartered
¼ teaspoon pepper
12 ounces boneless beef top
    sirloin steak, cut 1 inch
    thick

1. For sauce, in a medium mixing bowl place dried tomatoes and chili peppers; add boiling water to cover. Let stand 30 minutes or till vegetables are softened. Drain, reserving liquid.

2. Cut up tomatoes; place in a food processor bowl or blender container. Wearing disposable plastic gloves, trim stems from chilies; scrape out seeds. Cut up chili peppers; add to tomatoes with ¼ cup reserved soaking liquid, wine or water and bouillon, onion, brown sugar, lime or lemon juice, garlic, and pepper. Cover and process till nearly smooth.

3. Place steak in a shallow glass bowl; pour sauce over steak. Cover and marinate in the refrigerator for 2 to 8 hours. Drain, reserving marinade. Grill steak directly over medium coals for 14 to 18 minutes for medium doneness, turning and brushing steak with reserved marinade halfway through grilling time. (Or, spray the unheated rack of a broiler pan with *nonstick spray coating*. Place steak on rack; broil 4 inches from heat for 13 to 17 minutes, turning and brushing with marinade halfway through the broiling time.) In a small saucepan heat remaining marinade till boiling; pass with meat. Makes 4 servings.

Nutrition facts per serving: 240 calories, 8 g total fat (3 g saturated fat), 57 mg cholesterol, 105 mg sodium, 12 g carbohydrate, 1 g fiber, 21 g protein. **Daily values:** 46% vitamin A, 17% vitamin C, 3% calcium, 20% iron.

Delectable Dried Tomatoes

Dried tomatoes add a burst of flavor to sauces, salads, soups, and many other dishes. They are vine-ripened tomatoes picked at their peak of freshness, cut in half, sometimes salted, then dried. The result is a chewy, meaty tomato with a concentrated flavor.

Look for dried tomatoes in supermarkets, gourmet shops, and specialty stores. They either are dry or packed in olive oil and come in halves, slices, and bits. To rehydrate the dry version (not in oil), cover the tomatoes with boiling water and let them stand about 2 minutes, then drain. To use the oil-packed tomatoes, simply remove them from the oil and pat them dry with paper towels.

Store the dry form in an airtight container out of direct light or in a refrigerator or freezer for up to 1 year. You can store oil-packed tomatoes in the refrigerator after opening for up to 6 months if the oil covers the tomatoes.

Low-fat
Low-sodium

KOREAN-STYLE BEEF SKEWERS

You won't miss the salt in reduced-sodium soy sauce, and the flavor is every bit as good.

3 tablespoons light soy sauce
3 tablespoons sliced green
    onion
1 tablespoon brown sugar
2 teaspoons toasted sesame seed
3 cloves garlic, minced
2 tablespoons dry sherry
1 teaspoon sesame oil
12 ounces lean boneless beef top
    sirloin steak or beef top
    round steak, partially
    frozen
2 cups hot cooked rice

1. In a small mixing bowl stir together soy sauce, green onion, brown sugar, sesame seed, garlic, sherry, and sesame oil. Thinly bias-slice meat into 3-inch strips; place meat in a shallow glass bowl. Pour soy sauce mixture over meat; cover and marinate in the refrigerator for 2 hours, stirring occasionally to distribute marinade. Drain meat, discarding marinade.

2. Thread meat strips on skewers, leaving ¼ inch between pieces. Grill over medium coals for 10 to 12 minutes for medium doneness, turning once. (Or, spray the unheated rack of a broiler pan with *nonstick spray coating*. Place skewers on the rack; broil 4 inches from the heat for 10 to 12 minutes, turning once.) Serve with hot cooked rice. Makes 4 servings.

Nutrition facts per serving: 308 calories, 10 g total fat (3 g saturated fat), 57 mg cholesterol, 441 mg sodium, 28 g carbohydrate, 0 g fiber, 23 g protein. **Daily values:** 1% vitamin A, 2% vitamin C, 2% calcium, 24% iron.

Thread the beef on the skewers, loosely folding the strips accordion-style. Remember to leave about ¼ inch between strips to allow the beef to cook evenly.

Low-calorie
Low-sodium

TOMATO-STUFFED FLANK STEAK WITH SAUCE

Pair this hearty entrée with hot cooked egg noodles or bow-tie pasta.

8 dried tomato halves (not oil pack)
½ cup boiling water
1¼ pounds beef flank steak
½ cup fine dry bread crumbs
¼ cup chopped onion
1 slightly beaten egg white
½ teaspoon dried basil, crushed
¼ teaspoon dillweed
½ cup no-salt-added tomato juice
2 cloves garlic, minced
1 tablespoon snipped fresh parsley

1. Place dried tomatoes in a small mixing bowl. Add boiling water to cover. Let stand for 30 minutes or till softened. Cover steak with clear plastic wrap. Pound with a meat mallet to ¼-inch thickness; set aside. Drain and chop tomatoes. In a mixing bowl combine tomatoes, bread crumbs, onion, egg white, basil, dillweed, and ¼ teaspoon *pepper*. Spread tomato mixture over steak. Starting from the narrow end, roll up steak jelly-roll style; tie with kitchen string.

2. Spray a large skillet with *nonstick spray coating*. Brown meat roll on all sides over medium heat. Add tomato juice and garlic to skillet. Bring to boiling; reduce heat and simmer for 50 to 60 minutes or till tender. Cut meat crosswise into 6 slices. Arrange on a serving platter. Stir parsley and ⅛ teaspoon *salt* into pan juices; pass juices to spoon over meat. Makes 6 servings.

Nutrition facts per serving: 217 calories, 8 g total fat (3 g saturated fat), 44 mg cholesterol, 271 mg sodium, 14 g carbohydrate, 1 g fiber, 21 g protein. **Daily values:** 2% vitamin A, 13% vitamin C, 2% calcium, 15% iron.

Low-fat
Low-calorie
Low-sodium

MIDWEST SWISS STEAK WITH TOMATO GRAVY

Serve this satisfying entrée with Quick Herbed Pita Rounds (see recipe, page 328) or Popovers (see recipe, page 326).

1½ pounds boneless beef round steak
2 tablespoons all-purpose flour
1 large red sweet pepper
1 cup beef broth
2 large onions, sliced
2 cups chopped peeled parsnips
1 14½-ounce can low-sodium tomatoes, cut up
1 teaspoon dried basil, crushed
1 teaspoon salt-free seasoning blend
1 clove garlic, minced
1 teaspoon cornstarch
2 tablespoons snipped fresh parsley

1. Trim fat from meat. Cut meat into 6 serving-size pieces. Sprinkle meat on both sides with flour. With a meat mallet, pound flour into meat. Spray a 12-inch skillet with *nonstick spray coating;* brown meat over medium heat on both sides. Meanwhile, chop sweet pepper (you should have 1 cup). Add sweet pepper, beef broth, onions, parsnips, *undrained* tomatoes, basil, seasoning blend, garlic, and ¼ teaspoon *pepper*. Bring mixture to boiling; reduce heat. Simmer, covered, for 1¼ hours or till meat and vegetables are tender.

2. Transfer meat and vegetables to a serving platter; skim all fat from pan drippings. In a small bowl stir together cornstarch and 1 tablespoon *water;* add to pan drippings. Cook and stir till thickened and bubbly; cook and stir for 2 minutes more. Stir in parsley. Pour sauce over meat and vegetables. Makes 6 servings.

Nutrition facts per serving: 211 calories, 5 g total fat (2 g saturated fat), 60 mg cholesterol, 321 mg sodium, 16 g carbohydrate, 3 g fiber, 25 g protein. **Daily values:** 16% vitamin A, 72% vitamin C, 4% calcium, 20% iron.

Low-fat

Low-sodium

High-fiber

HOT AND SOUR BEEF WITH BROCCOLI

Partially freezing the round steak for about 30 minutes makes it easy to cut the meat into strips. (See photo, right.)

12 ounces boneless beef top
    round steak, partially
    frozen

⅓ cup water

2 tablespoons light soy sauce

2 tablespoons rice wine vinegar
    or white wine vinegar

4 teaspoons cornstarch

1 teaspoon sugar

¼ teaspoon pepper
    Several dashes bottled hot
    pepper sauce

8 shiitake mushrooms or
    medium brown mushrooms
    Nonstick spray coating

2 cloves garlic, minced

½ cup reduced-sodium chicken
    broth

2 cups broccoli flowerets

1 medium red or green sweet
    pepper, julienned (1 cup)

1 cup fresh pea pods, strings
    removed and halved

2 cups cooked cellophane
    noodles

1. Thinly slice steak across the grain into bite-size strips. In a small mixing bowl stir together water, soy sauce, vinegar, cornstarch, sugar, pepper, and hot pepper sauce; set aside.

2. Trim stems from mushrooms; discard stems. Slice mushroom caps; set aside.

3. Spray a large wok or skillet with nonstick spray coating. Place over medium-high heat. Stir-fry beef and garlic for 2 to 3 minutes or to desired doneness. Remove from wok. Turn heat to medium. Carefully add chicken broth; bring to boiling. Add broccoli; reduce heat and simmer, covered, for 3 minutes. Add sweet pepper and mushrooms; simmer, covered, for 2 minutes more. Add pea pods and simmer, covered, for 1 minute more. Push vegetables aside.

4. Stir soy sauce mixture; pour into center of wok. Cook and stir till thickened and bubbly; cook and stir 2 minutes more. Add beef mixture to wok; stir in all ingredients and heat through. Serve over cooked noodles. Makes 4 servings.

Nutrition facts per serving: 437 calories, 5 g total fat (1 g saturated fat), 54 mg cholesterol, 390 mg sodium, 75 g carbohydrate, 4 g fiber, 25 g protein. **Daily values:** 24% vitamin A, 178% vitamin C, 6% calcium, 37% iron.

Julienne

To julienne food, slice it into thin, matchlike sticks about 2 inches long. Speed up julienne cutting by first slicing the food into pieces about 2 inches long and ¼ inch thick. Then stack the slices and cut them lengthwise into thinner strips about ⅛ to ¼ inch wide.

Low-fat

Low-calorie

Low-sodium

BEEF AND VEGETABLE KABOBS WITH GARLIC MARINADE

If new potatoes aren't available, cut large russet or sweet potatoes into 1½-inch pieces and steam them the same way.

1 cup low-sodium vegetable
   juice
¼ cup red wine vinegar
½ cup sliced green onion
4 cloves garlic, minced
¼ teaspoon chili oil
¼ teaspoon pepper
12 ounces beef top round steak,
   cut into 1-inch cubes
8 small new potatoes, halved
2 yellow summer squash or
   zucchini, cut into ½-inch-
   thick slices
12 whole mushrooms, trimmed

1. In a shallow glass bowl stir together juice, vinegar, green onion, garlic, chili oil, and pepper. Add meat; cover and marinate in the refrigerator for 8 to 24 hours. Before grilling, steam potatoes over simmering water for 10 minutes; add squash during the last 3 minutes of steaming; cool. Drain meat, reserving marinade.

2. Thread meat chunks on skewers, alternating with mushrooms, potatoes, and squash slices, leaving about ¼ inch between pieces. Brush meat and vegetables with reserved marinade. Grill over medium coals for 12 to 14 minutes or to desired doneness, turning once and brushing with reserved marinade halfway through grilling time. (Or, spray the unheated rack of a broiler pan with *nonstick spray coating*. Broil skewers 4 inches from the heat for 12 to 14 minutes or to desired doneness, turning once and brushing with reserved marinade halfway through broiling time.) Makes 4 servings.

Nutrition facts per serving: 227 calories, 4 g total fat (1 g saturated fat), 54 mg cholesterol, 50 mg sodium, 23 g carbohydrate, 2 g fiber, 23 g protein. **Daily values:** 4% vitamin A, 30% vitamin C, 3% calcium, 27% iron.

Low-fat

Low-sodium

BEEF AND ASPARAGUS STIR-FRY

You can substitute sliced pork tenderloin or lamb loin chops, trimmed and cut into bite-size strips, for the beef.

12 ounces boneless beef top
   round steak
½ cup orange juice
½ cup beef broth
2 tablespoons dry sherry
1 tablespoon cornstarch
1 teaspoon toasted sesame seed
1 clove garlic, minced
2 tablespoons beef broth
1 large onion, cut into thin
   wedges
1 red or yellow sweet pepper,
   cut into 1-inch pieces
1 pound asparagus spears, bias-
   sliced into 1-inch pieces
2 cups hot cooked rice

1. Partially freeze steak. Trim fat from steak; thinly bias-slice meat into bite-size strips. Set aside. In a small mixing bowl stir together orange juice, the ½ cup broth, sherry, cornstarch, and sesame seed; set aside.

2. Spray a wok or large nonstick skillet with *nonstick spray coating*. Preheat over medium-high heat till a drop of water sizzles. Stir-fry beef and garlic for 2 to 3 minutes or to desired doneness. Remove beef mixture from wok. Add 2 tablespoons beef broth and onion. Cover and simmer for 2 minutes or till tender. Add sweet pepper and asparagus. Cover and simmer for 3 to 4 minutes or till crisp-tender. Remove all vegetables from wok. Stir orange juice mixture; pour into wok. Cook and stir till mixture is thickened and bubbly. Return beef mixture and vegetables to wok; toss to coat with sauce. Cover and cook for 2 minutes more or till heated through. Serve with hot cooked rice. Makes 4 servings.

Nutrition facts per serving: 306 calories, 5 g total fat (2 g saturated fat), 54 mg cholesterol, 167 mg sodium, 37 g carbohydrate, 3 g fiber, 26 g protein. **Daily values:** 19% vitamin A, 111% vitamin C, 3% calcium, 24% iron.

Low-fat

Low-calorie

Low-sodium

COUNTRY POT ROAST WITH BABY VEGETABLES

If you prefer a thicker gravy, purée a few of the cooked vegetables and stir them into the fat-skimmed pan juices.

1 3-pound boneless beef bottom
  round or rump roast
  Nonstick spray coating
1¼ cups beef broth
½ cup dry red wine or beef
  broth
2 medium onions, cut into
  wedges
2 cloves garlic, minced
1½ teaspoons dried basil, crushed
¼ teaspoon pepper
1 bay leaf
1 pound whole baby carrots
  or 6 medium carrots
1½ pounds whole tiny new
  potatoes or 2 medium
  potatoes
1 pound baby turnips or beets,
  or medium turnips or beets

1. Trim fat from roast. Spray a 4-quart Dutch oven with nonstick spray coating. Brown meat on all sides over medium-high heat. Drain off excess fat. In a small mixing bowl stir together broth, wine, onions, garlic, basil, pepper, and bay leaf; pour over roast. Bring to boiling; reduce heat. Cover and simmer for 2 hours.

2. Peel and trim baby carrots, or peel and cut medium carrots into fourths. Remove a narrow strip of peel from the center of each new potato, or peel and cut each medium potato into eighths. Peel baby turnips or beets, or peel and chop medium turnips or beets. Add carrots, potatoes, and turnips or beets to Dutch oven.

3. Cover and simmer for 45 to 60 minutes or till meat and vegetables are tender, adding additional broth or water, if necessary. Remove meat and vegetables from pan. Remove bay leaf. Skim fat from pan drippings; season to taste. Pass pan drippings with meat and vegetables. Makes 12 servings.

Nutrition facts per serving: 259 calories, 6 g total fat (2 g saturated fat), 72 mg cholesterol, 186 mg sodium, 20 g carbohydrate, 3 g fiber, 30 g protein. **Daily values:** 85% vitamin A, 22% vitamin C, 3% calcium, 26% iron.

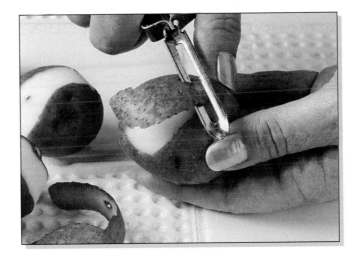

Use a vegetable peeler to remove a thin strip of peel from around the center of each new potato.

Low-fat

Low-calorie

Low-sodium

BEER-BRAISED RUMP ROAST WITH CABBAGE

Beer, red onion, and brown sugar give this tender roast a robust, well-rounded flavor. (See photo, right.)

1 3-pound boneless beef round
    rump roast
1½ cups light beer (12 ounces)
1 medium onion, sliced
1 tablespoon brown sugar
1 teaspoon instant beef bouillon
    granules
½ teaspoon dried thyme,
    crushed
½ teaspoon salt-free seasoning
    blend
1 bay leaf
1 medium head cabbage, cored
8 medium carrots, bias-sliced
    into 1-inch pieces

1. Trim fat from roast. Spray a 4-quart Dutch oven with *nonstick spray coating*. Brown meat on all sides over medium-high heat.

2. Add the beer, onion, brown sugar, bouillon granules, thyme, seasoning blend, bay leaf, 1 cup *water* and ½ teaspoon *pepper*. Bring to boiling; reduce heat. Simmer, covered, about 1¾ hours or till meat is nearly tender. Cut cabbage into 10 wedges.

3. Add cabbage and carrots to meat; cover and cook about 20 minutes more or till cabbage and carrots are crisp-tender and meat is very tender. Remove bay leaf. Transfer meat and vegetables to a serving platter; cover and keep warm. Skim fat from pan juices. Thinly slice meat; pass meat and vegetables with pan juices. Makes 10 servings.

Nutrition facts per serving: 243 calories, 7 g total fat (2 g saturated fat), 86 mg cholesterol, 180 mg sodium, 9 g carbohydrate, 2 g fiber, 34 g protein. **Daily values:** 69% vitamin A, 45% vitamin C, 4% calcium, 24% iron.

Low-fat

Low-calorie

Low-sodium

BEEF WITH VEGETABLE GRAVY

These slices of roast beef topped with chunky gravy prove that homestyle cooking can be healthy and taste great, too.

1 1½-pound boneless beef eye
    of round roast or round
    rump roast
½ cup chopped onion
½ cup chopped carrot
½ cup chopped celery
2 cloves garlic, minced
1 tablespoon tomato paste
1 teaspoon dried basil, crushed
½ teaspoon instant beef bouillon
    granules
1 tablespoon cornstarch

1. Trim fat from meat, if necessary. Spray a cold Dutch oven with *nonstick spray coating*. Brown beef on all sides in the Dutch oven over medium heat. Add onion, carrot, celery, garlic, tomato paste, basil, bouillon granules, 1 cup *water*, and ⅛ teaspoon *pepper*. Bring to boiling; reduce heat. Cover and simmer about 1½ hours or till meat is tender. Transfer meat to a serving platter; cover to keep warm.

2. For gravy, measure vegetables and liquid in pan. If necessary add enough water to make 1½ cups. Return all to Dutch oven. Stir together cornstarch and 2 tablespoons *cold water;* add to Dutch oven. Cook and stir till thickened and bubbly. Cook and stir for 2 minutes more. Slice beef and serve with gravy. Makes 6 servings.

Nutrition facts per serving: 166 calories, 3 g fat (1 g saturated fat), 66 mg cholesterol, 169 mg sodium, 6 g carbohydrate, 1 g fiber, 27 g protein. **Daily value:** 40% vitamin A, 6% vitamin C, 1% calcium, 18% iron.

FESTIVE TACO BURGERS

Low-sodium

A flour tortilla has about the same number of calories as a hamburger bun, and it's twice the fun with these burgers. (See photo, left.)

1 cup finely chopped tomato

¼ cup green or red taco sauce

2 tablespoons snipped fresh
   cilantro

5 7-inch flour tortillas

1 4-ounce can diced mild green
   chili peppers, drained

¼ cup fine dry bread crumbs

¼ cup finely chopped green
   onion

2 tablespoons skim milk

1 teaspoon dried oregano,
   crushed

½ teaspoon ground cumin

¼ teaspoon pepper

⅛ teaspoon salt

1 pound extra-lean ground beef
   Nonstick spray coating

1 cup shredded lettuce or red
   cabbage

1. In a medium mixing bowl stir together tomato, taco sauce, and cilantro. Cover and set aside. Wrap tortillas in aluminum foil; bake in a 350° oven for 15 minutes. Remove from oven, but do not open foil packet.

2. Meanwhile, in a large mixing bowl stir together chili peppers, bread crumbs, green onion, milk, oregano, cumin, pepper, and salt till well mixed. Add meat and mix well. Shape mixture into 5 oval patties about 4½ to 5 inches long and ½ inch thick. Spray the unheated rack of a broiler pan with nonstick spray coating; arrange patties on broiler pan. Broil 4 inches from the heat for 10 to 12 minutes or to desired doneness, turning halfway through broiling time.

3. To serve, place a patty on each warm tortilla; spoon some of the shredded lettuce and tomato mixture over the patty. If desired, serve with *salsa* and *cilantro sprigs*. Wrap tortillas around patties. Makes 5 servings.

Nutrition facts per serving: 303 calories, 12 g total fat (4 g saturated fat), 57 mg cholesterol, 456 mg sodium, 27 g carbohydrate, 1 g fiber, 21 g protein. **Daily values:** 5% vitamin A, 28% vitamin C, 6% calcium, 23% iron.

Is It Done?

Ground-meat patties with no other ingredients added should be cooked at least till their centers are brownish pink (medium doneness). Ground-meat patties and meat loaves with additional ingredients, such as eggs, bread crumbs, onions, or liquid, should be cooked to 170° or till no pink remains. Check for doneness by cutting into a patty or the loaf to see if the inside color of the meat is brown, or check the temperature of a baked loaf with a meat thermometer.

GREEK TOWN PIZZA

Low-sodium

Be sure to drain all liquid from the spinach so it doesn't add moisture to the crust or filling. (See photo, right.)

Nonstick spray coating
1 loaf frozen honey wheat bread dough, thawed
2 10-ounce packages frozen chopped spinach, thawed
1 pound extra-lean ground beef
1 cup chopped onion
2 cloves garlic, minced
1 cup lower-calorie, lower-sodium, and lower-fat spaghetti sauce
2 cups chopped tomato
1 cup shredded reduced-fat Monterey Jack or mozzarella cheese (4 ounces)
½ cup crumbled feta cheese (2 ounces)

1. Spray a 12-inch pizza pan or 13x9x2-inch baking pan with nonstick spray coating. Press bread dough into pan, forming a 1-inch-thick edge. Using tines of a fork, prick the dough several times. Bake in a 375° oven for 10 minutes.

2. Meanwhile, squeeze all liquid from spinach. Sprinkle spinach over prebaked crust. In a large skillet, cook beef, onion, and garlic for 5 minutes or till meat is no longer pink. Drain off excess fat; stir in spaghetti sauce. Spoon meat mixture over spinach layer; sprinkle with tomato, then cheeses.

3. Bake in a 375° oven for 30 to 35 minutes or till cheese is golden brown. Let stand 5 minutes. Cut into wedges or squares. Makes 8 servings.

Nutrition facts per serving: 341 calories, 12 g total fat (5 g saturated fat), 52 mg cholesterol, 288 mg sodium, 37 g carbohydrate, 3 g fiber, 23 g protein. **Daily values:** 63% vitamin A, 35% vitamin C, 26% calcium, 26% iron.

Lean Ground Beef

Cooking with the leanest ground beef available can help you meet your lower-fat goals. Look for 90 percent lean (10 percent fat) ground beef at your supermarket to use in dishes such as chili, tacos, and meat casseroles. In some parts of the country, you can buy 95 percent lean ground beef. This beef has some of its fat replaced with water and plant-derived ingredients so it still will be moist when cooked.

Low-fat

Low-calorie

GRILLED REUBENS

½ cup shredded green cabbage

½ cup shredded red cabbage

¼ cup coarsely shredded carrot

2 tablespoons nonfat Thousand Island salad dressing

1 teaspoon Dijon-style mustard

¼ teaspoon caraway seed

8 slices thin-sliced pumpernickel or rye bread

4 ounces thinly sliced, fully cooked corned beef

4 ¾-ounce slices Swiss-flavored nonfat process cheese product

1. In a medium mixing bowl stir together red and green cabbage, carrot, salad dressing, mustard, and caraway seed. Divide cole slaw mixture among 4 slices of bread, spreading nearly to edges. Layer meat slices over slaw; top with cheese slices and remaining bread.

2. Spray a nonstick skillet with *nonstick spray coating*. Add sandwiches and cook over medium-low heat for 2 to 3 minutes per side or till heated through, turning once. Halve sandwiches diagonally; serve hot. Makes 4 servings.

Nutrition facts per serving: 245 calories, 3 g total fat (0 g saturated fat), 11 mg cholesterol, 1,147 mg sodium, 38 g carbohydrate, 1 g fiber, 17 g protein. **Daily values:** 27% vitamin A, 18% vitamin C, 17% calcium, 13% iron.

Low-calorie

Low-sodium

NEW-STYLE MEAT LOAF

Baking a meat loaf on a rack over a roasting pan allows the fatty juices to drip away from the loaf.

1 egg white

1¼ cups soft whole wheat bread crumbs

⅓ cup skim milk

½ cup peeled and shredded white or sweet potato

½ cup shredded carrot or zucchini

⅓ cup sliced green onion

1 teaspoon dried thyme, crushed

½ teaspoon ground sage

¼ teaspoon salt-free seasoning blend

1 pound extra-lean ground beef

8 ounces lean ground pork or lamb

3 tablespoons catsup

1. In a large mixing bowl stir together egg white, bread crumbs, milk, potato, carrot, green onion, thyme, sage, seasoning blend, and ¼ teaspoon *pepper;* add ground beef and pork or lamb and mix well.

2. Place a rack in a shallow roasting pan; spray rack with *nonstick spray coating*. Shape meat mixture into a loaf (about 8 x 5 inches); place meat loaf on rack in roasting pan. Brush catsup over top of loaf.

3. Bake in a 350° oven about 1 hour or till juices run clear and a meat thermometer inserted in the center reads 170°. Remove from rack; cover and let stand 10 minutes. Cut into 8 slices. Makes 8 servings.

Nutrition facts per serving: 185 calories, 9 g total fat (3 g saturated fat), 49 mg cholesterol, 237 mg sodium, 9 g carbohydrate, 1 g fiber, 16 g protein. **Daily values:** 25% vitamin A, 10% vitamin C, 3% calcium, 12% iron.

Low-fat

Low-calorie

Low-sodium

High-fiber

VEAL WITH MUSHROOMS AND BABY CORN

1 9-ounce package frozen whole
    baby sweet corn
12 fresh shiitake mushrooms or
    white mushrooms
2 medium carrots
¼ cup reduced-sodium chicken
    broth
3 tablespoons dry vermouth or
    sherry
2 teaspoons cornstarch
1 teaspoon hoisin sauce
½ teaspoon dried thyme,
    crushed
12 ounces veal cutlets, cut
    ⅛ inch thick
½ cup sliced green onion
1 clove garlic, minced

1. Thaw baby corn and cut into 1-inch pieces. Slice mushrooms. Julienne carrots. Set vegetables aside. In a small mixing bowl stir together broth, vermouth, cornstarch, hoisin sauce, and thyme; set aside.

2. Spray a nonstick skillet generously with *nonstick spray coating.* Cook veal cutlets over medium heat for 3 to 4 minutes, turning once. Remove from pan. Cover and keep warm.

3. In the same skillet cook corn, mushrooms, carrots, green onion, and garlic for 3 to 4 minutes or till vegetables are crisp-tender. Stir broth mixture; pour over vegetables. Cook and stir till thickened and bubbly. Return veal to skillet; heat through. Makes 4 servings.

Nutrition facts per serving: 202 calories, 4 g total fat (1 g saturated fat), 69 mg cholesterol, 179 mg sodium, 17 g carbohydrate, 4 g fiber, 22 g protein. **Daily values:** 87% vitamin A, 14% vitamin C, 1% calcium, 8% iron.

Low-fat

Low-sodium

High-fiber

VEAL PAPRIKASH

1 pound boneless veal
2 cups fresh mushrooms
2 medium red sweet peppers
1 clove garlic, minced
2 onions, cut into wedges
1 cup reduced-sodium chicken
    broth
2 tablespoons paprika
1 teaspoon dried thyme,
    crushed
¼ teaspoon crushed red pepper
½ cup light dairy sour cream
2 tablespoons all-purpose flour
1 cup no-salt-added tomato
    juice
2 cups cooked egg noodles

1. Cut veal into 1-inch pieces. Halve mushrooms. Cut sweet peppers into 1-inch pieces. Set meat and vegetables aside.

2. Spray a nonstick skillet with *nonstick spray coating.* Brown veal and garlic on all sides in skillet over medium-high heat. Add mushrooms, sweet peppers, onions, chicken broth, paprika, thyme, and red pepper. Bring to boiling; cover and simmer for 45 to 60 minutes or till meat is tender.

3. In a small bowl stir together sour cream and flour; add to meat mixture along with tomato juice. Cook and stir till thickened and bubbly; cook and stir for 1 minute more. Serve with hot cooked noodles. Makes 4 servings.

Nutrition facts per serving: 370 calories, 9 g total fat (3 g saturated fat), 122 mg cholesterol, 129 mg sodium, 41 g carbohydrate, 4 g fiber, 34 g protein. **Daily values:** 54% vitamin A, 133% vitamin C, 6% calcium, 30% iron.

Low-fat

Low-calorie

Low-sodium

VEAL ROAST WITH HERB CRUST

A veal leg round roast may require a special order from your butcher. (See photo, left.)

1 3-pound boneless veal leg round roast

¼ cup fine dry bread crumbs

1 teaspoon dried basil, crushed

1 teaspoon dried thyme, crushed

1 tablespoon Dijon-style mustard

1 tablespoon lemon juice

½ teaspoon coarsely ground pepper

2 tablespoons water

2 tablespoons all-purpose flour

1 cup beef broth

¼ cup light dairy sour cream

1. Place roast on a rack in a roasting pan. In a small mixing bowl stir together bread crumbs, basil, thyme, mustard, lemon juice, and pepper. Stir in water to moisten. Spread mixture over surface of roast. Insert meat thermometer. Roast in a 325° oven for 2½ to 3 hours or till thermometer registers 170°. (If crust becomes too dry, cover roast loosely with foil after 1½ to 2 hours.) Transfer roast to a warm platter; cover and keep warm.

2. For sauce, skim fat from pan drippings. In a small saucepan stir beef broth into flour; add beef drippings. Cook and stir till thickened and bubbly; cook for 1 minute more. Stir in sour cream; heat through, but do not boil. Pass sauce with meat. Makes 10 to 12 servings.

Nutrition facts per serving: 200 calories, 6 g total fat (2 g saturated fat), 111 mg cholesterol, 214 mg sodium, 4 g carbohydrate, 0 g fiber, 31 g protein. **Daily values:** 0% vitamin A, 1% vitamin C, 1% calcium, 8% iron.

Low-fat

Low-calorie

Low-sodium

VEAL SCALLOPS MILANO

Thin scallops, or slices, of veal, pork, or turkey make elegant fast food with the addition of lemon, onion, and wine.

1 pound veal cutlets, cut ⅛ inch thick

¼ teaspoon pepper

⅛ teaspoon salt

1 to 2 teaspoons cooking oil

2 medium onions, sliced (1½ cups)

½ cup reduced-sodium chicken broth

½ teaspoon grated lemon peel

2 tablespoons lemon juice

2 tablespoons snipped fresh parsley

Lemon wedges

1. Sprinkle veal with pepper and salt. In a 10-inch nonstick skillet, heat 1 teaspoon oil over medium-high heat. Cook *half* of the veal for 1 to 2 minutes on each side till browned. Remove from pan. Repeat with remaining veal, adding remaining cooking oil, if necessary. Keep veal warm on a serving platter.

2. Add onions and chicken broth to skillet; bring to boiling. Reduce heat. Cover and simmer onion for 5 minutes or till tender. Stir in lemon peel and juice. Heat through. Spoon over veal. Sprinkle with parsley; serve with lemon wedges. Makes 6 servings.

Nutrition facts per serving: 125 calories, 4 g total fat (1 g saturated fat), 61 mg cholesterol, 141 mg sodium, 5 g carbohydrate, 1 g fiber, 17 g protein. **Daily values:** 0% vitamin A, 9% vitamin C, 1% calcium, 5% iron.

Low-calorie

Low-sodium

GINGER PORK WITH MANGO SAUCE

Substitute peaches, pears, or nectarines if mangoes or papayas are not available.

Nonstick spray coating
1 2-pound boneless pork single loin roast
2 tablespoons grated fresh gingerroot
4 cloves garlic, minced
½ teaspoon ground allspice
¼ teaspoon pepper
Dash salt
1 8-ounce can crushed pineapple (juice pack)
⅔ cup reduced-sodium chicken broth
2 tablespoons cornstarch
1 cup chopped, peeled mango or papaya
1 tablespoon snipped fresh parsley
1 to 2 jalapeño peppers, seeded and finely chopped

1. Spray a roasting rack with nonstick spray coating; set in a shallow roasting pan. With a small sharp knife, cut 1-inch slits about ½ inch deep all around top and sides of roast. Set roast aside.

2. In a small mixing bowl stir together gingerroot, garlic, and allspice. Spoon mixture into slits in roast. Sprinkle roast with pepper and salt. Insert a meat thermometer. Roast in a 325° oven for 1 to 1½ hours or till meat thermometer registers 160°. Transfer to a warm platter; cover and keep warm.

3. For sauce, in a small saucepan stir together *undrained* pineapple, chicken broth, and cornstarch. Cook and stir till mixture is thickened and bubbly. Stir in mango, parsley, and jalapeño pepper; cook and stir for 2 minutes more. Pass sauce with meat. Makes 8 servings.

Nutrition facts per serving: 185 calories, 8 g total fat (3 g saturated fat), 51 mg cholesterol, 111 mg sodium, 12 g carbohydrate, 1 g fiber, 17 g protein. **Daily values:** 10% vitamin A, 28% vitamin C, 1% calcium, 5% iron.

Spoon some of the gingerroot mixture into each slit in the roast.

Low-calorie

Low-sodium

BAYOU PORK ROAST

Another time, try the spice combination on a boned turkey breast.

1 teaspoon paprika
1 teaspoon dried oregano or
    marjoram, crushed
1 teaspoon dried thyme,
    crushed
½ teaspoon ground cumin
½ teaspoon ground allspice
¼ teaspoon pepper
1 clove garlic, halved
1 2½- to 3-pound boneless
    pork single loin roast
1 lime, quartered

1. In a small mixing bowl stir together paprika, oregano or marjoram, thyme, cumin, allspice, and pepper. Rub garlic over pork roast, then rub spice mixture over top and sides of roast.

2. Place roast on a rack in a shallow roasting pan; insert a meat thermometer. Roast in a 325° oven for 1 to 1¾ hours or till juices run clear and thermometer registers 160° to 170°. Transfer roast to a serving platter. Squeeze lime juice over roast. Makes 8 to 10 servings.

Nutrition facts per serving: 173 calories, 9 g total fat (3 g saturated fat), 64 mg cholesterol, 49 mg sodium, 1 g carbohydrate, 0 g fiber, 20 g protein. **Daily values:** 1% vitamin A, 3% vitamin C, 0% calcium, 7% iron.

Low-fat

Low-sodium

PORK CHOPS WITH ORANGE-DIJON SAUCE

Try these sweet and tangy chops with baked acorn squash and peas.

⅔ cup orange juice
¼ cup reduced-calorie orange
    marmalade
1 tablespoon Dijon-style
    mustard
¼ teaspoon ground sage
⅛ teaspoon salt
⅛ teaspoon pepper
4 boneless pork loin chops, cut
    ¾ inch thick (12 ounces)
1 medium onion, thinly sliced
1 clove garlic, minced
2 teaspoons cornstarch
8 ounces fettuccine, cooked

1. In a small mixing bowl stir together orange juice, marmalade, mustard, sage, salt, and pepper; set aside. Trim excess fat from chops. Spray a large nonstick skillet with *nonstick spray coating.* Brown chops over medium heat for 2 minutes on each side; remove from skillet. Add onion and garlic to skillet; cook for 3 minutes. Reduce heat to low; stir in orange juice mixture. Return chops to skillet. Cover and cook about 10 minutes or till chops are just slightly pink in the center and juices run clear. Remove chops from skillet and keep warm.

2. In a small mixing bowl stir together cornstarch and 1 tablespoon *cold water.* Add to skillet. Cook and stir till thickened and bubbly; cook 2 minutes more. Serve chops and sauce over hot cooked fettuccine. Makes 4 servings.

Nutrition facts per serving: 396 calories, 7 g total fat (2 g saturated fat), 38 mg cholesterol, 211 mg sodium, 61 g carbohydrate, 2 g fiber, 21 g protein. **Daily values:** 0% vitamin A, 40% vitamin C, 2% calcium, 20% iron.

Low-calorie

Low-sodium

Apple-Stuffed Pork Roast

Serve this roast on a bed of steamed white or brown rice. (See photo, right.)

1 3- to 3½-pound boneless
    pork single loin roast
½ cup chunky-style applesauce
½ cup finely chopped celery
2 tablespoons raisins
1 teaspoon ground cinnamon
½ teaspoon ground sage
¼ teaspoon pepper
    Dash salt
¼ cup finely chopped red apple
1¼ cups apple cider or
    apple juice
4 teaspoons cornstarch

1. To butterfly the roast, make a single lengthwise cut down the center of the roast, cutting to within ½ inch of the other side. Spread the meat open. At the center of the roast, make one slit to the right and perpendicular to the cut and one slit to the left and perpendicular to the cut. Cover roast with clear plastic wrap. Pound with a meat mallet to about 10 inches wide. Set roast aside.

2. In a small mixing bowl stir together applesauce, celery, raisins, cinnamon, sage, pepper, and salt. Remove plastic wrap from roast. Spread the applesauce mixture over the roast to within ½ inch of edges.

3. To roll the roast, start at one long side and roll up jelly-roll style. Secure the roll with a kitchen string, tying the roast crosswise at several places to prevent it from unrolling during cooking.

4. Place on a rack in a roasting pan; insert a meat thermometer. Roast, uncovered, in a 325° oven for 1¾ to 2½ hours or till meat thermometer registers 160° to 170°. Transfer to a warm platter; cover and keep warm.

5. For sauce, in a small saucepan cook the apple in *½ cup* of the apple cider for 3 to 5 minutes or till tender. In a small bowl stir remaining cider into cornstarch; add to saucepan. Cook and stir till thickened and bubbly; cook for 2 minutes more. Untie roast; slice thinly. Serve sauce with roast. Makes 10 to 12 servings.

Nutrition facts per serving: 201 calories, 9 g total fat (3 g saturated fat), 61 mg cholesterol, 72 mg sodium, 10 g carbohydrate, 1 g fiber, 20 g protein. **Daily values:** 0% vitamin A, 3% vitamin C, 1% calcium, 7% iron.

Low-fat

Low-calorie

Low-sodium

OVEN-BARBECUED PORK SANDWICHES

If you're fond of pork sandwiches, try this one made with lean roast pork tenderloin.

Nonstick spray coating

1 1-pound pork tenderloin

½ cup reduced-sodium, fat-free, hickory-smoked-flavor barbecue sauce

2 medium onions, thinly sliced

6 whole wheat hamburger buns, split and toasted

1 cup shredded lettuce

1. Trim fat from pork. Spray a roasting rack with nonstick spray coating; place rack in a shallow roasting pan. Place pork tenderloin on rack; folding thin end under; secure folded end with a wooden toothpick, if necessary. Brush with *1 tablespoon* of the barbecue sauce. Insert meat thermometer. Roast in a 425° oven for 25 to 35 minutes or till meat thermometer registers 160°. Let stand 5 minutes.

2. Meanwhile, spray a nonstick skillet with nonstick spray coating. Cook onions over medium heat about 10 minutes or till tender but not brown. Stir *2 tablespoons* of the barbecue sauce into onions; heat through. Slice meat thinly. For sandwiches, sprinkle bottom halves of buns with shredded lettuce; arrange meat slices over lettuce. Brush with some of the remaining barbecue sauce. Spoon onions over meat; add bun tops. Makes 6 servings.

Nutrition facts per serving: 257 calories, 6 g total fat (2 g saturated fat), 54 mg cholesterol, 418 mg sodium, 30 g carbohydrate, 1 g fiber, 21 g protein. **Daily values:** 3% vitamin A, 3% vitamin C, 4% calcium, 22% iron.

Low-calorie

Low-sodium

PORK CHOPS WITH CORN AND CILANTRO SALSA

Cilantro contributes a distinctive flavor to this chili-spiked Southwestern entrée.

⅔ cup canned whole kernel corn, drained

½ cup finely chopped red or green sweet pepper

⅓ cup chopped onion

2 tablespoons snipped fresh cilantro or parsley

2 tablespoons lime juice

1 jalapeño, serrano, fresno, or banana chili pepper, seeded and minced

¼ teaspoon ground cumin

4 boneless pork loin chops, cut ¾ inch thick (12 ounces)

½ teaspoon salt-free seasoning blend

1. For salsa, in a medium mixing bowl stir together corn, sweet pepper, onion, cilantro, lime juice, jalapeño pepper, and cumin. Cover and refrigerate for 1 to 24 hours.

2. At serving time, trim excess fat from chops. Sprinkle with seasoning blend.

3. Spray the unheated rack of a broiler pan with *nonstick spray coating.* Arrange chops on rack. Broil 3 inches from the heat for 12 to 14 minutes or till chops are no longer pink and juices run clear. Serve salsa with chops. Makes 4 servings.

Nutrition facts per serving: 140 calories, 6 g total fat (2 g saturated fat), 38 mg cholesterol, 120 mg sodium, 9 g carbohydrate, 1 g fiber, 13 g protein. **Daily values:** 11% vitamin A, 49% vitamin C, 1% calcium, 6% iron.

Low-calorie
Low-sodium

PORK AU POIVRE

If you prefer a less peppery taste, use half the amount of peppercorns.

4 boneless pork loin chops, cut
    ¾ inch thick (12 ounces)
1 tablespoon peppercorns,
    coarsely cracked
1½ teaspoons finely shredded
    orange or lemon peel
    Nonstick spray coating
½ cup dry red or white wine
½ cup sliced shallots or onions
1 clove garlic, minced
    Orange or lemon slices
    (optional)
    Parsley sprigs (optional)

1. Trim excess fat from chops. Combine peppercorns and orange peel; rub mixture over both sides of chops. Cover and chill in the refrigerator for 30 minutes to 2 hours.

2. Spray the unheated rack of a broiler pan with nonstick spray coating; arrange chops on rack. Place rack in broiler pan. Broil 4 inches from heat for 10 to 12 minutes, turning once, or till chops are no longer pink and juices run clear.

3. Meanwhile, in a small skillet bring wine to boiling; add shallots or onion and garlic. Simmer, uncovered, for 5 minutes. Arrange chops on a serving platter; spoon shallot mixture over chops. If desired, garnish with orange or lemon slices and parsley sprigs. Makes 4 servings.

Nutrition facts per serving: 143 calories, 6 g total fat (2 g saturated fat), 38 mg cholesterol, 52 mg sodium, 5 g carbohydrate, 0 g fiber, 13 g protein. **Daily values:** 25% vitamin A, 8% vitamin C, 1% calcium, 8% iron.

Crush peppercorns with a mortar and pestle.

Low-fat

Low-calorie

Low-sodium

GRILLED APRICOT-STUFFED PORK CHOPS

The tangy flavor of apricots pairs deliciously with the smoky taste of grilled pork. (See photo, left.)

½ cup cooked brown rice or
long grain rice

¼ cup snipped dried apricots

¼ cup finely chopped onion

1 tablespoon reduced-calorie
apricot spread

¼ teaspoon dried thyme, minced

¼ teaspoon pepper

4 pork center loin chops,
cut 1 inch thick

¼ cup reduced-calorie apricot
spread

1. For stuffing, in a medium mixing bowl stir together the rice, apricots, onion, 1 tablespoon apricot spread, thyme, and pepper. Trim fat from chops. Make a pocket in each chop by cutting horizontally from the fat side almost to the bone. Spoon ¼ of the stuffing into each pocket. If necessary, secure the openings with wooden toothpicks.

2. In a covered grill arrange preheated coals around a drip pan. Test for medium heat above the drip pan. Grill chops over medium heat for 30 to 40 minutes or till juices run clear, turning chops halfway through grilling time.

3. Meanwhile, in a saucepan heat ¼ cup apricot spread till melted. Brush over chops the last 5 minutes of grilling time. (Or, spray the unheated rack of a broiler pan with *nonstick spray coating*. Broil chops 4 inches from heat for 22 to 27 minutes or till juices run clear, turning chops halfway through broiling time. Brush with apricot spread the last 3 minutes of broiling time.) Makes 4 servings.

Nutrition facts per serving: 208 calories, 7 g total fat (2 g saturated fat), 48 mg cholesterol, 59 mg sodium, 19 g carbohydrate, 2 g fiber, 16 g protein. **Daily values:** 6% vitamin A, 5% vitamin C, 1% calcium, 9% iron.

Low-calorie
Low-sodium

BROILED PORK CHOPS WITH HORSERADISH SAUCE

Nonfat yogurt takes the place of sour cream in this spunky horseradish sauce for pork chops. Try it with roast beef, too.

4 boneless pork loin chops,
   cut ½ inch thick
   (about 1 pound)
  Nonstick spray coating
1 teaspoon olive oil or
   vegetable oil
¼ teaspoon pepper
½ cup plain nonfat yogurt
1 tablespoon prepared
   horseradish
1 tablespoon snipped fresh
   chives or 1 teaspoon dried
   chives
  Several dashes bottled hot
   pepper sauce
1 large tomato, cut into wedges
  Fresh chives (optional)

1. Trim fat from chops. Spray the unheated rack of a broiler pan with nonstick coating. Arrange chops on broiler rack; brush chops with oil and sprinkle with pepper. Broil chops 4 inches from heat for 8 to 14 minutes or till meat is no longer pink in the center, turning halfway through the broiling time.

2. For sauce, in a small mixing bowl stir together yogurt, horseradish, chives, and hot pepper sauce till blended. Garnish chops with tomato wedges and, if desired, fresh chives. Pass sauce with chops. Makes 4 servings.

Nutrition facts per serving: 135 calories, 7 g total fat (2 g saturated fat), 39 mg cholesterol, 94 mg sodium, 4 g carbohydrate, 1 g fiber, 14 g protein. **Daily values:** 2% vitamin A, 12% vitamin C, 5% calcium, 4% iron.

Keep It Lean

Once you get your healthy cut of meat home from the store, take a few more steps to make sure it is as lean as possible when it gets to the table.

Trim it. Even the leanest cuts of meat contain some separable fat that can be cut away with a sharp knife before cooking. This reduces the total fat in the cooked portion.

Cook it lean. The best cooking methods are broiling, grilling, pan-broiling, poaching, or roasting. Always roast and broil meats on a rack so the fat drips away from the meat.

Don't make gravy from it. Forget about using the fatty drippings for gravy. If you want to serve a gravy with your meat, try one of the low-fat versions available at your grocery store.

Cook it light. Eliminate or reduce the amount of fat used to cook your meat. Use nonstick spray coating instead of oil to brown your meat, and use low-fat or nonfat ingredients in your recipes.

Don't overcook it. For juicy results, cook lean meats to no more than medium doneness (160° to 170°). Lean meats cooked past this temperature tend to dry out and lose their flavor.

Low-fat
Low-sodium

PORK AND PLUM STIR-FRY

When fresh plums are in season, try this stir-fry recipe. You also can use turkey instead of pork.

2 cups sliced plums or peaches
¼ cup orange juice
2 tablespoons dry sherry
2 cloves garlic, minced
½ teaspoon five-spice powder
⅛ teaspoon pepper
12 ounces boneless pork loin
   Nonstick spray coating
2 teaspoons grated fresh
   gingerroot
6 green onions, bias-sliced into
   1-inch pieces
1 8-ounce can sliced water
   chestnuts, drained
2 cups hot cooked rice

1. For plum sauce, in a food processor bowl or blender container combine *½ cup* of the plums, the orange juice, sherry, garlic, five-spice powder, and pepper. Cover and process or blend till mixture is smooth; set aside. Cut pork tenderloin into thin bite-size strips.

2. Spray a wok or large nonstick skillet generously with nonstick spray coating. Preheat over medium heat. Stir-fry gingerroot for 15 seconds. Add green onions. Stir-fry 1½ minutes or till crisp-tender. Remove green onion mixture from wok. Add meat to hot wok or skillet and stir-fry 2 to 3 minutes or till no pink remains. Return green onion mixture to wok. Stir in remaining plums, plum sauce, and water chestnuts; toss to coat with sauce and heat through. Serve over hot cooked rice. Makes 4 servings.

Nutrition facts per serving: 320 calories, 7 g total fat (2 g saturated fat), 38 mg cholesterol, 33 mg sodium, 47 g carbohydrate, 2 g fiber, 16 g protein. **Daily values:** 8% vitamin A, 40% vitamin C, 2% calcium, 13% iron.

Low-fat
Low-calorie
Low-sodium

ITALIAN PORK AND PEPPER SANDWICHES

With low-cal Italian dressing and fat-trimmed marinara sauce, you can enjoy this traditional hot sandwich guilt-free.

1 1-pound pork tenderloin
   Nonstick spray coating
¼ cup reduced-calorie Italian
   salad dressing
1 medium red or yellow sweet
   pepper, cut into ¼-inch
   rings
1 medium green sweet pepper,
   cut into ¼-inch rings
1 medium onion, sliced
¾ cup lower-calorie, low-
   sodium, and low-fat
   traditional marinara
   spaghetti sauce
6 French rolls, split and toasted

1. Trim fat from pork. Spray a roasting rack with nonstick spray coating; place rack in a shallow roasting pan. Place pork tenderloin on rack; brush with *1 tablespoon* of the Italian salad dressing. Insert a meat thermometer. Roast, uncovered, in a 425° oven for 25 to 35 minutes or till juices run clear and the thermometer registers 160°. Let stand for 5 minutes.

2. Meanwhile, spray a large nonstick skillet with nonstick spray coating; cook pepper rings and onion slices over medium heat about 10 minutes or till tender. Stir *1 tablespoon* of the Italian salad dressing into vegetables. Heat spaghetti sauce just till warm. Using a clean brush, spread remaining dressing over toasted surfaces of rolls. Thinly slice pork. Layer pork slices, pepper rings, and onion slices onto bottom bun halves. Drizzle warm spaghetti sauce over sandwiches before adding bun tops. Serve hot. Makes 6 servings.

Nutrition facts per serving: 242 calories, 6 g total fat (1 g saturated fat), 54 mg cholesterol, 359 mg sodium, 27 g carbohydrate, 1 g fiber, 21 g protein. **Daily values:** 11% vitamin A, 56% vitamin C, 4% calcium, 14% iron.

SPICY PORK SATAY WITH PEANUT SAUCE

Low-calorie

This is an easy make-ahead recipe that you can grill once family or guests arrive. (See photo, right.)

12 ounces pork tenderloin
⅓ cup light soy sauce
2 tablespoons lemon juice
1½ teaspoons chili powder
   Peanut Sauce
8 green onions, cut into
   1-inch pieces
   Green onion brushes
   (optional)

1. Trim fat from pork. Cut meat diagonally into strips about 3 inches long and ¼ inch thick. In a shallow glass dish stir together soy sauce, lemon juice, and chili powder; add pork strips. Cover and marinate pork in the refrigerator for 1 to 2 hours, stirring occasionally. Meanwhile, prepare Peanut Sauce.

2. Drain pork strips, reserving marinade. Thread pork strips and green onion pieces onto skewers, leaving about ¼ inch between pieces.

3. Arrange preheated coals around a drip pan. Test for medium heat above drip pan. Grill pork skewers over drip pan, covered, for 12 to 14 minutes or till pork juices run clear, brushing with reserved marinade halfway through grilling time. (Or, spray the unheated rack of a broiler pan with *nonstick spray coating*. Broil skewers 4 to 5 inches from the heat for 6 to 8 minutes or till pork juices run clear, brushing with reserved marinade halfway through broiling time.)

4. Serve pork skewers with Peanut Sauce for dipping. If desired, garnish with green onion brushes and serve with hot cooked brown or white rice. Serves 4.

Peanut Sauce: In a small mixing bowl stir together 2 tablespoons *creamy peanut butter*, 2 tablespoons *hot water*, 4 teaspoons *light soy sauce*, ½ teaspoon grated *fresh gingerroot*, ½ teaspoon *sugar*, ¼ to ½ teaspoon *bottled hot pepper sauce*, and 1 small clove *garlic*, minced. Stir before serving.

Nutrition facts per serving: 165 calories, 7 g total fat (2 g saturated fat), 60 mg cholesterol, 925 mg sodium, 5 g carbohydrate, 1 g fiber, 22 g protein. **Daily values:** 8% vitamin A, 11% vitamin C, 2% calcium, 12% iron.

Low-fat
Low-calorie

SAUSAGE WITH APPLES AND CABBAGE

2 medium apples
12 ounces 97% fat-free, fully
    cooked, smoked sausage
1 medium onion, thinly sliced
2 tablespoons brown sugar
1 tablespoon cornstarch
1 tablespoon brown mustard
1 teaspoon caraway seed
¼ teaspoon ground allspice
⅛ teaspoon pepper
⅔ cup apple juice
2 tablespoons vinegar
4 cups shredded cabbage
    Fresh parsley (optional)

1. Core apples and cut into wedges. Cut sausage into ½-inch-thick slices. Set apples and sausage aside. Spray a 12-inch skillet with *nonstick spray coating.* Cook onion in skillet for 3 minutes.

2. Meanwhile, in a small mixing bowl stir together brown sugar, cornstarch, brown mustard, caraway seed, allspice, and pepper. Stir in apple juice, vinegar, and ½ cup *water.* Add to onion; cook and stir till mixture is thickened and bubbly.

3. Add cabbage and apples. Top with sausage. Bring to boiling; reduce heat. Simmer, covered, about 15 minutes or till apples and cabbage are tender. If desired, garnish with snipped fresh parsley. Makes 4 servings.

Nutrition facts per serving: 208 calories, 4 g total fat (0 g saturated fat), 30 mg cholesterol, 1,108 mg sodium, 31 g carbohydrate, 3 g fiber, 14 g protein. **Daily values:** 1% vitamin A, 55% vitamin C, 4% calcium, 7% iron.

Low-fat
Low-sodium

LAMB WITH SWEET POTATO PILAF

1 4- to 5-pound leg of lamb,
    boned and butterflied
2 tablespoons snipped fresh
    parsley
3 juniper berries, crushed
1 tablespoon Dijon-style
    mustard
¾ teaspoon dried thyme,
    crushed
½ teaspoon ground cumin
2 cloves garlic, minced
½ teaspoon salt-free seasoning
    blend
¾ cup wild rice
¾ cup wheat berries
2 cups coarsely shredded sweet
    potato

1. Untie roast; trim any white membrane and excess fat. In a small mixing bowl stir together parsley, juniper berries, mustard, ½ *teaspoon* of the thyme, cumin, and garlic. Spread mixture over cavity in meat. Reroll and tie roast with kitchen string. Place lamb on a rack in a shallow roasting pan; sprinkle with seasoning blend and ¼ teaspoon *pepper.* Insert a meat thermometer. Roast in a 325° oven for 2 to 3 hours or till thermometer registers 160° (medium).

2. Meanwhile, about 1 hour before meat is done, in a saucepan stir together wild rice, wheat berries, the remaining thyme, 3 cups *water,* ¼ teaspoon *salt,* and ⅛ teaspoon *pepper.* Bring to boiling; reduce heat. Simmer, covered, for 50 to 60 minutes or till berries are tender. Add sweet potato during the last 10 minutes of cooking, stirring once; drain, if necessary. Serve with lamb. Serves 10 to 12.

Nutrition facts per serving: 319 calories, 9 g total fat (3 g saturated fat), 92 mg cholesterol, 168 mg sodium, 26 g carbohydrate, 2 g fiber, 34 g protein. **Daily values:** 58% vitamin A, 13% vitamin C, 2% calcium, 22% iron.

Low-fat
Low-calorie
Low-sodium

HERB-ROASTED LAMB WITH SPRING VEGETABLES

Spreading an herb paste over a roast, as in this recipe, is a great way to add lots of flavor without adding fat.

1 4- to 5-pound leg of lamb
    roast, boned and butterflied
2 tablespoons snipped fresh
    basil or 2 teaspoons dried
    basil, crushed
1 tablespoon snipped fresh
    thyme or 1 teaspoon dried
    thyme, crushed
1 tablespoon snipped fresh
    rosemary or 1 teaspoon
    dried rosemary, crushed
2 cloves garlic, minced
¼ teaspoon pepper
2 tablespoons lemon juice
    Nonstick spray coating
½ teaspoon salt-free seasoning
    blend
1 pound asparagus spears
2 pounds tiny new potatoes,
    halved, or 6 medium
    potatoes, cut into 1-inch
    pieces
4 large carrots, cut into ½-inch
    pieces
3 tablespoons all-purpose flour
1½ teaspoons beef bouillon
    granules
⅛ teaspoon pepper
    Fresh herb sprigs (optional)

1. Untie roast on a flat surface; trim any excess white membrane and fat. In a small mixing bowl stir together basil, thyme, rosemary, garlic, and the ¼ teaspoon pepper. Add lemon juice. Spread herb mixture evenly over center cavity of roast. Reroll and tie roast with kitchen string. Spray a roasting rack with nonstick spray coating; place in a shallow roasting pan. Place roast on rack; sprinkle with seasoning blend. Insert a meat thermometer. Roast in a 325° oven for 2 to 3 hours or till meat thermometer registers 160° (medium).

2. Meanwhile, to trim asparagus, break off woody bases where spears snap easily; scrape off scales. Place a steamer rack in a Dutch oven; fill with water 1 to 2 inches deep. Place new potatoes and carrots on rack; cover and steam for 12 minutes. Add asparagus; steam 5 to 8 minutes more or till potatoes are tender and carrots and asparagus are crisp-tender. Transfer lamb and vegetables to a serving platter; cover and keep warm.

3. For gravy, skim fat from pan drippings; add enough *water* to measure 1 cup. In a small saucepan stir together flour, bouillon granules, the ⅛ teaspoon pepper, and ½ cup *cold water*. Add pan drippings. Cook and stir till mixture is thickened and bubbly; cook for 2 minutes more. If desired, garnish roast with fresh herbs; pass gravy with roast and vegetables. Makes 12 servings.

Nutrition facts per serving: 245 calories, 6 g total fat (2 g saturated fat), 67 mg cholesterol, 182 mg sodium, 22 g carbohydrate, 2 g fiber, 24 g protein. **Daily values:** 59% vitamin A, 30% vitamin C, 2% calcium, 22% iron.

After spreading the herb mixture over the meat, reroll the roast and tie it with kitchen string.

Low-calorie

Low-sodium

LAMB CHOPS AND PEPPERS

Enjoy this quick-cooking skillet dish in the summertime, when sweet peppers and zucchini are at their peak. (See photo, left.)

4 lamb leg sirloin chops, cut
    ¾ inch thick (1¼ pounds)
  Nonstick spray coating
1 cup julienned green sweet
    pepper
1 cup julienned red or yellow
    sweet pepper
1 cup julienned zucchini
½ cup thinly sliced leeks
1 clove garlic, minced
½ cup dry white wine or water
1 teaspoon instant beef bouillon
    granules
1 teaspoon dried basil, crushed
½ teaspoon dried oregano,
    crushed
⅛ teaspoon pepper

1. Trim excess fat from chops. Spray a large nonstick skillet with nonstick spray coating. Cook chops over medium-high heat for 2 minutes per side or till browned. Remove chops from pan. In pan drippings cook sweet peppers, zucchini, leeks, and garlic for 3 minutes. Return chops to skillet.

2. In a small mixing bowl stir together wine, bouillon granules, basil, oregano, and pepper. Add to skillet; bring to boiling. Reduce heat; cover and simmer for 8 to 10 minutes more or till chops are pink in the center for medium doneness. Makes 4 servings.

Nutrition facts per serving: 181 calories, 6 g total fat (2 g saturated fat), 58 mg cholesterol, 268 mg sodium, 8 g carbohydrate, 2 g fiber, 19 g protein. **Daily values:** 15% vitamin A, 80% vitamin C, 3% calcium, 16% iron.

Nonstick Spray Secrets

Nonstick spray coating is a handy kitchen staple for the time-pressed and health-conscious cook. What makes this simple spray work like magic? Vegetable oils and lecithin (from soybeans) prevent sticking, and alcohol helps the spray action but evaporates on contact. Here are a few secrets for success.

  Spray sparingly. A 1¼-second spray is like using 1 tablespoon of cooking oil, margarine, butter, or shortening.

  Hold the pan you are spraying over your sink so you don't make the floor or counter slippery.

  Spray only onto cold baking pans, skillets, and other cooking surfaces because nonstick spray coating can burn or smoke if applied to hot surfaces.

  Spray kitchen shears or scissors with nonstick coating when snipping dried fruit. This keeps the fruit from sticking to them.

  Make grilling cleanup easier by spraying your cold barbecue rack with nonstick coating before firing up the coals.

Low-sodium

High-fiber

CHUTNEY LAMB BURGERS

Shredded apple and carrot keep these low-fat burgers juicy and flavorful.

½ **cup shredded apple**

½ **cup shredded carrot**

1 **tablespoon snipped fresh parsley**

¼ **teaspoon curry powder**

⅛ **teaspoon ground red pepper**

8 **ounces ground lamb**

8 **ounces extra-lean ground beef**

 Nonstick spray coating

5 **whole wheat buns, split and toasted**

¼ **cup finely snipped chutney**

5 **slices red onion**

 Watercress sprigs or shredded lettuce

1. In a large mixing bowl stir together apple, carrot, parsley, curry powder, and red pepper. Add ground lamb and beef; mix well. Shape mixture into five ½-inch-thick patties.

2. Spray the rack of an unheated broiler pan with nonstick coating. Arrange patties on rack. Broil 4 inches from the heat for 10 to 12 minutes or till no longer pink, turning once halfway through the broiling time.

3. Place burgers on bun halves; spoon some of the chutney over each burger. Top with onion slices and watercress or lettuce. Add bun tops. Makes 5 servings.

Nutrition facts per serving: 316 calories, 12 g total fat (5 g saturated fat), 59 mg cholesterol, 278 mg sodium, 33 g carbohydrate, 4 g fiber, 20 g protein. **Daily values:** 34% vitamin A, 8% vitamin C, 5% calcium, 17% iron.

POPULAR POULTRY

When it comes to main dishes, poultry always scores well in popularity contests. It's easy to see why. Both chicken and turkey are readily available, economical, and make sensible low-fat choices for light cooking. Also, the mild taste perfectly complements a wide variety of flavors. For family-pleasing dishes, choose Oven-Fried Buttermilk Chicken, Green and Red Chicken Enchiladas, or Chicken and Biscuit Pie. For more adventurous dining, sample Indian-Style Chicken or Jamaican Chicken. And for a special occasion, cook up Turkey Piccata with Artichokes. You will find many more delights in this chapter. Sandwiches, stir-fries, casseroles, and grilled specialties are all represented. In fact, poultry offers so many options, it's difficult to choose.

Low-fat

Low-sodium

MANGO CHICKEN

To complement this Caribbean-style dish, cook your rice with a bit of fresh ginger and chopped mint. (See photo, right.)

½ cup reduced-sodium chicken
    broth
2 tablespoons lime juice
2 teaspoons finely shredded
    lime peel or orange peel
2 teaspoons brown sugar
2 teaspoons curry powder
1 teaspoon cornstarch
12 ounces skinless, boneless
    chicken breast halves or
    thighs
2 teaspoons peanut oil or
    cooking oil
2 cloves garlic, minced
1 cup sliced red onion
2 cups chopped, peeled mango
    or papaya
2 cups hot cooked rice
    Lime peel strips (optional)

1. For sauce, in a small bowl stir together broth, lime juice, lime peel, brown sugar, curry powder, and cornstarch; set aside. Rinse chicken; pat dry with paper towels. Cut chicken into bite-size strips; set aside.

2. In a large wok or 12-inch skillet heat oil till very hot. Stir-fry garlic for 30 seconds. Add onion slices; stir-fry for 3 minutes. Remove onion from wok or skillet. Add chicken and stir-fry for 2 to 3 minutes or till chicken is tender and no longer pink. Push chicken from center of wok.

3. Stir sauce mixture. Pour sauce into center of wok; cook and stir till thickened and bubbly. Return onion to the wok. Add mango or papaya. Stir all ingredients together to coat with sauce. Cook 2 minutes more or till mixture is heated through. Serve chicken mixture over rice. If desired, garnish with lime peel strips. Makes 4 servings.

Nutrition facts per serving: 301 calories, 5 g total fat (1 g saturated fat), 45 mg cholesterol, 125 mg sodium, 44 g carbohydrate, 3 g fiber, 20 g protein. **Daily values:** 30% vitamin A, 46% vitamin C, 3% calcium, 13% iron.

Mango Magic

This tropical fruit has a spicy peach flavor and a sweet aroma. It is oval, round, or kidney shaped with green to yellow skin tinged with red. The yellow meat clings tightly to the flat oval seed. To remove the meat, cut through the mango, sliding a sharp knife next to the seed. Repeat the cutting process on the other side of the seed, resulting in two large pieces. Then cut away all the meat that remains around the seed. Peel all the pieces. Mangos are high in beta carotene and contain about 55 calories per ½ cup serving.

Low-fat

Low-calorie

Low-sodium

OVEN-FRIED BUTTERMILK CHICKEN

This crispy coated chicken offers all the great flavor of deep-fat fried chicken, but a fraction of the fat.

4 cups cornflakes, crushed
  (1⅓ cups crushed)
2 tablespoons grated Parmesan
  cheese
⅔ cup all-purpose flour
1 teaspoon salt-free seasoning
  blend
1 teaspoon dried oregano,
  crushed
½ teaspoon paprika
¼ teaspoon garlic powder
¼ teaspoon pepper
1 cup buttermilk or skim milk
2½ to 3 pounds meaty chicken
  pieces, skinned (breast
  halves, thighs, and
  drumsticks)

1. In a shallow bowl or pie plate combine crushed cornflakes and cheese. In another bowl or pie plate combine flour, seasoning blend, oregano, paprika, garlic powder, and pepper. Pour buttermilk or skim milk into another shallow bowl. Place rack in a shallow roasting pan.

2. Rinse chicken; pat dry with paper towels. Dip chicken pieces in buttermilk to moisten on all sides; place in bowl with flour mixture. Turn to coat chicken. Remove chicken from flour mixture; dip in buttermilk again. Place chicken pieces in bowl with crushed cornflakes mixture. Turn to coat chicken. Arrange chicken pieces, not touching, on rack in pan.

3. Bake, uncovered, in a 425° oven for 35 to 40 minutes or till chicken is tender and no longer pink. Makes 6 servings.

Nutrition facts per serving: 277 calories, 7 g total fat (2 g saturated fat), 70 mg cholesterol, 331 mg sodium, 26 g carbohydrate, 1 g fiber, 26 g protein. **Daily values:** 23% vitamin A, 14% vitamin C, 7% calcium, 17% iron.

For a crispy coating, place the chicken pieces on a rack in a shallow roasting pan. Leave a little space between the pieces.

Low-fat

Low-calorie

Low-sodium

INDIAN-STYLE CHICKEN

Serve this exotic entrée with a fresh melon, cucumber salad, and brown rice.

½ cup nonfat plain yogurt
1 tablespoon lemon juice
2 teaspoons Dijon-style mustard
½ teaspoon salt-free seasoning
    blend
½ teaspoon ground turmeric
¼ teaspoon ground coriander
¼ teaspoon ground cinnamon
⅛ teaspoon ground ginger
⅛ teaspoon pepper
4 skinless, boneless chicken
    breast halves or large thighs
    (1 pound total)
Nonstick spray coating
Orange slices (optional)

1. For marinade, in a small bowl stir together yogurt, lemon juice, mustard, seasoning blend, turmeric, coriander, cinnamon, ginger, and pepper till well combined. Rinse chicken; pat dry with paper towels. Place chicken in a shallow, nonmetal dish. Brush marinade liberally over chicken; turn chicken to coat with mixture. Cover and marinate 4 to 24 hours to allow flavors to blend; turn chicken occasionally.

2. Spray the unheated rack of a broiler pan with nonstick spray coating. Remove chicken from marinade and place on broiler pan rack; discard marinade.

3. Broil chicken 4 inches from the heat for 10 to 12 minutes or till chicken is tender and no longer pink, turning once about halfway through the broiling time. If desired, garnish with orange slices. Makes 4 servings.

Nutrition facts per serving: 147 calories, 4 g total fat (1 g saturated fat), 60 mg cholesterol, 138 mg sodium, 3 g carbohydrate, 0 g fiber, 23 g protein. **Daily values:** 0% vitamin A, 2% vitamin C, 5% calcium, 6% iron.

Low-calorie

Low-sodium

HERBED CHICKEN BREASTS WITH WINE

Lightly buttered sweet potatoes and steamed summer squash are all you need to accompany this oven-baked main dish.

2 ounces feta cheese, crumbled
    (¼ cup)
1 tablespoon snipped fresh
    parsley
1 tablespoon snipped fresh basil
2 teaspoons snipped fresh
    thyme or oregano
1 clove garlic, minced
4 small chicken breast halves,
    skinned
½ cup dry white wine or
    reduced-sodium chicken
    broth
¼ teaspoon paprika

1. In a small bowl combine feta cheese, parsley, basil, thyme or oregano, and garlic. Rinse chicken; pat dry with paper towels. Cut a slit horizontally into the meaty side of each chicken breast half; stuff herb mixture into slits.

2. Arrange chicken pieces, skinned side up, in a 2-quart rectangular baking dish. Pour wine over chicken and sprinkle with the paprika.

3. Bake, uncovered, in a 375° oven for 40 to 45 minutes or till chicken is tender and no longer pink. Brush with pan juices. Transfer chicken to serving platter. If desired, garnish chicken with fresh herbs and lemon wedges. Makes 4 servings.

Nutrition facts per serving: 181 calories, 6 g total fat (3 g saturated fat), 72 mg cholesterol, 214 mg sodium, 1 g carbohydrate, 0 g fiber, 24 g protein. **Daily values:** 3% vitamin A, 2% vitamin C, 7% calcium, 8% iron.

Low-fat

Low-calorie

Low-sodium

High-fiber

CHUTNEY CHICKEN AND SQUASH BAKE

Chutney is a versatile condiment that you can add to baked main dishes, stir into a sauce or salad dressing, or mix with light sour cream for a fresh-fruit dip. (See photo, left.)

Nonstick spray coating

2 pounds meaty chicken pieces, skinned (breast halves, thighs, and drumsticks)

2 small acorn squash, quartered

2 teaspoons cooking oil

¼ teaspoon salt-free seasoning blend

⅛ teaspoon pepper

¼ cup chutney, snipped

1 tablespoon snipped fresh chives or 1 teaspoon dried snipped chives (optional)

Hot cooked pasta (optional)

1. Spray a 3-quart rectangular baking dish with nonstick spray coating. Rinse chicken; pat dry with paper towels. Arrange chicken and squash pieces, cut sides up, in dish. Brush chicken pieces with oil; sprinkle with seasoning blend and pepper. Spoon chutney over chicken and, if desired, sprinkle with chives.

2. Bake, uncovered, in a 400° oven for 40 to 45 minutes or till chicken and squash are tender and chicken is no longer pink; baste occasionally with pan drippings. Transfer chicken and squash to a serving platter; cover and keep warm. Skim fat from pan drippings; spoon juices over chicken and squash. If desired, serve over hot cooked pasta tossed with a few vegetables. Makes 4 servings.

Nutrition facts per serving: 269 calories, 7 g total fat (2 g saturated fat), 80 mg cholesterol, 82 mg sodium, 25 g carbohydrate, 4 g fiber, 27 g protein. **Daily values:** 102% vitamin A, 37% vitamin C, 6% calcium, 13% iron.

So Long, Skin

Chicken meat can be a healthy part of your diet. Chicken skin, however, is another story because it contains a lot of fat. The obvious and easy solution is to discard the skin. You can remove it either before or after cooking. If the chicken is cooking in a broth mixture, remove the skin before cooking. If you're baking or broiling the chicken, then remove the skin after cooking. This keeps the meat moist and retains flavor while the fat drips away from the chicken.

Low-fat

Low-calorie

Low-sodium

High-fiber

GRILLED CHICKEN THIGHS WITH BLACK BEANS

Warm some tortillas, wrapped in plastic wrap, for about 30 seconds in the microwave, to serve alongside this dish.

1 pound skinless, boneless large
 chicken thighs
3 tablespoons lime juice
2 cloves garlic, minced
¼ teaspoon crushed red pepper
1 15-ounce can black beans,
 drained
½ cup chunky salsa
1 tablespoon snipped fresh
 cilantro

1. Rinse chicken; pat dry with paper towels. In a small bowl stir together lime juice, garlic, and red pepper.

2. Place chicken on the rack of an uncovered grill directly over medium coals. Brush with half of the lime juice mixture. Grill, uncovered, for 12 to 15 minutes or till chicken is tender and no longer pink, turning once and basting with the remaining lime mixture halfway through grilling time.

3. Meanwhile, in a medium saucepan heat beans, salsa, and half of the cilantro till heated through. To serve, arrange chicken on a serving platter; ladle beans alongside chicken. Sprinkle with remaining cilantro. Makes 4 servings.

Nutrition facts per serving: 203 calories, 7 g total fat (2 g saturated fat), 54 mg cholesterol, 430 mg sodium, 18 g carbohydrate, 5 g fiber, 23 g protein. **Daily values:** 6% vitamin A, 21% vitamin C, 4% calcium, 14% iron.

Low-fat

Low-calorie

Low-sodium

CHICKEN WITH SHALLOT-WINE SAUCE

Shallots are small French onions that have a delicate flavor. Serve the chicken and sauce with egg noodles and a mushroom salad.

4 skinless, boneless chicken
 breast halves or large thighs
 (1 pound total)
 Nonstick spray coating
¼ cup sliced shallots or finely
 chopped onion
1 clove garlic, minced
½ cup dry white wine
2 teaspoons cornstarch
½ cup reduced-sodium chicken
 broth
¼ teaspoon dried thyme,
 crushed
⅛ teaspoon pepper
2 tablespoons snipped fresh
 parsley

1. Rinse chicken; pat dry with paper towels. Spray the unheated rack of a broiler pan with nonstick spray coating. Arrange chicken pieces on broiler rack. Broil chicken 4 inches from the heat for 10 to 12 minutes or till chicken is tender and no longer pink, turning once about halfway through the broiling time.

2. Meanwhile, for sauce, in a medium saucepan combine shallots or onion, garlic, and wine; bring to boiling. Reduce heat and simmer for 2 minutes. In a small bowl stir cornstarch into chicken broth; stir into mixture in saucepan along with the thyme and pepper. Cook and stir till thickened and bubbly; cook and stir for 2 minutes more. To serve, arrange chicken pieces on a platter; spoon sauce over chicken. Sprinkle with parsley. Makes 4 servings.

Nutrition facts per serving: 158 calories, 3 g total fat (1 g saturated fat), 59 mg cholesterol, 138 mg sodium, 4 g carbohydrate, 0 g fiber, 22 g protein. **Daily values:** 14% vitamin A, 6% vitamin C, 1% calcium, 8% iron.

Low-fat

Low-calorie

Low-sodium

JAMAICAN CHICKEN

Serve this spicy, broiled chicken with fresh pineapple, melon, or mango slices.

2 tablespoons lime or lemon
   juice
1 tablespoon prepared mustard
½ cup sliced green onions
2 fresh jalapeño or serrano chili
   peppers, seeded and finely
   chopped
1 tablespoon brown sugar
2 teaspoons grated gingerroot
1 teaspoon dried rosemary,
   crushed
1 teaspoon dried thyme,
   crushed
¼ teaspoon salt
2 cloves garlic, minced
4 skinless, boneless chicken
   breast halves (1 pound
   total)
   Nonstick spray coating

1. In a blender container or food processor bowl combine lime juice, mustard, green onions, jalapeño peppers, brown sugar, gingerroot, rosemary, thyme, salt, and garlic. Cover and blend or process till mixture is smooth, stopping and scraping sides as necessary.

2. Rinse chicken; pat dry with paper towels. Spray the unheated rack of a broiler pan with nonstick spray coating. Arrange chicken pieces on broiler rack. Brush some of the spice mixture over chicken. Broil chicken 4 inches from the heat for 6 minutes; turn and brush with remaining spice mixture. Broil 6 to 9 minutes more or till chicken is tender and no longer pink. Makes 4 servings.

Nutrition facts per serving: 153 calories, 4 g total fat (1 g saturated fat), 59 mg cholesterol, 239 mg sodium, 6 g carbohydrate, 0 g fiber, 22 g protein. **Daily values:** 4% vitamin A, 46% vitamin C, 2% calcium, 9% iron.

Because hot peppers contain oils that can burn your eyes, lips, and skin, protect yourself when working with them by wearing disposable plastic gloves or covering your hands with plastic bags. Use a sharp knife to remove the seeds and membranes from the pepper. Wash your hands before touching your eyes or face.

Low-fat

Low-sodium

High-fiber

THAI CHICKEN-CURRY STIR-FRY

You can make this dish as spicy as desired by adding more or less jalapeño pepper. (See photo, right.)

⅔ **cup skim milk**

2 **tablespoons snipped fresh cilantro**

1 **tablespoon soy sauce**

2 **teaspoons cornstarch**

1 **teaspoon curry powder**

½ **teaspoon coconut flavoring (optional)**

¼ **teaspoon crushed red pepper**

⅛ **teaspoon salt**

12 **ounces skinless, boneless chicken breast halves**

Nonstick spray coating

1 **large green sweet pepper, cut into 1-inch pieces**

1 **large red sweet pepper, cut into 1-inch pieces**

1 **fresh jalapeño or serrano chili pepper, seeded and finely chopped**

1 **cup sliced fresh shiitake mushrooms (stems removed)**

3 **green onions, cut into 1-inch pieces**

2 **teaspoons peanut oil or cooking oil**

3 **cups hot cooked Chinese egg noodles or rice**

Cilantro sprigs (optional)

1. For sauce, in a small bowl stir together milk, cilantro, soy sauce, cornstarch, curry powder, coconut flavoring (if desired), crushed red pepper, and salt; set aside.

2. Rinse chicken; pat dry with paper towels. Cut chicken into bite-size strips; set aside.

3. Spray an unheated wok or large nonstick skillet with nonstick spray coating. Preheat over medium heat. Add green sweet pepper, red sweet pepper, and jalapeño pepper pieces; stir-fry for 2 minutes. Add mushrooms and green onions and stir-fry for 2 minutes more or till vegetables are crisp-tender. Remove from wok. Add oil to wok or skillet. Add chicken to the hot wok. Stir-fry for 3 to 4 minutes or till chicken is tender and no longer pink. Push chicken from the center of wok.

4. Stir sauce. Pour sauce into center of wok; cook and stir till thickened and bubbly. Return cooked vegetables to wok; toss to coat with sauce. Cook and stir about 1 minute more or till heated through. Serve immediately with noodles or rice. If desired, garnish with cilantro sprigs. Makes 4 servings.

Nutrition facts per serving: 430 calories, 7 g total fat (1 g saturated fat), 83 mg cholesterol, 394 mg sodium, 66 g carbohydrate, 5 g fiber, 24 g protein. **Daily values:** 31% vitamin A, 157% vitamin C, 7% calcium, 18% iron.

Stir-Frying the Low-Fat Way

Chock-full of vegetables, stir-fried dishes generally are low in fat. Our Test Kitchen has a few guidelines for keeping them that way. First, start with lean cuts of meat or poultry and allow 12 ounces for four servings. Tossed with the vegetables and served over rice, this will make a satisfying serving for even the heartiest of eaters. Before you start stir-frying, spray your cold wok or skillet with nonstick spray coating. Then heat the wok over medium heat and proceed as directed in the recipe. If necessary, add a little cooking oil to the wok between cooking steps to keep the food from sticking. Never spray a hot wok or skillet with nonstick spray coating.

Low-fat

Low-calorie

Low-sodium

LEMON CHICKEN WITH ORIENTAL RICE STUFFING

Never stuff a bird until you are ready to roast it. You can prepare this stuffing ahead of time and chill it separately from the bird. The nutrition information assumes that the skin of the chicken is not eaten. If skin is included, add about 33 calories and about 5 grams of fat per serving.

1½ **cups reduced-sodium chicken broth**
¾ **cup long grain rice**
1 **cup shredded bok choy or Chinese cabbage**
1 **cup sliced fresh shiitake mushrooms (stems removed)**
½ **of an 8-ounce can water chestnuts, drained and chopped (½ cup)**
¼ **cup sliced green onions**
1 **teaspoon finely shredded lemon peel**
1 **tablespoon lemon juice**
1 **tablespoon light soy sauce**
½ **teaspoon grated gingerroot**
⅛ **teaspoon pepper**
1 **2½- to 3-pound whole broiler-fryer chicken**

1. In a medium saucepan bring broth to boiling. Stir in rice; cover and simmer for 5 minutes. Sprinkle bok choy and mushrooms atop rice; cover and cook 10 minutes more or till liquid is absorbed. Remove from heat. Stir in water chestnuts, green onions, lemon peel, lemon juice, soy sauce, gingerroot, and pepper; set aside.

2. Rinse chicken; pat dry with paper towels. Spoon some of the rice mixture into body and neck cavities. Place remaining stuffing in a casserole; cover and chill. Pull neck skin (if present) to the back and fasten with a skewer. Tie legs to tail. Twist wing tips under back. Place chicken, breast side up, on a rack in a shallow roasting pan. If desired, insert a meat thermometer into the center of an inside thigh muscle. Do not allow bulb of thermometer to touch bone.

3. Roast, uncovered, in a 375° oven for 1¼ to 1½ hours or till drumsticks move easily in their sockets, chicken is no longer pink, and meat thermometer registers 180°. If necessary, cover bird loosely with foil after about 45 minutes to prevent overbrowning. Bake remaining stuffing in casserole for the last 30 minutes of roasting time. Transfer bird to a serving platter. Makes 6 servings.

Nutrition facts per serving: 250 calories, 6 g total fat (2 g saturated fat), 68 mg cholesterol, 320 mg sodium, 22 g carbohydrate, 1 g fiber, 25 g protein. **Daily values:** 4% vitamin A, 22% vitamin C, 3% calcium, 16% iron.

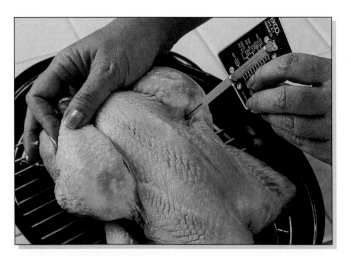

Insert the meat thermometer into the center of an inside thigh muscle. To ensure an accurate reading, do not allow the bulb of the thermometer to touch the bone. The chicken is done when the thermometer registers 180°.

Low-fat

Low-calorie

Low-sodium

GARLIC AND PEPPER CHICKEN WITH BROCCOLI

Next time, try tossing this stir-fry mixture with hot cooked linguine or bow-tie pasta.

¾ cup reduced-sodium chicken broth
1 tablespoon oyster sauce
2 teaspoons cornstarch
¼ teaspoon crushed red pepper
12 ounces skinless, boneless chicken breast halves
   Nonstick spray coating
4 cloves garlic, minced
1 medium onion, cut into thin wedges
2 cups broccoli flowerets
6 cherry tomatoes, halved
2 cups hot cooked rice

1. For sauce, in a bowl combine *½ cup* broth, oyster sauce, cornstarch, and red pepper; set aside. Rinse chicken; pat dry with paper towels. Cut into bite-size strips.

2. Spray an unheated wok or large nonstick skillet with nonstick spray coating. Over medium heat stir-fry chicken strips and garlic for 3 to 4 minutes or till chicken is tender and no longer pink. Remove chicken mixture from wok.

3. Add *2 tablespoons* broth to the wok; add onion and cook for 3 minutes. Remove from wok. Add more broth if necessary; add broccoli and cook for 3 minutes. Push broccoli to one side of wok. Stir sauce mixture. Pour sauce into center of wok; cook and stir till mixture is thickened and bubbly. Return chicken mixture and onion to wok; toss to coat with sauce. Cook and stir about 1 minute or till mixture is heated through. Stir in tomato halves. Serve with the hot cooked rice. Makes 4 servings.

Nutrition facts per serving: 236 calories, 3 g total fat (1 g saturated fat), 45 mg cholesterol, 210 mg sodium, 30 g carbohydrate, 3 g fiber, 21 g protein. **Daily values:** 9% vitamin A, 86% vitamin C, 4% calcium, 14% iron.

Low-calorie

Low-sodium

CHINESE CHICKEN

Place marinating poultry in the coldest part of your refrigerator, tightly wrapped.

2½ to 3 pounds meaty chicken pieces, skinned (breast halves, thighs, and drumsticks)
3 tablespoons reduced-sodium soy sauce
2 tablespoons water
1½ teaspoons grated gingerroot
1 teaspoon five-spice powder
¼ teaspoon onion powder
2 cloves garlic, minced
   Nonstick spray coating

1. Rinse chicken; pat dry with paper towels. Place chicken in a large plastic bag set in a shallow dish. For marinade, in a small bowl stir together soy sauce, water, gingerroot, five-spice powder, onion powder, and garlic till combined.

2. Pour marinade over chicken in bag. Close bag; turn bag to coat chicken with marinade. Place in dish in refrigerator for 4 to 24 hours, turning bag occasionally to distribute marinade. Drain chicken, discarding any remaining marinade.

3. Spray the unheated rack of a broiler pan with nonstick spray coating. Arrange chicken pieces on broiler rack. Broil chicken 4 to 5 inches from the heat for 15 minutes; turn and broil 10 to 15 minutes more or till chicken is tender and no longer pink. Makes 6 servings.

Nutrition facts per serving: 151 calories, 6 g total fat (2 g saturated fat), 67 mg cholesterol, 339 mg sodium, 1 g carbohydrate, 0 g fiber, 22 g protein. **Daily values:** 0% vitamin A, 0% vitamin C, 1% calcium, 8% iron.

Low-fat

Low-sodium

High-fiber

CHICKEN AND BISCUIT PIE

Nonfat dry milk powder makes a creamy gravy in this hearty one-dish meal. (See photo, left.)

1½ **pounds chicken breast halves,**
skinned
2¼ **cups water**
1 **bay leaf**
2 **cups cubed, peeled potatoes**
(2 medium)
1 **cup chopped onion**
½ **cup nonfat dry milk powder**
5 **tablespoons all-purpose flour**
1 **teaspoon dried basil, crushed**
¾ **teaspoon poultry seasoning**
¼ **teaspoon salt**
⅛ **teaspoon pepper**
1 **cup loose-pack frozen peas**
Green Onion Biscuits

1. Rinse chicken; pat dry with paper towels. In a 4-quart Dutch oven combine chicken, water, and bay leaf. Bring to boiling; reduce heat. Cover and simmer for 20 to 25 minutes or till chicken is tender and no longer pink. Drain, reserving cooking liquid. Discard bay leaf. Cool chicken slightly; discard bones and cut chicken into bite-size pieces.

2. Meanwhile, in a medium saucepan cook potatoes and onion in a small amount of boiling water about 10 minutes or till potatoes are tender. Drain; keep warm.

3. For sauce, in a small saucepan stir together the dry milk powder, flour, basil, poultry seasoning, salt, and pepper. Add 2 cups of the reserved chicken cooking liquid, stirring till smooth. Cook and stir over medium heat till thickened and bubbly. Gently stir together the cut-up chicken, drained vegetables, peas, and sauce; keep warm while preparing Green Onion Biscuits.

4. Spoon chicken mixture into four 14-ounce individual casserole dishes or a 2-quart rectangular baking dish. Drop biscuit topping onto warm mixture to form 8 small biscuits. For individual casserole dishes, drop 2 biscuits on each. Bake in a 400° oven for 20 to 25 minutes or till biscuits are golden and a wooden toothpick inserted into biscuits comes out clean. Makes 4 servings.

Green Onion Biscuits: In a medium mixing bowl stir together ⅔ cup *all-purpose flour*; 1 tablespoon thinly sliced *green onion*; 1 teaspoon *baking powder*; 1 teaspoon *sugar*; ¼ teaspoon *dried basil, crushed*; and dash *salt*. Stir together ⅓ cup *skim milk* and 4 teaspoons *cooking oil*. Stir milk mixture into flour mixture just till combined.

Nutrition facts per serving: 462 calories, 14 g total fat (3 g saturated fat), 61 mg cholesterol, 315 mg sodium, 52 g carbohydrate, 4 g fiber, 32 g protein. **Daily values:** 12% vitamin A, 19% vitamin C, 15% calcium, 23% iron.

Low-sodium

High-fiber

CHICKEN WITH HERB DUMPLINGS

If you need to thaw chicken, do it in the refrigerator and allow 5 hours for every pound of poultry.

2 pounds meaty chicken pieces,
  skinned (breast halves,
  thighs, and drumsticks)
2½ cups water
3 carrots, julienned
3 cups thinly sliced leeks
2 stalks celery, sliced
2 teaspoons dried basil, crushed
½ teaspoon dried dillweed
½ teaspoon poultry seasoning
⅛ teaspoon salt
⅛ teaspoon pepper
1 bay leaf
  Herb Dumplings
2 tablespoons snipped fresh
  parsley

1. Rinse chicken; pat dry with paper towels. In a 4½-quart Dutch oven combine chicken, water, carrots, leeks, celery, basil, dillweed, poultry seasoning, salt, pepper, and bay leaf. Bring to boiling; reduce heat. Cover and simmer for 25 minutes.

2. Meanwhile, prepare Herb Dumplings. Drop dumpling mixture in 6 mounds directly atop hot chicken mixture. Cover and simmer about 12 minutes or till a wooden toothpick inserted into dumplings comes out clean.

3. Using a slotted spoon, transfer chicken and dumplings to soup plates; cover and keep warm. Remove bay leaf from pan drippings. Skim fat from broth; discard fat. Stir in parsley. Spoon broth over chicken and dumplings. Makes 6 servings.

Herb Dumplings: In a medium mixing bowl stir together 1 cup *all-purpose flour*; 1½ teaspoons *baking powder*; ½ teaspoon *dried Italian seasoning, crushed*; and ⅛ teaspoon *salt*. In a small bowl combine ¼ cup *skim milk*, 2 tablespoons *water*, and 2 tablespoons *margarine*, melted; stir into flour mixture with a fork just till combined.

Nutrition facts per serving: 322 calories, 10 g total fat (2 g saturated fat), 67 mg cholesterol, 364 mg sodium, 33 g carbohydrate, 8 g fiber, 26 g protein. **Daily values:** 93% vitamin A, 19% vitamin C, 16% calcium, 29% iron.

Low-calorie

Low-sodium

ROSEMARY ROASTED CHICKEN

1 cup reduced-sodium chicken
  broth
5 cloves garlic, peeled
2 tablespoons lemon juice
2 tablespoons minced fresh
  rosemary or 2 teaspoons
  dried rosemary, crushed
2 teaspoons olive oil
¼ teaspoon pepper
⅛ teaspoon salt
1 2½- to 3½-pound whole
  broiler-fryer chicken
3 tablespoons all-purpose flour
½ cup skim milk

1. In a saucepan combine broth and garlic. Bring to boiling; reduce heat. Cover; simmer for 15 minutes. Remove garlic, reserve broth in refrigerator. In blender container combine lemon juice, garlic, rosemary, olive oil, pepper, and salt. Cover and blend till mixture is smooth; set aside. Rinse chicken; pat dry with paper towels. Place chicken, breast side up, on a rack in a shallow roasting pan. Brush chicken with some of the garlic mixture. Insert meat thermometer into the center of one of the inside thigh muscles. Roast in a 375° oven for 1¼ to 1¾ hours or till thermometer registers 180°, brushing several times with the garlic mixture.

2. Stir flour into milk; add to reserved garlic broth. Cook and stir till thickened and bubbly; cook 2 minutes more. Pass sauce with chicken. Serves 6.

Nutrition facts per serving: 222 calories, 12 g total fat (3 g saturated fat), 66 mg cholesterol, 224 mg sodium, 5 g carbohydrate, 0 g fiber, 22 g protein. **Daily values:** 4% vitamin A, 4% vitamin C, 3% calcium, 8% iron.

Low-fat

Low-calorie

Low-sodium

SKILLET-STYLE CHICKEN DRUMSTICKS

You'll find this recipe easy to prepare for your family. Serve these spunky drumsticks with hot cooked rice or noodles.

8 chicken drumsticks or thighs, skinned
Nonstick spray coating
½ cup reduced-sodium chicken broth
1 tablespoon prepared horseradish
1 teaspoon Worcestershire sauce
1 teaspoon honey
½ teaspoon dry mustard
¼ teaspoon pepper
1 teaspoon cornstarch
1 tablespoon water

1. Rinse chicken; pat dry with paper towels. Spray an unheated large nonstick skillet with nonstick spray coating. Place over medium heat. Add chicken and brown on all sides, about 10 minutes.

2. In a small bowl stir together broth, horseradish, Worcestershire sauce, honey, mustard, and pepper. Pour mixture over chicken in skillet; cook, covered, about 35 minutes or till chicken is tender and no longer pink. Transfer chicken to a serving platter; cover and keep warm.

3. In a small bowl combine cornstarch and water. Add to pan juices; cook and stir till thickened and bubbly; cook and stir 1 minute more. Spoon juices over chicken. Makes 4 servings.

Nutrition facts per serving: 166 calories, 5 g total fat (1 g saturated fat), 80 mg cholesterol, 215 mg sodium, 3 g carbohydrate, 0 g fiber, 25 g protein. **Daily values:** 1% vitamin A, 5% vitamin C, 1% calcium, 8% iron.

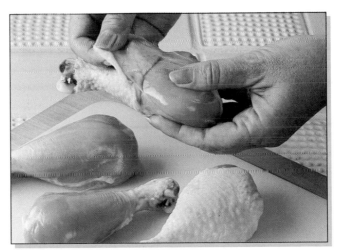

To remove the skin from a drumstick, pull it away from the meat with your fingers. You may need to use kitchen shears to snip off the skin at the bottom of the drumstick.

CHICKEN IN PHYLLO

Low-sodium

Phyllo dough can be found in the freezer case in large supermarkets, delis, and specialty food shops. (See photo, right.)

½ of an 8-ounce package
    reduced-fat cream cheese
    (Neufchâtel), softened
¼ cup sliced green onion
1 tablespoon skim milk
½ teaspoon dried basil, crushed
½ teaspoon dried rosemary,
    crushed
4 skinless, boneless chicken
    breast halves (1 pound
    total)
6 sheets phyllo dough
    Nonstick spray coating
2 teaspoons margarine, melted
1 tablespoon grated Parmesan
    cheese
    Sugar snap peas (optional)

1. In blender container or food processor bowl combine cream cheese, green onion, milk, basil, and rosemary. Cover and blend or process till well mixed; set aside.

2. Rinse chicken; pat dry with paper towels. Lay one sheet of the phyllo dough on a flat surface; spray with nonstick spray coating. Top with a second sheet; spray again. Repeat with a third sheet of phyllo dough. Cut stack of phyllo in half crosswise. On each half, lay a chicken breast diagonally across one corner of dough.

3. Spoon ¼ of the cheese mixture over chicken. Fold corner nearest chicken over filling; fold in sides and roll up. Repeat with remaining phyllo dough, chicken, and cheese mixture. Spray a 13x9x2-inch baking pan with nonstick spray coating. Place bundles, seam sides down, in pan. Brush bundles with melted margarine; sprinkle with Parmesan cheese.

4. Bake, uncovered, in a 400° oven for 20 to 30 minutes, or till chicken is no longer pink and phyllo is a deep golden brown. Place a phyllo bundle on each serving plate. If desired, serve with sugar snap peas. Makes 4 servings.

Nutrition facts per serving: 309 calories, 15 g total fat (6 g saturated fat), 83 mg cholesterol, 358 mg sodium, 16 g carbohydrate, 0 g fiber, 27 g protein. **Daily values:** 14% vitamin A, 2% vitamin C, 5% calcium, 12% iron.

Phyllo Know-How

Phyllo (FEE low) is a Greek pastry made from a mixture of flour and water that is stretched until paper thin, then cut into sheets. Look for frozen phyllo in the freezer case at your grocery store.

Allow frozen phyllo dough to thaw while it is still wrapped. Once unwrapped, sheets of phyllo dough quickly dry out and become unusable. To preserve the phyllo sheets while you're preparing the recipe, keep the opened stack of dough covered with plastic wrap or a slightly moistened cloth. Rewrap remaining sheets of dough and return them to the freezer.

Low-fat

Low-calorie

Low-sodium

STIR-FRIED LEMONGRASS CHICKEN

If you can't find lemongrass at your local grocery store, check produce markets or an Oriental food market.

**2 stalks fresh lemongrass or
1 teaspoon finely shredded
lemon peel**

**½ cup reduced-sodium chicken
broth**

2 teaspoons cornstarch

**2 teaspoons rice vinegar or
white wine vinegar**

2 teaspoons light soy sauce

**12 ounces skinless, boneless
chicken breast halves
Nonstick spray coating**

2 cloves garlic, minced

1 teaspoon grated gingerroot

**6 green onions, cut into 1-inch
pieces**

**2 small zucchini, quartered
lengthwise and sliced**

**2 teaspoons peanut oil or
cooking oil**

**1 11-ounce can mandarin
orange sections, drained**

**2 cups hot cooked rice
Green onion strips (optional)**

1. Peel off and discard the heavy outer stalks of lemongrass; finely chop the tender inner stalks. For sauce, in a small bowl stir together chopped lemongrass, broth, cornstarch, vinegar, and soy sauce till combined; set aside. Rinse chicken; pat dry with paper towels. Cut chicken into 1-inch pieces; set aside.

2. Spray an unheated wok or large skillet with nonstick spray coating. Preheat over medium heat. Stir-fry garlic and gingerroot for 15 seconds. Add onions and zucchini and stir-fry for 2 minutes. Remove vegetables from wok.

3. Add oil to wok or skillet. Add chicken and stir-fry for 3 to 4 minutes or till chicken is tender and no longer pink. Push chicken from center of wok.

4. Stir sauce. Pour sauce into center of wok; cook and stir till mixture is thickened and bubbly. Return cooked vegetables to wok; toss chicken and vegetables to coat with sauce. Cook and stir about 1 minute more or till mixture is heated through. Gently stir in mandarin oranges. Spoon rice onto a serving platter; spoon chicken mixture over rice. If desired, garnish with green onion strips. Makes 4 servings.

Nutrition facts per serving: 286 calories, 6 g total fat (1 g saturated fat), 45 mg cholesterol, 216 mg sodium, 39 g carbohydrate, 1 g fiber, 20 g protein. **Daily values:** 5% vitamin A, 9% vitamin C, 2% calcium, 14% iron.

Looking for Lemongrass

Lemongrass is a lemon-flavored plant that looks like a green onion. Often used in Oriental cooking, you can purchase it either fresh or dried in Oriental markets. If you have difficulty obtaining lemongrass, lemon peel makes a good alternative. In a recipe that calls for 1 tablespoon finely chopped lemongrass (about 2 stalks), you can substitute ½ teaspoon finely shredded lemon peel.

Low-calorie
Low-sodium

CHICKEN AND GOAT-CHEESE PIZZAS

If you have flour tortillas on hand, you have the beginnings of quick, individual pizzas.

4 **7- to 8-inch flour tortillas**
2 **small tomatoes, thinly sliced**
1 **green onion, sliced**
1 **cup shredded cooked chicken**
   or turkey
¼ **cup salsa**
2 **ounces goat cheese (chèvre)**
   or feta cheese
1 **tablespoon snipped fresh basil**
   or 1 teaspoon dried basil,
   crushed
4 **pitted ripe olives, sliced**

1. Place tortillas on an ungreased baking sheet. Bake in a 350° oven about 8 minutes or till crisp, turning tortillas once. Remove from oven.

2. Top each tortilla with ¼ of the tomato slices, onion, and chicken or turkey. Spoon 1 tablespoon salsa over each pizza. Dollop ¼ of the goat cheese or sprinkle ¼ of the feta cheese over each pizza. Top with basil and olives. Return to oven. Bake 5 to 10 minutes more or till cheese is melted and ingredients are heated through. Makes 4 servings.

Nutrition facts per serving: 264 calories, 12 g total fat (4 g saturated fat), 42 mg cholesterol, 356 mg sodium, 23 g carbohydrate, 1 g fiber, 17 g protein. **Daily values:** 8% vitamin A, 23% vitamin C, 6% calcium, 14% iron.

Low-calorie
Low-sodium

SESAME-SAUCED CHICKEN THIGHS

Don't overlook economical chicken thighs at your meat counter; they can be the basis for tasty main dishes like this one.

⅓ **cup reduced-sodium, fat-free,**
   hickory-flavored barbecue
   sauce
2 **tablespoons honey**
1 **tablespoon lemon juice**
8 **chicken thighs (about**
   2 pounds total)
1 **tablespoon thinly sliced green**
   onion
2 **teaspoons sesame seed**

1. In a small bowl stir together barbecue sauce, honey, and lemon juice. Remove skin from chicken thighs. Rinse chicken; pat dry with paper towels. Arrange chicken, meaty side down, in a shallow baking dish so that pieces are not touching. Brush chicken with half of the barbecue sauce mixture.

2. Bake in a 375° oven for 20 minutes. Turn pieces over; brush with remaining barbecue sauce mixture. Bake 25 to 30 minutes more or till chicken is tender and no longer pink. With tongs, transfer chicken to a serving platter. Sprinkle with green onion and sesame seed. Makes 4 servings.

Nutrition facts per serving: 281 calories, 11 g total fat (3 g saturated fat), 93 mg cholesterol, 268 mg sodium, 17 g carbohydrate, 0 g fiber, 26 g protein. **Daily values:** 5% vitamin A, 3% vitamin C, 1% calcium, 13% iron.

GREEN AND RED CHICKEN ENCHILADAS

Low-sodium

Look for firm tomatillos with tight fitting, dry husks. (See photo, left.)

1 pound fresh tomatillos,
   husked and chopped, or
   1 18-ounce can tomatillos,
   rinsed, drained, and cut up
1½ cups chopped onion
¼ cup firmly packed fresh
   cilantro leaves or fresh
   parsley sprigs
1 4-ounce can diced green chili
   peppers, drained
¼ teaspoon ground cumin
¼ teaspoon pepper
1 cup chopped tomato
3 cups shredded cooked
   chicken or turkey
   (1 pound)
Nonstick spray coating
⅔ cup low-sodium tomato juice
12 6-inch corn tortillas
⅔ cup shredded reduced-fat
   Monterey Jack cheese

1. In a blender container or food processor bowl combine tomatillos, *1 cup* of the onion, cilantro or parsley, chili peppers, cumin, and pepper. Cover and blend or process till puréed; set aside.

2. In a nonstick skillet cook tomato and remaining onion for 3 minutes. Stir in chicken and 1 cup of the tomatillo mixture; heat through. Spray a 3-quart rectangular baking dish with nonstick spray coating.

3. To assemble enchiladas, pour tomato juice into a shallow dish. Dip a tortilla in tomato juice, coating both sides. Place tortilla on a work surface. Spoon about *3 tablespoons* of the chicken mixture down center of tortilla; roll up. Place seam side down in dish. Repeat with remaining tomato juice, tortillas, and chicken filling. Spoon remaining tomatillo mixture over enchiladas.

4. Bake, covered, in a 350° oven about 30 minutes or till hot. Sprinkle with cheese; bake 5 minutes more or till cheese melts. If desired, serve with a tossed salad. Makes 6 servings.

Nutrition facts per serving: 375 calories, 13 g total fat (4 g saturated fat), 67 mg cholesterol, 313 mg sodium, 35 g carbohydrate, 2 g fiber, 30 g protein. **Daily values:** 10% vitamin A, 48% vitamin C, 17% calcium, 15% iron.

Low-fat

Low-calorie

Low-sodium

High-fiber

CHICKEN BREASTS WITH MUSHROOM SAUCE

4 skinless, boneless chicken
  breast halves (1 pound
  total)
½ cup reduced-sodium chicken
  broth
½ teaspoon dried thyme,
  crushed
1 cup chopped fresh
  mushrooms
2 teaspoons cornstarch
½ cup light dairy sour cream
¼ teaspoon ground sage
⅛ teaspoon pepper
  Watercress or parsley sprigs

1. Rinse chicken; pat dry with paper towels. Place chicken in a large nonstick skillet. Add chicken broth. Sprinkle with thyme. Bring to boiling; reduce heat. Cover and simmer for 10 to 12 minutes or till chicken is tender and no longer pink. Remove chicken from skillet; keep warm.

2. For sauce, add mushrooms to cooking liquid in skillet. Cover and simmer for 5 minutes or till mushrooms are tender. In a small bowl stir cornstarch into sour cream; add to broth with sage and pepper. Cook and stir till mixture is thickened; cook and stir for 2 minutes more. Spoon ¼ of the sauce over each chicken breast on a serving plate; garnish with watercress or parsley. Makes 4 servings.

Nutrition facts per serving: 174 calories, 5 g total fat (2 g saturated fat), 63 mg cholesterol, 171 mg sodium, 6 g carbohydrate, 0 g fiber, 24 g protein. **Daily values:** 5% vitamin A, 3% vitamin C, 4% calcium, 7% iron.

Low-calorie

Low-sodium

POTATO-CRUSTED CHICKEN

Mashed potatoes and chicken bake in one dish for an easy oven meal.

2 pounds meaty chicken pieces,
  skinned (breast halves and
  thighs)
½ cup water
½ cup skim milk
1 cup packaged instant mashed
  potato flakes
¼ cup light dairy sour cream
1 tablespoon snipped fresh
  parsley
½ teaspoon dried tarragon,
  crushed
⅛ teaspoon salt
¼ teaspoon paprika

1. Rinse chicken; pat dry with paper towels. Spray a 2-quart rectangular baking dish with *nonstick spray coating.* Arrange chicken in baking dish, meaty side up. Bake, uncovered, in a 375° oven for 20 minutes.

2. Meanwhile, in a small saucepan heat water and milk to almost boiling. Remove from heat; stir in potato flakes, sour cream, parsley, tarragon, and salt till well combined. Spread potato mixture liberally over chicken pieces, and sprinkle with paprika. Return to oven. Bake, uncovered, for 20 to 30 minutes more or till chicken is tender and no longer pink. Makes 4 servings.

Nutrition facts per serving: 240 calories, 8 g total fat (2 g saturated fat), 83 mg cholesterol, 120 mg sodium, 13 g carbohydrate, 0 g fiber, 29 g protein. **Daily values:** 5% vitamin A, 18% vitamin C, 6% calcium, 9% iron.

YUCATAN CHICKEN WITH PLANTAINS

Low-sodium

Plantains bring the flavor of Mexico to this one-dish meal.

1 8-ounce can crushed
  pineapple (juice pack)
3 tablespoons lime juice
1 tablespoon finely shredded
  orange peel
2 cloves garlic, minced
1 teaspoon dried oregano,
  crushed
½ teaspoon ground cumin
½ teaspoon chili powder
¼ teaspoon ground allspice
  Nonstick spray coating
2 pounds chicken thighs,
  skinned
2 to 3 medium-ripe plantains,
  peeled and sliced ¼ inch
  thick (about 2 cups)
2 tablespoons snipped fresh
  parsley

1. In a blender container or food processor bowl combine *undrained* pineapple, lime juice, orange peel, garlic, oregano, cumin, chili powder, and allspice. Blend or process till almost smooth.

2. Spray a 2-quart rectangular baking dish with nonstick spray coating. Rinse chicken; pat dry with paper towels. Arrange chicken in prepared baking dish. Arrange plantain slices around chicken. Spoon pineapple mixture over chicken and plantains.

3. Bake, covered, in a 350° oven for 40 to 50 minutes or till chicken is tender and no longer pink. Transfer chicken and plantains to a serving platter. Skim fat from pan drippings; spoon pan juices over chicken and plantains. Sprinkle with parsley. Makes 4 servings.

Nutrition facts per serving: 319 calories, 10 g total fat (3 g saturated fat), 81 mg cholesterol, 86 mg sodium, 36 g carbohydrate, 2 g fiber, 24 g protein. **Daily values:** 11% vitamin A, 37% vitamin C, 3% calcium, 15% iron.

Pleasures of Plantains

Recently you may have noticed in your grocery's produce section a fruit that looks like a banana but has a thick green skin and a longer, more squared-off shape. These tropical fruits are called plantains, and unlike bananas, they must be cooked to be enjoyed. The flavor of plantains is very mild, and they often are served in place of potatoes.

Look for plump, undamaged plantains, but don't be concerned about slight bruises. The skin is tough enough to absorb most bumps. Ripen plantains at room temperature. It takes one week for them to turn from totally green to yellow-brown and another week or two until the plantains are black and fully ripe. They can be cooked at various stages of ripeness. A ½-cup serving of cooked, sliced plantains contains about 90 calories.

Low-fat

Low-calorie

CHICKEN BURGERS WITH PESTO SAUCE

Ground chicken coupled with easy low-fat pesto sauce produces a perfectly seasoned burger. (See photo, right.)

1 beaten egg white
½ cup shredded carrot
½ cup sliced green onion
2 tablespoons cornstarch
2 tablespoons fat-free
   mayonnaise dressing or
   salad dressing
1 tablespoon Dijon-style
   mustard
¼ teaspoon pepper
1 pound ground chicken or
   turkey
   Nonstick spray coating
⅓ cup reduced-sodium chicken
   broth
3 tablespoons reduced-calorie
   margarine
2 tablespoons snipped fresh
   parsley
2 tablespoons snipped fresh
   basil or 2 teaspoons dried
   basil, crushed
2 tablespoons grated Parmesan
   cheese
1 clove garlic, minced
5 whole wheat hamburger buns,
   split and toasted
   Lettuce leaves (optional)
   Cherry tomatoes (optional)

1. In a medium mixing bowl combine egg white, carrot, green onion, cornstarch, mayonnaise dressing, mustard, and pepper. Add ground chicken or turkey; mix well. On waxed paper, shape mixture into five ½-inch-thick patties.

2. Spray an unheated nonstick 10- or 12-inch skillet with nonstick spray coating. Cook chicken patties over medium heat till brown on both sides. Add chicken broth. Bring to boiling; reduce heat. Cover and simmer for 15 to 20 minutes or till patties are no longer pink in the center.

3. Meanwhile, for pesto sauce, in a small mixing bowl stir together margarine, parsley, basil, Parmesan cheese, and garlic till well mixed and creamy. If desired, line bottoms of hamburger buns with lettuce leaves. Top with chicken patties. Spoon pesto sauce over burgers; add bun tops. If desired, serve with cherry tomatoes. Makes 5 servings.

Nutrition facts per serving: 277 calories, 8 g total fat (2 g saturated fat), 50 mg cholesterol, 604 mg sodium, 27 g carbohydrate, 3 g fiber, 24 g protein. **Daily values:** 42% vitamin A, 8% vitamin C, 8% calcium, 12% iron.

CORNISH HENS WITH APRICOT SAUCE

If you wish, ask the butcher to halve the game hens for you.

2 1- to 1¼-pound Cornish
  game hens
1 teaspoons cooking oil
½ teaspoon salt-free seasoning
  blend
¼ teaspoon pepper
6 dried apricots
1 cup reduced-sodium chicken
  broth
2 teaspoons cornstarch
½ teaspoon ground ginger
2 tablespoons snipped fresh
  parsley (optional)

1. Rinse hens; pat dry with paper towels. With a sharp knife, cut hens lengthwise in half. Place hens, skin side up, in a shallow roasting pan. Brush with oil and sprinkle with salt-free seasoning blend and pepper. Cover with foil. Bake in a 375° oven for 30 minutes. Remove foil; bake 25 to 30 minutes more or till juices run clear and meat is no longer pink.

2. Meanwhile, in a small saucepan combine apricots and *half* of the broth. Bring to boiling; reduce heat. Cover and simmer for 15 minutes. Transfer mixture to a blender container or food processor bowl; cover and blend or process till puréed. Return mixture to saucepan. Stir cornstarch into remaining broth; add to saucepan along with ginger. Cook and stir over medium heat till thickened and bubbly. Cook and stir for 2 minutes more. Spoon sauce over hens. If desired, sprinkle with parsley. Makes 4 servings.

Nutrition facts per serving: 272 calories, 16 g total fat (4 g saturated fat), 80 mg cholesterol, 221 mg sodium, 7 g carbohydrate, 1 g fiber, 25 g protein. **Daily values:** 5% vitamin A, 0% vitamin C, 0% calcium, 3% iron.

Use kitchen shears to cut a Cornish game hen in half. Begin by cutting through the breastbone, just off-center. Then cut through the center of the backbone.

CORNISH HENS WITH SPICED-APPLE STUFFING

▼ *Low-sodium*

Always wash your hands, countertops, and utensils in hot soapy water between each step of food preparation when handling poultry.

2 1- to 1½-pound Cornish game hens
1½ cups chopped peeled apple
⅓ cup finely chopped celery
2 tablespoons raisins
2 tablespoons chopped onion
2 teaspoons cooking oil
½ cup soft whole wheat or white bread crumbs
¼ teaspoon ground ginger
¼ teaspoon ground nutmeg
2 tablespoons apple cider or apple juice
⅔ cup apple cider or apple juice
2 tablespoons apple brandy, brandy, or apple cider
1 tablespoon cornstarch
⅛ teaspoon salt
⅛ teaspoon pepper

1. Rinse hens; pat dry with paper towels. In a nonstick skillet cook apple, celery, raisins, and onion in hot oil for 5 minutes. Remove from heat. Stir in bread crumbs, ginger, and nutmeg. Spoon mixture into birds; skewer neck skin to back. Twist wing tips under back. Place birds, breast side up, on a rack in a shallow roasting pan. Brush with *1 tablespoon* of the apple cider. Cover loosely with foil.

2. Roast in a 375° oven for 30 minutes. Uncover birds; brush again with *1 tablespoon* cider. Roast for 45 to 55 minutes more or till juices run clear and drumsticks move easily in their sockets. Transfer birds to a cutting board; spoon stuffing onto a platter. With a sharp knife or kitchen scissors cut hens lengthwise in half. Place hens on serving platter. Cover and keep warm.

3. Skim fat from pan juices; reserve 2 tablespoons pan drippings. In a small saucepan stir together the ⅔ cup apple cider, brandy, and cornstarch. Stir in reserved pan drippings, salt, and pepper. Cook and stir over medium heat till thickened and bubbly; cook and stir for 2 minutes more. Serve sauce with hens and stuffing. Makes 4 servings.

Nutrition facts per serving: 358 calories, 18 g total fat (4 g saturated fat), 80 mg cholesterol, 173 mg sodium, 23 g carbohydrate, 2 g fiber, 25 g protein. **Daily values:** 0% vitamin A, 4% vitamin C, 1% calcium, 4% iron.

Testing for Doneness

Whether you are roasting a turkey, chicken, or Cornish game hen, the same tests will tell you when your poultry is done cooking. Grasp the end of a drumstick with a paper towel and twist. It should move easily in the socket. Or, pierce the thigh meat with a fork. The juices should run clear, not pink.

Low-fat

Low-calorie

Low-sodium

TURKEY PICCATA WITH ARTICHOKES

Serve this with a cooked wild rice blend and a salad of sliced oranges, ripe olives, and mushrooms. (See photo, left.)

Nonstick spray coating
1 pound turkey breast
    tenderloin steaks
¼ cup skim milk
1½ cups soft whole wheat bread
    crumbs
1 teaspoon dried Italian
    seasoning, crushed
1 9-ounce package frozen
    artichoke hearts, thawed
1¼ cups reduced-sodium chicken
    broth
2 shallots, sliced, or
    2 tablespoons finely
    chopped onion
2 tablespoons lemon juice
1 tablespoon cornstarch
1 tablespoon Dijon-style
    mustard
½ teaspoon dried Italian
    seasoning, crushed
⅛ teaspoon pepper
Lemon slice twists (optional)

1. Spray a 15x10x1-inch baking pan with nonstick spray coating. Rinse turkey; pat dry with paper towels. Cut turkey steaks into 6 serving-size pieces. Pour milk into a shallow bowl. In another shallow bowl stir together bread crumbs and the 1 teaspoon Italian seasoning. Dip turkey pieces first in milk and then into the bread crumb mixture to coat.

2. Arrange turkey in a single layer in the prepared pan. Bake, uncovered, in a 450° oven about 12 minutes or till turkey is tender and no longer pink and crumb coating is crisp.

3. Meanwhile, for sauce, cut any large artichoke hearts in half. In a medium saucepan combine artichoke hearts, broth, and shallots. Bring to boiling; reduce heat. Cover and simmer for 5 minutes. In a small bowl combine lemon juice, cornstarch, mustard, the ½ teaspoon Italian seasoning, and pepper; add to saucepan. Cook and stir till thickened and bubbly; cook and stir 2 minutes more. Serve sauce over turkey. If desired, garnish with lemon slice twists. Makes 6 servings.

Nutrition facts per serving: 142 calories, 3 g total fat (1 g saturated fat), 33 mg cholesterol, 333 mg sodium, 12 g carbohydrate, 3 g fiber, 18 g protein. **Daily values:** 5% vitamin A, 10% vitamin C, 4% calcium, 11% iron.

Shallot Savvy

Shallots are one of the smaller members of the onion family. A thin, papery skin of reddish brown to yellow-brown covers off-white meat that is tinged with green or purple. Shallots have a mild, delicate flavor and tender texture. They can be eaten raw or cooked. Look for firm, well-shaped shallots that are not sprouting. Avoid those that are wrinkled or shriveled. Peel shallots before chopping or slicing them.

Low-fat

Low-calorie

Low-sodium

TURKEY SAUTÉ WITH MUSTARD SAUCE

Here's a 15-minute entrée that goes well with a purchased salad from the deli and fresh steamed asparagus or broccoli.

4 turkey breast tenderloin
  steaks (about 1 pound total)
  Nonstick spray coating
½ cup light dairy sour cream
¼ cup skim milk
1 tablespoon honey
2 teaspoons dry mustard
¼ teaspoon dried thyme,
  crushed
⅛ teaspoon pepper
2 tablespoons snipped fresh
  parsley
2 cups hot cooked noodles

1. Rinse turkey; pat dry with paper towels. Spray an unheated large skillet with nonstick spray coating. Cook turkey in skillet over medium heat for 3 to 4 minutes on each side till turkey is tender and no longer pink. Transfer turkey to a serving platter; cover and keep warm.

2. Remove skillet from heat for 1 to 2 minutes to cool slightly. In the skillet stir together sour cream, milk, honey, dry mustard, thyme, and pepper. Cook and stir till heated through, but do not boil. Stir in parsley. Spoon some of the sauce over turkey. Pass remaining sauce. Serve with hot cooked noodles. Makes 4 servings.

Nutrition facts per serving: 280 calories, 6 g total fat (2 g saturated fat), 79 mg cholesterol, 91 mg sodium, 28 g carbohydrate, 2 g fiber, 28 g protein. **Daily values:** 5% vitamin A, 4% vitamin C, 6% calcium, 12% iron.

Low-fat

Low-calorie

Low-sodium

TURKEY TENDERLOINS IN PAPRIKA SAUCE

2 tablespoons lemon juice
1 clove garlic, minced
¼ teaspoon pepper
4 turkey breast tenderloin
  steaks or 2 whole turkey
  breast tenderloins (about 1
  pound total)
½ of a 14½-ounce can low-
  sodium tomatoes, cut up
¼ cup light dairy sour cream
1 tablespoon dry sherry
  (optional)
1 teaspoon paprika
1 cup sliced fresh mushrooms
2 tablespoons snipped fresh
  parsley
2 cups hot cooked rice

1. In a bowl combine lemon juice, garlic, and pepper. Rinse turkey; pat dry with paper towels. If using whole turkey tenderloins, halve them horizontally to make 4 tenderloin steaks about ½ inch thick. Spray the broiler pan with *nonstick spray coating*. Arrange turkey steaks on broiler pan. Brush with half of the lemon juice mixture.

2. Broil 4 inches from the heat for 3 minutes. Turn; brush with remaining lemon juice mixture. Broil 3 to 5 minutes more or till turkey is tender and no longer pink.

3. For sauce, in blender container combine *undrained* tomatoes, sour cream, sherry (if desired), and paprika. Blend or process till mixture is smooth.

4. Spray a medium nonstick skillet with *nonstick spray coating*. Cook mushrooms for 3 minutes. Add tomato mixture; heat through but do not boil. Stir in parsley. Spoon sauce over turkey. Serve with hot cooked rice. Makes 4 servings.

Nutrition facts per serving: 254 calories, 4 g total fat (1 g saturated fat), 54 mg cholesterol, 66 mg sodium, 27 g carbohydrate, 1 g fiber, 25 g protein. **Daily values:** 9% vitamin A, 22% vitamin C, 5% calcium, 17% iron.

Low-fat

Low-calorie

Low-sodium

BARBECUED TURKEY WITH FRUIT SAUCE

To keep the turkey juicy, roast it with the skin on. Be sure to remove the skin before serving to save on calories.

1 8- to 12-pound turkey

1 onion, quartered

1 apple, quartered

1 14½-ounce can reduced-
   sodium chicken broth

½ cup dried cranberries,
   cherries, or apricots

1 cup low-calorie orange
   marmalade spread

2 teaspoons cornstarch

1 teaspoon grated gingerroot or
   ¼ teaspoon ground ginger

1. Remove neck and giblets from turkey. Rinse turkey; pat dry with paper towels. Remove all visible fat. Place onion and apple pieces in cavity of bird. Skewer neck skin to back of bird. Tie legs to tail; twist wing tips under back. Insert a meat thermometer into the center of the inside thigh muscle; do not allow tip to touch bone.

2. In a covered grill, arrange medium-hot coals for indirect cooking (see below). Test for medium heat above drip pan. (To test for medium heat, hold your hand, palm side down, where the turkey will cook; for medium heat, you should need to remove your hand after 4 seconds.) Place the turkey, breast side up, on a rack in a roasting pan on the grill rack above the drip pan. Reserve *1 cup* broth for sauce. Brush the turkey with some of the remaining broth.

3. Lower the grill hood. Grill for 2½ to 3½ hours or till thermometer registers 180°, drumsticks move easily in their sockets, and meat is no longer pink, brushing with remaining chicken broth and adding coals as necessary to maintain heat.

4. For sauce, in saucepan bring the 1 cup broth and the cranberries to boiling; reduce heat. Cover; simmer 10 minutes. Cool slightly. Transfer to blender container. Cover; blend till nearly smooth. Return to saucepan; stir in marmalade, cornstarch, and gingerroot. Heat and stir till bubbly. Let bird stand 20 minutes before carving. Discard onion and apple in cavity. Pass sauce with turkey. Serves 10 to 14.

Nutrition facts per serving: 265 calories, 6 g total fat (2 g saturated fat), 95 mg cholesterol, 229 mg sodium, 15 g carbohydrate, 0 g fiber, 37 g protein. **Daily values:** 0% vitamin A, 0% vitamin C, 2% calcium, 15% iron.

To grill indirectly, you'll need a disposable foil drip pan. You can make your own by shaping heavy foil into a shallow pan that is large enough to cover the surface below the food. Place the pan in the center of the firebox and mound the coals around the edge of the pan with long tongs.

Low-calorie

Low-sodium

SPINACH-STUFFED TURKEY BREAST

A turkey breast is a great way to enjoy the flavor of roast turkey without days of leftovers. (See photo, right.)

1 10-ounce package frozen chopped spinach, thawed
½ of an 8-ounce package reduced-fat cream cheese (Neufchâtel), softened
3 tablespoons grated Parmesan cheese
2 tablespoons water
1 teaspoon dried basil, crushed
¼ teaspoon ground nutmeg
¼ teaspoon pepper
1 2½- to 3½-pound turkey breast half with bone

1. Drain spinach thoroughly and squeeze out excess liquid. Place spinach in food processor bowl with cream cheese, Parmesan cheese, water, basil, nutmeg, and pepper. Cover and process till well combined.

2. Rinse turkey; pat dry with paper towels. With a small sharp knife loosen breast skin from meat and pull skin back, leaving skin attached along one side. Spread spinach mixture over exposed portion of meat; pull skin back over filling. Secure skin with wooden picks along sides of breast. Place turkey, skin side up, on a rack in a shallow roasting pan. Insert meat thermometer into center of breast, below stuffing and not touching bone. Cover turkey loosely with foil.

3. Roast in a 325° oven for 2 hours. Remove foil. Roast ½ to 1 hour more or till thermometer registers 180° and juices run clear. Let stand, covered, for 15 minutes before carving. To carve, start at outside of breast half; slice downward, keeping slices thin. Continue slicing slightly higher up on the breast. Makes 8 servings.

Nutrition facts per serving: 170 calories, 6 g total fat (3 g saturated fat), 62 mg cholesterol, 176 mg sodium, 3 g carbohydrates, 1 g fiber, 25 g protein. **Daily values:** 32% vitamin A, 7% vitamin C, 9% calcium, 10% iron.

Poultry Pointers

Follow these tips to ensure the safe handling and storage of poultry.

Always wash your hands, counter tops, and utensils in hot, soapy water between each step of food preparation. Bacteria on raw poultry can contaminate other foods that are exposed to the same surfaces, causing food poisoning.

When cutting raw poultry, use a plastic cutting board because it is easier to clean than a wooden one. A wooden cutting surface that isn't thoroughly cleaned may retain harmful bacteria.

Never leave poultry at room temperature for more than 2 hours. Cooked poultry that is not eaten immediately should be kept hot (140° to 165°) or chilled at 40° or less.

CHINESE TURKEY BURRITO

▼ *Low-fat*

If desired, you can substitute thin strips of turkey breast or tenderloin meat for the ground turkey; stir-fry until it's no longer pink.

1½ cups fresh shiitake
    mushrooms
½ of an 8-ounce can bamboo
    shoots, drained
8 7- or 8-inch flour tortillas
8 ounces ground raw turkey
1 tablespoon grated gingerroot
1½ cups julienned carrots
2 to 3 tablespoons water
2 cups thinly sliced or shredded
    bok choy or Chinese
    cabbage
½ cup sliced green onion
1 tablespoon light soy sauce
1 tablespoon hoisin sauce
    (optional)
3 tablespoons bottled plum
    sauce

1. Remove stems from mushrooms; discard. Slice caps very thinly; set aside. Julienne the bamboo shoots; set aside. Stack tortillas and wrap tightly in foil. Heat in a 350° oven for 10 minutes to soften.

2. Meanwhile, spray a large wok or nonstick skillet with *nonstick spray coating;* heat over medium-high heat. Cook ground turkey and gingerroot in wok for 3 minutes or till turkey is no longer pink. Remove turkey mixture from wok. Drain off excess fat. Stir-fry carrots in wok for 3 minutes. Remove carrots from wok.

3. If necessary, add water to wok. Add bok choy, mushrooms, and green onions; cook and stir for 2 minutes. Push vegetables to one side. Add soy sauce and, if desired, hoisin sauce to wok. Add turkey mixture, bamboo shoots, and carrots; toss all ingredients to coat with sauce. Cover; cook 2 minutes more to heat through.

4. To serve, brush some plum sauce over a tortilla. Spoon ⅛ of the turkey mixture down center of the tortilla. Roll up jelly-roll style. Repeat with remaining tortillas, plum sauce, and filling. Makes 4 servings.

Nutrition facts per serving: 358 calories, 10 g total fat (2 g saturated fat), 21 mg cholesterol, 537 mg sodium, 52 g carbohydrate, 3 g fiber, 16 g protein. **Daily values:** 136% vitamin A, 43% vitamin C, 12% calcium, 28% iron.

TURKEY FRANKS WITH ONION RELISH

▼ *Low-calorie*

If you like, double the onion relish and refrigerate half of it to use on meat or turkey sandwiches later.

Nonstick spray coating
1 cup thinly sliced red onion
2 tablespoons water
1 tablespoon red wine vinegar
1 teaspoon brown sugar
⅛ teaspoon pepper
1 tablespoon snipped fresh
    parsley
4 fully cooked turkey franks
4 frankfurter buns or French-
    style rolls, split and toasted
1 tablespoon brown mustard

1. Spray an unheated nonstick skillet with nonstick spray coating. Cook onion over medium heat for 5 minutes or till tender. Combine water, vinegar, brown sugar, and pepper; add to skillet. Cook 5 minutes more, stirring frequently. Stir in parsley.

2. Meanwhile, slit turkey franks in half lengthwise, splitting them open but not cutting through them. Place franks on unheated rack of a broiler pan. Broil 4 inches from the heat for 5 to 8 minutes or till slightly charred and heated through; turn once. Place franks on rolls; spread with mustard. Spoon ¼ of the onion mixture over each frank. Makes 4 servings.

Nutrition facts per serving: 243 calories, 11 g total fat (3 g saturated fat), 48 mg cholesterol, 892 mg sodium, 25 g carbohydrate, 1 g fiber, 11 g protein. **Daily values:** 0% vitamin A, 6% vitamin C, 8% calcium, 18% iron.

Low-calorie

Low-sodium

TURKEY LOAF

*When purchasing ground turkey, ask what the percentage of white meat is in the mixture,
as well as its fat content, since they can vary considerably.*

1 beaten egg white
½ cup quick-cooking rolled oats
¼ cup plain nonfat yogurt
1 cup finely shredded carrot
½ cup finely chopped onion
½ cup finely chopped red or
    green sweet pepper
1 teaspoon poultry seasoning
½ teaspoon salt
¼ teaspoon pepper
1½ pounds ground raw turkey
    or chicken

1. In a large bowl combine egg white, oats, yogurt, carrot, onion, sweet pepper, poultry seasoning, salt, and pepper. Add ground turkey and mix well. Turn mixture into an ungreased 9x5x3-inch loaf pan.

2. Bake, uncovered, in a 350° oven about 1¼ hours or till juices run clear and meat is no longer pink. Transfer turkey loaf to a serving platter. Makes 8 servings.

Nutrition facts per serving: 144 calories, 7 g total fat (2 g saturated fat), 32 mg cholesterol, 195 mg sodium, 7 g carbohydrate, 1 g fiber, 13 g protein. **Daily values:** 44% vitamin A, 10% vitamin C, 3% calcium, 8% iron.

Low-fat

Low-calorie

TURKEY SAUSAGE AND POTATO HASH

This is an excellent dish to prepare when you have leftover cooked potatoes or vegetables.

3 cups chopped peeled potatoes
1 10-ounce package frozen
    mixed vegetables
8 ounces fully cooked smoked
    turkey sausage, quartered
    lengthwise and sliced
    ¼ inch thick
½ cup chopped onion
1 tomato, cut into thin wedges
2 tablespoons snipped fresh
    parsley
½ teaspoon dried oregano,
    crushed
½ teaspoon salt-free seasoning
    blend
⅛ to ¼ teaspoon pepper

1. In a saucepan cook potatoes in enough water to cover for 10 minutes; add mixed vegetables and cook 5 minutes more or till tender. Drain; set aside.

2. In a 10- or 12-inch nonstick skillet cook turkey sausage and onion for 5 minutes. Stir in cooked vegetable mixture, tomato, parsley, oregano, seasoning blend, and pepper. Cook for 3 minutes more or till mixture is heated through. Makes 4 servings.

Nutrition facts per serving: 240 calories, 4 g total fat (1 g saturated fat), 36 mg cholesterol, 512 mg sodium, 37 g carbohydrate, 2 g fiber, 15 g protein. **Daily values:** 32% vitamin A, 33% vitamin C, 7% calcium, 14% iron.

Low-fat
Low-calorie

TURKEY AND TOMATO SANDWICHES

If you're tired of the same old sandwiches, try these mustard-sauced tenderloins on French-style rolls. (See photo, left.)

1 cup water
12 dried tomatoes (not oil-packed)
4 turkey breast tenderloin steaks, cut ¼ inch thick (about 1 pound total)
Nonstick spray coating
1 tablespoon red wine vinegar
¼ teaspoon pepper
3 tablespoons fat-free mayonnaise dressing or salad dressing
1 tablespoon Dijon-style mustard
4 French-style or sourdough rolls, split and toasted
Watercress sprigs, radicchio leaves, or lettuce leaves
Small tomatoes (optional)

1. In a medium saucepan bring water to boiling; add tomatoes. Simmer about 5 minutes or till tomatoes are soft. Drain tomatoes and cut into thin slivers; set aside.

2. Rinse turkey; pat dry with paper towels. Spray the unheated rack of a broiler pan with nonstick spray coating. Arrange turkey on rack.

3. In a small bowl combine vinegar and pepper. Brush half of the mixture over turkey. Broil 4 inches from the heat for 4 minutes. Turn; brush with remaining vinegar mixture. Broil 4 to 6 minutes more or till turkey is tender and no longer pink.

4. Meanwhile, in a small bowl combine mayonnaise dressing and mustard. Line rolls with watercress, radicchio, or lettuce leaves. Place a turkey tenderloin steak on each roll. Top each steak with ¼ of the mayonnaise mixture and ¼ of the dried tomato pieces. Add tops of rolls. If desired, garnish with small tomatoes. Makes 4 servings.

Nutrition facts per serving: 252 calories, 4 g total fat (1 g saturated fat), 50 mg cholesterol, 665 mg sodium, 26 g carbohydrate, 0 g fiber, 26 g protein. **Daily values:** 0% vitamin A, 5% vitamin C, 5% calcium, 13% iron.

Smart Sandwiches

Sandwiches are not only quick and easy to prepare, but they can be a healthy part of anyone's diet. So start stacking, keeping these healthy tips in mind.

Use whole grain bread or rolls for increased fiber. Choose bread or rolls that list whole wheat flour (or another whole grain flour) as the first ingredient.

Take control of the amount of fat and sodium in your sandwich meat by cooking and thinly slicing your own meat instead of using processed luncheon meats. A good choice is to roast a 2½- to 3-pound skinless turkey breast half with bone in a 325° oven for 2½ to 3 hours or till a meat thermometer registers 165°.

Eliminate fat-laden mayonnaise, margarine, and butter. Spread full-flavored mustard, nonfat mayonnaise dressing, or fat-free salad dressing on your bread.

Check out the dairy case to find the growing selection of reduced-fat and fat-free cheeses. Use these instead of their higher fat cousins.

Don't forget the veggies! Leaf lettuce, colorful sweet peppers, red onions, cucumbers, tomatoes, and shredded carrots all add color, texture, flavor, fiber, and vitamins to your sandwich.

Low-fat

Low-calorie

Low-sodium

TURKEY AND HAM ROLL-UPS

You don't have to attend a cooking school to prepare a classy entrée like this one. Try it with steamed baby vegetables and a mixed lettuce salad with a raspberry vinegar dressing.

4 turkey breast tenderloin
　steaks or skinless, boneless
　chicken breast halves
　(about 1 pound total)
2 teaspoons Dijon-style mustard
⅛ teaspoon pepper
2 ounces very thinly sliced fully
　cooked ham
2 tablespoons grated Parmesan
　cheese
　Nonstick spray coating
1 egg white
1 tablespoon skim milk
⅓ cup fine dry bread crumbs
2 teaspoons reduced-calorie
　margarine, melted
½ teaspoon dried basil, crushed
　Lemon wedges (optional)

1. Rinse turkey; pat dry with paper towels. Pound turkey steaks between pieces of waxed paper to ¼-inch thickness. Spread each steak with Dijon-style mustard and sprinkle with pepper. Place ham, cutting to fit if necessary, and some of the Parmesan cheese over each turkey steak. Roll up from the short end and set aside, seam side down.

2. Spray a shallow baking dish with nonstick spray coating. In a shallow bowl whisk together egg white and milk. In another shallow bowl stir together bread crumbs, margarine, and basil. Coat each turkey roll by dipping it in the egg white mixture, then in crumbs. Place in prepared baking dish with seam sides down.

3. Bake in a 400° oven for 30 to 35 minutes or till lightly browned and turkey is tender and no longer pink. If desired, garnish with lemon wedges. Makes 4 servings.

Nutrition facts per serving: 202 calories, 6 g total fat (2 g saturated fat), 60 mg cholesterol, 453 mg sodium, 7 g carbohydrate, 0 g fiber, 29 g protein. **Daily values:** 3% vitamin A, 0% vitamin C, 6% calcium, 9% iron.

Roll up the turkey steaks with the ham and the cheese, starting from a short end. Place the rolled breasts, seam sides down, in a shallow baking dish that has been sprayed with nonstick spray coating.

Low-fat

Low-calorie

Low-sodium

TURKEY WITH TOMATOES, MOZZARELLA, AND BASIL

Serve these sautéed turkey stacks over thin slices of toasted sourdough bread.

4 turkey breast tenderloin
    steaks (about 1 pound total)
⅛ teaspoon salt
    Nonstick spray coating
1 shallot, sliced
1 clove garlic, minced
4 thin tomato slices
1 tablespoon chopped fresh
    basil or 1 teaspoon dried
    basil, crushed
½ cup shredded reduced-fat
    mozzarella cheese
    (2 ounces)
    Fresh basil leaves (optional)

1. Rinse turkey; pat dry with paper towels. Sprinkle turkey with the salt. Spray an unheated large nonstick skillet with nonstick spray coating. Cook turkey with shallot and garlic in skillet over medium heat for 3 to 4 minutes on each side or till turkey is tender and no longer pink.

2. Place a tomato slice on each steak in the skillet; sprinkle basil and shredded cheese over tomatoes. Cover skillet; heat 2 minutes more or till cheese melts. If desired, garnish with fresh basil leaves. Makes 4 servings.

Nutrition facts per serving: 152 calories, 4 g total fat (1 g saturated fat), 55 mg cholesterol, 190 mg sodium, 3 g carbohydrate, 0 g fiber, 26 g protein. **Daily values:** 7% vitamin A, 8% vitamin C, 1% calcium, 7% iron.

High-fiber

TURKEY AND VEGETABLE-STUFFED PASTA SHELLS

Accompany these jumbo shells with a mixture of tossed greens topped by a light salad dressing.

12 jumbo macaroni shells
 8 ounces ground turkey sausage
 1 cup finely chopped carrot
 1 cup finely chopped zucchini
 1 cup finely chopped red or
    green sweet pepper
¼ cup finely chopped onion
½ of an 8-ounce package
    reduced-fat cream cheese
 1 teaspoon dried basil, crushed
½ teaspoon dried dillweed
¼ teaspoon garlic powder
1½ cups light home-style
    spaghetti sauce
 2 tablespoons grated Parmesan
    cheese

1. Spray a 2-quart rectangular baking dish with *nonstick spray coating*. Cook pasta according to package directions; drain.

2. Meanwhile, spray an unheated nonstick skillet with *nonstick spray coating*. Cook turkey sausage with carrot, zucchini, pepper, and onion for 7 to 8 minutes or till sausage is no longer pink and vegetables are tender. Drain off fat. Stir in cream cheese, basil, dillweed, and garlic powder till combined.

3. Spoon about ¼ cup of turkey mixture into each pasta shell and arrange, filled side up, in prepared baking dish. Pour spaghetti sauce over shells.

4. Bake, covered, in a 350° oven for 30 to 40 minutes or till hot. Sprinkle with Parmesan cheese before serving. Makes 4 servings.

Nutrition facts per serving: 364 calories, 16 g total fat (8 g saturated fat), 46 mg cholesterol, 658 mg sodium, 36 g carbohydrate, 4 g fiber, 21 g protein. **Daily values:** 118% vitamin A, 82% vitamin C, 9% calcium, 19% iron.

Low-fat

Low-calorie

Low-sodium

ASPARAGUS-STUFFED TURKEY ROLLS

If you're preparing this dish for guests, you can roll the turkey bundles ahead; cover and refrigerate. (See photo, right.)

 4 **turkey breast tenderloin**
   steaks (about 1 pound total)
16 **asparagus spears**
   Nonstick spray coating
⅔ **cup reduced-sodium chicken**
   broth
 2 **tablespoons lemon juice**
 2 **tablespoons orange juice**
¼ **teaspoon salt-free seasoning**
   blend
⅛ **teaspoon pepper**
 1 **tablespoon water**
 2 **teaspoons cornstarch**
   Slivered orange or lemon peel
   (optional)
   Hot cooked pasta or rice
   (optional)

1. Rinse turkey; pat dry with paper towels. Pound turkey steaks between pieces of waxed paper to ¼-inch thickness. Trim asparagus spears, breaking off woody ends. Arrange 4 asparagus spears on the short end of each turkey piece. Roll up turkey; secure with wooden toothpicks, if necessary.

2. Spray an unheated large nonstick skillet with nonstick spray coating. Cook turkey rolls in skillet over medium heat till browned on all sides. Add broth, lemon juice, orange juice, seasoning blend, and pepper. Bring to boiling; reduce heat. Cover and simmer for 8 to 10 minutes or till turkey is tender and no longer pink.

3. Transfer turkey to serving platter; discard toothpicks. Keep turkey warm. In a small bowl stir together water and cornstarch; add to liquid in skillet. Cook and stir till thickened and bubbly. Cook and stir for 2 minutes more. Spoon over turkey. If desired, sprinkle with slivered orange or lemon peel and serve with hot cooked pasta or rice. Makes 4 servings.

Nutrition facts per serving: 137 calories, 3 g total fat (1 g saturated fat), 50 mg cholesterol, 154 mg sodium, 4 g carbohydrate, 1 g fiber, 23 g protein. **Daily values:** 2% vitamin A, 24% vitamin C, 1% calcium, 7% iron.

Make-Ahead Pasta

Take advantage of a few spare minutes now to cook pasta to use later. Simply cook the desired amount of pasta according to package directions, except omit salt and margarine or butter. Rinse pasta and drain well. Line 6-ounce custard cups with clear plastic wrap. Spoon ½ cup cooked pasta into each lined custard cup. Freeze till firm. Remove from custard cups and wrap each portion in the clear plastic wrap. Place wrapped portions in a large freezer bag. Seal, label, and freeze for up to 6 months.

To reheat pasta, unwrap desired amount. Using a large spoon, carefully lower frozen pasta into a saucepan of boiling water. Return water to boiling and cook for 1 minute; drain. Or, to reheat pasta in a microwave oven, unwrap frozen pasta and return portions to custard cups. Cover with waxed paper and cook on 100% power (high) till hot. Allow 1½ to 2 minutes for one ½-cup portion or 2 to 2½ minutes for 2 portions.

Low-fat

Low-calorie

Low-sodium

Turkey Marsala

Try this dish with thinly sliced pork tenderloin or pounded boneless chicken breasts, too. (See photo, left.)

4 turkey breast tenderloin steaks
    (about 1 pound total)
  Nonstick spray coating
2 cloves garlic, minced
½ cup reduced-sodium chicken
    broth
¼ cup marsala wine
1 tablespoon lemon juice
½ teaspoon salt-free seasoning
    blend
⅛ teaspoon pepper
2 tablespoons snipped fresh
    parsley
  Steamed carrots and zucchini
    (optional)
  Grapes (optional)

1. Rinse turkey; pat dry with paper towels. Spray an unheated large skillet with nonstick spray coating. Cook turkey steaks with garlic in skillet over medium heat for 3 to 4 minutes on each side or till turkey is tender and no longer pink. Transfer to a serving platter; cover and keep warm.

2. For sauce, in same skillet stir together broth, wine, lemon juice, seasoning blend, and pepper. Bring to boiling; boil gently, uncovered, about 4 minutes or till reduced to ¼ cup liquid. Stir in parsley. Spoon sauce over turkey. If desired, serve over thinly sliced steamed carrots and zucchini and garnish with grapes. Makes 4 servings.

Nutrition facts per serving: 139 calories, 3 g total fat (1 g saturated fat), 50 mg cholesterol, 56 mg sodium, 2 g carbohydrate, 0 g fiber, 22 g protein. **Daily values:** 0% vitamin A, 7% vitamin C, 1% calcium, 8% iron.

Low-fat

Low-calorie

HOT TURKEY-SALAD DOGS

These are a natural make-ahead for families with different eating schedules. Just wrap and refrigerate the sandwiches to heat later when the troops come drifting in.

1½ cups chopped cooked turkey
   or chicken
½ cup chopped red or green
   sweet pepper
¼ cup sliced green onion
2 tablespoons plain nonfat
   yogurt
2 tablespoons fat-free
   mayonnaise dressing or
   salad dressing
2 tablespoons sweet pickle
   relish, drained
4 frankfurter or hamburger
   buns, split
½ cup shredded reduced-fat
   cheddar or Monterey Jack
   cheese (2 ounces)

1. In a medium bowl stir together turkey or chicken, sweet pepper, green onion, yogurt, mayonnaise dressing, and pickle relish. Divide mixture among frankfurter or hamburger buns. Sprinkle *one-fourth* of the cheese over filling in each sandwich.

2. Wrap each sandwich in foil leaving space above sandwich for steam; seal well. Bake foil-wrapped bundles in a 350° oven for 25 to 30 minutes or till mixture is heated through. Makes 4 servings.

Nutrition facts per serving: 273 calories, 6 g total fat (3 g saturated fat), 47 mg cholesterol, 536 mg sodium, 28 g carbohydrate, 0 g fiber, 24 g protein. **Daily values:** 17% vitamin A, 41% vitamin C, 15% calcium, 14% iron.

MEAT-FREE MAIN DISHES

Planning meals around protein sources other than meat frees us to explore all kinds of new dishes. Lentils, beans, eggs, low-fat cheeses, pasta, and rice are the beginnings of many great-tasting dishes that are sure to become your family's favorites. If you think you'll have trouble convincing family members that meatless meals are worth trying, serve them Vegetarian Chili with Biscuits. This zesty concoction is so full of beans, they'll never miss the meat. Or try Baked Macaroni, Vegetables, and Cheese, a twist on a classic brightened with broccoli, carrots, and sweet peppers. And for a weekend breakfast, forget the bacon and dish up Stuffed French Toast with Strawberries. Give meat-free dining a try—you'll discover a wealth of healthful foods low in fat, yet high in taste.

Low-fat

Low-calorie

Low-sodium

High-fiber

SWISS LENTIL BURGERS

Serve these burgers with a spinach salad, and melon and pineapple slices.

⅓ **cup dry lentils**

¼ **cup bulgur**

1 **egg white, slightly beaten**

⅓ **cup fine dry bread crumbs**

¼ **cup shredded reduced-fat Swiss cheese**

¼ **cup shredded carrots**

2 **tablespoons snipped parsley**

½ **teaspoon dried basil, crushed**

¼ **teaspoon ground cumin**

1 **clove garlic, minced**

¼ **cup toasted wheat germ**

1 **medium onion, sliced**

1 **cup sliced fresh mushrooms**

1 **tablespoon margarine**

1 **cup chopped fresh tomatoes**

1. Rinse lentils; drain well. In a small saucepan combine lentils, bulgur, and 1¾ cups *water*. Bring to boiling; reduce heat. Cover and simmer for 45 to 60 minutes or till tender. Drain off any liquid.

2. In mixing bowl mash lentil mixture slightly. Add egg white, bread crumbs, cheese, carrots, parsley, basil, cumin, garlic, ⅛ teaspoon *salt*, and ⅛ teaspoon *pepper*. Mix well. Shape into four ¾-inch-thick patties. Coat patties in wheat germ. Spray a large skillet with *nonstick spray coating*. Cook patties in skillet over medium heat for 6 minutes or till golden, turning once.

3. Meanwhile, in another skillet cook onion and mushrooms in margarine for 4 to 5 minutes or till tender. Stir in tomatoes and heat through. Spoon tomato mixture over each patty. Sprinkle with additional parsley, if desired. Makes 4 servings.

Nutritional facts per serving: 226 calories, 6 g total fat (1 g saturated fat), 4 mg cholesterol, 279 mg sodium, 34 g carbohydrate, 4 g fiber, 12 g protein. **Daily values:** 28% vitamin A, 30% vitamin C, 7% calcium, 25% iron.

Low-fat

Low-calorie

Low-sodium

High-fiber

CURRIED LENTILS WITH VEGETABLES

Spice up your dining with this zesty, healthy dish.

⅔ **cup dry lentils**

1⅓ **cups reduced-sodium chicken broth**

1 **cup chopped, peeled parsnips**

1 **cup carrots cut into strips**

1 **cup sliced onions**

1 **cup cauliflower flowerets**

1 **small zucchini, sliced**

1 **cup shredded cabbage**

2 **teaspoons curry powder**

½ **teaspoon salt-free seasoning blend**

¼ **teaspoon crushed red pepper**

1 **clove garlic, minced**

1. Rinse lentils and drain well. Place lentils and broth in a large saucepan. Bring to boiling; reduce heat. Simmer, covered, for 20 minutes.

2. Stir in parsnips, carrots, onions, cauliflower, zucchini, cabbage, curry powder, seasoning blend, red pepper, and garlic. Bring to boiling; reduce heat. Simmer for 10 to 15 minutes more or till vegetables are tender. Makes 4 servings.

Nutritional facts per serving: 214 calories, 1 g total fat (0 g saturated fat), 0 mg cholesterol, 169 mg sodium, 41 g carbohydrate, 5 g fiber, 13 g protein. **Daily values:** 85% vitamin A, 64% vitamin C, 5% calcium, 38% iron.

Low-fat

High-fiber

FABULOUS FALAFEL

Traditionally these Middle Eastern bean patties are fried in oil, but here they're baked till crisp.

1 15-ounce can garbanzo
   beans, rinsed and drained
¼ cup sliced green onions
3 tablespoons sesame tahini
1 egg white
2 tablespoons snipped parsley
2 teaspoons lemon juice
1 teaspoon ground cumin
2 cloves garlic, minced
¼ teaspoon crushed red pepper
⅓ cup toasted wheat germ
¼ cup fine dry bread crumbs
5 tomato slices
5 6-inch pita bread rounds, slit
   Yogurt-Chive Spread
⅓ cup alfalfa sprouts

1. In a food processor bowl or blender container combine garbanzo beans, green onions, tahini, egg white, parsley, lemon juice, cumin, garlic, and red pepper. Cover, and process or blend till nearly smooth. Stir in wheat germ and bread crumbs. Shape mixture into five patties, each 3½ inches in diameter.

2. Spray a shallow baking pan with *nonstick spray coating.* Place patties in baking pan. Bake in a 350° oven for 15 minutes or till heated through. Place a patty and tomato slice in each pita. Spoon on some of the Yogurt-Chive Spread and add some sprouts to each sandwich. Makes 5 servings.

Yogurt-Chive Spread: In a small bowl stir together 1 cup *plain fat-free yogurt* and 1 tablespoon snipped fresh *chives* or 1 teaspoon dried *chives.*

Nutritional facts per serving: 390 calories, 8 g total fat (1 g saturated fat), 1 mg cholesterol, 700 mg sodium, 63 g carbohydrate, 5 g fiber, 18 g protein. **Daily values:** 4% vitamin A, 23% vitamin C, 17% calcium, 36% iron.

Low-fat

Low-calorie

High-fiber

PINTO BEAN AND CHEESE BURRITOS

For a quick, well-rounded lunch or dinner, serve these burritos with a cabbage salad and fresh melon wedges.

8 8-inch whole wheat or flour
   tortillas
2 15-ounce cans pinto beans
   with jalapeños, rinsed and
   drained
   Nonstick spray coating
½ cup sliced green onion
1 cup shredded reduced-fat
   Monterey Jack or cheddar
   cheese (4 ounces)
½ cup salsa
¼ cup light dairy sour cream

1. Wrap tortillas in foil. Heat in a 350° oven for 15 minutes or till heated through. Meanwhile, mash beans slightly with back of a spoon.

2. On each tortilla, place ⅛ of the beans, green onion, and cheese. Fold in two sides, then roll up. Spray a baking sheet with nonstick coating. Arrange burritos, seam sides down, on prepared baking sheet. Bake for 15 minutes or till heated through. Serve burritos topped with salsa, light sour cream, and, if desired, snipped *cilantro or parsley.* Makes 8 burritos.

Nutritional facts per burrito: 263 calories, 6 g total fat (2 g saturated fat), 11 mg cholesterol, 677 mg sodium, 39 g carbohydrate, 5 g fiber, 14 g protein. **Daily values:** 6% vitamin A, 9% vitamin C, 15% calcium, 15% iron.

Low-fat

High-fiber

VEGETARIAN CHILI WITH BISCUITS

Your family will never notice that there's no meat in this full-flavored chili that's spiked with beer and molasses. (See photo, right.)

¼ cup reduced-sodium vegetable broth

1 cup chopped celery

1 cup chopped red or green sweet pepper

1 cup chopped onion

2 cloves garlic, minced

3 14½-ounce cans low-sodium whole tomatoes, diced

1 15-ounce can kidney or garbanzo beans, rinsed and drained

1 15-ounce can black beans, rinsed and drained

1½ teaspoons chili powder

2 teaspoons molasses

1 teaspoon ground cumin

¼ teaspoon salt

¼ teaspoon pepper

1 bay leaf

1 12-ounce can light beer

Sour Cream Biscuits

1 cup shredded low-fat cheddar or Monterey Jack cheese product (4 ounces)

1. Bring broth to boiling in a 4-quart Dutch oven or kettle. Add celery, sweet pepper, onion, and garlic and cook for 5 to 8 minutes or till tender. Stir in *undrained* tomatoes, kidney or garbanzo beans, black beans, chili powder, molasses, cumin, salt, pepper, and bay leaf. Bring mixture to boiling; reduce heat. Simmer, covered, for 1½ hours.

2. Remove bay leaf. Stir in beer. Drop biscuit dough in 8 dollops into simmering chili. Cover and cook about 15 minutes more or till a toothpick inserted into biscuits comes out clean. Uncover and simmer for 5 minutes. Ladle into bowls and sprinkle with cheese. Makes 8 servings.

Sour Cream Biscuits: In a medium bowl stir together ½ cup *all-purpose flour,* ½ cup *whole wheat flour,* 1½ teaspoons *baking powder,* and ⅛ teaspoon *salt.* Add ½ cup *skim milk* and ¼ cup *light sour cream,* stirring just till mixture is moistened.

Nutritional facts per serving: 482 calories, 7 g total fat (2 g saturated fat), 11 mg cholesterol, 650 mg sodium, 91 g carbohydrate, 17 g fiber, 27 g protein. **Daily values:** 93% vitamin A, 367% vitamin C, 44% calcium, 67% iron.

Freezing Onions and Sweet Peppers

When you have a spare minute, chop some extra onion or green sweet pepper to use when time is sparse. Spread the chopped onion or sweet pepper in a single layer in a shallow baking pan. Place the pan in the freezer till the pieces are frozen (about 1 hour). Transfer the frozen vegetables to freezer bags or containers; seal, label, and freeze for up to 1 month. To use, just measure and add to your recipe as if the vegetables were fresh.

Low-fat

Low-sodium

High-fiber

BLACK AND RED BEAN STEW

Spinach and couscous are added to this savory bean stew.

½ cup dry black beans

½ cup dry red kidney beans

1 medium onion, sliced and
   separated into rings

2 teaspoons curry powder

2 teaspoons instant chicken
   bouillon granules

2 cloves garlic, minced

2 medium parsnips or carrots,
   sliced

1 14-ounce can low-sodium
   diced tomatoes

2 cups shredded fresh spinach
   or kale

1 cup quick-cooking couscous

1. Rinse beans. In a 4½-quart kettle or Dutch oven combine the dry beans and 3 cups *water.* Bring to boiling; boil for 2 minutes. Remove from heat. Cover; let stand 1 hour. (Or, soak beans in water overnight in a covered pan.)

2. Drain beans. In same pan mix beans, onion, curry powder, bouillon granules, garlic, and 8 cups *water.* Bring to boiling; reduce heat. Cover; simmer for 1 hour.

3. Meanwhile, in a small saucepan cook parsnips, covered, in ½ cup boiling *water* about 10 minutes or till very tender; cool. In blender container or food processor bowl place *undrained* parsnips. Cover, and blend or process till smooth.

4. Add pureed parsnips, *undrained* tomatoes, spinach, and couscous to bean mixture. Simmer for 5 to 8 minutes or till couscous is tender. Makes 6 servings.

Nutritional facts per serving: 377 calories, 2 g total fat (0 g saturated fat), 0 mg cholesterol, 390 mg sodium, 76 g carbohydrate, 13 g fiber, 18 g protein. **Daily values:** 46% vitamin A, 158% vitamin C, 18% calcium, 45% iron.

Low-fat

Low-calorie

High-fiber

CHEESY MEXICAN LASAGNA

This twist on the traditional main dish uses tortillas instead of pasta and enchilada sauce instead of tomato sauce.

1 cup chopped sweet pepper

1 cup chopped celery

½ cup chopped onion

1 15-ounce can pinto beans,
   rinsed and drained

1 15-ounce can black beans,
   rinsed and drained

½ cup frozen whole kernel corn

1 cup chopped tomatoes

1 4-ounce can diced green
   chilies, drained

1 10-ounce can enchilada sauce

1 8-ounce jar chunky salsa

8 6-inch corn tortillas

1 cup shredded low-fat
   mozzarella cheese

1. In a medium saucepan cook sweet pepper, celery, and onion in ¼ cup boiling *water* for 5 minutes or till vegetables are tender; drain. Stir in both kinds of beans, corn, tomatoes, and chilies; heat through. Remove from heat.

2. In a medium bowl stir together enchilada sauce and salsa. Spray a 2-quart rectangular baking dish with *nonstick spray coating.* Arrange *half* of the tortillas in the baking dish, cutting as necessary to fit. Spread with *half* of the bean mixture. Top with *half* of the enchilada sauce mixture and *half* of the cheese. Repeat layers. Bake, covered, in a 400° oven for 20 minutes. Uncover and bake for 10 minutes more or till hot and bubbly. Let stand 5 minutes before serving. If desired, sprinkle with 2 tablespoons snipped *cilantro or parsley.* Makes 6 servings.

Nutritional facts per serving: 301 calories, 7 g total fat (2 g saturated fat), 29 mg cholesterol, 1195 mg sodium, 50 g carbohydrate, 9 g fiber, 18 g protein. **Daily values:** 37% vitamin A, 94% vitamin C, 22% calcium, 20% iron.

Low-fat

Low-calorie

BENEDICT-STYLE EGGS FLORENTINE

Another time, try this easy mock hollandaise sauce over steamed vegetables or baked potatoes.

4 **large eggs**

½ **cup fat-free mayonnaise**
   dressing or salad dressing

¼ **cup skim milk**

1 **teaspoon lemon juice**

1 **teaspoon Dijon-style mustard**

¼ **teaspoon dried dillweed**

¼ **teaspoon paprika**

2 **English muffins, split and**
   toasted

4 **slices tomato**

½ **of a 10-ounce package frozen**
   leaf spinach, cooked and
   drained

   Fresh dill (optional)

1. Fill a large skillet half full of *water*. Bring to boiling; reduce heat to simmering. Break one egg into a small dish or measuring cup; slide the egg into simmering water. Repeat with remaining eggs, keeping eggs separate. Simmer eggs, uncovered, about 5 minutes or till yolks are just set.

2. Meanwhile, for sauce, in a small saucepan combine mayonnaise dressing, milk, lemon juice, mustard, dillweed, and paprika. Whisk over medium-low heat just till mixture is heated through; do not boil. Remove from heat.

3. To serve, arrange a muffin half on each plate and top with a tomato slice. Top each tomato slice with ¼ of the cooked spinach and 1 tablespoon sauce. With a slotted spoon transfer a poached egg to cover spinach and sauce. Spoon an additional 2 tablespoons of the sauce atop each egg. If desired, garnish with fresh dill. Serve immediately. Makes 4 servings.

Nutritional facts per serving: 190 calories, 6 g total fat (2 g saturated fat), 213 mg cholesterol, 649 mg sodium, 24 g carbohydrate, 1 g fiber, 10 g protein. **Daily values:** 40% vitamin A, 17% vitamin C, 12% calcium, 14% iron.

To poach the eggs, break one at a time into a custard cup or other small dish. Carefully slide the egg into the simmering water, holding the lip of the dish as close to the liquid as possible. Repeat with the remaining eggs, keeping them separate.

Low-calorie

Low-sodium

Zucchini-Tofu Cakes

You also can use these herbed vegetable pancakes (photo, left) as an appetizer for six.

5 egg whites
1 egg
1½ cups coarsely shredded
    zucchini or yellow summer
    squash
½ cup finely chopped red or
    green sweet pepper
½ cup coarsely shredded carrots
⅓ cup fine dry bread crumbs
1 tablespoon snipped fresh basil
    or 1 teaspoon dried basil,
    crushed
1 tablespoon snipped fresh
    chives or 1 teaspoon dried
    chives
½ teaspoon Worcestershire
    sauce
⅛ teaspoon salt
⅛ teaspoon pepper
1 cup crumbled tofu
⅔ cup skim milk
¾ cup water
2 tablespoons all-purpose flour
½ teaspoon curry powder
¼ teaspoon ground nutmeg
⅛ teaspoon salt
    Nonstick spray coating
    Fresh basil or chives
    (optional)

1. In a medium bowl beat egg whites and egg till frothy. Stir in zucchini or yellow summer squash, sweet pepper, carrots, bread crumbs, basil, chives, Worcestershire sauce, ⅛ teaspoon salt, and pepper. Drain tofu on paper towels. Stir into zucchini mixture; set aside.

2. For sauce, in medium saucepan combine milk, water, and flour. Add curry powder, nutmeg, and ⅛ teaspoon salt. Cook and stir till mixture is thickened and bubbly. Cook for 1 minute more. Cover and keep warm.

3. Spray a large nonstick skillet or griddle with nonstick coating. Drop zucchini mixture, ¼ cup at a time, into hot skillet or onto griddle. Spread slightly to about 3½ inches in diameter. Cook for 1 to 2 minutes or till browned on one side. Turn and cook for 1 to 2 minutes more or till set. Place pancakes on a heated platter. Cover and keep warm till all are cooked. Serve pancakes with sauce and if desired, garnish with fresh basil or chives. Makes 4 servings.

Nutritional facts per serving: 221 calories, 8 g total fat (1 g saturated fat), 54 mg cholesterol, 331 mg sodium, 21 g carbohydrate, 3 g fiber, 20 g protein. **Daily values:** 130% vitamin A, 39% vitamin C, 18% calcium, 52% iron.

Tofu Tidbits

Tofu, which is popular in Oriental cooking, is made from soybean milk in a process similar to cheese-making. Although it is almost tasteless by itself, tofu easily absorbs other flavors. A ½-cup portion of regular tofu contains about 95 calories, 10 grams protein, 6 grams fat (all unsaturated), and no cholesterol.

Tofu can be purchased fresh or in an aseptic package. Fresh tofu generally is sold packed in water and can be found in a store's refrigerator case. At home, fresh tofu should be kept in the refrigerator, covered with water, in an airtight container. It can be stored this way for up to 1 week. Change the water daily to keep the tofu fresh and moist.

Aseptically packaged tofu is shelf stable and should be kept in a cool place. Because of the sterile packaging method it undergoes, this type of tofu needs no refrigeration until it is opened.

Tofu is available in soft, firm, and extra-firm styles. The soft type is good for whipping, blending, and crumbling. Use firm tofu for slicing and cubing. Extra-firm tofu is a good choice for stir-fried dishes.

BAKED MACARONI, VEGETABLES, AND CHEESE

Low-fat

A combination of low-fat cottage cheese and low-fat sharp cheddar cheese keeps the fat content down but the cheesiness high.

8 ounces elbow macaroni
1 cup broccoli flowerets
½ cup julienned carrots or yellow squash
½ cup chopped sweet pepper
3 tablespoons all-purpose flour
1½ cups skim milk
½ teaspoon Worcestershire sauce
Dash crushed red pepper
1½ cups low-fat cottage cheese
¾ cup shredded low-fat sharp cheddar cheese (3 ounces)
½ cup soft whole wheat bread crumbs
1 tablespoon snipped parsley

1. Cook macaroni in a Dutch oven in boiling water for 5 minutes. Add broccoli, carrots or yellow squash, and sweet pepper. Return to boiling and cook for 5 minutes more or till macaroni is tender; drain. Return mixture to Dutch oven.

2. Meanwhile, in a medium saucepan stir together flour and skim milk. Add Worcestershire sauce, crushed red pepper, and ⅛ teaspoon *black pepper.* Cook and stir till mixture is thickened and bubbly. Remove from heat; stir in cottage cheese and cheddar cheese. Add to macaroni mixture.

3. Spray a 2-quart rectangular baking dish with *nonstick spray coating.* Spoon macaroni mixture into dish. Stir together bread crumbs and parsley; sprinkle over mixture. Bake in a 350° oven for 25 to 30 minutes or till hot and bubbly. Serves 4.

Nutritional facts per serving: 435 calories, 7 g total fat (3 g saturated fat), 20 mg cholesterol, 596 mg sodium, 63 g carbohydrate, 3 g fiber, 30 g protein. **Daily values:** 69% vitamin A, 93% vitamin C, 29% calcium, 22% iron.

WHEAT NOODLES IN PEANUT SAUCE

High-fiber

Beans, wheat noodles, and peanut butter combine to make a complete high-protein main dish.

8 ounces whole wheat or plain noodles
1 cup thinly sliced carrots
1 cup sliced fresh mushrooms
1 large green sweet pepper, cut in ½-inch cubes
1 15-ounce can cannellini, great northern, or pinto beans, rinsed and drained
Peanut Sauce

1. Cook noodles in a large saucepan in boiling water according to package directions, adding carrots, mushrooms, and sweet pepper 5 minutes before end of cooking time. Simmer till vegetables and pasta are tender. Add beans; heat through.

2. Drain pasta and vegetables, reserving ⅓ cup of the cooking liquid for the Peanut Sauce. Place pasta mixture in serving bowl; keep warm while preparing the Peanut Sauce. Pour Peanut Sauce over noodle mixture. Makes 4 servings.

Peanut Sauce: In a small bowl gradually stir 3 tablespoons *reduced-sodium soy sauce* into 2 tablespoons *reduced-fat creamy peanut butter.* Stir in 3 tablespoons *rice wine vinegar* or *white wine vinegar,* 2 tablespoons sliced *green onion,* ½ teaspoon *toasted sesame oil,* and ⅛ to ¼ teaspoon *crushed red pepper.* Add ⅓ cup reserved *cooking liquid,* stirring well. Pour mixture into saucepan; heat through.

Nutritional facts per serving: 345 calories, 5 g total fat (1 g saturated fat), 0 mg cholesterol, 625 mg sodium, 68 g carbohydrate, 8 g fiber, 18 g protein. **Daily values:** 86% vitamin A, 31% vitamin C, 5% calcium, 27% iron.

Low-fat

High-fiber

WHEAT BERRY AND PASTA PILAF

Wheat berries, which are whole unprocessed wheat kernels, lend a whole-grain flavor to this Italian favorite.

1¼ cups wheat berries
¾ cup orzo
2 cups sliced fresh mushrooms
2 medium carrots, thinly sliced
1 14½-ounce can pasta-style chunky tomatoes
1 8-ounce can low-sodium tomato sauce
½ cup dry white wine
½ teaspoon instant beef or chicken bouillon granules
½ teaspoon fennel seed, crushed
Dash ground red pepper

1. For pilaf, bring 5 cups *water* to boiling. Add wheat berries. Reduce heat. Simmer, covered, for 60 minutes. Add orzo. Cook, uncovered, about 10 minutes or till wheat berries and orzo are tender. Drain off any liquid. Cover to keep warm.

2. Meanwhile, for sauce, in a medium saucepan cook mushrooms and carrots, covered, in a small amount of boiling water about 4 minutes or till carrots are crisp-tender; drain. Stir *undrained* tomatoes, tomato sauce, wine, bouillon granules, fennel, and red pepper into the mushroom mixture. Bring to boiling; reduce heat. Simmer about 25 minutes or to desired consistency, stirring occasionally.

3. To serve, spoon pilaf on plates and top with sauce. Makes 4 servings.

Nutritional facts per serving: 433 calories, 2 g total fat (0 g saturated fat), 0 mg cholesterol, 600 mg sodium, 85 g carbohydrate, 6 g fiber, 17 g protein. **Daily values:** 98% vitamin A, 35% vitamin C, 7% calcium, 32% iron.

Low-calorie

Low-sodium

High-fiber

TOFU-STUFFED PEPPERS

Sprinkle the Cheesy Crumb Topping over other baked casseroles.

4 medium sweet peppers
8 ounces firm-style tofu
1 cup chopped broccoli
½ cup chopped carrots
⅓ cup sliced green onion
1 clove garlic, minced
½ cup chopped tomato
½ cup frozen whole kernel corn
½ teaspoon dried basil, crushed
½ teaspoon dried thyme, crushed
Cheesy Crumb Topping
2 cups low-sodium spaghetti sauce, warmed

1. Cut tops from peppers. Discard stems, seeds, and membranes. Chop tops for ¾ cup; set aside. Cook peppers in boiling water for 5 minutes; drain well.

2. Drain tofu; crumble into small pieces. Spray a large nonstick skillet with *nonstick spray coating*. Add chopped pepper, broccoli, carrots, green onion, and garlic; cook over medium heat till crisp-tender. Stir in tomato, corn, basil, and thyme; remove from heat. Stir in tofu. Spray a 2-quart square baking dish with *nonstick spray coating*. Place peppers, cut sides up, in dish; spoon tofu mixture into peppers. Sprinkle with Cheesy Crumb Topping. Bake, loosely covered, in a 350° oven for 30 minutes or till hot. Serve with spaghetti sauce. Makes 4 servings.

Cheesy Crumb Topping: Toss together ¼ cup *soft bread crumbs*, ¼ cup *shredded reduced-fat cheddar cheese*, and 1 tablespoon *snipped parsley*.

Nutritional facts per serving: 229 calories, 8 g total fat (2 g saturated fat), 5 mg cholesterol, 131 mg sodium, 30 g carbohydrate, 6 g fiber, 16 g protein. **Daily values:** 121% vitamin A, 273% vitamin C, 18% calcium, 50% iron.

Low-fat

Low-sodium

MU SHU VEGETABLE ROLL-UPS

See Mu Shu photo, right. Remember this Plum Sauce as a delicious complement when you serve grilled chicken and turkey.

10 dried Oriental mushrooms,
    such as shiitake or oyster
8 spring roll wrappers or 8-inch
    flour tortillas
1 tablespoon hoisin sauce
1 tablespoon low-sodium soy
    sauce
1 tablespoon dry sherry
    Nonstick spray coating
1 tablespoon grated gingerroot
2 cloves garlic, minced
1 egg, slightly beaten
2 cups shredded Chinese (napa)
    cabbage or green cabbage
1 8-ounce can water chestnuts,
    rinsed, drained, and
    chopped
1 cup julienned carrots
½ cup sliced green onion
1½ cups crumbled tofu, drained
    Plum Sauce

1. In a medium bowl cover dried mushrooms with boiling water. Cover and let stand for 30 minutes or till softened. Drain, reserving liquid. Remove stems from mushrooms; discard. Slice mushrooms; set aside.

2. If using spring roll wrappers, dip each wrapper into warm water in a shallow dish and place between damp cotton dish towels. Let stand for 10 minutes or till needed. If using tortillas, wrap them in foil and place in a steamer basket over simmering water for 10 minutes.

3. Meanwhile, in a small bowl stir together hoisin sauce, soy sauce, and sherry; set aside. Spray a wok or large nonstick skillet generously with nonstick spray coating. Heat wok over medium-high heat; stir-fry gingerroot and garlic for 15 seconds. Add beaten egg; rotate wok to evenly distribute egg. Cook for 5 seconds more or till egg is set. Remove egg mixture and cut into shreds; set aside.

4. Add 2 tablespoons reserved mushroom liquid to wok; add cabbage and cook and stir for 3 minutes. Remove cabbage from wok. Add more liquid to wok, if necessary. Add water chestnuts and carrots; cook and stir for 3 minutes or till carrots are nearly tender; remove from wok. Add more liquid if necessary; add green onion and cook and stir for 1 minute. Stir hoisin sauce mixture; add to center of wok. Stir in mushrooms, shredded egg mixture, cooked vegetables, and tofu. Cover and cook for 1 minute more or till heated through.

5. With a slotted spoon, place about ½ cup of the tofu mixture on each wrapper or tortilla; drizzle with some of the Plum Sauce. Fold wrapper over filling. Serve with remaining Plum Sauce. Makes 4 servings.

Plum Sauce: In a small saucepan combine ½ cup *plum preserves,* ⅓ cup *low-calorie orange marmalade spread,* 2 tablespoons *vinegar,* and ¼ teaspoon *crushed red pepper.* Bring mixture to boiling; remove from heat. Cool; cover and chill. Makes ¾ cup.

Nutritional facts per serving: 376 calories, 8 g total fat (1 g saturated fat), 36 mg cholesterol, 419 mg sodium, 66 g carbohydrate, 2 g fiber, 13 g protein. **Daily values:** 60% vitamin A, 20% vitamin C, 13% calcium, 39% iron.

BRUNCH FRUIT CHEESE CREPES

Low-fat

Crepes can be made up to 24 hours in advance. To store, stack with waxed paper between layers, wrap in plastic wrap, and chill.

1 16-ounce carton low-fat
   cottage cheese
1 egg white
2 tablespoons sugar
1½ teaspoons finely shredded
   orange or lemon peel
1 teaspoon vanilla
   Crepes
   Nonstick spray coating
2 cups sliced fresh fruit
   (strawberries, peaches, kiwi
   fruit, bananas, pears,
   plums, mangoes, or
   papayas)
2 tablespoons powdered sugar
   Fresh mint sprigs (optional)

1. In food processor bowl or blender container combine cottage cheese, egg white, sugar, orange or lemon peel, and vanilla. Cover, and process or blend till mixture is nearly smooth.

2. Spoon about ⅓ cup cheese mixture onto each crepe, spreading slightly to within ½ inch of edges. Fold left and right edges to center. Then roll up jelly-roll style. Spray a 2-quart rectangular baking dish with nonstick spray coating. Arrange crepes, seam sides down, in baking dish. Bake in a 400° oven for 12 to 15 minutes or till heated through.

3. To serve, place 2 crepes on a each plate. Top with *½ cup* of the fresh fruit and sprinkle with some of the powdered sugar. If desired, garnish with mint sprig. Makes 4 servings.

Crepes: In a large mixing bowl combine 1 cup *all-purpose flour*, 1½ cups *skim milk*, and 1 *egg*. Beat with a rotary beater till well mixed. Heat a lightly greased 10-inch nonstick skillet over medium heat. Remove from heat. Spoon in a scant ¼ cup of the batter. Lift and tilt skillet to spread batter. Return to heat; brown crepe on one side only. Invert skillet over paper towels. Remove crepe. Repeat to make 8 crepes, greasing skillet occasionally. Cover crepes and chill till needed.

Nutritional facts per serving: 307 calories, 3 g total fat (1 g saturated fat), 60 mg cholesterol, 541 mg sodium, 45 g carbohydrate, 2 g fiber, 23 g protein. **Daily values:** 9% vitamin A, 73% vitamin C, 17% calcium, 13% iron.

To fold a crepe, first bring two opposite edges to the center. Then, starting from an unfolded edge, roll up the crepe like a jelly roll.

STEAMED VEGETABLE PLATTER WITH FETA

High-fiber

With all of the vegetable and rice possibilities, you can make this dish different every time.

2 cups bias-sliced carrots, parsnips, or potatoes

1 cup broccoli flowerets

2 cups sliced mushrooms or zucchini, or halved pea pods

1 medium tomato, cut into wedges

1 teaspoon dried fines herbes, crushed or dried basil, crushed

1 teaspoon sesame seed

⅛ teaspoon pepper

3 cups hot cooked brown rice, wild rice, or couscous

⅔ cup crumbled feta cheese

1. Place carrots, parsnips, or potatoes in a steamer basket over simmering water. Cover and steam for 8 minutes. Add broccoli. Steam for 5 minutes more or till vegetables are nearly tender. Add mushrooms, zucchini, or pea pods and tomato wedges. Cover and steam for 2 to 3 minutes more or till tender.

2. Stir fines herbes or basil, sesame seed, and pepper into hot rice or couscous. Spoon rice or couscous onto a serving platter and top with steamed vegetables. Sprinkle with cheese. Cover platter with foil. Let stand for 3 minutes before serving to soften cheese. Serves 4.

Nutritional facts per serving: 356 calories, 11 g total fat (7 g saturated fat), 38 mg cholesterol, 514 mg sodium, 53 g carbohydrate, 6 g fiber, 13 g protein. **Daily values:** 95% vitamin A, 56% vitamin C, 21% calcium, 21% iron.

ITALIAN POTATO PIZZA

Low-fat

Potatoes on a pizza? Italians in central Italy have been enjoying it for years.

¼ cup reduced-sodium chicken broth

1½ cups thinly sliced sweet onion

½ pound tiny new potatoes, thinly sliced

4 cloves garlic, minced

2 teaspoons snipped fresh thyme, basil, or oregano

1 11-ounce package refrigerated French bread dough

2 teaspoons olive or cooking oil

2 cups chopped tomato

1½ cups shredded low-fat mozzarella cheese

1. In a large nonstick skillet heat broth to boiling. Add onion, potatoes, garlic, and herb. Cook for 4 minutes or till onion is tender. Drain, if necessary.

2. Spray a 13x9x2-inch baking pan with *nonstick spray coating*. Unroll dough and pat into pan; form a 1-inch edge. Brush dough with oil. Spoon potato mixture evenly over dough. Sprinkle with chopped tomato and ⅛ teaspoon *pepper*. Top with mozzarella cheese. Bake in a 425° oven for 20 minutes or till crust is lightly browned. Cut into rectangles. Makes 4 servings.

Nutritional facts per serving: 413 calories, 11 g total fat (5 g saturated fat), 24 mg cholesterol, 620 mg sodium, 58 g carbohydrate, 2 g fiber, 21 g protein. **Daily values:** 13% vitamin A, 49% vitamin C, 26% calcium, 28% iron.

Low-fat

Low-calorie

Low-sodium

High-fiber

VEGETABLE LASAGNA PIE

Round out this cheesy vegetable entrée (photo, left) with breadsticks and a crisp green salad.

9 or 10 lasagna noodles
1½ cups fat-free ricotta cheese
3 tablespoons skim milk
½ teaspoon dried basil, crushed
¼ teaspoon pepper
¼ cup reduced-sodium chicken broth
1½ cups finely chopped broccoli
1 cup frozen French-cut green beans
1 cup finely chopped carrots
½ cup chopped onion
1 clove garlic, minced
1 15-ounce can low-sodium tomato sauce
½ teaspoon dried oregano, crushed
¼ teaspoon salt
Nonstick spray coating
2 tablespoons Romano or Parmesan cheese
2 small tomatoes, thinly sliced
1 tablespoon snipped parsley

1. Cook noodles according to package directions, except omit the salt; drain. In a small mixing bowl combine ricotta cheese, milk, basil, and pepper; set aside.

2. For filling, in a large skillet combine broth, broccoli, green beans, carrots, onion, and garlic. Bring to boiling; reduce heat. Cover and cook about 5 minutes or till vegetables are tender. Stir in tomato sauce, oregano, and salt. Cook, covered, over medium heat till heated through.

3. Spray a 9-inch springform pan with nonstick spray coating. Line pan with noodles, extending noodles over sides of pan. Layer half of the vegetable mixture, 1 cup of the ricotta mixture, and remaining vegetable mixture over noodles. Trim noodles so 3 inches extend over top of vegetable mixture. Discard trimmings. Fold noodle ends over vegetable mixture. Place springform pan on a 15x10x1-inch baking pan. Cover and bake in a 375° oven for 30 minutes.

4. Stir Romano or Parmesan cheese into remaining ricotta mixture. Spread ricotta mixture over top of pie. Place tomato slices around edges, slightly overlapping the slices. Cover; bake 20 minutes more or till heated through. Let stand 10 minutes. Sprinkle with parsley. Cut into wedges. Makes 6 servings.

Nutritional facts per serving: 228 calories, 2 g total fat (1 g saturated fat), 9 mg cholesterol, 217 mg sodium, 40 g carbohydrate, 4 g fiber, 16 g protein. **Daily values:** 77% vitamin A, 68% vitamin C, 15% calcium, 16% iron.

Low-calorie

Low-sodium

STUFFED FRENCH TOAST WITH STRAWBERRIES

Here's a delectable, low-fat variation of French toast that's perfect for a weekend brunch. (See photo, right.)

4 slices sourdough bread cut
    1 inch thick
½ of an 8-ounce package light
    cream cheese, softened
3 tablespoons strawberry or
    raspberry fruit spread
⅔ cup skim milk
1 egg
1 egg white
1 teaspoon granulated sugar
1 teaspoon vanilla
½ teaspoon ground cinnamon
2 cups sliced strawberries
2 tablespoons powdered sugar

1. Cut each bread slice in half crosswise. With a sharp knife, cut a horizontal slit in each half slice to make a pocket. In a medium bowl combine cream cheese and fruit spread. Stir till smooth. Spread ⅛ of the mixture inside each bread pocket. Pinch edges of bread together to hold filling.

2. In a shallow bowl whisk together milk, egg, egg white, granulated sugar, vanilla, and cinnamon. Dip filled bread slices in egg mixture to coat. Spray a large nonstick skillet with *nonstick spray coating*. Cook about 6 minutes or till golden brown, turning once. Top with strawberries and sprinkle with powdered sugar. Serves 4.

Nutritional facts per serving: 255 calories, 9 g total fat (5 g saturated fat), 76 mg cholesterol, 316 mg sodium, 35 g carbohydrate, 1 g fiber, 9 g protein. **Daily values:** 14% vitamin A, 71% vitamin C, 9% calcium, 8% iron.

Whole Wheat Stuffed French Toast with Strawberries: Prepare as above, except substitute *whole wheat bread* slices for the sourdough bread.

Low-calorie

Low-sodium

CHEESE AND CHILI SOUFFLÉ

Serve a fresh fruit salad for the first course and follow with the soufflé hot from your oven.

2 tablespoons margarine
3 tablespoons all-purpose flour
1 cup skim milk
½ cup shredded low-fat sharp
    cheddar cheese (2 ounces)
¾ cup low-fat ricotta cheese
1 4-ounce can diced green
    chilies, drained
½ teaspoon paprika
¼ teaspoon salt-free seasoning
    blend
⅛ teaspoon pepper
2 beaten egg yolks
5 egg whites

1. Spray a 2-quart soufflé dish with *nonstick spray coating;* set aside.

2. In a medium saucepan melt margarine; stir in flour. Add milk all at once; cook and stir till mixture is thickened and bubbly. Remove from heat. Stir in cheddar cheese till melted. Add ricotta cheese, chilies, paprika, seasoning blend, and pepper. Add egg yolks, stirring till blended. Beat egg whites with an electric mixer on high speed till stiff (tips stand straight). Gently fold into cheese mixture. Spoon soufflé mixture into prepared dish. If desired, sprinkle *cilantro* over soufflé mixture.

3. Bake in a 350° oven for 40 to 45 minutes or till puffed and light golden brown and a knife inserted off center comes out clean. Serve immediately. Serves 5.

Nutritional facts per serving: 190 calories, 11 g total fat (4 g saturated fat), 102 mg cholesterol, 311 mg sodium, 9 g carbohydrate, 0 g fiber, 13 g protein. **Daily values:** 27% vitamin A, 13% vitamin C, 20% calcium, 5% iron.

Low-fat

High-fiber

VEGETARIAN WHOLE WHEAT PIZZA

Frozen bread dough makes an easy crust for this veggie-topped pizza. (See photo, left.)

3 cups sliced or julienned vegetables (sliced mushrooms; julienned zucchini, yellow squash, carrots, baby eggplant, onions, or sweet peppers; or small broccoli or cauliflower flowerets)

1 14½-ounce can Italian-style stewed tomatoes

1 6-ounce can low-sodium tomato paste

2 teaspoons red wine vinegar

Nonstick spray coating

1 16-ounce loaf frozen whole wheat bread dough, thawed

1 15½-ounce can lower-sodium red kidney beans, rinsed and drained

1½ cups shredded part-skim mozzarella cheese or reduced-fat Monterey Jack cheese (6 ounces)

½ cup crumbled feta cheese, shredded reduced-fat cheddar cheese, or grated Parmesan cheese (2 ounces)

2 tablespoons snipped cilantro or parsley

1. Place vegetables in a steamer basket over simmering water for 2 to 5 minutes or till crisp-tender. Drain on paper towels; set aside.

2. For tomato sauce, in blender container or food processor bowl combine *undrained* stewed tomatoes, tomato paste, and vinegar. Cover, and blend or process till smooth.

3. For crust, spray two 12-inch pizza pans with nonstick spray coating. Divide dough in half. In the prepared pizza pans pat dough to 11-inch circles and build up edges slightly. Do not let rise. Bake in a 425° oven about 10 minutes or till browned. Remove from oven; spread sauce mixture over crusts to within ½ inch of edges. Layer with kidney beans, cooked vegetables, and cheeses. Sprinkle cilantro or parsley on top. Bake for 10 to 15 minutes more or till bubbly. Cut into wedges. Makes 8 servings.

Nutritional facts per serving: 331 calories, 9 g total fat (5 g saturated fat), 26 mg cholesterol, 513 mg sodium, 45 g carbohydrate, 5 g fiber, 18 g protein. **Daily values:** 58% vitamin A, 30% vitamin C, 28% calcium, 24% iron.

Rinsing Canned Beans

For the time-pressed healthy cook, canned beans are helpful. Low in fat and high fiber, they are a quick-to-cook source of protein. Unfortunately, they can be high in sodium. Look for canned beans labeled lower sodium. Before using, rinse them in cold water to further reduce the sodium content.

Low-fat

Low-calorie

Low-sodium

High-fiber

SPINACH AND ARTICHOKE STRATA

Perfect for brunch, this cheesy egg and vegetable casserole can be mixed up the night before and baked the following morning.

¼ **cup reduced-sodium chicken broth**

2 **cups sliced fresh mushrooms**

1 **9-ounce package frozen artichoke hearts, thawed and chopped**

½ **of a 10-ounce package frozen chopped spinach, thawed and well drained**

1 **15-ounce container fat-free ricotta cheese**

¼ **cup grated Parmesan cheese**

½ **teaspoon dried basil, crushed**

½ **teaspoon dried thyme, crushed**

1½ **cups skim milk**

2 **large eggs**

2 **egg whites**

¼ **teaspoon ground nutmeg**

¼ **teaspoon pepper**

Nonstick spray coating

8 **thin slices whole wheat or sourdough bread, halved**

1½ **cups lower-sodium marinara spaghetti sauce**

1. In a medium saucepan bring broth to boiling. Add mushrooms and simmer for 3 minutes; drain.

2. In a medium bowl toss together cooked mushrooms, artichoke hearts, and spinach. In a medium bowl combine ricotta cheese, Parmesan cheese, basil, and thyme. In another bowl whisk together milk, eggs, egg whites, nutmeg, and pepper.

3. Spray a 2-quart rectangular baking dish with nonstick spray coating. Arrange 8 bread-slice halves in dish. Top with the spinach mixture and then the ricotta mixture. Arrange remaining bread-slice halves on top. Pour egg mixture slowly over top of bread, pressing down on bread with a spatula till all of the egg mixture is absorbed. Cover and chill strata for 8 to 24 hours. Bake in a 350° oven for 50 to 60 minutes or till set and golden brown. Let stand for 10 minutes. Cut into squares. Meanwhile, heat spaghetti sauce. Serve with strata. Makes 6 servings.

Nutritional facts per serving: 270 calories, 5 g total fat (1 g saturated fat), 83 mg cholesterol, 499 mg sodium, 38 g carbohydrate, 8 g fiber, 24 g protein. **Daily values:** 39% vitamin A, 23% vitamin C, 29% calcium, 21% iron.

To drain thawed spinach, place it in a colander and shake gently. Then pick up handfuls of spinach and squeeze gently, removing excess liquid.

Low-calorie

Low-sodium

KALE AND MUSHROOM FRITTATA

Kale, a member of the cabbage family, is extremely high in fiber and calcium.

¼ cup reduced-sodium chicken
    broth
2 cups shredded kale or spinach
1 cup sliced fresh mushrooms
¼ cup chopped onion
5 egg whites
1 egg
½ teaspoon dried basil, crushed
¼ teaspoon dried thyme,
    crushed
¼ cup shredded low-fat
    mozzarella cheese (1 ounce)

1. In a medium saucepan heat broth to boiling. Add kale or spinach, mushrooms, and onion. Cover and cook over medium heat for 9 to 12 minutes or till vegetables are tender; drain well.

2. In a medium bowl lightly beat together egg whites and whole egg. Stir in basil, thyme, ⅛ teaspoon *salt,* and ⅛ teaspoon *pepper;* set aside. Spray a cold 8- to 10-inch ovenproof skillet with *nonstick spray coating.* Preheat the skillet over medium heat. Add kale mixture. Pour egg mixture over vegetables in skillet. Bake in a 350° oven for 6 to 8 minutes or till eggs are set. Sprinkle with mozzarella cheese. Bake for 1 to 2 minutes more or till cheese melts. Cut into wedges. Makes 3 servings.

Nutritional facts per serving: 111 calories, 4 g total fat (2 g saturated fat), 76 mg cholesterol, 285 mg sodium, 7 g carbohydrate, 2 g fiber, 12 g protein. **Daily values:** 36% vitamin A, 32% vitamin C, 11% calcium, 8% iron.

Low-calorie

Low-sodium

High-fiber

SPINACH-FETA SHELLS WITH MINTED TOMATO SAUCE

A little cinnamon adds a nice spiciness to these plump cheese-filled shells.

1 10-ounce package frozen
    chopped spinach, thawed
    and well drained
½ cup crumbled feta cheese
½ cup low-fat ricotta cheese
¼ cup toasted chopped walnuts
1 slightly beaten egg white
¼ teaspoon ground cinnamon
12 jumbo macaroni shells,
    cooked and drained
    Minted Tomato Sauce
¼ cup shredded low-fat
    mozzarella cheese (1 ounce)

1. For filling, combine spinach, feta cheese, ricotta cheese, *3 tablespoons* of the walnuts, egg white, cinnamon, ¼ teaspoon *salt,* and ⅛ teaspoon *pepper.* Stuff macaroni shells with filling. Place in an ungreased 2-quart square baking dish. Top with Minted Tomato Sauce. Sprinkle with remaining nuts.

2. Bake, covered, in a 350° oven for 25 minutes. Uncover; sprinkle with mozzarella cheese; bake for 2 minutes more. Makes 4 servings.

Minted Tomato Sauce: Combine one 14½-ounce can *low-sodium whole tomatoes,* cut up and undrained; ⅓ cup *reduced-sodium tomato paste;* 2 tablespoons *water;* 1½ teaspoons dried *mint,* crushed; 1 teaspoon *sugar;* and ¼ teaspoon *garlic powder.* Bring to boiling; reduce heat. Simmer about 5 minutes or till slightly thickened.

Nutritional facts per serving: 276 calories, 10 g total fat (3 g saturated fat), 19 mg cholesterol, 466 mg sodium, 35 g carbohydrate, 4 g fiber, 15 g protein. **Daily values:** 72% vitamin A, 61% vitamin C, 21% calcium, 21% iron.

Low-sodium

High-fiber

PRUDENT EGGPLANT PARMIGIANA

In this recipe, to save calories from fat, broil the eggplant slices instead of frying them.

1 medium eggplant, peeled and
    trimmed (1 pound)
  Nonstick spray coating
1 tablespoon lemon juice
1½ cups soft whole wheat bread
    crumbs (2 slices)
1 teaspoon dried Italian
    seasoning, crushed
¼ teaspoon lemon-pepper
    seasoning
¼ teaspoon garlic powder
½ cup skim milk
1 29-ounce jar low-sodium
    spaghetti sauce
6 slices part-skim mozzarella
    cheese (6 ounces), cut into
    1-inch strips
2 tablespoons grated Parmesan
    or Romano cheese
2 tablespoons snipped parsley

1. Slice eggplant crosswise into ¼-inch slices. Spray the unheated rack of a broiler pan with nonstick spray coating. Arrange *half* of the eggplant slices on the rack. Brush with some of the lemon juice. Broil 6 inches from the heat for about 5 to 6 minutes per side or till tender when pierced with a fork. Repeat with remaining eggplant slices and lemon juice; cool.

2. In a shallow bowl stir together the bread crumbs, Italian seasoning, lemon-pepper seasoning, and garlic powder. Pour milk into a second shallow dish. Spray a 2-quart square baking dish or four 10- to 14-ounce individual casseroles with nonstick spray coating. Dip eggplant slices first in milk, then in crumb mixture to coat both sides. Arrange ⅓ of the eggplant slices in dish(es). Top with ⅓ of the spaghetti sauce and ⅓ of the mozzarella cheese strips. Repeat layers twice, ending with cheese strips. Sprinkle with Parmesan cheese. Bake in a 350° oven about 40 minutes (30 to 35 minutes for individual casseroles) or till hot and bubbly. Sprinkle with parsley. Makes 4 servings.

Nutritional facts per serving: 304 calories, 10 g total fat (5 g saturated fat), 27 mg cholesterol, 473 mg sodium, 41 g carbohydrate, 7 g fiber, 18 g protein. **Daily values:** 26% vitamin A, 41% vitamin C, 34% calcium, 13% iron.

Bread Crumbs

Some of the recipes in this cookbook call for soft bread crumbs while others call for fine, dry bread crumbs. It's important to note the difference. Soft bread crumbs are made from fresh or slightly stale bread that is torn into small pieces. Fine, dry bread crumbs are made from very dry bread that is finely crushed. Fine, dry crumbs also are available commercially in plain and seasoned forms.

To make soft bread crumbs, use a blender or food processor to break the bread into fluffy pieces. One slice of bread yields about ¾ cup crumbs.

When making fine, dry bread crumbs, minimize the mess by placing the dried bread in a plastic bag and then crushing it with a rolling pin. One slice of bread yields about ¼ cup fine, dry crumbs.

PLEASING PASTA, RICE, & GRAINS

Today's savvy cooks are exploring pasta, rice, and grains as never before. These versatile foods are low in fat, and when tastefully paired with vegetables, meats, and seasonings, can be the foundation for many treasured meals. From fat-reduced classics to creative new combinations, you'll find a delightful collection of main dishes and side dishes on the following pages. Our updated version of Seafood Pasta Alfredo is so creamy, you wouldn't dream it's good for you, too. Are you in a hurry? Frozen vegetables make Pasta with Primavera Sauce as quick as it is delicious. Istanbul Pilaf is an easy way to add exotic flavors to your table, and Roasted Pepper Pasta with Basil Pesto brightens any meal. Take a look for yourself and sample these taste-tempting possibilities.

ROASTED PEPPER PASTA WITH BASIL PESTO

Low-fat

In this garden-fresh pesto sauce (photo, left) chicken broth replaces the oil while roasted sweet peppers add extra body.

3 large red, yellow, or green
  sweet peppers
1 cup firmly packed fresh basil
  leaves, torn
½ cup firmly packed fresh
  parsley, snipped
¼ cup reduced-sodium chicken
  broth
3 tablespoons grated Parmesan
  cheese
2 tablespoon lemon juice
2 cloves garlic, quartered
¼ teaspoon pepper
⅛ teaspoon salt
8 ounces angel hair pasta
  (capellini) or linguine
  Fresh basil leaves (optional)

1. Halve all of the peppers; remove stems, seeds, and membranes. Place peppers, cut sides down, on a foil-lined baking sheet. Bake in a 425° oven for 20 to 25 minutes or till skin is bubbly and browned. Place peppers in a clean brown paper bag; seal and let stand for 10 to 30 minutes or till cool enough to handle. Peel skin from peppers. Julienne peppers. Measure ½ cup pepper strips; set remaining pepper strips aside.

2. For pesto, in food processor bowl or blender container combine the ½ cup pepper strips, basil, parsley, broth, Parmesan cheese, lemon juice, garlic, pepper, and salt. Cover, and process or blend till mixture is nearly smooth; set aside.

3. Cook pasta in a large saucepan or Dutch oven in lightly salted water according to package directions; drain. Return to pan; toss with remaining pepper strips and pesto till coated. Turn into a serving dish. If desired, garnish with fresh basil leaves. Makes 6 side-dish servings.

Nutrition facts per serving: 176 calories, 2 g total fat (1 g saturated fat), 2 mg cholesterol, 210 mg sodium, 33 g carbohydrate, 1 g fiber, 7 g protein. **Daily values:** 32% vitamin A, 128% vitamin C, 5% calcium, 11% iron.

Hot Tips on Pasta

Here are three simple tricks for keeping cooked pasta hot:

Drain the pasta quickly. Don't let it stand in the colander longer than necessary.

Return the pasta to the hot cooking pan immediately. The heat of the pan will help keep the pasta warm.

Always use a warm serving dish. To warm your serving dish, simply run hot water into it. Let it stand a few minutes to absorb the heat. Then empty the dish and wipe it dry. Add the cooked pasta and serve immediately.

Low-fat

Low-calorie

Low-sodium

High-fiber

HOMEMADE PASTA

2¼ **cups all-purpose flour**
¼ **teaspoon salt**
1 **beaten egg**
1 **egg white**
⅓ **cup water**
1 **teaspoon olive or cooking oil**

1. In a medium mixing bowl stir together *2 cups* of the flour and the salt. Make a well in the center. In a small bowl combine egg, egg white, water, and oil; add to the flour mixture. Stir till thoroughly mixed. Sprinkle the kneading surface with remaining flour. Turn dough out onto floured surface. Knead till dough is smooth and elastic (8 to 10 minutes). Cover; let rest 10 minutes. (Dough can be refrigerated for 3 days or can be frozen for longer storage.)

2. Divide dough into thirds; use a rolling pin or pasta machine to roll out dough. Cut as desired. Cook pasta in a large pot of boiling unsalted water for 1 to 2 minutes for thinly cut pasta; 2 to 3 minutes for wider noodles or shapes. Drain and use as desired. Makes 1 pound fresh pasta or 4 servings.

Note: To make dough with a food processor, place steel blade in dry work bowl; add *all* of the flour, the salt, egg, and egg white. Process till mixture is the consistency of cornmeal. With the machine running, slowly pour water and oil through feed tube. Process till a smooth ball forms. Divide dough into thirds; use a rolling pin or pasta machine to roll out dough. Cut as desired.

Nutrition facts per serving: 269 calories, 3 g total fat (1 g saturated fat), 53 mg cholesterol, 164 mg sodium, 50 g carbohydrate, 2 g fiber, 9 g protein. **Daily values:** 2% vitamin A, 0% vitamin C, 1% calcium, 21% iron.

Rolling Homemade Pasta

Rolling pin method:
On floured surface, roll each portion of dough into a 16x12-inch rectangle about 1⁄16 inch thick. (If dough becomes too elastic, cover and let rest 5 minutes.)

Pasta machine method:
Follow manufacturer's directions.

Whole Wheat Pasta: Prepare Homemade Pasta as directed above, except substitute *whole wheat flour* for the all-purpose flour.

Spinach Pasta: Prepare Homemade Pasta as directed above, except increase the all-purpose flour to 3¼ cups. Combine *2¾ cups* with the salt. Reduce the water to 1 tablespoon. Add one 10-ounce package frozen chopped *spinach,* cooked and thoroughly drained, with the water. Divide dough into 4 portions and continue as directed. Makes about 1⅓ pounds.

Carrot Pasta: Prepare Homemade Pasta as directed above, except increase the all-purpose flour to 3¾ cups. Combine *3¼ cups* flour with the salt. Substitute one 16-ounce can *carrots,* drained and mashed (1 cup), for the water. Divide dough into 5 portions. Makes 1¾ pounds.

To knead the dough, fold it and then push down on it with the heel of your hand, curving your fingers over the dough. Turn, fold, and push down again.

Storing Homemade Pasta

Spread cut pasta out on a rack. Let dry overnight or till completely dry. Wrap in clear plastic wrap or foil, or place in an airtight container. Store in a dry place. To freeze, let cut pasta dry at least 1 hour. Place in a freezer container or wrap in freezer wrap, label, and freeze for up to 8 months.

Cutting and Shaping Homemade Pasta

After rolling out dough, let it stand for 20 to 30 minutes to dry the surface slightly. While shaping dough, keep unused portion covered to prevent it from drying out too much.

Linguine: To cut by hand, roll up the rectangle of dough loosely. Cut into 1/8-inch-wide slices. Lift and shake to separate. To cut with a pasta machine, pass dough through a 1/8-inch-wide cutting blade. Use a sharp knife to cut strips to desired length.

Fettuccine: To cut by hand, roll up the rectangle of dough loosely. Cut into 1/4-inch-wide slices. Lift and shake to separate. To cut with a pasta machine, pass the dough through a 1/4-inch-wide cutting blade. Use a sharp knife to cut strips to desired length.

Lasagna: With a sharp knife or fluted pastry wheel, cut the rectangle of dough into 3-inch-wide strips. Cut strips to desired length.

Low-fat
Low-calorie

FRESH TOMATO SAUCE FOR PASTA

This easy sauce is perfect with homemade, fresh, refrigerated, or dried pasta.

Nonstick spray coating
1 cup chopped onion
1/2 cup finely shredded carrots
1 clove garlic, minced
2 pounds ripe fresh tomatoes, cored and chopped, or two 14 1/2-ounce cans low-sodium diced tomatoes
2 tablespoons snipped fresh basil or 2 teaspoons dried basil, crushed
1/2 teaspoon sugar
1/4 teaspoon salt
1/8 teaspoon pepper

1. Spray a large nonstick skillet with nonstick spray coating. Cook onion, carrots, and garlic over medium heat for 5 minutes or till vegetables are tender. Stir in fresh tomatoes or *undrained* canned tomatoes, basil, sugar, salt, and pepper. Simmer for 10 to 20 minutes or till most of the liquid is evaporated. Cool slightly.

2. Pour mixture into a blender container or food processor bowl. Cover, and blend or process till desired consistency is reached. Makes about 3 cups sauce.

Nutrition facts per 1/2 cup: 62 calories, 1 g total fat (0 g saturated fat), 0 mg cholesterol, 114 mg sodium, 13 g carbohydrate, 1 g fiber, 2 g protein. **Daily values:** 42% vitamin A, 56% vitamin C, 1% calcium, 6% iron.

Low-fat

Low-calorie

Low-sodium

FENNEL AND CARROT PASTA

When preparing this dish (photo, right),you will save time and pans by cooking the vegetables with the simmering pasta.

1 bulb (about 1 pound) fennel

4 ounces bow-tie, gemelli,
   or corkscrew pasta

2 large carrots, julienned
   (1 cup)

½ cup chopped onion

2 cloves garlic, minced

2 teaspoons olive oil

¼ teaspoon pepper

⅛ teaspoon salt

1½ cups shredded radicchio or
   fresh spinach

2 tablespoons grated Parmesan
   cheese

1. Remove upper stalks from fennel, including feathery leaves. Discard any wilted outer layers on fennel bulb; cut off a thin slice from the base. Wash fennel and pat dry. Quarter fennel bulb lengthwise and discard core; julienne each quarter lengthwise.

2. Cook pasta in a large pot of lightly salted boiling water for 5 minutes. Add fennel and carrots; cook for 5 minutes more or till pasta is al dente (tender but slightly firm); drain.

3. Meanwhile, in a small skillet cook onion and garlic in hot oil for 3 minutes or till onion is tender. Stir in pepper and salt. Transfer pasta and vegetables to a serving dish; add onion mixture, radicchio or spinach, and Parmesan cheese. Toss well to mix. Makes 4 side-dish servings.

Nutrition facts per serving: 247 calories, 4 g total fat (1 g saturated fat), 2 mg cholesterol, 242 mg sodium, 44 g carbohydrate, 2 g fiber, 10 g protein. **Daily values:** 86% vitamin A, 49% vitamin C, 13% calcium, 9% iron.

Low-fat

Low-sodium

SPINACH LINGUINE WITH SPICY GARLIC SAUCE

This makes a great addition to a meal featuring grilled chicken breasts or salmon steaks.

8 ounces dry spinach linguine
   or fettuccine

2 tablespoons dry white wine or
   reduced-sodium chicken
   broth

4 cloves garlic, minced

1 4-ounce jar diced pimiento,
   drained

¼ cup reduced-sodium chicken
   broth

2 tablespoon snipped fresh
   parsley

1 tablespoon lemon juice

¼ teaspoon pepper

⅛ teaspoon crushed red pepper

1. Cook pasta in a large saucepan of unsalted boiling water according to package directions; drain.

2. Meanwhile, in a small skillet heat wine; add garlic and simmer for 2 minutes. Stir in pimiento, broth, parsley, lemon juice, pepper, and crushed red pepper; simmer for 2 minutes more. Transfer pasta to a serving bowl; spoon sauce over and toss well to coat. Makes 4 side-dish servings.

Nutrition facts per serving: 229 calories, 1 g total fat (0 g saturated fat), 0 mg cholesterol, 38 mg sodium, 45 g carbohydrate, 1 g fiber, 8 g protein. **Daily values:** 10% vitamin A, 53% vitamin C, 5% calcium, 15% iron.

Low-fat
Low-calorie

PASTA WITH STIR-FRIED PEPPERS

For this stunning side dish, bright strips of sweet pepper nestle in pasta nests.

4 ounces tri-colored angel hair
   pasta (capellini) or fine egg
   noodles
3 medium red, green, yellow,
   and/or orange sweet
   peppers, julienned (3 cups)
1 tablespoon snipped fresh basil
⅛ teaspoon pepper
2 tablespoons grated Parmesan
   cheese
1 tablespoon reduced-calorie
   margarine

1. Cook pasta according to package directions; drain. Spray a large nonstick skillet with *nonstick spray coating*. Add sweet peppers; cook and stir over medium heat for 3 to 4 minutes or till crisp-tender. Remove from heat. Stir in snipped basil and pepper.

2. Toss drained pasta with Parmesan cheese and margarine. Twirl ¼ of the pasta around a long-tine fork to form a nest shape. Slide the pasta onto a plate keeping nest upright. Repeat with remaining pasta; spoon sweet pepper mixture into pasta nests. If desired, garnish with additional fresh basil. Makes 4 side-dish servings.

Nutrition facts per serving: 148 calories, 3 g total fat (1 g saturated fat), 3 mg cholesterol, 103 mg sodium, 25 g carbohydrate, 1 g fiber, 5 g protein. **Daily values:** 46% vitamin A, 156% vitamin C, 6% calcium, 7% iron.

Low-fat
Low-sodium

ORZO IN SAFFRON AND GREEN ONION SAUCE

Just a bit of saffron (or turmeric), wine, and Dijon-style mustard transforms tiny macaroni into a delightful dish without added fat.

2 cups reduced-sodium chicken
   broth
1 cup orzo
1 4-ounce jar diced pimiento,
   drained
¼ cup sliced green onion
2 tablespoons dry white wine
1 teaspoon Dijon-style mustard
⅛ teaspoon saffron threads
⅛ teaspoon pepper
1 tablespoon snipped fresh
   parsley

1. In a medium saucepan bring chicken broth to boiling; stir in orzo. Simmer, covered, for 10 minutes or till tender. Drain off any excess liquid.

2. Add pimiento, green onion, wine, mustard, saffron, and pepper to orzo; cook for 2 minutes more. Sprinkle with parsley. Makes 4 side-dish servings.

Nutrition facts per serving: 191 calories, 1 g total fat (0 g saturated fat), 0 mg cholesterol, 75 mg sodium, 36 g carbohydrate, 1 g fiber, 7 g protein. **Daily values:** 8% vitamin A, 48% vitamin C, 1% calcium, 16% iron.

CHILI PESTO PASTA

Spread the chili pesto on broiled poultry, meats, and fish, too.

1 cup boiling water
2 to 3 dried ancho or pasilla
    peppers
1 cup fresh parsley sprigs
1 cup chopped tomato
¼ cup fat-free mayonnaise
    dressing or salad dressing
2 tablespoons snipped fresh
    cilantro
2 tablespoons lime juice
1 clove garlic, quartered
¼ teaspoon pepper
8 ounces bow-ties (farfalle) or
    corkscrew macaroni
    (rotelle)
½ cup sliced green onion
    Fresh cilantro sprigs
    (optional)
    Lime wedges (optional)

1. For chili pesto, pour boiling water over dried peppers. Cover and let stand for 30 minutes or till softened; drain. Wearing gloves, remove stems from peppers; halve peppers lengthwise. Scrape out seeds; discard. Place peppers in food processor bowl or blender container. Add parsley, tomato, mayonnaise dressing or salad dressing, the 2 tablespoons cilantro, lime juice, garlic, and pepper. Cover, and process or blend till mixture is nearly smooth.

2. Cook pasta in lightly salted boiling water according to package directions till al dente (tender but slightly firm), adding the green onion to the water for the last minute of cooking time. Drain pasta and onion; return mixture to pan. Add pesto and toss well to coat. Heat through. Transfer to a serving bowl. If desired, garnish pasta with cilantro sprigs and lime wedges. Makes 6 side-dish servings.

Nutrition facts per serving: 174 calories, 1 g total fat (0 g saturated fat), 0 mg cholesterol, 167 mg sodium, 36 g carbohydrate, 2 g fiber, 6 g protein. **Daily values:** 28% vitamin A, 37% vitamin C, 2% calcium, 18% iron.

Spaghetti Etiquette

Is there a proper way to eat spaghetti? That question has been argued for years. One school of thought says you should catch a few strands of pasta on a fork. Then, with the tines resting against a large spoon, twist the fork to wrap up the pasta. Yet others say you should spear a few strands on a fork. Then, with the tip of the fork resting against the plate (not a spoon), twirl the fork and pasta.

Our advice? Use whatever works best for you.

Low-fat

Low-calorie

Low-sodium

PASTA PUFF

If you're ready for a new twist on macaroni and cheese, try this healthful version that puffs up like a soufflé. (See photo, left.)

6 ounces tiny shell macaroni (conchigliette) or elbow macaroni

2 beaten egg yolks

1¼ cups skim milk

2 tablespoons all-purpose flour

½ cup chopped red or green sweet pepper

½ cup shredded carrots

1 teaspoon dried basil, crushed

½ teaspoon dried dillweed

⅛ teaspoon pepper

1½ cups shredded reduced-fat cheddar, Monterey Jack or Swiss cheese (6 ounces)

1½ cups soft bread crumbs (2 slices bread)

4 egg whites

Chopped red sweet pepper (optional)

Grated Parmesan cheese (optional)

Dill sprigs (optional)

1. Cook pasta in a large amount of boiling water for 6 to 8 minutes or till al dente (tender but slightly firm); drain.

2. In a large bowl combine egg yolks, milk, and flour; beat till mixed. Add sweet pepper, carrots, basil, dillweed, and pepper. Stir in drained pasta, cheese, and *1 cup* of the bread crumbs. In a medium mixing bowl beat egg whites with an electric mixer on high speed till stiff peaks form (tips stand straight); fold into pasta mixture. Transfer mixture to a greased shallow 2-quart baking dish. Sprinkle remaining bread crumbs atop.

3. Bake in a 350° oven for 30 to 35 minutes or till puffed and knife inserted near center comes out clean. If desired, garnish with chopped sweet pepper, Parmesan cheese, and dill sprigs. Serve immediately. Makes 6 main-dish servings.

Nutrition facts per serving: 283 calories, 8 g total fat (4 g saturated fat), 92 mg cholesterol, 310 mg sodium, 33 g carbohydrate, 1 g fiber, 18 g protein. **Daily values:** 45% vitamin A, 24% vitamin C, 24% calcium, 12% iron.

Measuring Dry and Cooked Pasta

If you don't have a kitchen scale, it's nice to know some cup measurements for pasta.

Four ounces of uncooked elbow macaroni or medium shell macaroni measures about 1 cup. When it's cooked, you'll have approximately 2½ cups pasta.

Four ounces of uncooked medium noodles measures about 3 cups. Noodles measure the same when cooked—about 3 cups.

Four ounces of uncooked 10-inch-long spaghetti, held together in a bunch, has about a 1-inch diameter. When it's cooked, you'll have about 2 cups of pasta.

ROTELLE WITH ARTICHOKES AND RED ONIONS

Low-fat

If desired, stir in shredded meat or chicken to make this side dish an entrée.

6 ounces corkscrew macaroni
   (rotelle)
1 9-ounce package frozen
   artichoke hearts, thawed
   and chopped
1 medium red onion, halved
   and thinly sliced
1 clove garlic, minced
2 teaspoons olive oil
¼ cup fat-free mayonnaise
   dressing or salad dressing
¼ cup skim milk
2 teaspoons snipped fresh
   oregano
¼ teaspoon pepper
2 tablespoons grated Parmesan
   cheese

1. Cook pasta in lightly salted boiling water according to package directions; drain.

2. Meanwhile, in a large nonstick skillet cook artichoke hearts, onion, and garlic in hot oil over medium heat for 5 to 7 minutes or till onion is tender. In a small bowl stir together mayonnaise dressing, milk, oregano, and pepper; stir into vegetables. Heat through. Transfer pasta to a serving bowl; add vegetable mixture and grated Parmesan cheese. Toss well to coat. Makes 6 side-dish servings.

Nutrition facts per serving: 171 calories, 3 g total fat (1 g saturated fat), 2 mg cholesterol, 223 mg sodium, 31 g carbohydrate, 3 g fiber, 7 g protein. **Daily values:** 2% vitamin A, 8% vitamin C, 7% calcium, 11% iron.

Low-fat

Low-calorie

Low-sodium

PASTA AND BROWN RICE WITH ASPARAGUS

It's fun to experiment with different tiny pastas and a variety of rices and grains for intriguing side dishes such as this one.

⅔ cup reduced-sodium chicken
   broth
¼ cup quick-cooking brown rice
¼ cup chopped red onion
1½ teaspoons snipped fresh
   tarragon
1½ teaspoons snipped fresh basil
4 ounces tiny tube macaroni
   (ditalini)
8 ounces asparagus spears,
   trimmed and cut into 1-inch
   pieces (about 1 cup)
½ cup chopped red or green
   sweet pepper

1. In a medium saucepan bring chicken broth to boiling; stir in rice, onion, tarragon, basil, and ⅛ teaspoon *pepper*. Cover and simmer for 10 minutes or till broth is absorbed.

2. Meanwhile, cook pasta according to package directions, adding asparagus and sweet pepper after the first 5 minutes of cooking time. Drain pasta and vegetables; transfer to a large serving bowl. Add rice mixture; toss well and serve. Makes 6 side-dish servings.

Nutrition facts per serving: 99 calories, 1 g total fat (0 g saturated fat), 0 mg cholesterol, 73 mg sodium, 20 g carbohydrate, 1 g fiber, 4 g protein. **Daily values:** 7% vitamin A, 31% vitamin C, 1% calcium, 6% iron.

Low-fat

Low-sodium

PASTA AND LENTILS WITH VEGETABLES

1 cup reduced-sodium chicken
   broth
½ cup dry lentils, rinsed and
   drained
½ cup chopped onion
1 teaspoon dried thyme,
   crushed
½ teaspoon salt-free seasoning
   blend
¼ teaspoon pepper
1 cup chopped carrots
1½ cups elbow macaroni
1 10-ounce package frozen
   chopped spinach, thawed
   and well drained
1 cup chopped tomato
2 tablespoons grated Parmesan
   cheese

1. In a medium saucepan combine chicken broth, lentils, onion, thyme, seasoning blend, and pepper. Bring to boiling; reduce heat. Cover and simmer for 20 minutes. Add carrots. Simmer for 10 minutes more or till carrots and lentils are tender.

2. Meanwhile, cook pasta in a large saucepan in unsalted boiling water according to package directions; drain. Return pasta to pan. Add lentil mixture, spinach, and tomato. Heat through. Sprinkle each serving with some Parmesan cheese. Makes 4 main-dish servings.

Nutrition facts per serving: 307 calories, 3 g total fat (1 g saturated fat), 2 mg cholesterol, 147 mg sodium, 57 g carbohydrate, 3 g fiber, 16 g protein. **Daily values:** 126% vitamin A, 32% vitamin C, 13% calcium, 35% iron.

Low-calorie

Low-sodium

SUMMER SQUASH FRITTATA WITH PASTA

This open-face omelet features colorful vegetables and tiny bow-tie shaped pasta for a filling brunch, lunch, or dinner entrée.

1 cup tiny bow-tie pasta
   (tripolini)
1 cup chopped zucchini
1 cup chopped yellow summer
   squash or patty pan squash
½ cup sliced fresh mushrooms
½ cup chopped red sweet
   pepper
3 eggs
3 egg whites
⅓ cup skim milk
½ teaspoon dried thyme,
   crushed
½ cup shredded reduced-fat
   cheddar cheese (2 ounces)

1. Cook pasta according to package directions. Drain and set aside.

2. Spray a large nonstick skillet with *nonstick spray coating*. Add zucchini, summer squash or patty pan squash, mushrooms, and sweet pepper; cook and stir over medium heat for 5 minutes or till tender. Stir in pasta.

3. Combine eggs, egg whites, milk, thyme, and ¼ teaspoon *pepper*. Pour egg mixture over vegetable mixture in skillet. Cook over medium heat. As egg mixture sets, run a spatula around edge of skillet, lifting mixture to allow uncooked portions to flow underneath. Continue cooking and lifting edges till egg mixture is almost set (about 5 minutes total). Surface will be moist. Remove from heat; sprinkle with cheddar cheese. Cover and let stand for 3 to 4 minutes or till top is set. If desired, garnish with *red sweet pepper rings*. Makes 4 main-dish servings.

Nutrition facts per serving: 161 calories, 7 g total fat (3 g saturated fat), 176 mg cholesterol, 202 mg sodium, 10 g carbohydrate, 1 g fiber, 14 g protein. **Daily values:** 21% vitamin A, 39% vitamin C, 13% calcium, 9% iron.

Low-fat

Low-sodium

Pasta with Primavera Sauce

Toss the cheesy yogurt sauce with any pasta you like—we chose cavatelli and mostaccioli. (See photo, right.)

8 ounces cavatelli and/or
    mostaccioli
3 cups frozen loose-pack
    broccoli, cauliflower, and
    carrots
¾ cup skim milk
2 tablespoons all-purpose flour
1 teaspoon instant chicken
    bouillon granules
¾ teaspoon fines herbes
¾ cup plain fat-free yogurt
3 ounces reduced-fat shredded
    Monterey Jack cheese
2 tablespoons snipped parsley
2 tablespoons grated Parmesan
    cheese

1. Cook pasta in a large saucepan in lightly salted boiling water according to package directions; add vegetables for the last 3 minutes of cooking time.

2. Meanwhile, in a medium saucepan stir together milk, flour, bouillon granules, fines herbes, and ¼ teaspoon *pepper*. Cook and stir over medium heat till mixture is thickened and bubbly. Stir in yogurt, Monterey Jack cheese, and parsley; cook and stir till cheese is melted (do not boil). Drain pasta and vegetables; transfer to a serving bowl. Add sauce; toss to coat. Sprinkle with Parmesan cheese. Makes 4 main-dish servings.

Nutrition facts per serving: 374 calories, 6 g total fat (3 g saturated fat), 19 mg cholesterol, 498 mg sodium, 58 g carbohydrate, 3 g fiber, 21 g protein. **Daily values:** 116% vitamin A, 58% vitamin C, 31% calcium, 21% iron.

Low-fat

Low-sodium

High-fiber

Bow-Tie Bolognese

Change the spaghetti-supper routine without losing the crowd's appreciation.

8 ounces bow-tie (farfalle) pasta
8 ounces lean ground beef
1 medium onion, chopped
½ cup finely chopped carrots
1 clove garlic, minced
2 16-ounce cans low-sodium
    tomatoes, cut up
1 6-ounce can low-sodium
    tomato paste
1½ teaspoons dried Italian
    seasoning, crushed
1 teaspoon sugar
2 tablespoons snipped fresh
    parsley

1. Cook pasta according to package directions. Drain and keep warm.

2. Meanwhile, for bolognese sauce, spray a large nonstick skillet with *nonstick spray coating*. Cook ground beef, onion, carrots, and garlic about 5 minutes or till meat is browned and vegetables are almost tender. Stir in *undrained* tomatoes, tomato paste, Italian seasoning, and sugar. Simmer, covered, for 10 minutes. Season to taste with *salt* and *pepper*. Stir in parsley.

3. Transfer cooked pasta to a serving platter; spoon bolognese sauce atop hot cooked pasta. If desired, sprinkle with grated *Parmesan cheese* and garnish with *parsley sprigs*. Toss to serve. Makes 4 main-dish servings.

Nutrition facts per serving: 445 calories, 10 g total fat (4 g saturated fat), 38 mg cholesterol, 295 mg sodium, 67 g carbohydrate, 5 g fiber, 24 g protein. **Daily values:** 74% vitamin A, 94% vitamin C, 12% calcium, 42% iron.

Low-fat

Low-calorie

VERMICELLI WITH ASPARAGUS AND HAM

Nonfat yogurt, reduced-calorie margarine, and lean cooked ham helped create a flavorful, low-fat substitute for this rich dish.

8 ounces vermicelli or fine
    noodles
8 ounces asparagus spears,
    cut into 1-inch pieces
2 tablespoons reduced-calorie
    margarine
1 cup low-fat, fully cooked
    ham, cut into thin strips
¼ cup sliced green onions
1 tablespoon lemon juice
½ cup nonfat plain yogurt
2 tablespoons grated Parmesan
    cheese
¼ teaspoon pepper

1. Cook pasta in unsalted boiling water according to package directions. About 4 minutes before end of cooking time, add asparagus pieces to boiling liquid. Cook till pasta and asparagus are al dente (tender but still firm).

2. Meanwhile, melt margarine in a medium nonstick skillet; sauté ham and green onions for 2 minutes. Stir in lemon juice, yogurt, Parmesan cheese, and pepper; heat through but do not boil. Drain pasta and asparagus; transfer to a serving bowl. Add ham mixture; toss and serve. Makes 4 main-dish servings.

Nutrition facts per serving: 313 calories, 8 g total fat (2 g saturated fat), 71 mg cholesterol, 606 mg sodium, 41 g carbohydrate, 1 g fiber, 19 g protein. **Daily values:** 13% vitamin A, 17% vitamin C, 89% calcium, 21% iron.

Low-fat

Low-sodium

SEAFOOD PASTA ALFREDO

Seafood lovers will feel like they're indulging with this rich-tasting, creamy pasta dish laced with garlic and Parmesan cheese.

1 pound refrigerated fettuccine
8 ounces shrimp in shells,
    peeled and deveined
8 ounces scallops or frozen
    lump crabmeat, thawed
    and flaked
1 12-ounce can evaporated
    skim milk
2 tablespoons all-purpose flour
2 cloves garlic, minced
¼ cup grated Parmesan cheese
2 tablespoons snipped fresh
    parsley
⅛ teaspoon pepper
⅛ teaspoon ground nutmeg

1. Cook pasta in a large pot of unsalted boiling water according to package directions; add shrimp and scallops (but not crab, if using) for the last 3 minutes of cooking time. Cook till pasta is al dente (tender but slightly firm) and shrimp are pink.

2. Meanwhile, in a medium saucepan stir together evaporated milk and flour. Stir in garlic. Cook and stir till mixture is thickened and bubbly. Cook and stir for 2 minutes more. Stir in crab (if using), Parmesan cheese, parsley, pepper, and nutmeg; heat through. Drain pasta and seafood; transfer to a serving bowl. Add sauce; toss to coat. Makes 4 main-dish servings.

Nutrition facts per serving: 388 calories, 4 g total fat (2 g saturated fat), 90 mg cholesterol, 398 mg sodium, 56 g carbohydrate, 0 g fiber, 31 g protein. **Daily values:** 17% vitamin A, 8% vitamin C, 36% calcium, 28% iron.

Low-fat

Low-calorie

Low-sodium

CHINESE NOODLE CAKE WITH SHRIMP

Noodle pancakes, typical of Chinese cuisine, convert easily to low-fat cooking. We topped this one with ginger-sauced shrimp.

**6 ounces fine noodles
    (vermicelli)**
Nonstick spray coating
**12 ounces shelled, deveined
    shrimp**
¼ cup sliced green onions
2 teaspoons grated gingerroot
1 clove garlic, minced
1 teaspoon cooking oil
**2 tablespoons dry sherry
    or water**
2 tablespoons water
1 tablespoon light soy sauce
1 teaspoon cornstarch

1. Cook pasta in a large saucepan in unsalted boiling water for 4 to 6 minutes or till tender. Drain and rinse with cold water; drain well. Spray a 9x1½-inch round baking pan with nonstick spray coating. Spread cooked noodles evenly in pan, pressing lightly. Bake, uncovered, in a 400° oven for 20 to 25 minutes or till top is crisp and light brown.

2. Meanwhile, cook shrimp in a medium saucepan in unsalted boiling water for 1 to 3 minutes or till opaque. Drain and set aside.

3. In the medium saucepan cook green onions, gingerroot, and garlic in hot oil about 2 minutes or till tender. Stir together sherry, water, soy sauce, and cornstarch. Add to saucepan. Cook and stir till slightly thickened and bubbly. Cook and stir for 1 minute more. Add shrimp; heat through.

4. Transfer noodle cake to a serving platter. Spoon shrimp mixture over noodle cake. Makes 4 main-dish servings.

Nutrition facts per serving: 242 calories, 4 g total fat (1 g saturated fat), 167 mg cholesterol, 290 mg sodium, 30 g carbohydrate, 0 g fiber, 20 g protein. **Daily values:** 7% vitamin A, 5% vitamin C, 3% calcium, 26% iron.

Loosen the noodle pancake from the pan with a thin spatula. Then, using a pancake turner, slide the pancake from the pan onto a serving plate.

CONFETTI VEGETABLE RISOTTO

Low-fat

Risotto, an Italian rice dish, (photo, right) requires constant attention while it's cooking, but the great taste is well worth the effort.

1 cup chopped mushrooms
½ cup chopped carrots
½ cup chopped zucchini
1 clove garlic, minced
2 teaspoons olive oil
1 cup Italian arborio rice or
    long grain rice
½ cup frozen loose-pack peas
½ cup frozen whole kernel corn
1¾ cups reduced-sodium chicken
    broth
1¾ cups water
¾ teaspoon dried basil, crushed
¼ teaspoon dried thyme,
    crushed
⅛ teaspoon pepper
¼ cup grated Parmesan cheese
Carrot curls (optional)

1. In a large saucepan cook mushrooms, carrots, zucchini, and garlic in hot oil for 3 minutes. Stir in rice, peas, and corn; cook and stir for 3 minutes.

2. In another saucepan combine broth, water, basil, thyme, and pepper. Bring to boiling. Add 1 cup of the boiling broth mixture to rice mixture. Cook over medium heat, stirring constantly, till nearly all the liquid is absorbed. Add enough additional broth mixture to barely cover rice; cook, stirring constantly, till broth is nearly absorbed. Continue adding broth and cooking and stirring rice mixture till rice is tender and nearly all the liquid has cooked away (this should take about 18 to 22 minutes). The rice will have a creamy consistency. Remove from heat; stir in Parmesan cheese. If desired, garnish with carrot curls. Makes 6 side-dish servings.

Nutrition facts per serving: 185 calories, 3 g total fat (1 g saturated fat), 3 mg cholesterol, 291 mg sodium, 33 g carbohydrate, 2 g fiber, 6 g protein. **Daily values:** 51% vitamin A, 5% vitamin C, 6% calcium, 14% iron.

Cook Rice Now; Serve Later

To save time later, cook up some extra rice and save it. Simply store the cooked rice in an airtight container in the refrigerator for up to 1 week or in the freezer for up to 6 months.

To reheat chilled or frozen rice, in a saucepan add 2 tablespoons of water for each cup of rice. Cover and heat on top of the range about 5 minutes or till the rice is heated through.

ISTANBUL PILAF

This fragrant spiced pilaf is a delightful accompaniment to grilled meats, fish, and barbecued chicken.

2¼ cups reduced-sodium chicken
    broth
 1 teaspoon finely shredded
    lemon peel
 ½ teaspoon ground cinnamon
 ¼ teaspoon pepper
 ¼ teaspoon cumin
 ⅛ teaspoon ground cardamom
 ⅛ to ¼ teaspoon ground saffron
 1 cup long grain rice
 1 cup chopped onion
 3 tablespoons golden raisins
 1 tablespoon snipped fresh
    cilantro or parsley

1. In a medium saucepan combine broth, lemon peel, cinnamon, pepper, cumin, cardamom, and saffron. Bring to boiling; stir in rice, onion, and raisins. Simmer, covered, about 15 minutes or till rice is tender and liquid is absorbed.

2. Let stand, covered, for 5 minutes. Sprinkle with cilantro or parsley. Makes 6 side-dish servings.

Nutrition facts per serving: 146 calories, 0 g total fat (0 g saturated fat), 0 mg cholesterol, 153 mg sodium, 32 g carbohydrate, 1 g fiber, 3 g protein. **Daily values:** 0% vitamin A, 21% vitamin C, 1% calcium, 11% iron.

LEMON RICE WITH GREEN BEANS

A package of frozen green beans makes this fat-free rice dish especially easy for the cook.

 2 cups water
1½ teaspoons finely shredded
    lemon peel
 ½ teaspoon instant chicken
    bouillon granules
 ⅛ teaspoon pepper
 1 cup long grain rice
 1 9-ounce package frozen
    French-cut green beans
 2 tablespoons snipped fresh
    parsley
 1 teaspoon lemon juice

1. In a medium saucepan combine water, lemon peel, bouillon granules, and pepper. Bring to boiling; stir in rice and beans. Return to boiling; reduce heat. Cover and simmer for 15 minutes or till rice and beans are nearly tender. Remove from heat; cover and let stand 5 minutes.

2. Stir in parsley and lemon juice; toss to mix. Makes 6 side-dish servings.

Nutrition facts per serving: 125 calories, 0 g total fat (0 g saturated fat), 0 mg cholesterol, 82 mg sodium, 28 g carbohydrate, 1 g fiber, 3 g protein. **Daily values:** 2% vitamin A, 10% vitamin C, 2% calcium, 11% iron.

RICE VERDE

 Low-fat

This recipe is named for the spinach which gives this easy, stove-top dish its green color (verde means green in Spanish).

1½ cups water
¾ cup long grain white or
    brown rice
½ cup sliced green onions
¼ teaspoon garlic salt
¼ teaspoon ground sage
⅛ teaspoon pepper
1½ cups chopped fresh spinach
¼ cup finely shredded reduced-
    fat sharp cheddar cheese
    (1 ounce)

1. In a medium saucepan bring water to boiling. Slowly stir in rice, green onions, garlic salt, sage, and pepper; return to boiling. Reduce heat. Cover and simmer for 15 minutes or till rice is tender and most of the water is absorbed.

2. Stir the spinach into the rice mixture. Transfer to a serving dish. Sprinkle with cheese. Cover and let stand for 3 to 4 minutes or till spinach is wilted and cheese is melted. Makes 4 side-dish servings.

Nutrition facts per serving: 155 calories, 2 g total fat (1 g saturated fat), 5 mg cholesterol, 199 mg sodium, 29 g carbohydrate, 1 g fiber, 5 g protein. **Daily values:** 17% vitamin A, 13% vitamin C, 7% calcium, 14% iron.

BROWN RICE PILAF

 Low-fat

High-fiber

High-fiber brown rice imparts a nutty flavor to this pilaf.

1 cup reduced-sodium
    chicken broth
1 cup water
1 cup brown rice
½ cup chopped onion
½ cup chopped yellow summer
    squash or zucchini
1 2-ounce jar sliced pimiento,
    drained
¼ cup snipped fresh parsley
¼ teaspoon dried thyme,
    crushed
¼ teaspoon dried basil, crushed
⅛ teaspoon salt
⅛ teaspoon pepper

1. In a medium saucepan bring broth and water to boiling. Stir in rice and onion. Return to boiling; reduce heat. Cover and simmer for 30 minutes.

2. Stir yellow summer squash or zucchini, pimiento, parsley, thyme, basil, salt, and pepper into the rice mixture. Return to boiling; reduce heat. Cover and simmer for 10 to 20 minutes more or till the rice is tender and the liquid is absorbed. Makes 4 side-dish servings.

Nutrition facts per serving: 194 calories, 2 g total fat (0 g saturated fat), 0 mg cholesterol, 239 mg sodium, 40 g carbohydrate, 4 g fiber, 5 g protein. **Daily values:** 5% vitamin A, 33% vitamin C, 2% calcium, 8% iron.

Low-fat

High-fiber

STIR-FRIED RICE WITH ORIENTAL VEGETABLES

A practical way to use up leftover rice, this dish is terrific for fans of fried rice. (See photo, left.)

1 cup sliced fresh shiitake,
    oyster, or button
    mushrooms
¼ cup reduced-sodium chicken
    broth or beef broth
1 cup Chinese long beans or
    fresh green beans, cut into
    1-inch pieces
1 cup sliced bok choy
1 cup sliced carrots
2 teaspoons grated gingerroot
2 cloves garlic, minced
4 green onions, bias-sliced into
    1-inch pieces
1 cup bean sprouts
2 cups cold cooked long grain
    white or brown rice
2 tablespoons light soy sauce
1 tablespoon water
    Green onion fans or curls
    (optional)

1. Trim stems from mushrooms and discard. Slice mushrooms; set aside.

2. Heat broth in a large nonstick wok or skillet. Add beans, bok choy, carrots, gingerroot, and garlic to wok; cook and stir for 3 to 4 minutes or till crisp-tender. Add green onions and sprouts to wok; cook and stir for 2 minutes. Add mushrooms to wok; cook and stir for 1 minute more. Add rice, soy sauce, and water to wok; cook for 2 minutes more or till heated through. If desired, garnish with green onion fans or curls. Makes 4 side-dish servings.

Nutrition facts per serving: 156 calories, 1 g total fat (0 g saturated fat), 0 mg cholesterol, 299 mg sodium, 33 g carbohydrate, 4 g fiber, 6 g protein. **Daily values:** 91% vitamin A, 27% vitamin C, 4% calcium, 16% iron.

Cooking Rice

When a recipe calls for cooked rice in the ingredient list, plan on 1 cup of uncooked long-grain rice for 3 cups of cooked rice (or six servings). Use twice as much water as rice (2 cups of water for each cup of rice). In a saucepan combine the water and rice. Cover with a tight-fitting lid. Bring to boiling. Reduce heat. Simmer for 15 minutes. Do not remove lid. Remove from heat. Let stand, covered, for 10 minutes. Then, fluff with a fork.

Low-fat

Low-calorie

ORIENTAL RICE

Stir some new life into pre-cooked rice!

¼ cup reduced-sodium
   chicken broth
 1 cup sliced fresh shiitake or
   brown mushrooms
 1 cup sliced bok choy or
   Chinese (Napa) cabbage
1½ cups cooked rice
 ½ cup chopped red or green
   sweet pepper
 2 tablespoons light soy sauce
 2 tablespoons dry sherry
 1 teaspoon toasted sesame seed

1. In a nonstick wok or skillet heat 1 tablespoon of the broth. Add mushrooms and bok choy or Chinese cabbage; cook and stir for 2 minutes. Remove from wok. Add more broth to wok as necessary. Add rice and sweet pepper and cook for 2 minutes.

2. Stir soy sauce and sherry into the rice mixture. Return mushroom-cabbage mixture to wok; toss to mix. Cover and heat for 2 minutes more. Sprinkle with sesame seed before serving. Makes 4 side-dish servings.

Nutrition facts per serving: 109 calories, 1 g total fat (0 g saturated fat), 0 mg cholesterol, 310 mg sodium, 21 g carbohydrate, 1 g fiber, 3 g protein. **Daily values:** 8% vitamin A, 36% vitamin C, 1% calcium, 9% iron.

White vs. Brown

No, it's not a legal battle—it's two kinds of rice. White rice is milled to completely remove the hull and bran layers resulting in a mild, delicately flavored grain. Only the hull is removed from brown rice. The bran layers left on the grain give it a tan color.

Cooked brown rice has a nutty flavor and a slightly chewy texture. Brown rice cooks in about 35 minutes; white rice cooks in 15 minutes.

SPANISH-STYLE RICE

Low-fat

A fresh jalapeño pepper zips up this healthful adaptation of Spanish rice.

¾ cup chopped onion

1 large clove garlic, minced

2 teaspoons cooking oil

¾ cup chopped tomatoes

¾ cup reduced-sodium
    chicken broth

¾ cup water

¾ cup low-sodium tomato juice

1 teaspoon salt-free seasoning
    blend

½ teaspoon dried basil, crushed

1 jalapeño pepper, seeded
    and finely chopped, or
    ⅛ teaspoon crushed red
    pepper

⅛ teaspoon pepper

1 cup long grain rice

1. In a 2-quart saucepan cook onion and garlic in hot oil till tender.

2. Stir in chopped tomatoes, chicken broth, water, tomato juice, seasoning blend, basil, jalapeño pepper or crushed red pepper, and pepper. Bring to boiling; stir in rice. Return to boiling. Reduce heat; simmer, covered, for 15 to 20 minutes or till rice is tender. Remove from heat; cover and let stand for 5 minutes. Makes 6 side-dish servings.

Nutrition facts per serving: 157 calories, 2 g total fat (0 g saturated fat), 0 mg cholesterol, 90 mg sodium, 31 g carbohydrate, 1 g fiber, 4 g protein. **Daily values:** 4% vitamin A, 35% vitamin C, 1% calcium, 12% iron.

Low-fat

Low-sodium

TROPICAL FRUIT AND BROWN RICE PILAF

A perfect accompaniment for chicken or pork, this fruit-spiked pilaf is amazingly simple to make.

2 cups water

1 teaspoon finely shredded
    orange peel

¼ teaspoon salt-free seasoning
    blend

¼ teaspoon coconut extract
    (optional)

¾ cup regular brown rice

¼ cup chopped onion

1 15¼-ounce can tropical fruit
    salad, drained and chopped

1. In a medium saucepan combine water, orange peel, seasoning blend, and, if desired, coconut extract. Bring to boiling; stir in rice and onion. Reduce heat. Cover and simmer for 40 to 45 minutes or till rice is tender and liquid is absorbed. Remove from heat.

2. Stir in drained tropical fruit salad into rice mixture. Cover and let stand for 5 minutes. Makes 4 side-dish servings.

Nutrition facts per serving: 206 calories, 1 g total fat (0 g saturated fat), 0 mg cholesterol, 17 mg sodium, 45 g carbohydrate, 2 g fiber, 3 g protein. **Daily values:** 10% vitamin A, 37% vitamin C, 1% calcium, 3% iron.

Low-fat

High-fiber

HOPPIN' JOHN

Traditionally, Southerners serve this dish of black-eyed peas and rice (photo, left) on New Year's Day for good luck.

Nonstick spray coating
8 ounces ground turkey sausage
1 large onion, chopped (1 cup)
1 medium green or red sweet
    pepper, chopped (1 cup)
2 medium carrots, chopped
    (1 cup)
2 cloves garlic, minced
8 ounces dry black-eyed peas
    (1¼ cups)
5 cups reduced-sodium chicken
    broth or water
½ teaspoon dried rosemary,
    crushed
½ teaspoon dried thyme,
    crushed
½ teaspoon salt-free seasoning
    blend
⅛ to ¼ teaspoon pepper
⅛ teaspoon ground red pepper
1 bay leaf
1¼ cups long grain rice

1. Spray a 4-quart Dutch oven with nonstick coating. Add turkey sausage, onion, sweet pepper, carrots, and garlic. Cook for 5 minutes or till sausage is brown, stirring frequently. Drain excess fat.

2. Rinse black-eyed peas; add to the Dutch oven. Stir in broth, rosemary, thyme, seasoning blend, pepper, ground red pepper, and bay leaf. Bring to boiling; reduce heat. Cover and simmer for 25 minutes. Stir in rice; cook for 15 to 20 minutes more or till rice and black-eyed peas are done and liquid is absorbed. Remove bay leaf. Makes 6 main-dish servings.

Nutrition facts per serving: 384 calories, 7 g total fat (2 g saturated fat), 14 mg cholesterol, 846 mg sodium, 60 g carbohydrate, 7 g fiber, 21 g protein. **Daily values:** 57% vitamin A, 23% vitamin C, 5% calcium, 35% iron.

The Long and Short of It

The next time you visit the grocery store, take a closer look at the packages of rice. Rice is available in several lengths—you'll find the packages marked as long grain, medium grain, or short grain. Long grain rice is four or five times as long as it is wide. When cooked, the grains tend to remain separate and are light and fluffy. Medium grain rice is plump but not round. When cooked, it is moister and more tender than long grain rice. Short grain rice is almost round. It tends to cling together when cooked. Unless otherwise specified, the recipes in this book were tested with long grain rice.

Low-calorie

Low-sodium

High-fiber

CABBAGE ROLLS WITH TURKEY AND RICE STUFFING

We replaced the classic beef filling with lean ground turkey, and added some turkey sausage for extra flavor.

12 large cabbage leaves
8 ounces ground raw turkey
8 ounces ground turkey sausage
1 cup chopped carrots
¼ cup chopped onion
1 cup cooked brown rice
1 teaspoon salt-free seasoning
    blend
½ teaspoon dried thyme,
    crushed
1½ cups light marinara sauce
½ teaspoon dried basil, crushed

1. Spray a 2-quart rectangular baking dish with *nonstick spray coating;* set aside. Trim center vein from cabbage leaves, keeping each leaf in 1 piece. Immerse leaves in boiling water just till limp, about 3 minutes; drain and set aside.

2. For filling, spray a large nonstick skillet with nonstick coating. Cook ground turkey and turkey sausage for 5 minutes. Add carrots and onion; cook for 3 minutes more. Drain excess fat. Stir in rice, seasoning blend, and thyme.

3. Place about ¼ cup of the filling in the center of each cabbage leaf. Fold in sides; fold ends so they overlap atop rice. Place rolls, seam sides down, in prepared baking dish. Combine marinara sauce and basil; pour over rolls. Cover; bake in a 350° oven for 45 to 50 minutes or till heated through. Makes 6 main-dish servings.

Nutrition facts per serving: 212 calories, 8 g total fat (3 g saturated fat), 28 mg cholesterol, 348 mg sodium, 20 g carbohydrate, 4 g fiber, 15 g protein. **Daily values:** 60% vitamin A, 25% vitamin C, 3% calcium, 13% iron.

Low-fat

Low-calorie

Low-sodium

LOUISIANA RED BEANS WITH RICE

This economical, high-protein, one-pot dish traditionally was prepared on wash day by cooks in the old South.

8 ounces dried red kidney
    beans (1¼ cups)
1 cup chopped onion
1 green sweet pepper, chopped
    (1 cup)
3 cloves garlic, minced
2 tablespoons snipped fresh
    parsley
½ teaspoon dried thyme,
    crushed
½ teaspoon dried basil, crushed
¼ teaspoon ground red pepper
1 bay leaf
8 ounces fully cooked, smoked
    turkey sausage, chopped
3 cups hot cooked rice

1. Rinse beans. In a large saucepan combine beans and 4 cups cold *water.* Bring to boiling; reduce heat. Simmer for 2 minutes. Remove from heat. Cover; let stand 1 hour. (Or, omit simmering; soak beans in cold water overnight in a covered pan.) Drain and rinse beans.

2. In the same pan combine beans and 3 cups fresh *water.* Add onion, sweet pepper, garlic, parsley, thyme, basil, red pepper, and bay leaf. Bring to boiling; reduce heat. Cover and simmer for 1 hour. Add sausage; cover and simmer for 20 to 30 minutes more or till beans are tender, stirring occasionally. Discard bay leaf. Using a potato masher or back of a fork, mash beans slightly. Season to taste with *salt* and *pepper.* To serve, spoon hot cooked rice onto dinner plates; ladle bean mixture over rice. If desired, garnish with *parsley sprigs.* Makes 6 main-dish servings.

Nutrition facts per serving: 295 calories, 3 g total fat (1 g saturated fat), 24 mg cholesterol, 412 mg sodium, 49 g carbohydrate, 3 g fiber, 17 g protein. **Daily values:** 12% vitamin A, 51% vitamin C, 6% calcium, 30% iron.

BULGUR-STUFFED ARTICHOKES

Bulgur, a cracked wheat product, adds a delicate nutty flavor.

4 medium artichokes
   Lemon juice
½ cup reduced-sodium chicken
   broth
½ cup water
½ cup bulgur
1 cup chopped fresh
   mushrooms
1 red, green, or yellow sweet
   pepper, chopped (1 cup)
3 leeks, sliced (about 1 cup)
1 clove garlic, minced
½ teaspoon salt-free seasoning
   blend
¼ teaspoon dried thyme,
   crushed
⅛ teaspoon pepper
½ cup shredded part-skim
   mozzarella cheese
   (2 ounces)

1. Wash artichokes; trim stems. Cut artichokes leaves 1 inch from the top, snipping off sharp leaf tips. Brush cut edges with lemon juice. Cook, covered, in a large amount of boiling water for 20 to 30 minutes or till you can pull a leaf out easily. Invert to drain; cool. Cut each artichoke in half vertically from top to stem. Remove fuzzy choke and heart. Discard choke; chop hearts.

2. For filling, in a medium saucepan combine broth, water, and bulgur; bring to boiling. Reduce heat; simmer for 5 minutes. Stir in mushrooms, sweet pepper, leeks, and garlic; cover and simmer for 7 to 10 minutes more or till most of the liquid is absorbed and bulgur is tender. Remove from heat. Stir in chopped artichoke hearts, seasoning blend, thyme, and pepper.

3. Arrange artichoke halves, cut sides up, in a 13x9x2-inch baking pan. Spoon filling into artichoke halves, mounding it on top. Sprinkle cheese over filling. Bake, uncovered, in a 350° oven for 25 to 30 minutes or till cheese is melted and artichokes are heated through. Makes 8 main-dish servings.

Nutrition facts per serving: 140 calories, 1 g total fat (0 g saturated fat), 2 mg cholesterol, 230 mg sodium, 28 g carbohydrate, 11 g fiber, 10 g protein. **Daily values:** 12% vitamin A, 61% vitamin C, 11% calcium, 18% iron.

Using kitchen shears, snip sharp tips from the leaves on the artichokes.

Low-fat

Low-calorie

Low-sodium

High-fiber

WARM TABBOULEH WITH TUNA

Need a new picnic menu? Pack this refreshing salad (photo, right) along with fresh fruit, bread sticks, and lemonade.

2 cups cold water

1 cup whole wheat bulgur

1 teaspoon olive oil

1 cup chopped cucumber

1 cup cherry tomatoes, halved

⅓ cup snipped fresh parsley

¼ cup snipped fresh mint or
   1 tablespoon dried mint,
   crushed

3 tablespoons lemon juice

⅛ teaspoon pepper

1 6½-ounce can low-sodium
   chunk light tuna, drained
   and broken up
   Cucumber slices (optional)
   Mint sprigs (optional)

1. In a medium saucepan stir together cold water and bulgur. Bring to boiling; reduce heat. Cover and simmer for 12 to 15 minutes or till bulgur is tender and all of the water is absorbed.

2. Meanwhile, in a large nonstick skillet, heat oil. Cook chopped cucumber for 1 minute. Stir in bulgur, tomatoes, parsley, mint, lemon juice, and pepper. Add tuna and heat through. Serve warm. If desired, garnish with cucumber slices and mint sprigs. Makes 4 main-dish servings.

Nutrition facts per serving: 205 calories, 3 g total fat (0 g saturated fat), 15 mg cholesterol, 34 mg sodium, 31 g carbohydrate, 9 g fiber, 17 g protein. **Daily values:** 7% vitamin A, 41% vitamin C, 3% calcium, 19% iron.

Give Bulgur a Try

Bulgur is fast-cooking, has a delicious nutty flavor, and is high in fiber. This nutritious whole grain is made by hulling, precooking, drying, and cracking whole wheat berries. Look for bulgur in the aisle with the flour at your grocery store. If you can't find bulgur, you might try cracked wheat, which is a similar product.

To cook bulgur, stir 1 cup bulgur into 2 cups boiling water. If you like, add ¼ to ½ teaspoon salt. Cover and simmer for 12 to 15 minutes or till the water is absorbed.

Try replacing some or all of the rice in pilaf with bulgur. (Use 2 parts cooking liquid to 1 part bulgur.) Or, serve a stir-fry or thick stew over hot cooked bulgur.

POLENTA WITH SPINACH

Low-fat

It's your choice—serve polenta right from the pot, or chill it to bake or broil at a later time.

¼ **cup finely chopped onion**
1 **tablespoon margarine**
1 **cup water**
1 **cup reduced-sodium chicken broth**
1 **teaspoon dried basil, crushed**
¼ **teaspoon ground nutmeg**
⅛ **teaspoon salt**
⅔ **cup yellow cornmeal**
⅔ **cup cold water**
½ **of a 10-ounce package frozen chopped spinach, thawed**

1. In a medium saucepan cook onion in hot margarine till tender but not brown. Stir in the 1 cup water, the chicken broth, basil, nutmeg, and salt; bring to boiling.

2. In a bowl combine cornmeal and the ⅔ cold cup water; slowly pour cornmeal mixture into boiling liquid. Return to boiling; reduce heat to low. Cook, uncovered, for 10 to 15 minutes or till very thick, stirring occasionally. Stir in spinach; heat through. Serve immediately. Makes 6 side-dish servings.

Baked Polenta with Spinach: Prepare Polenta with Spinach as directed above, except spread hot mixture in a 9-inch pie plate. Cover and chill 30 minutes or till firm. Cover with foil. Bake in a 350° oven for 20 minutes or till heated through.

Nutrition facts per serving (soft or baked): 194 calories, 4 g total fat (1 g saturated fat), 0 mg cholesterol, 295 mg sodium, 35 g carbohydrate, 1 g fiber, 5 g protein. **Daily values:** 32% vitamin A, 8% vitamin C, 5% calcium, 7% iron.

Broiled Polenta with Spinach: Prepare Polenta with Spinach as directed above, except transfer hot mixture to an 8x4x2-inch loaf pan. Cover and chill at least 30 minutes or till firm. Turn out onto a cutting board. Cut into ½-inch-thick slices. Spray the unheated rack of a broiler pan with *nonstick spray coating*. Place slices on rack. Brush tops with 1 teaspoon *olive oil* or *cooking oil*; sprinkle with 1 tablespoon grated *Parmesan cheese*. Broil 4 inches from heat for 4 minutes or till light brown. Turn; brush other sides with 1 teaspoon oil and sprinkle with 1 tablespoon grated Parmesan cheese. Broil for 4 to 6 minutes more or till light brown. Makes 16 slices.

Cook the polenta until it is very thick, stirring occasionally with a wooden spoon.

HERBED KASHA PILAF

Kasha, also called toasted buckwheat groats, has a more intense flavor than other whole grains. Cooking softens its texture.

Nonstick spray coating
¾ cup buckwheat groats (kasha)
1 cup reduced-sodium chicken broth
1 cup water
½ cup sliced celery
⅓ cup sliced green onions
1 teaspoon dried basil, crushed
½ teaspoon dried thyme, crushed
¼ teaspoon ground sage
¼ teaspoon pepper
2 tablespoons snipped fresh chives or parsley

1. Spray a large nonstick skillet with nonstick spray coating. Add kasha and cook for 3 minutes, stirring frequently.

2. Stir cold broth, water, celery, green onions, basil, thyme, sage, and pepper into kasha; cover and bring to boiling. Reduce heat; simmer, covered, about 15 minutes or till nearly all the liquid is absorbed. Stir in snipped chives or parsley. Makes 4 side-dish servings.

Nutrition facts per serving: 121 calories, 2 g total fat (0 g saturated fat), 0 mg cholesterol, 183 mg sodium, 25 g carbohydrate, 3 g fiber, 4 g protein. **Daily values:** 2% vitamin A, 6% vitamin C, 2% calcium, 7% iron.

WILD RICE AND PEA PODS

If you don't have pea pods, frozen green peas make a tasty substitute.

1½ cups reduced-sodium chicken broth
⅔ cup wild rice
1 cup fresh pea pods, halved
½ of an 8-ounce can sliced water chestnuts, drained (about ½ cup)
½ cup chopped red or green sweet pepper
¼ cup chopped onion
2 teaspoons snipped fresh chives or ½ teaspoon dried chives
½ teaspoon salt-free seasoning blend

1. In a medium saucepan bring broth to boiling. Stir in wild rice; return to boiling. Reduce heat; simmer, covered, for 45 minutes.

2. Stir peas pods, water chestnuts, sweet pepper, onion, chives, and seasoning blend into wild rice. Cover and simmer for 2 to 3 minutes more or till wild rice is tender and most of the liquid is absorbed; drain, if necessary. Makes 4 side-dish servings.

Nutrition facts per serving: 137 calories, 1 g total fat (0 g saturated fat), 0 mg cholesterol, 271 mg sodium, 28 g carbohydrate, 2 g fiber, 6 g protein. **Daily values:** 14% vitamin A, 77% vitamin C, 2% calcium, 10% iron.

Low-fat

High-fiber

TOASTED BARLEY WITH APPLES AND RAISINS

If you've only considered barley as a soup ingredient, try it toasted till golden and mixed with apples and spices.

1¼ **cups quick-cooking barley**
 2 **cups reduced-sodium chicken broth**
 1 **cup chopped peeled apple**
⅓ **cup sliced green onions**
 2 **tablespoons raisins**
½ **teaspoon ground cinnamon**
¼ **teaspoon ground allspice**
⅛ **teaspoon pepper**

1. In a large skillet cook and stir barley over medium heat about 5 minutes or till toasted and golden brown.

2. Carefully stir broth, apple, green onions, raisins, cinnamon, allspice, and pepper into skillet. Bring to boiling; reduce heat. Cover; simmer for 10 to 12 minutes or till barley is tender and most of the liquid is absorbed. Remove from heat. Let stand, covered, for 5 minutes. Makes 6 side-dish servings.

Nutrition facts per serving: 166 calories, 1 g total fat (0 g saturated fat), 0 mg cholesterol, 138 mg sodium, 36 g carbohydrate, 42 g fiber, 5 g protein. **Daily values:** 1% vitamin A, 18% vitamin C, 0% calcium, 4% iron.

SUPER SALADS AND DRESSINGS

Whether it's a simple salad of fresh greens tossed with just the right amount of dressing or grilled chicken strips artfully arranged with the freshest fruits and vegetables, salads appeal to the eyes as well as the palate. On these pages, you'll find an impressive array to complement your meal. Sample either a fat-slashed classic, such as Caesar-Style Salad, or try an all-new creation, such as Jicama-Berry Salad with Shallot-Mint Vinaigrette. If you enjoy the ease of serving one-dish meals, take a look at the main-dish salads. Broiled Pineapple Chicken Salad drizzled with a curried yogurt dressing stars as a tantalizing main attraction; the Vegetable and Ham Pasta Salad makes a stick-to-the-ribs main course perfect for picnics and potlucks. These super salads don't require special occasions. Serve one tonight!

Low-calorie

Low-sodium

JICAMA-BERRY SALAD WITH SHALLOT-MINT VINAIGRETTE

This light, bright salad makes a perfect first course for a dinner featuring fish or poultry. (See photo, left.)

Romaine leaves and/or
    white kale
2 cups sliced strawberries
1 cup peeled jicama cut in
    julienne strips
3 tablespoons white wine
    vinegar
3 tablespoons orange juice
2 shallots, finely chopped
1 tablespoon snipped fresh mint
    or 1 teaspoon dried mint,
    crushed
1 tablespoon olive or salad oil
    Dash salt-free seasoning blend

1. Line 4 salad plates with romaine and/or kale. Arrange strawberries and jicama on top.

2. For dressing, in a screw-top jar combine vinegar, orange juice, shallots, mint, oil, and seasoning blend. Cover and shake well. Drizzle dressing over salads. Garnish with whole strawberries, if desired. Makes 4 side-dish servings.

Nutritional facts per serving: 80 calories, 4 g total fat (0 g saturated fat), 0 mg cholesterol, 4 mg sodium, 11 g carbohydrate, 3 g fiber, 2 g protein. **Daily values:** 14% vitamin A, 115% vitamin C, 2% calcium, 8% iron.

Low-calorie

SMOKED SALMON ON MIXED GREENS

For the mixed greens, try a combination of romaine, red cabbage, curly endive, and watercress.

4 cups torn mixed salad greens
½ cup thinly sliced cucumber
2 ounces hot smoked salmon,
    flaked
¼ cup chopped red onion
2 teaspoons snipped fresh dill
    or ½ teaspoon dried
    dillweed
2 tablespoons white wine
    vinegar
2 tablespoons orange juice
1 teaspoon olive or salad oil
¼ teaspoon pepper
    Fresh dill sprigs (optional)

1. Line 4 salad plates with mixed greens. Arrange cucumber slices on lettuce, top with salmon, and sprinkle with onion and dill.

2. For dressing, in a screw-top jar combine vinegar, orange juice, oil, and pepper. Cover and shake well. Drizzle mixture over salads. Garnish with fresh dill sprigs, if desired. Makes 4 side-dish servings.

Nutritional facts per serving: 64 calories, 4 g total fat (1 g saturated fat), 3 mg cholesterol, 121 mg sodium, 4 g carbohydrate, 1 g fiber, 4 g protein. **Daily values:** 11% vitamin A, 23% vitamin C, 2% calcium, 3% iron.

Low-fat

Low-calorie

PICNIC COLESLAW

For a more colorful coleslaw, use a combination of green and red cabbage.

2½ cups shredded cabbage
¾ cup shredded carrot
¾ cup red or green sweet
    pepper cut in julienne strips
⅓ cup sliced green onions
⅓ cup fat-free mayonnaise
    dressing or salad dressing
1 tablespoon vinegar
1 tablespoon skim milk
¼ teaspoon celery seed
¼ teaspoon dillweed

1. In a large bowl toss together cabbage, carrot, sweet pepper, and green onions.

2. For dressing, in a small mixing bowl combine mayonnaise or salad dressing, vinegar, skim milk, celery seed, dillweed, and ⅛ teaspoon *pepper*. Add dressing to cabbage mixture. Toss gently to coat. Serve on cabbage leaves, if desired. Makes 6 side-dish servings.

Nutritional facts per serving: 29 calories, 0 g total fat (0 g saturated fat), 0 mg cholesterol, 178 mg sodium, 7 g carbohydrate, 1 g fiber, 1 g protein. **Daily values:** 54% vitamin A, 67% vitamin C, 2% calcium, 2% iron.

Low-fat

Low-calorie

High-fiber

TOSSED SALAD WITH DRIED TOMATO DRESSING

A basil-scented vinaigrette-style dressing perks up a combo of lettuce, garbanzo beans, and sweet peppers.

½ cup dried tomatoes (dry pack)
¼ cup red or white wine vinegar
2 tablespoons snipped fresh
    basil or 1 teaspoon dried
    basil, crushed
1 clove garlic, minced
1 teaspoon sugar
¼ teaspoon pepper
4 cups torn lettuce
1 8-ounce can garbanzo beans,
    rinsed and drained
1 medium red or green sweet
    pepper, julienned
½ cup sliced onion

1. In a shallow bowl place dried tomatoes and cover with ⅓ cup *boiling water*. Cover and let stand 30 minutes or till softened. Drain, reserving liquid. Add enough water to equal ⅓ cup liquid. Chop tomatoes; set aside.

2. For dressing, in blender container or food processor bowl combine ¼ *cup* of the chopped tomatoes, ⅓ cup reserved liquid, vinegar, basil, garlic, sugar, and pepper. Cover, and blend or process till smooth.

3. In a large bowl toss together lettuce, the remaining dried tomatoes, garbanzo beans, sweet pepper, and onion. Add dressing. Toss gently to coat. Makes 4 side-dish servings.

Nutritional facts per serving: 101 calories, 1 g total fat (0 g saturated fat), 0 mg cholesterol, 390 mg sodium, 20 g carbohydrate, 4 g fiber, 4 g protein. **Daily values:** 23% vitamin A, 73% vitamin C, 3% calcium, 12% iron.

Low-fat

Low-calorie

Low-sodium

ORANGE, ONION, AND FENNEL SALAD

Licorice-flavored fennel and sweet, tangy oranges team up for a delightful side salad.

3 cups shredded romaine or
  leaf lettuce
2 oranges, peeled, cut into
  halves and sliced
1 medium fennel bulb,
  trimmed, quartered and
  thinly sliced
⅔ cup sliced red onion
3 tablespoons white wine
  vinegar
3 tablespoons orange juice
2 teaspoons snipped fresh basil
  or thyme or ½ teaspoon
  dried basil or thyme,
  crushed
⅛ teaspoon salt
⅛ teaspoon pepper

1. In a large bowl combine romaine or leaf lettuce, orange slices, fennel, and onion.

2. For dressing, in a screw-top jar combine vinegar, orange juice, basil or thyme, salt, and pepper. Cover and shake well. Pour over salad. Toss gently to coat. Makes 4 side-dish servings.

Nutritional facts per serving: 47 calories, 0 g total fat (0 g saturated fat), 00 mg cholesterol, 88 mg sodium, 11 g carbohydrate, 2 g fiber, 2 g protein. **Daily values:** 11% vitamin A, 62% vitamin C, 4% calcium, 4% iron.

To prepare the fennel, cut off and discard the upper stalks, including the feathery leaves (save the leaves for a garnish, if desired). Remove wilted outer layer; cut off a thin slice from the base. Cut into quarters lengthwise and then slice.

Low-calorie

Low-sodium

Roasted Pepper and Onion Salad

For a burst of color, use a combination of green, red, and yellow sweet peppers. (See photo, right.)

5 medium sweet peppers
1 red onion, cut into thin
   wedges
2 tablespoons white wine
   vinegar
1 tablespoon olive or salad oil
1 tablespoon snipped fresh basil
   or 1 teaspoon dried basil,
   crushed
¼ teaspoon salt-free seasoning
   blend
   Lettuce leaves
1 tablespoon snipped fresh
   chives or 1 teaspoon dried
   snipped chives

1. Halve peppers lengthwise, removing stems, seeds, and membranes. Arrange peppers, cut side down, with onions on a foil-lined baking sheet. Bake in a 425° oven for 20 to 25 minutes or till pepper skin is browned and bubbly. (Cover onions loosely with foil to prevent overbrowning after 10 to 15 minutes). Place peppers in a clean brown paper bag. Close bag; let stand 20 to 30 minutes. Set onions aside. Strip off pepper skins. Cut peppers into ½-inch-wide strips.

2. For dressing, in a blender container or food processor bowl place *⅓ cup* of one color of pepper strips, the vinegar, oil, basil, seasoning blend, and 2 tablespoons *water.* Cover, and blend or process till mixture is smooth.

3. Line 4 salad plates with lettuce leaves. Arrange remaining pepper strips and onions on lettuce. Sprinkle salads with chives. Drizzle some of the dressing over salad. Serve with remaining dressing. Makes 4 side-dish servings.

Nutritional facts per serving: 81 calories, 4 g total fat (1 g saturated fat), 0 mg cholesterol, 5 mg sodium, 12 g carbohydrate, 3 g fiber, 2 g protein. **Daily values:** 10% vitamin A, 184% vitamin C, 1% calcium, 5% iron.

Low-fat

Low-calorie

High-fiber

Southwestern Three-Bean Salad

The simple step of rinsing the canned beans removes some of the excess sodium.

1 16-ounce can black beans
1 8-ounce can garbanzo beans
1 9-ounce package frozen cut
   green beans
1 cup loose-pack frozen whole
   kernel corn
1½ cups chopped carrots
1 medium red onion, thinly
   sliced
½ cup red wine vinegar
3 tablespoons orange juice
1 tablespoon snipped cilantro or
   parsley
1 clove garlic, minced
¼ teaspoon ground turmeric

1. Rinse the black beans and the garbanzo beans under cold running water; drain well. In a medium saucepan cook green beans and corn in a small amount of boiling water for 5 minutes or till crisp-tender. Drain. Rinse with cold water; drain again.

2. In a large bowl combine black beans, garbanzo beans, green beans, corn, carrots, and red onion.

3. For dressing, in a screw-top jar combine vinegar, orange juice, cilantro or parsley, garlic, and turmeric. Cover and shake well. Pour dressing over bean mixture; toss to coat. Cover and chill for 2 to 24 hours, stirring occasionally. Serve on lettuce-lined plates, if desired. Makes 8 side-dish servings.

Nutritional facts per serving: 101 calories, 1 g total fat (0 g saturated fat), 0 mg cholesterol, 243 mg sodium, 21 g carbohydrate, 5 g fiber, 6 g protein. **Daily values:** 61% vitamin A, 15% vitamin C, 4% calcium, 11% iron.

CAESAR-STYLE SALAD

Low-calorie

Traditionally, this classic salad contains more than 30 grams of fat per serving! We trimmed our version to just 6 grams.

Nonstick spray coating
3 slices Italian bread, cut into
    1-inch cubes
2 tablespoons bottled fat-free
    Italian salad dressing
2 tablespoons dry white wine
4 teaspoons lemon juice
2 tablespoons grated Parmesan
    cheese
1 tablespoon olive or salad oil
1½ teaspoons anchovy paste
1 teaspoon Worcestershire
    sauce
¼ teaspoon pepper
5 cups torn romaine lettuce
    Anchovy fillets (optional)

1. Spray a shallow baking pan with nonstick coating. Arrange bread cubes in the pan. Drizzle with Italian dressing. Bake in a 375° oven for 10 to 15 minutes or till lightly toasted, stirring several times.

2. For dressing, in a small mixing bowl stir together wine, lemon juice, cheese, oil, anchovy paste, Worcestershire, and pepper. In a large bowl combine romaine, croutons, and dressing. Toss gently to coat. Serve immediately. Garnish with anchovy fillets, if desired. Makes 4 side-dish servings.

Nutritional facts per serving: 136 calories, 6 g total fat (1 g saturated fat), 5 mg cholesterol, 388 mg sodium, 14 g carbohydrate, 1 g fiber, 5 g protein. **Daily values:** 19% vitamin A, 35% vitamin C, 7% calcium, 11% iron.

Chicken Caesar-Style Salad: Prepare as directed above, *except* add 1½ cups bite-size strips cooked *chicken* to the romaine mixture. Makes 4 main-dish servings.

Nutritional facts per serving: 235 calories, 10 g total fat (2 g saturated fat), 52 mg cholesterol, 433 mg sodium, 14 g carbohydrate, 1 g fiber, 21 g protein. **Daily values:** 19% vitamin A, 35% vitamin C, 8% calcium, 15% iron.

Low-fat

Low-calorie

Low-sodium

YUCATAN JICAMA-MANGO SALAD

Pack this tasty salad in a plastic container to enjoy with a brown-bag lunch.

1½ cups chopped peeled jicama
1 ripe mango, pitted, peeled,
    and chopped
1 cup chopped zucchini or
    yellow summer squash
¼ cup sliced green onions
2 tablespoons white wine
    vinegar
1 tablespoon snipped cilantro or
    parsley
⅛ to ¼ teaspoon crushed red
    pepper
    Lettuce leaves

1. In a medium bowl combine jicama, mango, zucchini or yellow squash, green onions, vinegar, cilantro or parsley, and pepper. Toss gently to coat.

2. Cover and chill for 2 to 24 hours before serving to blend flavors. Serve on lettuce leaves. Makes 6 side-dish servings.

Nutritional facts per serving: 46 calories, 0 g total fat (0 g saturated fat), 0 mg cholesterol, 4 mg sodium, 11 g carbohydrate, 1 g fiber, 1 g protein. **Daily values:** 15% vitamin A, 34% vitamin C, 1% calcium, 4% iron.

Low-calorie
Low-sodium

SPINACH AND MUSHROOM SALAD WITH CHIPOTLE VINAIGRETTE

A chipotle pepper is a smoked, dried jalapeño. Look for them in Mexican grocery stores or other specialty stores.

½ to 1 dried chipotle chili
    pepper or 1 canned whole
    chili pepper, seeded and
    finely chopped
½ cup low-sodium tomato juice
2 tablespoons snipped cilantro
    or parsley
1 tablespoon salad oil
1 teaspoon sugar
1 clove garlic, minced
¼ teaspoon salt-free seasoning
    blend
5 cups shredded spinach
2 cups sliced fresh mushrooms
⅔ cup sliced red onion

1. If using dried chili pepper, cover with boiling water. Let soak for 20 minutes or till softened. Remove stems and seeds from pepper; chop finely.

2. For dressing, in a blender container or food processor bowl place the chili pepper, tomato juice, cilantro or parsley, oil, sugar, garlic, and seasoning blend. Cover, and blend or process till mixture is nearly smooth. Set aside.

3. In a large bowl combine spinach, mushrooms, and onion. Add dressing. Toss gently to coat. Serve immediately. Makes 5 side-dish servings.

Nutritional facts per serving: 62 calories, 3 g total fat (0 g saturated fat), 0 mg cholesterol, 49 mg sodium, 8 g carbohydrate, 3 g fiber, 3 g protein. **Daily values:** 39% vitamin A, 53% vitamin C, 5% calcium, 14% iron.

Low-fat
Low-calorie

SWEET PEPPER SLAW

For a fun salad bowl, spoon this colorful slaw into hollowed bell pepper halves.

2 cups shredded red or green
    cabbage
3 red, green, and/or yellow
    sweet peppers, julienned
½ cup sliced radishes
⅓ cup buttermilk
3 tablespoons fat-free
    mayonnaise dressing or
    salad dressing
1 tablespoon cider vinegar
½ teaspoon salt-free seasoning
    blend
¼ teaspoon sugar
¼ teaspoon celery seed

1. In a large bowl combine cabbage, sweet peppers, and radishes.

2. For dressing, in a small mixing bowl combine buttermilk, mayonnaise dressing, vinegar, seasoning blend, sugar, and celery seed. Using a wire whisk, mix till smooth. Pour over salad and toss to coat. Serve, or cover and chill for up to 24 hours before serving. Makes 5 side-dish servings.

Nutritional facts per serving: 46 calories, 0 g total fat (0 g saturated fat), 1 mg cholesterol, 140 mg sodium, 10 g carbohydrate, 2 g fiber, 2 g protein. **Daily values:** 20% vitamin A, 201% vitamin C, 3% calcium, 3% iron.

Low-fat

Low-calorie

Low-sodium

RASPBERRY YOGURT SALAD MOLD

This dazzling salad (see photo, left) doubles as a dessert when garnished with whipped topping and raspberries.

1 3-ounce package sugar-free raspberry- or strawberry-flavored gelatin

1 cup boiling water

1 6-ounce carton raspberry or strawberry fat-free yogurt

¼ cup orange juice

Nonstick spray coating

1 cup raspberries or sliced strawberries

Raspberries or strawberries (optional)

Fresh mint sprigs (optional)

1. In a medium bowl dissolve gelatin in boiling water. Stir in yogurt and orange juice with a wire whisk. Cover and chill for 1½ hours or till slightly thickened (consistency of unbeaten egg white).

2. Spray a 3-cup mold with nonstick coating. Fold 1 cup raspberries or strawberries into gelatin mixture and pour into mold. Cover and chill several hours or till firm. Unmold onto a serving plate. Garnish with raspberries or strawberries and mint sprigs, if desired. Makes 6 side-dish servings.

Nutritional facts per serving: 49 calories, 0 g total fat (0 g saturated fat), 1 mg cholesterol, 72 mg sodium, 9 g carbohydrate, 1 g fiber, 2 g protein. **Daily values:** 1% vitamin A, 39% vitamin C, 4% calcium, 1% iron.

Low-calorie

High-fiber

FLORIDA AVOCADO SALAD

Add color to winter menus with this conversation-piece salad.

2 tablespoons fat-free
   mayonnaise dressing or
   salad dressing
2 tablespoons plain fat-free
   yogurt
1 teaspoon finely shredded
   orange or grapefruit peel
3 tablespoons orange or
   grapefruit juice
2 teaspoons snipped fresh mint
   or ¼ teaspoon dried mint,
   crushed
   Lettuce leaves
3 seedless oranges, peeled and
   sectioned
2 large pink or white grapefruit,
   peeled and sectioned
½ of an avocado, peeled, pitted
   and thinly sliced

1. For dressing, in a small bowl stir together mayonnaise dressing, yogurt, orange or grapefruit peel, orange or grapefruit juice, and mint.

2. Line 4 salad plates with lettuce leaves. Arrange orange sections, grapefruit sections, and avocado slices on the lettuce. Spoon the dressing over the salads. Makes 4 side-dish servings.

Nutritional facts per serving: 111 calories, 4 g total fat (0 g saturated fat), 0 mg cholesterol, 103 mg sodium, 18 g carbohydrate, 6 g fiber, 2 g protein. **Daily values:** 6% vitamin A, 132% vitamin C, 5% calcium, 3% iron.

Section the oranges and grapefruit, working over a bowl to catch the juices. Cut between one fruit section and the membrane. Cut to the center of the fruit. Turn the knife and slide it up the other side of the section next to the membrane. Repeat with remaining sections. Remove any seeds from the fruit sections.

Low-fat

Low-calorie

Low-sodium

DILLED CARROT AND CUCUMBER SALAD

This colorful cucumber salad is a tasty, low-fat version of cucumbers in sour cream dressing.

1 medium cucumber, cut in half
    lengthwise and sliced
1½ cups shredded carrots
½ teaspoon salt-free seasoning
    blend
½ cup plain fat-free yogurt
2 tablespoons white wine
    vinegar
1 tablespoon snipped fresh dill
    or ½ teaspoon dried
    dillweed
1 radish, thinly sliced (optional)
    Fresh dill sprigs (optional)

1. In a medium bowl combine cucumber and carrot. Sprinkle with salt-free seasoning blend.

2. For dressing, in a small bowl stir together yogurt, vinegar, and dill. Add to cucumber mixture and toss gently to coat. Cover and chill at least 1 hour before serving. Garnish with radish slices and fresh dill sprigs, if desired. Makes 4 side-dish servings.

Nutritional facts per serving: 44 calories, 0 g total fat (0 g saturated fat), 1 mg cholesterol, 38 mg sodium, 9 g carbohydrate, 1 g fiber, 3 g protein. **Daily values:** 117% vitamin A, 13% vitamin C, 6% calcium, 3% iron.

NEW-STYLE WALDORF SALAD

Low-calorie

For a kid-pleasing snack, spread this creamy apple salad over low-fat crackers.

1 cup chopped celery or peeled
    jicama
1 cup chopped apples or
    ripe pears
⅔ cup halved red or green
    seedless grapes
3 tablespoons fat-free
    mayonnaise dressing or
    salad dressing
1 teaspoon lemon juice
¼ teaspoon ground cinnamon
    Dash ground nutmeg
2 cups shredded lettuce
2 tablespoons chopped pecans
    or walnuts

1. In a medium bowl toss together celery or jicama, apples or pears, and grapes.

2. For dressing, in a small bowl stir together mayonnaise dressing, lemon juice, cinnamon, and nutmeg till blended. Add to apple mixture. Toss gently to coat. Cover and chill up to 2 hours. Serve salad on lettuce-lined plate. Sprinkle with nuts. Makes 4 side-dish servings.

Nutritional facts per serving: 77 calories, 3 g total fat (0 g saturated fat), 0 mg cholesterol, 172 mg sodium, 14 g carbohydrate, 2 g fiber, 1 g protein. **Daily values:** 6% vitamin A, 20% vitamin C, 3% calcium, 5% iron.

Low-fat
Low-calorie

NEW POTATO-GREEN BEAN SALAD

This salad is a wonderful choice for potlucks and summertime picnics and parties. (See photo, left.)

2 pounds whole tiny new
    potatoes, halved or
    quartered, or 6 medium
    red potatoes, cubed
1 9-ounce package frozen
    French-style green beans
    or cut green beans, cooked
    and drained
    Shredded lettuce
4 plum tomatoes, cut into
    wedges
    Yogurt-French Dressing

1. In a large saucepan cook potatoes, covered, in boiling water for 15 to 20 minutes or till just tender. Drain; cool 20 minutes. Cover and chill potatoes and beans for 2 to 24 hours.

2. To serve, line a platter with lettuce. Arrange potatoes, green beans, and tomato wedges on lettuce. Drizzle Yogurt-French Dressing over salad and serve immediately. Makes 6 side-dish servings.

Yogurt-French Dressing: Stir together ¼ cup bottled *fat-free French salad dressing;* 3 tablespoons *plain fat-free yogurt;* 1 tablespoon *fat-free mayonnaise dressing or salad dressing;* and 1 *green onion,* sliced.

Nutritional facts per serving: 110 calories, 1 g total fat (0 g saturated fat), 1 mg cholesterol, 134 mg sodium, 24 g carbohydrate, 2 g fiber, 3 g protein. **Daily values:** 4% vitamin A, 30% vitamin C, 3% calcium, 11% iron.

Low-caloric
Low-sodium
High-fiber

BROILED SUMMER SQUASH SALAD

Fresh basil and rosemary emphasize the garden-fresh taste of the sweet pepper dressing.

½ cup chopped red or yellow
    sweet pepper
¼ cup red wine vinegar
1 tablespoon snipped fresh basil
1 tablespoon snipped fresh
    rosemary
2 cloves garlic, minced
1 tablespoon olive or salad oil
2 medium zucchini
2 medium yellow summer
    squash
    Lettuce leaves
1 medium tomato, cut into thin
    wedges
2 teaspoons sugar

1. In a blender container or food processor bowl combine the sweet pepper, vinegar, basil, rosemary, garlic, oil, 2 tablespoons *water,* and ¼ teaspoon *pepper.* Cover, and blend or process till almost smooth. Set aside.

2. Spray the unheated rack of a broiler pan with *nonstick spray coating.* Cut the zucchini and yellow squash lengthwise into ¼-inch slices; place on broiler rack. Brush with some of the sweet pepper mixture. Broil 3 inches from heat for 4 to 5 minutes or till just slightly charred. Turn and brush with more of the sweet pepper mixture. Broil for 3 to 5 minutes more or till just slightly charred.

2. Line 4 salad plates with lettuce leaves. Arrange zucchini and yellow squash on lettuce. Top with tomato wedges. Stir sugar into sweet pepper mixture; drizzle over salads. Makes 4 side-dish servings.

Nutritional facts per serving: 140 calories, 5 g total fat (1 g saturated fat), 0 mg cholesterol, 54 mg sodium, 22 g carbohydrate, 8 g fiber, 7 g protein. **Daily values:** 32% vitamin A, 93% vitamin C, 11% calcium, 23% iron.

Low-fat

Low-calorie

High-fiber

ARTICHOKE, ASPARAGUS, AND HEARTS OF PALM SALAD

Hearts of palm are the cream-colored interior of a young palm tree and look like fat stalks of white asparagus.
They have a silken texture and a delicate flavor that will remind you of artichokes.

12 asparagus spears, trimmed
½ of a 10-ounce package frozen
    artichoke hearts, thawed
1 14-ounce can hearts of palm,
    drained
    Lettuce leaves
8 thin tomato slices
¼ cup light dairy sour cream
2 tablespoons fat-free
    mayonnaise dressing or
    salad dressing
1 2-ounce jar diced pimiento,
    drained
1 tablespoon dry sherry
1 tablespoon skim milk
⅛ teaspoon pepper

1. In a saucepan cook asparagus spears and artichoke hearts, covered, in a small amount of boiling water for 3 minutes or till crisp-tender. Drain. Rinse with cold water. Drain and set aside.

2. Cut any large hearts of palm in half lengthwise. Line 4 salad plates with lettuce leaves. On each plate arrange tomato slices, hearts of palm, artichoke hearts, and 3 asparagus spears.

3. For dressing, stir together sour cream, mayonnaise dressing, pimiento, sherry, milk, and pepper. Drizzle dressing over salads. Makes 4 side-dish servings.

Nutritional facts per serving: 86 calories, 2 g total fat (1 g saturated fat), 2 mg cholesterol, 169 mg sodium, 15 g carbohydrate, 5 g fiber, 5 g protein. **Daily values:** 11% vitamin A, 59% vitamin C, 5% calcium, 9% iron.

Low-fat

Low-calorie

Low-sodium

FRUIT SALAD WITH CREAM DRESSING

This rich ambrosia salad is a healthy version made with fat-free yogurt and light sour cream.

    Lettuce leaves
1 cup sliced apricots,
    nectarines, or peaches
1 cup sliced plums or pears
1 banana, sliced
½ cup vanilla fat-free yogurt
2 tablespoons light dairy sour
    cream
1 tablespoon toasted coconut or
    chopped toasted pecans

1. Arrange lettuce leaves on a salad platter. Arrange apricots, nectarines, or peaches, plums or pears, and bananas on lettuce.

2. For dressing, in a small bowl stir together yogurt, sour cream, and coconut or pecans. Drizzle over salad. Makes 4 side-dish servings.

Nutritional facts per serving: 119 calories, 2 g total fat (1 g saturated fat), 2 mg cholesterol, 28 mg sodium, 25 g carbohydrate, 2 g fiber, 3 g protein. **Daily values:** 11% vitamin A, 22% vitamin C, 5% calcium, 2% iron.

Low-fat

Low-calorie

Low-sodium

High-fiber

BARLEY-VEGETABLE MARINATED SALAD

Barley cooks quickly and adds a chewy texture and nutty flavor to this vegetable salad.

1¼ cups water

½ cup quick-cooking barley

1 cup broccoli or cauliflower flowerets

1 cup fresh pea pods, stringed and halved crosswise or one 6-ounce package frozen pea pods, thawed and halved

½ cup seeded, chopped cucumber

1 medium red sweet pepper, julienned

¼ cup sliced green onions

2 tablespoons lime or lemon juice

2 tablespoons white wine vinegar

2 tablespoons water

1 tablespoon olive or salad oil

2 teaspoons sugar

1 teaspoon dried thyme, crushed

2 cloves garlic, minced

¼ teaspoon crushed red pepper

¼ teaspoon pepper

1. In a medium saucepan bring 1¼ cups water to boiling; stir in barley. Reduce heat. Cover and simmer for 5 minutes. Stir in broccoli or cauliflower; cover and cook 5 minutes more. Add fresh pea pods (if using). Cover and cook 1 minute more or till barley is tender. Rinse mixture with cold water; drain well.

2. In a shallow glass dish combine barley mixture with thawed pea pods (if using), cucumber, sweet pepper, and onions. For dressing, in a screw-top jar combine lime or lemon juice, vinegar, 2 tablespoons water, oil, sugar, thyme, garlic, red pepper, and pepper. Cover and shake well. Pour over salad. Toss gently to mix. Cover and chill for 2 to 6 hours, stirring occasionally. Makes 8 side-dish servings.

Nutritional facts per serving: 84 calories, 2 g total fat (0 g saturated fat), 0 mg cholesterol, 12 mg sodium, 15 g carbohydrate, 14 g fiber, 3 g protein. **Daily values:** 6% vitamin A, 72% vitamin C, 2% calcium, 6% iron.

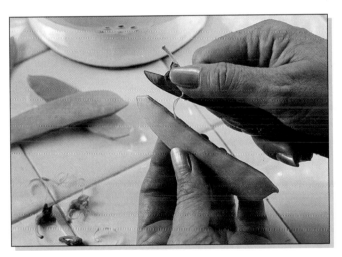

To remove strings from pea pods, use a knife or your fingers to pull off the tip of the pea pod without breaking the string. Then pull the string down the entire length of the pod and discard the string.

Low-fat
Low-calorie
Low-sodium
High-fiber

FRUIT SALAD PLATTER WITH STRAWBERRY VINAIGRETTE

This salad (see photo, right) can become the main course by adding rolled-up thin slices of smoked turkey or chicken.

Kale or lettuce leaves
2 cups sliced strawberries and/or whole raspberries
2 kiwi fruit, peeled and thinly sliced
1 orange, peeled and sectioned
2 bananas, sliced
1 medium peach, plum, or nectarine, sliced
1 small apple or pear, cored and sliced
2 tablespoons raspberry or red wine vinegar
2 tablespoons water
2 teaspoons sugar

1. Line a large serving platter with kale or lettuce leaves. Arrange half of the strawberries and/or raspberries, the kiwi fruit, orange sections, bananas, peach, plum, or nectarine slices, and apple or pear slices decoratively over kale or lettuce.

2. For dressing, in blender container or food processor bowl place remaining strawberries and/or raspberries, vinegar, water, and sugar. Cover, and blend or process till smooth. Drizzle a little of the dressing over salad. Serve with remaining dressing. Makes 6 side-dish servings.

Nutritional facts per serving: 120 calories, 1 g total fat (0 g saturated fat), 0 mg cholesterol, 3 mg sodium, 28 g carbohydrate, 4 g fiber, 2 g protein. **Daily values:** 3% vitamin A, 124% vitamin C, 2% calcium, 4% iron.

A Variety of Vinegars

Gone are the days when distilled and cider vinegar were your only vinegar choices. Here's a rundown of old and new vinegar varieties to splash in your next recipe.

Distilled vinegar, also called white vinegar, is made from grains such as corn, rye, and barley. Its somewhat harsh flavor lends itself best to pickling.

Malt vinegar is made from ale and fermented potatoes or grain, giving it a brownish color and yeasty flavor. It's best known for splashing on English fish and chips, but can be used in recipes calling for cider vinegar.

Wine vinegars are made from wine, sherry, or champagne, and are the mildest and most versatile of all vinegars. Use them in salad dressings or sprinkled over fish.

Rice wine vinegar starts with sake (Japanese rice wine) and has a clean, mild taste. The slightly sweet taste complements salads as well as Japanese rice dishes.

Fruit and herb vinegars are made from either cider, distilled, or wine vinegars, and flavored with natural flavors of fruits and herbs. Try them in marinades or salad dressings.

Balsamic vinegar is made from the unfermented juice of high sugar grapes and aged in wooden barrels. The finished vinegar must be at least 6 years old, resulting in an intense, dark brown vinegar that is both sour and sweet. It makes an outstanding vinegar for salad dressing.

Low-fat

Low-calorie

Low-sodium

CARROT-APPLE SLAW

Chopped apple sweetens this creamy coleslaw.

2 cups shredded carrots
1 cup finely chopped apple
1 cup shredded red or green
    cabbage
2 tablespoons raisins
¼ cup plain low-fat yogurt
2 tablespoons light dairy sour
    cream
½ teaspoon finely shredded
    lemon or orange peel
2 tablespoons toasted, sliced
    almonds

1. In a medium bowl combine carrots, apples, cabbage, and raisins. Add yogurt, sour cream, and lemon or orange peel. Toss gently to coat.

2. Cover and chill for 1 to 24 hours. (If salad becomes too dry, stir in a little skim milk.) Stir in almonds. If desired, serve in a cabbage- or lettuce-lined bowl. Makes 6 side-dish servings.

Nutritional facts per serving: 76 calories, 2 g total fat (0 g saturated fat), 1 mg cholesterol, 50 mg sodium, 14 g carbohydrate, 3 g fiber, 2 g protein. **Daily values:** 115% vitamin A, 27% vitamin C, 5% calcium, 4% iron.

Low-calorie

High-fiber

BULGUR-SPINACH SALAD WITH CORN AND FETA

Feta cheese is soft, white and crumbly with a sharp, salty flavor that adds pizzazz to this high-fiber salad.

½ cup bulgur wheat
3 cups torn spinach
1 cup julienned carrot or
    zucchini
1 medium tomato, cut into thin
    wedges
⅔ cup loose-pack frozen whole
    kernel corn, thawed
⅓ cup sliced green onions
2 tablespoons lemon juice
2 tablespoons red wine vinegar
1 tablespoon olive or salad oil
¼ teaspoon paprika
½ cup crumbled feta cheese

1. In a medium saucepan combine bulgur and 1 cup *water.* Bring to boiling; reduce heat. Cover and simmer for 12 to 15 minutes or till nearly all water is absorbed and bulgur is tender. Drain off any excess liquid; cool 10 minutes.

2. In a large bowl toss together spinach, bulgur, carrot or zucchini, tomato, corn, and green onions.

3. For dressing, in a screw-top jar combine lemon juice, vinegar, oil, paprika, 2 tablespoons *water,* and ⅛ teaspoon *pepper.* Cover and shake well. Pour over salad. Toss gently to coat. Sprinkle with cheese. Makes 6 side-dish servings.

Nutritional facts per serving: 123 calories, 5 g total fat (2 g saturated fat), 8 mg cholesterol, 142 mg sodium, 18 g carbohydrate, 5 g fiber, 5 g protein. **Daily values:** 91% vitamin A, 30% vitamin C, 7% calcium, 10% iron.

Low-fat

Low-calorie

Low-sodium

High-fiber

MANGO AND PAPAYA SALAD WITH ORANGE DRESSING

Brighten a blustery winter day with this tropical fruit salad.

Romaine leaves

2 ripe mangoes, pitted, peeled, and cubed or thinly sliced

1 papaya, peeled, seeded, and thinly sliced

1 cup sliced strawberries, or whole raspberries or blueberries

1 tablespoon snipped fresh mint or 1 teaspoon dried mint, crushed

¼ cup light dairy sour cream

2 tablespoons frozen orange juice concentrate, thawed

2 teaspoons sugar

Fresh mint leaves (optional)

1. Line a serving platter with romaine leaves. Arrange mangoes, papaya, and strawberries, raspberries or blueberries decoratively over lettuce. Sprinkle with chopped mint. (If desired, cover and chill for 1 to 2 hours.)

2. For dressing, in a small bowl stir together sour cream, orange juice concentrate, and sugar. Drizzle dressing over salad. Garnish with additional fresh mint, if desired. Makes 6 side-dish servings.

Nutritional facts per serving: 123 calories, 1 g total fat (0 g saturated fat), 1 mg cholesterol, 20 mg sodium, 28 g carbohydrate, 4 g fiber, 2 g protein. **Daily values:** 35% vitamin A, 167% vitamin C, 4% calcium, 4% iron.

To pit, peel and cube a mango, cut through the mango, sliding a sharp knife next to the seed along one side. Repeat on the other side of the seed to get two large pieces. In each piece, make crosshatch cuts through the meat just to the peel. Bend the peel back and carefully slide the knife between the peel and meat to separate.

Low-sodium

LIGHT CHINESE CHICKEN SALAD

Uncooked ramen noodles add a crunchy note to this flavor-packed salad. (See photo, left.)

¼ cup water

3 tablespoons rice wine vinegar
   or white wine vinegar

1 tablespoon sesame tahini

1 tablespoon reduced-sodium
   soy sauce

2 teaspoons sugar

2 teaspoons finely chopped beni
   shoga (pickled ginger),
   drained, or 1 teaspoon
   grated gingerroot

1 clove garlic, minced

⅛ teaspoon pepper

4 cups shredded Chinese (napa)
   cabbage or lettuce

2 cups shredded cooked
   chicken or turkey

1 cup carrots cut in julienne
   strips

1 cup pea pods, halved
   lengthwise

1 cup seeded cucumber cut in
   julienne strips

1 cup red sweet pepper cut in
   julienne strips

½ cup sliced green onions

1 3-ounce package low-fat
   ramen noodles

1. For dressing, in blender container or food processor bowl combine water, vinegar, tahini, soy sauce, sugar, beni shoga or gingerroot, garlic, and pepper. Cover, and blend or process till smooth. Set aside.

2. In a large salad bowl toss together cabbage or lettuce, chicken or turkey, carrots, pea pods, cucumber, pepper, and onions. Remove seasoning mix from ramen noodle package; save for another use. With hands, break noodles over salad. Pour dressing over salad and toss gently to mix. Serve immediately. Makes 4 main-dish servings.

Nutritional facts per serving: 329 calories, 12 g total fat (3 g saturated fat), 76 mg cholesterol, 220 mg sodium, 28 g carbohydrate, 3 g fiber, 28 g protein. **Daily values:** 139% vitamin A, 177% vitamin C, 9% calcium, 26% iron.

Caring for Salad Greens

In order for salad greens to be their freshest when you bring your salad to the table, follow a few easy steps once you get them home from the store.

To clean leafy greens: Remove and discard any outer leaves that are bruised, discolored, tough, or wilted. Wash the remaining leaves under cold water. Drain thoroughly and place on paper towels or a clean kitchen towel. Place a second towel over them and gently pat dry. Or, dry them in a salad spinner.

To clean iceberg lettuce: Remove and discard any outer leaves that are bruised, discolored, tough, or wilted.

Remove the core by hitting the stem end sharply on a countertop. Then twist the core and lift it out. Place the head of lettuce, core side up, under cold running water to rinse the leaves. Invert the head and let it drain thoroughly.

To store greens: Place the clean and dry greens in a plastic bag or airtight container, and store them in the refrigerator. They should stay crisp and fresh for three or four days.

To crisp greens that are limp: Wash greens and place them in a plastic bag while they're still slightly damp. Refrigerate for at least 8 hours.

Low-calorie

Low-sodium

BISTRO-STYLE CHICKEN SALAD

Toss strips of chicken with leafy greens and an easy vinaigrette to create this exquisite yet simple salad.

   3 cups torn spinach or romaine
      leaves
1 ½ cups cooked chicken cut in
      bite-size strips
   1 cup torn radicchio or red leaf
      lettuce
1 ½ cups chopped tomatoes
   2 shallots, halved and thinly
      sliced
   ⅓ cup white wine vinegar
   2 tablespoons water
   2 teaspoons olive or salad oil
   1 teaspoon sugar
   ½ teaspoon dried Italian
      seasoning, crushed
   ¼ teaspoon pepper
      Spinach or romaine leaves

1. In a large bowl toss together spinach or romaine, chicken, radicchio or leaf lettuce, tomatoes, and shallots.

2. For dressing, in a screw-top jar combine vinegar, water, oil, sugar, Italian seasoning, and pepper. Cover and shake well. Add dressing to salad; toss gently to mix. Serve on 4 spinach- or romaine-lined plates. Makes 4 main-dish servings.

Nutritional facts per serving: 229 calories, 13 g total fat (4 g saturated fat), 56 mg cholesterol, 176 mg sodium, 8 g carbohydrate, 2 g fiber, 21 g protein. **Daily values:** 51% vitamin A, 48% vitamin C, 7% calcium, 18% iron.

Ravishing Radicchio

Radicchio (raa DICK ee oh) is an Italian red chicory that's used as a salad green. The brilliant ruby-red leaves with thick white veins come from small, round, compact heads. Eaten alone, the fresh leaves are quite bitter and peppery tasting, but when mixed with other salad greens, radicchio adds a nice flavor and color accent to salads. To prepare radicchio, cut out and discard the white core. Separate the leaves; rinse and dry well. Tear into bite-size pieces and use fresh in salads.

Low-calorie
Low-sodium

Spicy Thai Beef Salad

The Spicy Thai Dressing also tastes great when brushed over grilled steaks, fish, and poultry.

Nonstick spray coating
8 ounces beef top sirloin steak,
    1 inch thick
Spicy Thai Dressing
5 cups shredded Chinese (napa)
    cabbage
1 cup seeded, julienned
    cucumber
1 cup sugar snap peas or pea
    pods, stringed and slivered
1 yellow, red, or green sweet
    pepper, cut into ½-inch
    squares
½ cup fresh bean sprouts

1. Spray the unheated rack of a broiler pan with nonstick coating. Place steak on broiler pan. Brush meat lightly with *1 tablespoon* of the Spicy Thai Dressing. Broil steak 4 to 5 inches from the heat for 13 to 17 minutes for medium, turning once and brushing second side with an additional *1 tablespoon* of the Spicy Thai Dressing. Slice meat into thin bite-size strips.

2. Toss together steak, cabbage, cucumber, peas, sweet pepper, and bean sprouts. Add remaining Spicy Thai Dressing; toss gently to mix. Makes 4 main-dish servings.

Spicy Thai Dressing: In a blender container or food processor bowl combine ¼ cup *red wine vinegar*; 3 tablespoons *lime or lemon juice*; ¼ cup sliced *green onions*; 1 *serrano or jalapeño pepper*, seeded and chopped; 2 tablespoons *water*; 1 tablespoon grated *gingerroot*; 1 tablespoon *brown sugar*; 1 tablespoon *fish sauce*; 1 tablespoon *salad oil*; and ¼ to ½ teaspoon *crushed red pepper*. Cover, and blend or process till mixture is pureed.

Nutritional facts per serving: 220 calories, 9 g total fat (3 g saturated fat), 39 mg cholesterol, 191 mg sodium, 19 g carbohydrate, 3 g fiber, 17 g protein. **Daily values:** 5% vitamin A, 192% vitamin C, 11% calcium, 3% iron.

Low-fat
Low-calorie
Low-sodium

Shrimp 'n' Shells Salad

This dressed-up macaroni salad features orange sections and shallots, in addition to shrimp.

4 ounces medium shell
    macaroni, small bow ties,
    or elbow macaroni, cooked
    and drained
12 ounces medium shrimp,
    cooked, shelled, and
    deveined
1 cup julienned red, yellow, or
    green sweet pepper
1 11-ounce can mandarin
    orange sections, drained
2 shallots, sliced, or ¼ cup
    sliced red onion
Easy Yogurt Dressing

1. In a mixing medium bowl toss together macaroni, shrimp, sweet pepper, orange sections, and shallots or onion.

2. Add Easy Yogurt Dressing to macaroni mixture; toss well to coat. Cover; chill 2 to 24 hours. If desired, serve on lettuce-lined plates. Makes 4 main-dish servings.

Easy Yogurt Dressing: In a small mixing bowl stir together 2 tablespoons *fat-free mayonnaise dressing* or *salad dressing*, 2 tablespoons *plain fat-free yogurt*, 2 tablespoons *orange or lemon juice*, ¼ teaspoon *crushed red pepper*, and ¼ teaspoon *dry mustard*.

Nutritional facts per serving: 226 calories, 1 g total fat (0 g saturated fat), 109 mg cholesterol, 235 mg sodium, 37 g carbohydrate, 1 g fiber, 17 g protein. **Daily values:** 35% vitamin A, 72% vitamin C, 4% calcium, 20% iron.

Low-fat

Low-calorie

Low-sodium

BROILED PINEAPPLE CHICKEN SALAD

Choose a fresh pineapple that is slightly soft to the touch, with a sweet aroma and deep green leaves for this recipe. (See photo, left.)

4 skinless, boneless chicken
    breasts or turkey breast
    tenderloin steaks (about
    1 pound)
  Nonstick spray coating
¼ of a medium pineapple,
    cored, and cut into wedges
6 cups shredded lettuce
1 cup peeled jicama cut into
    bite-size pieces
1 cup coarsely shredded carrot
1 6-ounce carton tropical or
    pineapple-flavored fat-free
    yogurt
2 tablespoons pineapple or
    orange juice
½ teaspoon curry powder
  Dash pepper

1. Rinse chicken; pat dry. Spray the unheated rack of a broiler pan with nonstick coating. Arrange chicken or turkey pieces on rack. Broil 4 to 5 inches from the heat for 6 minutes. Turn chicken or turkey. Add pineapple wedges to broiler pan. Broil 6 to 9 minutes more or till chicken or turkey is no longer pink in the center, turning pineapple once during broiling time.

2. Line 4 salad plates with lettuce. Cut chicken or turkey into bite-size strips. Arrange chicken or turkey and pineapple on each plate. Sprinkle with jicama and carrot.

3. For dressing, stir together yogurt, pineapple or orange juice, curry powder, and pepper. Drizzle over salads. Makes 4 main-dish servings.

Nutritional facts per serving: 221 calories, 4 g total fat (1 g saturated fat), 61 mg cholesterol, 95 mg sodium, 21 g carbohydrate, 2 g fiber, 25 g protein. **Daily values:** 80% vitamin A, 31% vitamin C, 8% calcium, 12% iron.

Oil-Free Dressing

Here's a fat-free salad dressing with only 7 calories per tablespoon. Fresher in taste than bottled dressing, it pairs well with most any salad.

  In a mixing bowl combine 1 tablespoon *powdered fruit pectin;* ¾ teaspoon snipped fresh or ¼ teaspoon dried *oregano, basil, thyme, tarragon, savory,* or *dillweed,* crushed; ½ teaspoon *sugar;* ⅛ teaspoon *dry mustard;* and ⅛ teaspoon *pepper.* Stir in ¼ cup *water;* 1 tablespoon *vinegar;* and 1 small clove *garlic,* minced. Cover and store in the refrigerator up to 3 days.

Low-fat

Low-calorie

Low-sodium

ELEGANT SEAFOOD SALAD

For an appetizer buffet, serve the Seafood Dressing as a dipping sauce for cooked shrimp.

6 cups torn lettuce

12 ounces medium shrimp,
   cooked, shelled, and
   deveined

8 ounces scallops, cooked and
   drained or one 6-ounce
   package frozen crabmeat,
   thawed and flaked

16 asparagus spears, cooked
   and drained

⅔ cup chopped red or green
   sweet pepper

1 medium tomato, chopped
   Seafood Dressing

1. Line 4 salad plates with lettuce.

2. Arrange ¼ of the shrimp, scallops, and asparagus spears on each plate. Sprinkle sweet pepper and tomato over salads. Serve dressing with salads. Makes 4 main-dish servings.

Seafood Dressing: In a small mixing bowl stir together one 8-ounce carton *plain fat-free yogurt*, 2 tablespoons *low-sodium chili sauce*, 1 tablespoon *pickle relish*, 1 teaspoon *vinegar*, and 1 teaspoon *prepared mustard*.

Nutritional facts per serving: 170 calories, 2 g total fat (0 g saturated fat), 149 mg cholesterol, 359 mg sodium, 12 g carbohydrate, 2 g fiber, 27 g protein. **Daily values:** 24% vitamin A, 77% vitamin C, 17% calcium, 26% iron.

Low-fat

Low-calorie

Low-sodium

CURRIED CHICKEN AND MELON SALAD

This refreshing salad tastes even better on a hot summer day with a tall glass of iced tea.

4 cups torn romaine or leaf
   lettuce

2 cups cooked chicken cut in
   bite-size strips

1½ cups cubed cantaloupe

1½ cups cubed watermelon or
   honeydew

2 tablespoons raisins

⅓ cup fat-free mayonnaise
   dressing or salad dressing

2 tablespoons mango chutney,
   chopped

1½ to 2 teaspoons curry powder

1 tablespoon snipped chives

1. Line 4 salad plates with romaine or leaf lettuce. In a large bowl toss together chicken, melon cubes, and raisins.

2. For dressing, in a small bowl stir together mayonnaise dressing, chutney, curry powder, and chives. Add to chicken mixture and toss gently to coat. Spoon chicken mixture over romaine on the salad plates. Makes 4 main-dish servings.

Nutritional facts per serving: 243 calories, 6 g total fat (2 g saturated fat), 68 mg cholesterol, 332 mg sodium, 23 g carbohydrate, 2 g fiber, 24 g protein. **Daily values:** 38% vitamin A, 75% vitamin C, 4% calcium, 13% iron.

BLACK-EYED PEA AND TOMATO SALAD

For this meat-free salad, two Southern specialties—black-eyed peas and rice—are tossed with a puréed tomato dressing.

5 cups torn lettuce
1 16-ounce can black-eyed
    peas, rinsed and drained
1 red, yellow, or green sweet
    pepper, chopped
1 cup cooked long grain rice
1 cup chopped tomatoes
⅓ cup chopped red onion
    Tomato-Basil Dressing
    Lettuce leaves

1. In a large bowl combine 5 cups lettuce, black-eyed peas, sweet pepper, rice, tomatoes, and onion.

2. Pour the Tomato-Basil Dressing over the black-eyed pea mixture and toss lightly to coat. Serve on a lettuce-lined platter or individual salad plates. Makes 4 main-dish servings.

Tomato-Basil Dressing: In a blender container or food processor bowl combine ½ cup chopped *tomato;* ¼ cup *red wine vinegar;* 2 tablespoons *water;* 1 tablespoon *olive* or *salad oil;* 1 tablespoon snipped *fresh basil* or 1 teaspoon *dried basil,* crushed; 2 teaspoons snipped *fresh thyme* or ½ teaspoon *dried thyme,* crushed; 1 clove *garlic,* minced; ⅛ to ¼ teaspoon *ground red pepper.* Cover, and blend or process till smooth.

Nutritional facts per serving: 200 calories, 5 g total fat (1 g saturated fat), 0 mg cholesterol, 287 mg sodium, 34 g carbohydrate, 9 g fiber, 9 g protein. **Daily values:** 34% vitamin A, 94% vitamin C, 4% calcium, 18% iron.

VEGETABLE AND HAM PASTA SALAD

To keep the dressing low in fat yet high on flavor, we replaced some of the oil with water and boosted the herbs.

6 ounces linguine or spaghetti,
    cooked and drained
4 ounces lean ham, julienned
1 cup julienned red or green
    sweet pepper
1 cup frozen peas, thawed
⅔ cup chopped carrots
¼ cup snipped parsley
¼ cup white wine vinegar
1 tablespoon olive or salad oil
1 tablespoon Dijon-style
    mustard
½ teaspoon sugar
½ teaspoon dried thyme, basil,
    or oregano crushed

1. In a large mixing bowl toss together the pasta, ham, sweet pepper, peas, carrots, and parsley.

2. For dressing, in a screw-top jar combine the vinegar, oil, mustard, sugar, herb, 2 tablespoons *water,* and ¼ teaspoon *pepper.* Cover and shake well. Drizzle over salad and toss gently to coat. If desired, serve on a lettuce-lined platter. Makes 4 main-dish servings.

Nutritional facts per serving: 273 calories, 6 g total fat (1 g saturated fat), 12 mg cholesterol, 442 mg sodium, 44 g carbohydrate, 2 g fiber, 13 g protein. **Daily values:** 69% vitamin A, 81% vitamin C, 2% calcium, 20% iron.

Low-fat

Low-calorie

Low-sodium

GARDEN-STYLE SALAD WITH TUNA

Prepare the vegetables and dressing the night before and serve this stylish tuna salad after work. (See photo, right.)

Lettuce leaves

1 6½-ounce can reduced-
    sodium chunk-style light
    tuna, drained and broken
    into chunks

8 ounces fresh asparagus, cut
    into 3-inch pieces, or whole
    green beans

12 yellow pear-shape cherry
    tomatoes, halved

1 cup yellow summer squash or
    zucchini cut in julienne
    strips

1 cup sliced fresh shiitake or
    button mushrooms

3 tablespoons skim milk

2 tablespoons fat-free
    mayonnaise dressing or
    salad dressing

2 tablespoons plain fat-free
    yogurt

1 tablespoon white wine vinegar

1½ teaspoons snipped fresh
    tarragon or ½ teaspoon
    dried tarragon, crushed

½ teaspoon sugar

⅛ teaspoon pepper

1. Line a salad platter with lettuce leaves. Arrange tuna, asparagus or green beans, tomatoes, zucchini or yellow squash, and mushrooms in sections on platter.

2. For dressing, stir together milk, mayonnaise or salad dressing, yogurt, vinegar, tarragon, sugar, and pepper. (If desired, cover and chill salad and dressing for 1 hour before serving.) Drizzle some of the dressing over salad. Serve with remaining dressing. Makes 3 main-dish servings.

Nutritional facts per serving: 132 calories, 2 g total fat (0 g saturated fat), 0 mg cholesterol, 287 mg sodium, 14 g carbohydrate, 3 g fiber, 17 g protein. **Daily values:** 14% vitamin A, 60% vitamin C, 6% calcium, 13% iron.

Mayonnaise Options

Although fat-free mayonnaise may sound like the best choice when selecting mayonnaise, it may not be, especially if you are concerned about sodium. The chart below compares a tablespoon of mayonnaise, reduced-fat mayonnaise, and fat-free mayonnaise dressing. As you can see, the sodium increases as the fat decreases.

	Calories	Fat	Sodium
Mayonnaise	100	12 g	70 mg
Reduced-fat mayonnaise	50	5 g	110 mg
Fat-free mayonnaise dressing	12	0 g	190 mg

Often, the best solution is to mix either reduced-fat mayonnaise or fat-free mayonnaise dressing with plain fat-free yogurt for a delicious tangy dressing.

Low-fat

Low-calorie

TODAY'S EGG SALAD

This revolutionary egg salad contains only 1 gram of fat and is virtually cholesterol free! Serve it as a salad or a sandwich filling.

Nonstick spray coating

1¼ **cups frozen egg product, thawed**

¾ **cup chopped red, yellow, or green sweet pepper**

⅓ **cup sliced green onions**

⅓ **cup chopped celery**

¼ **cup fat-free mayonnaise dressing or salad dressing**

¼ **cup plain fat-free yogurt**

1 **tablespoon pickle relish**

1 **teaspoon lemon juice**

Lettuce leaves

⅛ **teaspoon paprika**

1. Spray a large nonstick skillet with nonstick coating. Heat over medium heat for 1 minute. Pour egg product into skillet. Cook, covered, without stirring for 4 minutes. Lift egg product and allow uncooked portion to flow underneath. Cover and continue cooking for 2 to 4 minutes or till set. Place on cutting board and cool 10 minutes. Coarsely chop.

2. In a medium bowl combine egg product, sweet pepper, onions, and celery. Add mayonnaise dressing, yogurt, pickle relish, and lemon juice. Toss to mix. Cover and chill for 2 to 24 hours. Spoon onto a lettuce-lined platter and sprinkle with paprika. Makes 2 main-dish servings.

Nutritional facts per serving: 137 calories, 1 g total fat (0 g saturated fat), 1 mg cholesterol, 682 mg sodium, 17 g carbohydrate, 1 g fiber, 15 g protein. **Daily values:** 123% vitamin A, 129% vitamin C, 10% calcium, 21% iron.

After cooking the frozen egg product for 4 minutes, lift the cooked portion with a spatula, allowing the uncooked portion to flow underneath. Cover and continue cooking till set.

Low-fat

Low-calorie

Low-sodium

High-fiber

BEAN SALAD WITH TUNA

For a pleasing accompaniment, top thin slices of Italian bread with grated Parmesan cheese and toast under the broiler.

1 15-ounce can cannellini or
   great northern beans,
   drained
1 6½-ounce can low-sodium
   chunk light tuna, drained
   and broken up
1 cup sliced celery
1 cup chopped red, yellow,
   or green sweet pepper
½ cup sliced radishes
2 tablespoons snipped parsley
   Dijon Vinaigrette
   Lettuce leaves

1. In a nonmetal bowl toss together beans, tuna, celery, sweet pepper, radishes, and parsley.

2. Pour Dijon Vinaigrette over salad; toss gently to coat. Cover and chill at least 1 hour to blend flavors. Serve on lettuce-lined plates. Makes 4 main-dish servings.

Dijon Vinaigrette: In a screw-top jar combine ¼ cup *water*; 3 tablespoons *lemon juice*; 4 teaspoons *Dijon-style mustard*; 1 tablespoon *olive* or *salad oil*; 1 teaspoon snipped *fresh thyme* or ¼ teaspoon *dried thyme*, crushed; ¼ teaspoon *pepper*; 1 clove *garlic*, minced. Cover and shake well.

Nutritional facts per serving: 174 calories, 5 g total fat (1 g saturated fat), 16 mg cholesterol, 341 mg sodium, 19 g carbohydrate, 6 g fiber, 20 g protein. **Daily values:** 32% vitamin A, 100% vitamin C, 4% calcium, 15% iron.

Low-fat

Low-calorie

Low-sodium

TENDERLOIN OF PORK SALAD WITH APPLES AND ENDIVE

Enjoy this roasted pork salad in the autumn when apples are at their peak.

12 ounces pork tenderloin
 2 teaspoons olive oil or salad oil
 1 clove garlic, minced
 1 teaspoon dried oregano,
    crushed
 1 teaspoon cornstarch
 ¼ teaspoon ground ginger
 ¾ cup apple cider or juice
 ¼ cup white wine vinegar
 2 teaspoons honey
 3 medium Belgian endives
 3 cups coarsely shredded
    romaine
 2 medium tart red apples
 ¼ cup sliced green onions

1. Trim fat from pork. Place pork on a rack in a shallow baking pan. Brush with *1 teaspoon* of the oil. Rub garlic and oregano on pork. Insert a meat thermometer. Roast in a 375° oven for 20 to 30 minutes or till meat thermometer registers 160°. Let stand 5 minutes; slice thinly.

2. Meanwhile, for dressing, in a small saucepan combine cornstarch and ginger. Stir in apple cider, vinegar, honey, and remaining 1 teaspoon oil. Cook, stirring constantly, till thickened and bubbly. Cook and stir 2 minutes more.

3. For salad, trim ½ inch from the bottom of the Belgian endives. Cut endives crosswise into quarters. Core and thinly slice apples. On 4 dinner plates, arrange romaine, Belgian endive, apple, and pork slices. Drizzle with dressing and sprinkle with green onions. Makes 4 main-dish servings.

Nutritional facts per serving: 211 calories, 6 g total fat (1 g saturated fat), 61 mg cholesterol, 52 mg sodium, 21 g carbohydrate, 2 g fiber, 20 g protein. **Daily values:** 12% vitamin A, 31% vitamin C, 2% calcium, 14% iron.

Low-fat

Low-calorie

Low-sodium

CRAB MACARONI SALAD

Lemon yogurt and light sour cream impart a tangy taste to the creamy dressing.

4 ounces elbow macaroni,
   ditalini, bow ties, or rotini,
   cooked and drained
1 6-ounce package frozen
   crabmeat, thawed, drained,
   and flaked
⅔ cup shredded carrot
1 11-ounce can mandarin
   orange sections, drained
⅓ cup sliced green onions
⅓ cup lemon fat-free yogurt
3 tablespoons light dairy sour
   cream
2 tablespoons snipped parsley
1 tablespoon lemon juice
1½ teaspoons Dijon-style mustard
⅛ teaspoon salt
2 tablespoons skim milk
   (optional)
   Lettuce leaves

1. In a large bowl toss together macaroni, crabmeat, carrot, orange sections, and green onions.

2. For dressing, in a small bowl stir together yogurt, sour cream, parsley, lemon juice, mustard, and salt. Add dressing to salad. Toss gently to coat. Cover and chill for 2 to 24 hours. If mixture is too dry, stir in a little skim milk. Serve in a lettuce-lined bowl. Makes 3 main-dish servings.

Nutritional facts per serving: 308 calories, 3 g total fat (1 g saturated fat), 53 mg cholesterol, 390 mg sodium, 52 g carbohydrate, 1 g fiber, 20 g protein. **Daily values:** 75% vitamin A, 20% vitamin C, 11% calcium, 15% iron.

SPLENDID SOUPS AND STEWS

Soups and stews are the ultimate comfort food. Hearty and wholesome, each savory spoonful offers a sum of flavors more delicious than the individual ingredients. And for the health-conscious cook, good taste prevails even when you eliminate the fat and calories. For this collection, we have lightened a host of familiar recipes, as well as created new combinations. Our updated Beef Burgundy is chock-full of succulent beef, baby carrots, and tiny onions. Corn Chowder with Ham makes a tummy-warming feast on the coldest days of winter and Easy Gazpacho pleases palates in the heat of the summer. For casual gatherings, pair steaming bowls of Leek and Potato Soup with a plateful of sandwiches. Don't wait to serve up some old-fashioned taste with health-wise nutrition—select a soup and start cooking.

Low-fat

Low-calorie

WILD RICE-CARROT SOUP

Pureed carrots and onions thicken this intriguing rice soup. (See photo, left.)

1 14½-ounce can reduced-
    sodium chicken broth
2½ cups sliced carrots
 ½ cup chopped onion
 1 bay leaf
 ⅛ teaspoon pepper
 ⅛ teaspoon ground cloves
    (optional)
1½ cups water
 ½ cup light dairy sour cream
 1 cup cooked wild rice or long
    grain rice
 1 tablespoon snipped fresh
    parsley

1. In a large saucepan combine broth, carrots, onion, bay leaf, pepper, and, if desired, cloves. Bring to boiling; reduce heat. Simmer, covered, for 15 to 20 minutes or till carrots are tender. Remove bay leaf.

2. In a blender container or food processor bowl place carrot mixture, half at a time. Cover, and blend or process till smooth. Return mixture to saucepan. Stir in water. Bring just to boiling. Stir a small amount of liquid into sour cream. Return to saucepan along with rice. Heat through but do not boil. Sprinkle with parsley. Makes 6 side-dish servings.

Nutrition facts per servings: 108 calories, 2 g total fat (1 g saturated fat), 3 mg cholesterol, 279 mg sodium, 20 g carbohydrate, 3 g fiber, 4 g protein. **Daily values:** 223% vitamin A, 6% vitamin C, 4% calcium, 5% iron.

Low-fat

Low-calorie

EASY GAZPACHO

Here's a soup you can make any time of the year, but it's especially refreshing in the summer.

3 cups reduced-sodium tomato
    juice
1½ cups reduced-sodium chicken
    broth
2 cups chopped tomatoes
1 cup diced cucumber
½ cup sliced green onions
2 tablespoons red wine vinegar
1 clove garlic, minced
1 tablespoon snipped fresh basil
    or 1 teaspoon dried basil,
    crushed
¼ teaspoon pepper
¼ teaspoon hot pepper sauce

1. In a large bowl stir together all ingredients. Cover and chill for 2 to 24 hours to blend flavors. Makes 6 side-dish servings.

Nutrition facts per serving: 51 calories, 1 g total fat (0 g saturated fat), 0 mg cholesterol, 200 mg sodium, 10 g carbohydrates, 2 g fiber, 1 g protein. **Daily values:** 27% vitamin A, 71% vitamin C, 2% calcium, 8% iron.

Low-fat

Low-calorie

CREAM OF VEGETABLE SOUP

Hot or cold, serve this soup as a first course or an accompaniment to a main-dish salad.

1 cup reduced-sodium chicken broth
1 cup water
1½ cups loose-pack frozen peas and carrots
1 cup evaporated skim milk
½ cup instant mashed potato flakes
½ teaspoon dried fines herbes, crushed
⅛ teaspoon pepper
1 green onion, sliced

1. In a 2-quart saucepan combine broth and water; bring to boiling. Add peas and carrots. Cover and cook till vegetables are crisp-tender. Stir in evaporated skim milk, potato flakes, fines herbes, and pepper. Heat through. Sprinkle with onion. Makes 4 side-dish servings.

Nutrition facts per serving: 103 calories, 1 g total fat (0 g saturated fat), 2 mg cholesterol, 280 mg sodium, 18 g carbohydrate, 2 g fiber, 8 g protein. **Daily values:** 51% vitamin A, 17% vitamin A, 16% calcium, 5% iron.

Low-fat

MUSHROOM BISQUE

Delicate and elegant, this soup is perfect for entertaining.

2 teaspoons olive or cooking oil
8 ounces fresh shiitake mushrooms, sliced (stems removed)
1 cup sliced fresh oyster, wood ear, or brown mushrooms
1 cup chopped onion
1 clove garlic, minced
1 12-ounce can evaporated skim milk
1 cup reduced-sodium chicken broth
1 teaspoon dried thyme, crushed
½ teaspoon salt-free seasoning blend
2 tablespoons all-purpose flour
⅓ cup light dairy sour cream
2 tablespoons snipped fresh parsley

1. Heat oil in a 3-quart saucepan. Add mushrooms, onion, and garlic and cook for 5 minutes.

2. Place mushroom mixture in a blender container or food processor bowl. Cover, and blend or process till smooth. Return mixture to saucepan. Stir in evaporated skim milk, broth, thyme, and seasoning blend. Bring to boiling; reduce heat. Simmer, covered, for 5 minutes.

3. Stir flour into sour cream. Gradually stir 1 cup hot soup into sour cream mixture. Return to saucepan. Cook and stir till thickened and bubbly. Cook and stir for 1 to 2 minutes more. Sprinkle with parsley. Makes 4 side-dish servings.

Nutrition facts per serving: 176 calories, 5 g total fat (1 g saturated fat), 5 mg cholesterol, 287 mg sodium, 24 g carbohydrate, 2 g fiber, 11 g protein. **Daily values:** 13% vitamin A, 15% vitamin C, 24% calcium, 14% iron.

ONION SOUP

Low-fat cheeses significantly reduce the total amount of fat in this classic soup.

1 tablespoon margarine
4 cups thinly sliced onion
2 cloves garlic, minced
1 teaspoon sugar
2 tablespoons all-purpose flour
1 14½-ounce can reduced-
    sodium chicken broth
1¼ cups water
½ cup dry white wine
4 slices French or Italian bread
4 teaspoons grated Parmesan
    cheese
1 tablespoon snipped fresh
    parsley

1. In a large saucepan melt margarine. Add onion, garlic, and sugar. Cook, covered, over medium-low heat for 18 to 20 minutes or till onions are very tender and golden.

2. Stir in flour. Add broth, water, and wine. Cook and stir till thickened and bubbly. Reduce heat. Simmer, uncovered, for 10 minutes.

3. Meanwhile, place bread slices on baking sheet. Broil bread 3 to 4 inches from the heat for 2 minutes or till toasted. Sprinkle bread with Parmesan cheese. Broil 1 minute more or till cheese begins to brown. To serve, ladle soup into bowls and float bread on top. Sprinkle with parsley. Makes 4 side-dish servings.

Nutrition facts per serving: 200 calories, 5 g total fat (1 g saturated fat), 2 mg cholesterol, 519 mg sodium, 29 g carbohydrate, 2 g fiber, 6 g protein. **Daily values:** 4% vitamin A, 11% vitamin C, 6% calcium, 8% iron.

SPINACH AND POTATO SOUP

Try this soup for a Sunday-night supper with a platter of sandwiches.

3 cups water
3 medium potatoes (about
    1 pound), peeled and diced
1 cup chopped onion
1 cup sliced celery
1 clove garlic, minced
4 cups torn spinach
1 12-ounce can evaporated
    skim milk
1 tablespoon snipped fresh
    chives or 1 teaspoon dried
    snipped chives
1 teaspoon dried basil, crushed
½ teaspoon dry mustard
¼ teaspoon salt
¼ teaspoon pepper
⅓ cup light dairy sour cream

1. In a large saucepan or Dutch oven combine water, potatoes, onion, celery, and garlic. Bring to boiling; reduce heat. Simmer about 20 minutes or till vegetables are tender. Stir in spinach.

2. Place mixture, one-third at a time, in a blender container or food processor bowl. Cover, and blend or process till smooth. Return mixture to saucepan.

3. Stir in evaporated skim milk, chives, basil, mustard, salt, and pepper. Cook 5 minutes more or till heated through. Top each serving with a dollop of sour cream. Makes 6 side-dish servings.

Nutrition facts per serving: 152 calories, 1 g total fat (1 g saturated fat), 4 mg cholesterol, 220 mg sodium, 29 g carbohydrate, 3 g fiber, 8 g protein. **Daily values:** 24% vitamin A, 20% vitamin C, 19% calcium, 9% iron.

Low-fat

High-fiber

MINESTRONE SOUP

Herb Pistou, a mixture of basil, rosemary, and garlic moistened with a bit of oil, flavors this familiar soup. (See photo, right.)

Nonstick spray coating

1 cup carrots cut in julienne
  strips

1 cup bias-cut celery

1 cup sliced zucchini or yellow
  summer squash

⅔ cup chopped onion

½ of a 15-ounce can cannellini,
  great northern, or red
  kidney beans, rinsed and
  drained

½ of a 15-ounce can garbanzo
  beans, rinsed and drained

4 cups reduced-sodium chicken
  broth

1 cup water

⅔ cup elbow macaroni, ditalini,
  bow-ties, small shells, or tri-
  colored rotini

1 14-ounce can low-sodium
  whole tomatoes, cut up

Herb Pistou

1. Spray a 4-quart Dutch oven with nonstick spray coating. Add carrots, celery, zucchini, and onion and cook for 10 minutes. Stir in beans, broth, and water. Bring to boiling; reduce heat. Simmer for 15 minutes.

2. Stir in pasta. Cook for 5 to 7 minutes more or till pasta is just tender. Stir in tomatoes and Pistou. Heat through. Makes 5 side-dish servings.

Herb Pistou: In a small bowl stir together 2 tablespoons snipped *fresh basil* or 2 teaspoons *dried basil,* crushed; 2 teaspoons snipped *fresh rosemary* or ¼ teaspoon *dried rosemary,* crushed; 2 cloves *garlic,* minced; ¼ teaspoon *pepper;* and ⅛ teaspoon *salt.* Stir in 1 teaspoon *cooking oil* to make a paste.

Nutrition facts per serving: 203 calories, 4 g total fat (0 g saturated fat), 0 mg cholesterol, 865 mg sodium, 37 g carbohydrate, 7 g fiber, 10 g protein. **Daily values:** 73% vitamin A, 33% vitamin C, 7% calcium, 20% iron.

To Peel or Not to Peel

To make a dish more nutritious, you can omit peeling many fruits and vegetables, such as potatoes, tomatoes, carrots, parsnips, pears, apples, and nectarines. You'll not only make the dish faster and easier to prepare, but you'll be increasing the fiber content since much of the fiber in fruits and vegetables is contained in the peels. Before cutting up unpeeled fruits and vegetables, scrub them thoroughly with a soft vegetable brush till clean. Do not use soap.

Low-fat
Low-calorie

LEEK AND POTATO SOUP

3 medium potatoes (about
     1 pound), peeled and diced
3 leeks, trimmed and thinly
     sliced (white part only)
1 clove garlic, minced
1 14½-ounce can reduced-
     sodium chicken broth
½ teaspoon dried thyme,
     crushed
⅛ teaspoon salt
⅛ teaspoon pepper
2 cups skim milk
1 tablespoon snipped fresh
     chives or 1 teaspoon dried
     snipped chives (optional)

1. In a 3-quart saucepan combine potatoes, leeks, garlic, broth, thyme, salt, and pepper. Bring to boiling; reduce heat. Cover and simmer about 15 minutes or till potatoes are tender. Do not drain. Mash slightly with potato masher. Stir in milk. Heat through. If desired, sprinkle with chives. Makes 5 side-dish servings.

Nutrition facts per serving: 127 calories, 1 g total fat (0 g saturated fat), 2 mg cholesterol, 344 mg sodium, 25 g carbohydrate, 3 g fiber, 6 g protein. **Daily values:** 6% vitamin A, 15% vitamin C, 12% calcium, 6% iron.

Low-fat
Low-calorie
High-fiber

SQUASH SOUP

This savory soup makes a flavorful first course for a special company meal.

3 pounds winter squash (such as
     butternut, acorn, banana,
     or turban squash)
1½ cups reduced-sodium chicken
     broth
½ cup water
1 cup chopped onion
½ cup chopped carrots
1 teaspoon dried thyme,
     crushed
1 teaspoon finely shredded
     orange peel (optional)
¼ teaspoon pepper
1 12-ounce can evaporated
     skim milk
   Orange slices (optional)
   Parsley (optional)

1. Halve squash; remove seeds and strings. Place halves, cut side down, in a baking dish. Bake in a 350° oven for 30 minutes. Turn cut side up. Bake, covered, for 20 to 25 minutes more or till tender. Scoop out pulp into a blender container or food processor bowl. Cover, and blend or process till squash is pureed; set aside.

2. In a large saucepan combine broth, water, onion, carrots, thyme, orange peel, and pepper. Bring to boiling; reduce heat. Simmer, covered, for 10 minutes or till vegetables are tender. Stir in squash puree and evaporated skim milk; heat through. If desired, garnish with orange slices and parsley. Makes 6 side-dish servings.

Nutrition facts per serving: 150 calories, 1 g total fat (0 g saturated fat), 2 mg cholesterol, 252 mg sodium, 32 g carbohydrate, 5 g fiber, 8 g protein. **Daily values:** 173% vitamin A, 53% vitamin C, 23% calcium, 11% iron.

Low-fat
Low-calorie

VEGETABLE SOUP WITH SHRIMP WONTONS

You'll find wonton wrappers in the produce department or in the supermarket freezer case.

½ cup chopped cooked shrimp
¼ cup sliced green onions
1 teaspoon light soy sauce
1 clove garlic, minced
20 wonton wrappers
3 cups reduced-sodium chicken broth
3 cups water
1½ cups shredded bok choy or Chinese (napa) cabbage
1 8-ounce can sliced water chestnuts, drained
1 cup carrots cut in julienne strips
1 cup sliced fresh shiitake mushrooms (stems removed)
1 tablespoon light soy sauce
1 tablespoon grated gingerroot
Dash bottled hot pepper sauce

1. In a small mixing bowl stir together shrimp, green onions, 1 teaspoon soy sauce, and garlic.

2. To make wontons, place one wrapper on a flat surface. Spoon 1 teaspoon of the shrimp mixture onto the center of the wrapper. Moisten edges of the wrapper with water. Bring opposite corners together to form a triangle. Press edges together to seal. Repeat with remaining filling and wrappers.

3. In a Dutch oven or very large saucepan bring broth, 3 cups water, bok choy, water chestnuts, carrots, mushrooms, 1 tablespoon soy sauce, gingerroot, and hot pepper sauce to boiling. Reduce heat. Simmer for 10 minutes. Add wontons to broth and simmer for 2 minutes more. Makes 6 side-dish servings.

Nutrition facts per serving: 135 calories, 1 g total fat, (0 g saturated fat), 26 mg cholesterol, 646 mg sodium, 24 g carbohydrate, 1 g fiber, 8 g protein. **Daily values:** 82% vitamin A, 12% vitamin C, 4% calcium, 13% iron.

To make wontons, bring the opposite corner of the wonton wrapper over the filling, forming a triangle. Then press the edges together to seal.

Low-fat

Low-calorie

High-fiber

BLACK BEAN SOUP

To give extra kick to this Cuban-style soup (photo, left), stir in a chopped fresh jalapeño pepper.

Nonstick spray coating

1 red, yellow, or green sweet pepper, chopped (¾ cup)

¾ cup chopped onion

¾ cup chopped carrots

2 cloves garlic, minced

1 14½-ounce can reduced-sodium chicken broth

1½ cups water

2 15-ounce cans black beans, rinsed and drained

2 tablespoons snipped fresh cilantro or parsley

1 tablespoon lemon juice

1 teaspoon dried oregano, crushed

½ teaspoon dried thyme, crushed

¼ teaspoon crushed red pepper

⅛ teaspoon black pepper

¼ cup light dairy sour cream (optional)

1. Spray a large saucepan with nonstick coating. Cook sweet pepper, onion, carrots, and garlic, covered, in the saucepan over medium-low heat about 5 minutes or till tender. Remove from heat. Stir in broth, water, beans, cilantro, lemon juice, oregano, thyme, crushed red pepper, and black pepper.

2. Place *half* of the soup mixture in a blender container or food processor bowl. Cover, and blend or process till nearly smooth. Repeat with remaining half of the mixture. Return mixture to saucepan. Bring to boiling; reduce heat. Simmer, covered, for 10 minutes. If desired, top each serving with a dollop of sour cream. Makes 4 main-dish servings.

Nutritional facts per serving: 193 calories, 2 g total fat (0 g saturated fat) 0 mg cholesterol, 848 mg sodium, 39 g carbohydrate, 12 g fiber, 16 g protein. **Daily values:** 113% vitamin A, 59% vitamin C, 8% calcium, 19% iron.

Make It Easy with Leftover Soup

Freeze or chill soup leftovers, and you'll have a quick meal for another day. (Don't freeze soups made with milk products.)

To reheat soup on the range top, use a covered saucepan and heat over medium heat till mixture is heated throughout; stir often. Break up frozen soup during reheating.

To reheat soup in your microwave oven, micro-cook frozen soup in a covered, microwave-safe container on 100% power (high). Allow about 2½ minutes for ¾ cup, 3 to 4 minutes for 1 cup, 8 minutes for 1½ cups, and 10 minutes for 2 cups; stir once or twice. To micro-cook chilled soup, allow 2 minutes for ¾ cup, 3 minutes for 1 cup, 3 to 4 minutes for 1½ cups, and 5 minutes for 2 cups; stir once.

Low-fat
Low-calorie

CORN CHOWDER WITH HAM

This chowder seems far too hearty to be both low-fat and low-calorie.

1 cup chopped zucchini
1 red or green sweet pepper,
    chopped
¾ cup chopped onion
1 14½-ounce can reduced-
    sodium chicken broth
1½ cups frozen whole kernel corn
1½ cups chopped peeled potatoes
1 teaspoon dried fines herbes,
    crushed
1 12-ounce can evaporated
    skim milk
3 tablespoons all-purpose flour
1 cup skim milk
4 ounces chopped fully-cooked
    lean ham (about 1 cup)
2 tablespoons snipped parsley
½ teaspoon salt-free seasoning
    blend

1. Spray a Dutch oven or 4-quart saucepan with *nonstick spray coating*. Add zucchini, sweet pepper, and onion. Cook, stirring occasionally, for 5 minutes. Stir in broth, corn, potatoes, fines herbes, and 1¾ cups *water*. Bring to boiling; reduce heat. Cover and simmer for 15 to 20 minutes or till potatoes are tender.

2. Stir in evaporated milk. Stir flour into skim milk. Add to soup with ham, parsley, and seasoning blend. Cook and stir till mixture is thickened and bubbly. Cook and stir for 2 minutes more. Makes 6 main-dish servings.

Nutrition facts per serving: 187 calories, 2 g total fat (1 g saturated fat), 12 mg cholesterol, 514 mg sodium, 31 g carbohydrate, 1 g fiber, 13 g protein. **Daily values:** 20% vitamin A, 56% vitamin C, 19% calcium, 8 % iron.

Low-fat
Low-calorie
High-fiber

CHICKEN NOODLE SOUP

2 14½-ounce cans reduced-
    sodium chicken broth
1 cup chopped carrots
1 cup sliced celery
1 cup chopped zucchini
½ cup sliced green onions
1 teaspoon dried basil, crushed
½ teaspoon dried dillweed
1 bay leaf
3 ounces wide noodles
1½ cups shredded cooked
    chicken breast
⅔ cup loose-pack frozen peas

1. In a Dutch oven combine broth, carrots, celery, zucchini, onions, basil, dillweed, bay leaf, 2 cups *water*, and ¼ teaspoon *pepper*. Bring to boiling; reduce heat. Cover and simmer for 20 minutes.

2. Stir in noodles, chicken, and peas; return to boiling. Reduce heat. Cover and cook for 5 to 7 minutes more or till noodles are just tender. Remove bay leaf. Makes 4 main-dish servings.

Nutrition facts per serving: 238 calories, 6 g total fat (1 g saturated fat), 62 mg cholesterol, 713 mg sodium, 26 g carbohydrate, 4 g fiber, 21 g protein. **Daily values:** 91% vitamin A, 16% vitamin C, 5% calcium, 18% iron.

SEAFOOD GUMBO

Full of tradition, this gumbo now can be served as a healthy new sensation.

1 cup chopped onion

1 cup chopped carrots

¼ cup chopped celery

½ cup chopped red or green
    sweet pepper

2 cloves garlic, minced

1 teaspoon cooking oil

2½ cups reduced-sodium chicken
    broth

2½ cups water

1 16-ounce can low-sodium
    whole tomatoes, cut up

1 teaspoon dried thyme,
    crushed

½ teaspoon salt-free seasoning
    blend

¼ to ½ teaspoon ground red
    pepper

¼ teaspoon black pepper

1 bay leaf

1 10-ounce package frozen cut
    okra

8 ounces medium shrimp,
    shelled and deveined

8 ounces firm-fleshed white fish
    fillets, cut into 1-inch
    chunks

8 ounces clams or mussels,
    rinsed, or flaked crabmeat

1 cup cooked rice

1. In a Dutch oven cook onion, carrots, celery, sweet pepper, and garlic in oil for 10 minutes. Stir in broth, water, undrained tomatoes, thyme, seasoning blend, red pepper, black pepper, and bay leaf. Bring to boiling; reduce heat. Simmer, covered, for 20 minutes.

2. Stir in okra and cook for 5 minutes. Stir in shrimp, fish chunks, clams or crabmeat, and rice. Return to boiling; reduce heat. Simmer for 3 minutes more or till seafood is opaque. Discard bay leaf and any clams that do not open. Makes 8 main-dish servings.

Nutrition facts per serving: 143 calories, 2 g total fat (0 g saturated fat), 57 mg cholesterol, 306 mg sodium, 17 g carbohydrate, 2 g fiber, 15 g protein. **Daily values:** 71% vitamin A, 47% vitamin C, 6% calcium, 33% iron.

LAMB STEW WITH HERBS

Low-sodium

To save yourself some preparation time for this stew (photo, right), look for boneless lamb or ask the butcher to bone and cut it.

1 pound boneless lamb, cut into
    1-inch pieces
2 teaspoons olive or cooking oil
1 cup chopped onion
1 cup dry red wine
½ cup reduced-sodium chicken
    broth
½ cup water
1 teaspoon dried basil, crushed
½ teaspoon dried rosemary,
    crushed
½ teaspoon dried oregano,
    crushed
⅛ teaspoon pepper
2 cloves garlic, minced
1 medium eggplant, peeled,
    if desired, and cut into
    1-inch cubes
1½ cups carrots cut in julienne
    strips
1½ cups chopped tomatoes
3 cups hot cooked rice
2 tablespoons snipped fresh
    parsley

1. In a kettle or large Dutch oven cook lamb, *half* at a time, in oil till browned. Drain off fat. Return all lamb to Dutch oven. Add onion, wine, broth, water, basil, rosemary, oregano, pepper, and garlic. Bring to boiling; reduce heat. Cover and simmer for 1 hour.

2. Stir in eggplant, carrots, and tomatoes. Cover and simmer for 30 minutes more. Serve over hot cooked rice. Sprinkle with parsley. Makes 6 main-dish servings.

Nutrition facts per serving: 314 calories, 11 g total fat (4 g saturated fat), 42 mg cholesterol, 134 mg sodium, 32 g carbohydrate, 3 g fiber, 14 g protein. **Daily values:** 68% vitamin A, 23% vitamin C, 3% calcium, 18% iron.

Herb Alternative Guide

Whether you're making an emergency substitution or experimenting with a new flavor, follow these suggestions for herb alternatives. Some of the suggestions are similar flavors, and others are acceptable flavor alternatives. As a general rule, start with half of the amount the recipe calls for unless directed otherwise, and add the herb until it suits your taste.

Basil: oregano or thyme
Chervil: tarragon or parsley
Chive: green onion, onion, or leek
Cilantro: parsley
Italian seasoning (a blend of any of these): basil, oregano, rosemary, and ground red pepper

Marjoram: basil, thyme, or savory
Mint: basil, marjoram, or rosemary
Oregano: thyme or basil
Parsley: chervil or cilantro
Poultry seasoning: sage plus (a blend of any of these): thyme, marjoram, savory, black pepper, and rosemary
Red pepper: dash bottled hot pepper sauce or black pepper
Rosemary: thyme, tarragon, or savory
Sage: poultry seasoning, savory, marjoram, or rosemary
Savory: thyme, marjoram, or sage
Tarragon: chervil, dash fennel seed, or dash aniseed
Thyme: basil, marjoram, oregano, or savory

Low-fat

Low-sodium

High-fiber

NEW BRUNSWICK STEW

1 pound skinless, boneless
   chicken breasts or thighs
1 14½-ounce can reduced-
   sodium chicken broth
2 medium potatoes, diced
1 10-ounce package frozen lima
   beans
1 cup loose-pack frozen whole
   kernel corn
1 cup sliced celery
1 cup chopped onion
1 cup chopped red, yellow, or
   green sweet pepper
¼ cup snipped fresh parsley
½ teaspoon dried thyme,
   crushed
1 14½-ounce can low-sodium
   whole tomatoes, cut up
¼ cup all-purpose flour

1. Rinse chicken; pat dry. Cut chicken into 1-inch pieces. In a large kettle or Dutch oven place chicken, broth, potatoes, beans, corn, celery, onion, sweet pepper, parsley, thyme, 1¾ cups *water*, ½ teaspoon *salt*, and ¼ teaspoon *pepper*. Bring to boiling; reduce heat. Simmer, covered, about 10 to 12 minutes or till chicken and vegetables are tender.

2. Add undrained tomatoes. Stir flour into ½ cup *water*. Stir into stew. Cook and stir till thickened and bubbly. Cook 1 minute more. Makes 6 main-dish servings.

Nutrition facts per serving: 342 calories, 3 g total fat (1 g saturated fat), 40 mg cholesterol, 456 mg sodium, 52 g carbohydrate, 5 g fiber, 28 g protein. **Daily values:** 15% vitamin A, 76% vitamin C, 6% calcium, 36% iron.

Low-calorie

Low-sodium

PORK STEW WITH SQUASH

2 pounds butternut squash
1¼ pounds lean boneless pork
2 teaspoons cooking oil
1 14½-ounce can beef broth
2 tablespoons quick-cooking
   tapioca
2 teaspoons dried thyme,
   crushed
2 bay leaves
½ teaspoon salt-free seasoning
   blend
½ of a 16-ounce package frozen
   small whole onions
1 cup loose-pack frozen whole
   kernel corn

1. Cut squash into 2-inch pieces. Cut pork into 1-inch pieces. Set squash and pork aside.

2. Heat oil in a large kettle or Dutch oven. Cook pork in oil till browned. Drain off excess fat. Stir in broth, tapioca, thyme, bay leaves, seasoning blend, 2¼ cups *water*, and ¼ teaspoon *pepper*. Add squash. Bring to boiling; reduce heat. Simmer, covered, for 1 hour.

3. Stir in onions and corn; simmer for 20 minutes more. Remove bay leaves. Makes 6 main-dish servings.

Nutrition facts per serving: 234 calories, 8 g total fat (2 g saturated fat), 43 mg cholesterol, 277 mg sodium, 22 g carbohydrate, 3 g fiber, 16 g protein. **Daily values:** 67% vitamin A, 29% vitamin C, 5% calcium, 12% iron.

Low-fat

Low-calorie

Low-sodium

High-fiber

TURKEY AND BEAN CHILI

1 15-ounce can black beans
1 15-ounce can red kidney
   beans or pinto beans
1 pound ground turkey
1 cup chopped red, yellow,
   or green sweet pepper
1 cup chopped onion
2 cloves garlic, minced
2 28-ounce cans low-sodium
   whole tomatoes, cut up
2 tablespoons red wine vinegar
1 tablespoon chili powder
1 teaspoon dried oregano,
   crushed
1 teaspoon dried basil, crushed
1 teaspoon ground cumin
¼ teaspoon bottled hot pepper
   sauce

1. Rinse and drain canned beans; set aside. Spray a Dutch oven with *nonstick spray coating.* Cook ground turkey, pepper, onion, and garlic till turkey is browned and vegetables are tender.

2. Stir in beans, undrained tomatoes, vinegar, chili powder, oregano, basil, cumin, and hot pepper sauce. Bring to boiling; reduce heat. Simmer, covered, for 20 minutes. If a thicker consistency is desired, cook, uncovered, for 10 to 15 minutes more. Makes 6 main-dish servings.

Nutrition facts per serving: 274 calories, 7 g total fat (2 g saturated fat), 28 mg cholesterol, 376 mg sodium, 38 g carbohydrate, 10 g fiber, 23 g protein. **Daily values:** 29% vitamin A, 106% vitamin C, 12% calcium, 32% iron.

Low-fat

Low-calorie

Low-sodium

VEAL STEW WITH BABY CARROTS

1 pound boneless veal
1 clove garlic, minced
2 teaspoons cooking oil
1 14½-ounce can reduced-
   sodium chicken broth
1 cup dry white wine
1 teaspoon dried thyme,
   crushed
1 bay leaf
8 ounces fresh mushrooms
2 cups baby carrots
1 10-ounce package frozen
   small whole onions
3 tablespoons all-purpose flour
¼ cup snipped fresh parsley

1. Cut veal into 1-inch cubes. In a kettle or Dutch oven cook veal, *half* at a time, and garlic in oil till meat is browned. Drain off excess fat. Add broth, wine, thyme, bay leaf, and ¼ teaspoon *pepper.* Bring to boiling; reduce heat. Simmer, covered, for 45 minutes.

2. Meanwhile, slice mushrooms. Add mushrooms, carrots, and onions to veal; simmer for 20 minutes more or till vegetables are tender. Stir together flour and ⅓ cup *water;* stir into stew. Cook and stir till thickened and bubbly. Cook for 1 minute more. Stir in parsley. Makes 6 main-dish servings.

Nutrition facts per serving: 259 calories, 6 g total fat (2 g saturated fat), 102 mg cholesterol, 269 mg sodium, 13 g carbohydrate, 1 g fiber, 31 g protein. **Daily values:** 11% vitamin A, 17% vitamin C, 3 % calcium, 16% iron.

Low-fat
Low-calorie

CHICKEN STEW WITH TORTELLINI

This one-dish, healthful meal has an Italian flair. (See photo, left.)

1 medium zucchini
1 red or green sweet pepper
1 medium onion
1 14½-ounce can sodium-reduced chicken broth
6 cups torn beet or turnip greens, or torn spinach
1½ cups sliced carrots
1 cup cheese-filled dried tortellini
1 teaspoon dried basil, crushed
½ teaspoon dried oregano, crushed
½ teaspoon salt-free seasoning blend
2 cups chopped cooked chicken

1. Halve zucchini lengthwise and cut into ½-inch slices. Coarsely chop red or green sweet pepper. Cut onion into bite-size wedges.

2. In a large kettle or Dutch oven bring broth and 2 cups *water* to boiling. Add zucchini or yellow squash, sweet pepper, onion, greens, carrots, tortellini, basil, oregano, seasoning blend, and ¼ teaspoon *pepper*. Reduce heat. Simmer, covered, about 15 minutes or till tortellini and vegetables are nearly tender.

3. Stir in cooked chicken. Cover and cook for 5 minutes more or till pasta and vegetables are tender. If desired, sprinkle with coarsely *ground pepper*. Makes 6 main-dish servings.

Nutrition facts per serving: 234 calories, 6 g total fat (1 g saturated fat), 45 mg cholesterol, 530 mg sodium, 22 g carbohydrate, 3 g fiber, 22 g protein. **Daily values:** 114% vitamin A, 55% vitamin C, 14% calcium, 13% iron.

Low-fat
Low-calorie
Low-sodium

OYSTER POTATO STEW

Flavorful and traditional, oyster stew now can be served as a smart and healthy dish.

1 cup chopped onion
1 cup red and/or green sweet pepper cut in julienne strips
1 cup sliced celery
2 teaspoons margarine or cooking oil
3 medium potatoes (about 1 pound), peeled and diced
1 8-ounce bottle clam juice
½ cup snipped parsley
1 teaspoon dried savory, crushed
¼ cup all-purpose flour
1 cup evaporated skim milk
12 ounces fresh whole oysters

1. In a large saucepan or Dutch oven cook onion, sweet pepper, and celery, covered, in margarine for 5 minutes or till celery is crisp-tender, stirring occasionally. Add potatoes, clam juice, parsley, savory, 2 cups *water*, and ¼ teaspoon *pepper*. Bring to boiling; reduce heat. Simmer, covered, for 20 to 25 minutes or till potatoes are tender.

2. Stir flour into milk; stir into stew. Cook and stir till thickened and bubbly. Reduce heat. Cook and stir for 2 minutes more. Stir in undrained oysters. Cook for 3 minutes more or till oysters are done (edges are curly). Makes 6 main-dish servings.

Nutrition facts per serving: 183 calories, 3 g total fat (1 g saturated fat), 32 mg cholesterol, 247 mg sodium, 29 g carbohydrate, 2 g fiber, 10 g protein. **Daily values:** 28% vitamin A, 73% vitamin C, 15% calcium, 72% iron.

Low-calorie

Low-sodium

High-fiber

LAMB STEW WITH BARLEY

This savory stew is a great reason to enjoy lamb more often.

1 **pound lean lamb stew meat**
2 **medium carrots**
2 **medium turnips, peeled**
1 **medium onion**
2 **teaspoons olive or cooking oil**
1 **14½-ounce can low-sodium**
   whole tomatoes, cut up
½ **of a 6-ounce can low-sodium**
   tomato paste (⅓ cup)
2 **stalks celery, sliced**
1 **14½-ounce can beef broth**
2 **teaspoons dried basil, crushed**
½ **teaspoon salt-free seasoning**
   blend
½ **cup pearl barley**

1. Cut meat into bite-size pieces. Cut carrots and turnips into 1-inch pieces. Cut onion into bite-size wedges.

2. In a large Dutch oven cook *half* of the meat in oil till browned. Remove from pan. Repeat with remaining meat. Drain off excess fat. Return meat to pan.

3. Stir in carrots, turnips, onion, undrained tomatoes, tomato paste, celery, broth, basil, seasoning blend, 1¼ cups *water,* and ¼ teaspoon *pepper.* Bring to boiling; reduce heat. Simmer, covered, for 45 minutes.

4. Stir in barley. Cook, covered, for 45 minutes more or till barley and lamb are tender. Makes 6 main-dish servings.

Nutrition facts per serving: 261 calories, 11 g total fat (4 g saturated fat), 42 mg cholesterol, 343 mg sodium, 24 g carbohydrate, 6 g fiber, 16 g protein. **Daily values:** 106% vitamin A, 37% vitamin C, 6% calcium, 19% iron.

Low-fat

Low-sodium

High-fiber

BEEF BURGUNDY

This all-time favorite dinner can be served in good health conscience.

1½ **pounds lean beef stew meat**
2 **cloves garlic, minced**
1 **10-ounce package frozen tiny**
   white onions
2 **cups Burgundy wine**
3 **cups baby carrots, peeled and**
   trimmed
1½ **teaspoons dried basil, crushed**
1 **bay leaf**
2 **tablespoons all-purpose flour**
½ **teaspoon beef bouillon**
   granules
1 **pound fresh mushrooms,**
   quartered
¼ **cup snipped parsley**

1. Cut meat into 1-inch pieces. Spray an oven-going kettle or Dutch oven with *nonstick spray coating.* Cook meat and garlic till browned. Remove from pan. In drippings cook onions, covered, about 5 minutes or till nearly tender. Remove from pan; cover and set aside. Drain off excess fat. Return meat to pan. Add wine, carrots, basil, bay leaf, ⅛ teaspoon *salt,* and ⅛ teaspoon coarsely *ground pepper.* Cover and bake in a 325° oven for 1½ to 2 hours or till meat is very tender.

2. Meanwhile, in a small bowl stir together flour and 2 tablespoons *water;* set aside. In a medium saucepan bring bouillon granules and 1 cup *water* to boiling. Add mushrooms. Simmer mushrooms, covered, for 5 minutes. Stir in flour mixture and reserved cooked onions. Stir mushroom mixture into Dutch oven; return to oven. Bake, covered, for 30 minutes more. Stir in *half* the parsley. Garnish with remaining parsley. Makes 6 main-dish servings.

Nutrition facts per serving: 316 calories, 9 g total fat (3 g saturated fat), 77 mg cholesterol, 259 mg sodium, 19 g carbohydrate, 4 g fiber, 29 g protein. **Daily values:** 172% vitamin A, 17% vitamin C, 4% calcium, 35% iron.

Low-fat

Low-calorie

Low-sodium

High-fiber

RATATOUILLE WITH CHICKEN

We added chicken to this classic vegetable stew, and created a sensational main-dish.

2 14½-ounce cans low-sodium
   whole tomatoes, cut up
1 cup reduced-sodium chicken
   broth
1 medium eggplant, peeled and
   cut into ½-inch cubes
1 red sweet pepper, cut into
   1-inch squares
1 yellow or green sweet pepper,
   cut into 1-inch squares
2 medium zucchini, halved
   lengthwise and cut into
   ¼-inch slices
1 cup sliced red onion
2 tablespoons snipped fresh
   basil or 2 teaspoons dried
   basil, crushed
4 teaspoons snipped fresh
   oregano or 1 teaspoon
   dried oregano, crushed
1 tablespoon snipped fresh
   rosemary or 1 teaspoon
   dried rosemary, crushed
2 cloves garlic, minced
¼ teaspoon pepper
12 ounces skinless, boneless
   chicken breasts, cut into
   bite-size strips
1 tablespoon grated Parmesan
   cheese

1. In a large kettle or Dutch oven combine undrained tomatoes, broth, eggplant, sweet peppers, zucchini, onion, basil, oregano, rosemary, garlic, and pepper. Bring to boiling; reduce heat. Simmer, covered, for 20 minutes or till vegetables are nearly tender.

2. Stir in chicken. Cook for 10 minutes more or till chicken is no longer pink. Sprinkle with Parmesan. Makes 4 main-dish servings.

Nutrition facts per serving: 225 calories, 4 g total fat (1 g saturated fat), 46 mg cholesterol, 263 mg sodium, 28 g carbohydrate, 7 g fiber, 22 g protein. **Daily values:** 29% vitamin A, 255% vitamin C, 10% calcium, 18% iron.

The easiest way to cut up the tomatoes is right in the cans. Use your kitchen shears to snip the tomatoes into coarse pieces.

Low-fat

Low-sodium

High-fiber

CARIBBEAN-STYLE PORK STEW

Slices of fresh mango or papaya make a cooling accompaniment to this spicy stew. (See photo, right.)

2 teaspoons cooking oil

12 ounces boneless lean pork,
cut into 1-inch cubes

1 cup chopped onion

1 cup chopped red, yellow, or
green sweet pepper

1 clove garlic, minced

1 14½-ounce can beef broth

1¾ cups water

1 cup chopped tomatoes

1 tablespoon grated gingerroot

1 teaspoon ground cumin

¼ teaspoon crushed red pepper

3 plantains, peeled and cubed

1 15-ounce can black beans,
rinsed and drained

3 cups hot cooked rice

1. Heat oil in a large kettle or Dutch oven. Add pork and cook till browned. Remove pork from pan. In drippings cook onion, sweet pepper, and garlic for 5 minutes. Drain off fat. Return pork to pan. Add broth, water, tomatoes, gingerroot, cumin, and crushed red pepper. Bring to boiling; reduce heat. Simmer, covered, for 45 minutes.

2. Add plantains and black beans. Simmer, covered, for 15 minutes more or till pork is tender. Serve with rice. Makes 6 main-dish servings.

Nutrition facts per serving: 383 calories, 8 g total fat (2 g saturated fat), 30 mg cholesterol, 433 mg sodium, 67 g carbohydrate, 6 g fiber, 18 g protein. **Daily values:** 22% vitamin A, 77% vitamin C, 4% calcium, 22% iron.

Serve It Hot

Serve soups and stews at just the right temperature by heating the individual bowls or mugs. Just before serving, run the containers under hot tap water, then dry with a towel. The warm containers help the soup stay hot.

Low-fat

Low-sodium

High-fiber

MULLIGATAWNY STEW

1 cup chopped onion
1 cup bias-cut carrots
1 cup chopped celery
3 cloves garlic, minced
1 14½-ounce can reduced-
   sodium chicken broth
1 cup chopped apple
2 tablespoons snipped fresh
   cilantro or parsley
1 tablespoon grated gingerroot
1 tablespoon curry powder
1 teaspoon ground cumin
1 pound skinless, boneless
   chicken breasts or thighs
1 14½-ounce can low-sodium
   whole tomatoes, cut up
2 tablespoons all-purpose flour
½ cup plain fat-free yogurt
2 cups hot cooked couscous or
   rice

1. Spray a Dutch oven with *nonstick spray coating*. Cook onion, carrots, celery, and garlic for 10 minutes. Stir in broth, apple, cilantro, gingerroot, curry, and cumin. Bring to boiling; reduce heat. Simmer, covered, for 10 minutes.

2. Rinse chicken; pat dry. Cut into 1-inch pieces. Add chicken and undrained tomatoes to stew. Simmer for 10 minutes or till chicken and vegetables are tender. Stir flour into yogurt. Stir into stew. Cook and stir till thickened and bubbly. Cook and stir for 1 minute more. Serve with couscous or rice. Makes 4 main-dish servings.

Nutrition facts per serving: 359 calories, 5 g total fat (1 g saturated fat), 60 mg cholesterol, 459 mg sodium, 49 g carbohydrate, 9 g fiber, 31 g protein. **Daily values:** 125% vitamin A, 40% vitamin C, 14% calcium, 24% iron.

Low-fat

Low-sodium

High-fiber

EASY BEEF GOULASH

1 pound lean beef stew meat
2 medium onions
2 teaspoons cooking oil
½ cup beef broth
1½ cups reduced-sodium tomato
   juice
¼ cup low-sodium tomato paste
4 teaspoons paprika
½ teaspoon caraway seed
8 ounces rutabagas or sweet
   potatoes
2 tablespoons snipped parsley
3 cups cooked wide noodles

1. Cut meat into 1-inch cubes; cut onions into bite-size wedges. Heat oil in a large Dutch oven. Add meat and onions and cook till meat is browned.

2. Add broth, tomato juice, tomato paste, paprika, caraway seed, ½ cup *water*, and ¼ teaspoon *pepper*. Bring to boiling; reduce heat. Simmer, covered, for 1 hour.

3. Meanwhile, peel and chop rutabagas or sweet potatoes. (You should have about 2½ cups.) Add rutabagas or sweet potatoes to Dutch oven. Cover and cook for 20 to 30 minutes more or till meat and rutabagas are tender. Stir in parsley. Serve with noodles. Makes 4 main-dish servings.

Nutrition facts per serving: 397 calories, 13 g total fat (4 g saturated fat), 107 mg cholesterol, 188 mg sodium, 38 g carbohydrate, 5 g fiber, 34 g protein. **Daily values:** 26% vitamin A, 68% vitamin C, 6% calcium, 39% iron.

Low-fat

Low-calorie

Low-sodium

WEST COAST CIOPPINO

This classic is usually served with crusty sourdough bread which is great for dipping into the flavorful broth.

  1 cup chopped yellow or green
     sweet pepper
¾ cup chopped onion
½ cup sliced celery
  2 cloves garlic, minced
  2 teaspoons cooking oil
  1 16-ounce can low-sodium
     whole tomatoes, cut up
  1 8-ounce can low-sodium
     tomato sauce
  1 cup reduced-sodium chicken
     broth
  1 cup dry white wine or
     reduced-sodium chicken
     broth
1½ teaspoons dried basil, crushed
  1 teaspoon dried oregano,
     crushed
  1 teaspoon paprika
¼ teaspoon pepper
  1 pound fresh or frozen fish
     fillets, thawed
  8 ounces medium shrimp,
     shelled and deveined
  1 6½-ounce can minced clams
  1 tablespoon snipped fresh
     parsley
    Lemon wedges

1. In a large saucepan cook sweet pepper, onion, celery, and garlic in oil for 5 minutes. Stir in undrained tomatoes, tomato sauce, broth, wine, basil, oregano, paprika, and pepper. Bring to boiling; reduce heat. Cover and simmer for 20 minutes.

2. Cut fish into 1-inch pieces. Add fish, shrimp, undrained clams, and parsley to tomato mixture. Bring just to boiling; reduce heat. Cover and simmer for 5 to 7 minutes more or till fish flakes easily with a fork. Serve with lemon wedges. Makes 6 main-dish servings.

Nutrition facts per serving: 189 calories, 3 g total fat (1 g saturated fat), 93 mg cholesterol, 251 mg sodium, 12 g carbohydrate, 2 g fiber, 22 g protein. **Daily values:** 14% vitamin A, 86% vitamin C, 6% calcium, 23% iron.

Low-fat

Low-calorie

Low-sodium

High-fiber

TURKEY STEW

This is probably one of the fastest stews you can make. Serve it over cooked egg noodles or brown rice.

12 ounces turkey tenderloins,
    cut into bite-size pieces
 2 teaspoons cooking oil
 1 large onion, cut into wedges
 2 cloves garlic, minced
 1 cup reduced-sodium chicken
    broth
¾ cup water
 1 16-ounce bag frozen zucchini,
    carrots, cauliflower, lima
    beans, and Italian beans
 1 8-ounce can low-sodium
    tomato sauce
 2 teaspoons dried Italian
    seasoning
¼ teaspoon pepper
 2 tablespoons all-purpose flour
¼ cup dry white wine, reduced-
    sodium chicken broth,
    or water
¼ cup snipped fresh parsley

1. In a large kettle or Dutch oven cook turkey in oil till browned. Remove from pan. In pan drippings cook onion and garlic for 3 minutes. Return turkey to pan. Add broth, water, vegetables, tomato sauce, Italian seasoning, and pepper. Bring to boiling; reduce heat. Simmer, covered, for 15 minutes.

2. Stir flour into wine, reduced-sodium chicken broth, or water. Stir into stew. Cook and stir till thickened and bubbly. Cook for 1 minute more. Sprinkle with parsley. Makes 4 main-dish servings.

Nutrition facts per serving: 215 calories, 4 g total fat (1 g saturated fat), 37 mg cholesterol, 242 mg sodium, 20 g carbohydrate, 4 g fiber, 21 g protein. **Daily values:** 87% vitamin A, 86% vitamin C, 5% calcium, 18% iron.

The Frozen Facts About Vegetables

To keep up with today's hectic pace and healthy lifestyle, look no further than your grocer's freezer case for frozen vegetables. They are quick and easy to prepare, and packed with as much or more nutrition than fresh vegetables. You'll also find a huge variety to choose from with all different package sizes to fit anyone's needs.

To keep the fat, calories, and sodium in line, avoid frozen vegetables in sauces and butter.

Need a few more good reasons to eat frozen vegetables? Consider these:

Frozen vegetables are often picked and frozen within 4 to 6 hours, locking in vitamins and minerals.

Frozen vegetables are convenient and easy to prepare because little or no preparation time is required.

Frozen vegetables are a good value because there's more usable portion per pound than fresh.

Frozen vegetables reduce waste because every vegetable in the package is usable.

Frozen vegetables are consistently priced from season to season.

Frozen vegetables are available year-round in your grocer's freezer case.

VALUABLE VEGETABLES

Calorie for calorie, few foods offer as much of a nutrition bargain as vegetables. These tantalizing morsels are packed with vitamins and minerals that are essential for good health and may even play a role in preventing certain diseases. Just as important, vegetables add deliciously colorful accents to meals. Steamed just till crisp-tender, Broccoli and Peppers are quick to prepare and pair well with meat, poultry, and fish. Family and guests alike will savor our fat-slashed version of Twice-Baked Potatoes and ask for them again and again. In Mediterranean-Style Vegetables, zucchini, broccoli, sweet peppers, tomatoes, and fresh basil team up for a tantalizing combination that looks as good as it tastes. Review the wide array of delightful, vitamin-rich dishes and choose one for today.

Low-fat

Low-calorie

High-fiber

STUFFED ARTICHOKES WITH TOMATOES, GARLIC, AND ONION

Artichokes are low in calories—one medium artichoke, steamed, has just 25! (See Stuffed Artichokes photo, left.)

4 medium artichokes
  Lemon juice
1 cup chopped mushrooms
½ cup chopped onion
3 cloves garlic, minced
2 teaspoons olive or cooking oil
2 cups chopped tomatoes
1 teaspoon dried Italian
  seasoning, crushed
⅛ teaspoon pepper
1 tablespoon fine dry bread
  crumbs
  Nonstick spray coating
2 tablespoons grated Parmesan
  cheese

1. Wash artichokes and trim stems. Cut off 1 inch from tops and snip off sharp leaf tips. Brush cut edges with lemon juice. Cook artichokes, covered, in a large amount of boiling water for 20 to 30 minutes or till a leaf pulls out easily. Invert to drain. Cool slightly.

2. Meanwhile, in a nonstick skillet, cook mushrooms, onion, and garlic in oil for 3 minutes. Stir in tomatoes, Italian seasoning, and pepper. Cook 1 minute. Remove from heat. Stir in bread crumbs and set aside.

3. Cut each artichoke in half from top to stem. Remove and discard fuzzy choke. Spray a shallow 2-quart rectangular baking dish with nonstick coating. Arrange artichokes, cut side up, in dish. Spoon tomato mixture into artichoke halves, mounding slightly on top. Sprinkle cheese over filling. Bake in a 350° oven for 15 to 20 minutes or till heated through. Makes 8 servings.

Nutritional facts per serving: 121 calories, 2 g total fat (1 g saturated fat), 1 mg cholesterol, 192 mg sodium, 23 g carbohydrate, 9 g fiber, 7 g protein. **Daily values:** 6% vitamin A, 45% vitamin C, 8% calcium, 16% iron.

Buying Vegetables

Take a few minutes in the produce section and inspect each vegetable before you buy. Look for plump, crisp, brightly colored vegetables that are heavy for their size (this indicates moistness). Avoid vegetables that are bruised, shriveled, moldy, or blemished.

Artichokes: Pick firm globes with large, tightly closed leaves. Darkened leaves do not affect quality.

Asparagus: Choose firm, straight stalks with compact, closed tips. Avoid stalks that are either very thin (less than ⅛ inch) or very thick (more than ½ inch), because they may be stringy.

Broccoli: Look for firm, tender stalks bearing small crisp leaves. The dark green buds should be tightly closed and show no sign of flowering.

Corn: Check for bright, green husks and well-filled, even rows of plump kernels.

Green beans: Buy long pods that snap crisply when you bend them.

Mushrooms: Pick plump, firm mushrooms with closed caps. Avoid open caps or mushrooms with blemishes.

Potatoes: Find firm, smooth spuds with shallow eyes. Don't buy potatoes with sprouts or green patches.

Low-calorie

BRUSSELS SPROUTS WITH GARLIC CREAM SAUCE

With convenient light products like fat-free mayonnaise dressing, you can enjoy creamed vegetables guilt-free!

1 10-ounce package frozen
  brussels sprouts
2 cloves garlic, minced
1 teaspoon olive or cooking oil
2 tablespoons fat-free
  mayonnaise dressing or
  salad dressing
2 tablespoons plain fat-free
  yogurt
4 to 5 tablespoons skim milk
1 tablespoon snipped parsley

1. Cook brussels sprouts in a small amount of boiling water according to package directions. Drain and transfer to a serving dish. Cover and keep warm.

2. In same pan cook garlic in oil for 1 minute. Stir in mayonnaise dressing or salad dressing, yogurt, and enough milk to make of desired consistency. Heat through. Do not boil. Stir in parsley. Pour sauce atop brussels sprouts. Makes 4 servings.

Nutritional facts per serving: 58 calories, 2 g total fat (0 g saturated fat), 0 mg cholesterol, 125 mg sodium, 10 g carbohydrate, 3 g fiber, 3 g protein. **Daily values:** 6% vitamin A, 83% vitamin C, 5% calcium, 6% iron.

Low-fat

Low-calorie

High-fiber

ORANGE GLAZED BRUSSELS SPROUTS AND CARROTS

Serve this winter specialty with roasted duck or poultry.

2 cups fresh brussels sprouts or
  one 10-ounce package
  frozen brussels sprouts
3 medium carrots, cut
  lengthwise into quarters,
  then into 1-inch pieces
1/3 cup orange juice
1 teaspoon cornstarch
1/2 teaspoon sugar
1/4 teaspoon salt
1/4 teaspoon ground nutmeg
  (optional)

1. Cut brussels sprouts in half. Cook brussels sprouts and carrots, covered, in a small amount of boiling water for 10 to 12 minutes or till crisp-tender. Drain; remove from pan.

2. In the same saucepan combine orange juice, cornstarch, sugar, salt, and nutmeg, if desired. Add brussels sprouts and carrots. Cook and stir the mixture till thickened and bubbly. Cook and stir for 1 minute more. Makes 4 servings.

Nutritional facts per serving: 61 calories, 1 g total fat (0 g saturated fat), 0 mg cholesterol, 184 mg sodium, 14 g carbohydrate, 4 g fiber, 3 g protein. **Daily values:** 90% vitamin A, 100% vitamin C, 3% calcium, 8% iron.

Low-fat

Low-calorie

MEXICAN GRILLED CORN

You'll never miss the butter when you grill corn on the cob with this seasoned topping.

2 tablespoons reduced-calorie
    margarine, melted
1 4-ounce can diced, mild
    green chilies, drained
2 tablespoons snipped cilantro
    or parsley
¼ teaspoon ground cumin
¼ teaspoon salt-free seasoning
    blend
6 ears corn, husked

1. In a small bowl combine margarine, chilies, cilantro, cumin, and seasoning blend. Set aside.

2. Rinse corn and pat dry with paper towels. Place each ear of corn on a piece of heavy foil. Brush corn with chili mixture. Wrap corn securely in heavy foil.

3. Grill corn on the rack of a grill directly over medium to medium-high coals about 20 minutes or till kernels are tender, turning twice. (Or, bake in a 375° oven for 20 to 25 minutes, turning twice.) Unwrap corn and spread remaining chili mixture on the foil over the corn. Makes 6 servings.

Nutritional facts per serving: 86 calories, 2 g total fat (0 g saturated fat), 0 mg cholesterol, 136 mg sodium, 17 g carbohydrate, 2 g fiber, 3 g protein. **Daily values:** 6% vitamin A, 12% vitamin C, 0% calcium, 2% iron.

Low-fat

Low-calorie

STIR-FRIED BROCCOLI AND CARROTS

If you like, buy pre-cut broccoli and carrots for this easy side dish.

⅓ cup orange juice
1 tablespoon reduced-sodium
    soy sauce
1 teaspoon cornstarch
    Nonstick spray coating
1 teaspoon grated gingerroot
1½ cups thinly bias-sliced carrots
1 cup broccoli flowerets

1. For sauce, stir together orange juice, soy sauce, and cornstarch. Set aside.

2. Spray a wok or large skillet with nonstick spray coating. Preheat over medium heat. Stir-fry gingerroot for 15 seconds. Add carrots. Stir-fry for 2 minutes. Add broccoli. Stir-fry about 4 minutes or till vegetables are crisp-tender. Push vegetables from center of wok or skillet.

3. Stir sauce. Add to center of wok. Cook and stir till thickened and bubbly. Cook and stir for 1 minute more. Stir all ingredients together to heat through. Makes 4 servings.

Nutritional facts per serving: 50 calories, 1 g total fat (0 g saturated fat), 0 mg cholesterol, 174 mg sodium, 10 g carbohydrate, 3 g fiber, 2 g protein. **Daily values:** 132% vitamin A, 54% vitamin C, 2% calcium, 4% iron.

Low-calorie

Low-sodium

BROCCOLI AND PEPPERS

If you don't have a steamer basket, improvise with a metal colander to prepare this dish. (See photo, right.)

1 pound broccoli, cut into
    flowerets

1 red or yellow sweet pepper,
    cut into 1-inch pieces

2 tablespoons reduced-calorie
    margarine

1 teaspoon finely shredded
    lemon peel

1 tablespoon lemon juice

1/8 teaspoon pepper

1. Place broccoli and pepper in a steamer basket over simmering water. Steam, covered, for 8 to 12 minutes or till vegetables are crisp-tender. Drain. Arrange on a serving platter.

2. Meanwhile, in a small saucepan melt the margarine. Stir in lemon peel, lemon juice, and pepper. Drizzle over broccoli mixture. Makes 6 servings.

Nutritional facts per serving: 42 calories, 2 g total fat (0 g saturated fat), 0 mg cholesterol, 63 mg sodium, 5 g carbohydrate, 3 g fiber, 2 g protein. **Daily values:** 23% vitamin A, 131% vitamin C, 3% calcium, 4% iron.

The Many Colors of Sweet Peppers

With its mild flavor, the familiar green bell pepper is still a favorite in salads, stir-fries, and casseroles, but more and more cooks are turning to sweet peppers in other hues to brighten their dishes. These varieties are available in most grocery stores.

    Chocolate: Brown bell pepper with a green stem and interior; turns green when cooked

    Golden or orange: Red-orange bell pepper with a green stem and orange interior

    Green: Traditional green bell pepper with a green stem and green interior

    Purple: Purple bell pepper with a green stem and interior; turns green when cooked

    Red: Vine-ripened green bell pepper that turns red and has a green stem and a red interior

    Yellow: Yellow bell pepper with a green stem and yellow interior

Low-fat

Low-calorie

Low-sodium

COLLARD GREENS WITH MUSHROOMS

Collards are mild-flavored greens that are actually a type of kale.

¼ **cup reduced-sodium chicken broth**

12 **cups torn collard greens or spinach (10 ounces)**

1½ **cups sliced mushrooms**

1 **teaspoon dried basil, crushed**

¼ **teaspoon pepper**

1. In a Dutch oven or large saucepan bring broth to boiling.

2. Add greens or spinach, mushrooms, basil, and pepper. Reduce heat. Cover and cook till just tender (9 to 12 minutes for collards; 3 to 5 minutes for spinach). Serves 4.

Nutritional facts per serving: 35 calories, 0 g total fat (0% saturated fat), 0 mg cholesterol, 76 mg sodium, 7 g carbohydrate, 3 g fiber, 3 g protein. **Daily values:** 42% vitamin A, 33% vitamin C, 12% calcium, 8% iron.

Microwave Magic

Press a few buttons, and 1 minute later your microwave melts margarine right before your eyes. Is it magic? No. Is it convenient? Yes. Here are a few other tricks you can pull out of your microwave oven to help save time in the kitchen. These tips were tested using 600- to 700-watt ovens, so if your oven has fewer watts, you may need to increase the cooking time. Remember to always use microwave-safe dishes.

Cooking frozen vegetables: In a 1-quart casserole place 1½ cups loose-pack frozen vegetables and 1 tablespoon water. Cover and cook on 100% power (high) till crisp-tender, stirring once. Drain. Allow 2½ to 3 minutes for broccoli cuts, whole kernel corn, and peas. Allow 4 to 5 minutes for cut green beans, crinkle-cut carrots, cauliflower flowerets, and mixed vegetables.

Baking potatoes: Prick medium potatoes (5 to 6 ounces each) with a fork. Cook, uncovered, on 100% power (high) till almost tender, rearranging once. Allow 5 to 7 minutes for 1 potato and 8 to 10 minutes for 2 potatoes. Let stand 5 minutes.

Melting margarine: Place margarine in a custard cup. Cook, uncovered, on 100% power (high) till melted. Allow 40 to 50 seconds for 2 tablespoons, 45 to 60 seconds for ¼ cup, and 1 to 2 minutes for ½ cup.

Softening margarine: Place margarine in a custard cup. Cook, uncovered, on 10% power (low) till softened. Allow 45 seconds for 2 tablespoons and 1 to 1½ minutes for ¼ to ½ cup.

Softening tortillas: Place four 6- to 8-inch flour tortillas between paper towels. Cook on 100% power (high) for 45 to 60 seconds or till softened.

Low-fat

Low-calorie

Low-sodium

High-fiber

PARSNIP AND APPLE SAUTÉ

A good rule of thumb is to purchase parsnips that are the size of carrots. Larger ones may have less flavor and a soft interior.

**12 ounces parsnips, peeled and
chopped**

**1 tablespoon reduced-calorie
margarine**

**1 medium red apple, cored
and diced**

**⅓ cup unsweetened apple cider
or juice**

**1 tablespoon snipped fresh
chives or 1 teaspoon dried
snipped chives**

Dash salt

⅛ teaspoon pepper

1. Place parsnips in a steamer basket over simmering water. Steam, covered, for 8 to 10 minutes or till nearly tender. Drain.

2. In a large nonstick skillet melt margarine. Add parsnips and apples. Cook and stir for 3 minutes. Stir in apple cider or juice, chives, salt, and pepper. Bring to boiling; reduce heat. Simmer about 2 minutes or till apples and parsnips are tender. Makes 4 servings.

Nutritional facts per serving: 133 calories, 2 g total fat (0 g saturated fat), 0 mg cholesterol, 79 mg sodium, 30 g carbohydrate, 6 g fiber, 2 g protein. **Daily values:** 3% vitamin A, 29% vitamin C, 4% calcium, 5% iron.

Low-fat

Low-calorie

Low-sodium

HONEY-GLAZED ONIONS

Serve these diminutive onions with sliced, roasted pork or ham, or oven-roasted chicken.

**2 cups fresh or frozen small
whole onions**

2 tablespoons honey

**2 tablespoons white wine
vinegar**

1 teaspoon dried basil, crushed

¼ teaspoon ground sage

1. Peel fresh onions. Cook, covered, in boiling water for 8 to 10 minutes or till just tender. (Or, cook frozen onions according to package directions.) Drain.

2. In same saucepan combine honey, vinegar, basil, and sage. Add onions. Cook and stir till onions are glazed and heated through. Makes 4 servings.

Nutritional facts per serving: 78 calories, 0 g total fat (0 g saturated fat), 0 mg cholesterol, 4 mg sodium, 19 g carbohydrate, 2 g fiber, 1 g protein. **Daily values:** 0% vitamin A, 8% vitamin C, 2% calcium, 2% iron.

Low-fat

Low-calorie

High-fiber

BAKED FENNEL WITH LEEKS

Here's an elegant vegetable that can bake right along with your beef, pork, or lamb. (See photo, left.)

4 8-ounce fennel bulbs
1 teaspoon cooking oil
2 cups sliced leeks
1 clove garlic, minced
½ cup reduced-sodium chicken
  broth
⅛ teaspoon pepper

1. Trim tops from fennel. Chop leaves to make 2 tablespoons. Set leaves aside. Cut bulbs into wedges.

2. In a large nonstick skillet heat oil over medium-high heat. Cook and stir fennel, leeks, and garlic in oil for 5 minutes or till lightly brown. Transfer vegetables to a 2-quart square baking dish. Pour broth over vegetables. Sprinkle with pepper. Cover and bake in a 350° oven about 30 minutes or till fennel is tender. Sprinkle with chopped fennel leaves over top. Makes 4 servings.

Nutritional facts per serving: 122 calories, 2 g total fat (0 g saturated fat), 0 mg cholesterol, 170 mg sodium, 26 g carbohydrate, 4 g fiber, 4 g protein. **Daily values:** 0% vitamin A, 54% vitamin C, 12% calcium, 9% iron.

Easy Cleanup

To help get you in and out of the kitchen in record time, follow these simple cleaning tips.

Crusty broiler pans: Coat surface of dirty pan with dish washing liquid. Cover with a damp paper towel and let stand till it softens.

Burned pots and pans: Do not run cold water into your hot pans because this can warp them. Instead, let the pans cool and fill with water, adding a little baking soda. Boil gently till the food loosens. Do not use baking soda to clean aluminum pots and pans. Just boil water in aluminum pans till the food loosens. Then wash the pots and pans with hot soapy water to complete the cleanup.

Low-fat

Low-calorie

Low-sodium

MINTED SWEET PEAS

For a colorful presentation, serve these peas inside a red or yellow bell pepper ring on each dinner plate.

1 green onion, sliced
1 tablespoon reduced-calorie
    margarine
2 cups shelled peas or
    one 10-ounce package
    frozen peas
¼ cup reduced-sodium chicken
    broth or water
½ teaspoon sugar
⅛ teaspoon pepper
2 teaspoons snipped fresh mint
    Lemon slices (optional)
    Mint leaves (optional)

1. In a medium saucepan cook green onion in margarine for 2 minutes. Stir in peas, broth or water, sugar, and pepper. Bring to boiling; reduce heat.

2. Simmer, covered, for 10 to 12 minutes or till crisp-tender. (Or, cook frozen peas according to package directions.) Stir in snipped mint. Garnish with lemon slices and mint leaves, if desired. Makes 4 servings.

Nutritional facts per serving: 73 calories, 2 g total fat (0 g saturated fat), 0 mg cholesterol, 75 mg sodium, 11 g carbohydrate, 2 g fiber, 4 g protein. **Daily values:** 8% vitamin A, 17% vitamin C, 1% calcium, 8% iron.

Low-fat

Low-calorie

High-fiber

BLACK BEAN-STUFFED PEPPERS

This side dish is a great accompaniment to a well-spiced chicken or pork dish.

2 medium red, yellow, or green
    sweet peppers
½ cup chopped red onion
½ cup chopped carrots
½ cup loose-pack frozen whole
    kernel corn
1 16-ounce can black or
    cannellini beans, rinsed and
    drained
3 tablespoons fat-free ranch-
    style or Italian salad
    dressing
¼ teaspoon pepper
    Nonstick spray coating
1 tablespoon grated Parmesan
    cheese

1. Halve peppers lengthwise, removing stem ends, seeds, and membranes. Cook peppers in boiling water for 3 to 5 minutes or till crisp-tender. Invert and drain on paper towels.

2. Cook onion and carrots in boiling water for 3 minutes. Stir in corn. Cook 2 minutes more. Drain well. Stir in beans, dressing, and pepper.

3. Spray a 2-quart square baking dish with nonstick spray coating. Arrange pepper halves, cut side up, in dish. Spoon bean mixture into peppers. Sprinkle with cheese. Bake in a 350° oven for 25 to 30 minutes or till heated through. Makes 4 servings.

Nutritional facts per serving: 129 calories, 1 g total fat (0 g saturated fat), 1 mg cholesterol, 419 mg sodium, 26 g carbohydrate, 6 g fiber, 9 g protein. **Daily values:** 76% vitamin A, 107% vitamin C, 5% calcium, 10% iron.

Low-fat

Low-sodium

TWO-POTATO GRATIN

Evaporated skim milk works well in cooking and in baked items like this casserole, because it won't separate or curdle.

Nonstick spray coating
2 medium sweet potatoes, peeled and shredded
2 large white, yellow Finnish, Yukon gold, or red potatoes, peeled and shredded
1 cup evaporated skim milk
1 tablespoon all-purpose flour
1 teaspoon dried basil, crushed
½ cup shredded reduced-fat Swiss cheese product or reduced-fat mozzarella cheese
¼ cup fine dry bread crumbs
3 tablespoons snipped parsley

1. Spray a 2-quart square baking dish with nonstick spray coating. Place potatoes in dish. In a small bowl combine milk, flour, and basil. Pour over potatoes.

2. Cover and bake in a 400° oven for 60 minutes, stirring after 30 and 45 minutes. Stir again. Sprinkle with a mixture of cheese, bread crumbs, and parsley. Bake, uncovered, 10 minutes more. Makes 6 to 8 servings.

Nutritional facts per serving: 176 calories, 2 g total fat (1 g saturated fat), 8 mg cholesterol, 74 mg sodium, 31 g carbohydrate, 2 g fiber, 9 g protein. **Daily values:** 93% vitamin A, 30% vitamin C, 19% calcium, 5% iron.

Low-fat

Low-calorie

ROASTED GARLIC MASHED POTATOES

Garlic is neither fattening, nor high in calories and adds a lot of flavor to these mashed potatoes.

5 cloves garlic, unpeeled
½ teaspoon olive oil
3 medium potatoes (1 pound), peeled and quartered
4½ teaspoons butter-flavored seasoning mix
1 tablespoon snipped fresh chives or 1 teaspoon dried snipped chives
¼ teaspoon salt-free seasoning blend
⅓ to ½ cup skim milk, warmed

1. Place unpeeled garlic cloves in a 6-ounce custard cup. Drizzle oil over garlic. Cover with foil. Bake in a 350° oven about 30 minutes or till garlic is tender. Cool 5 minutes. Squeeze garlic pulp from skins.

2. Meanwhile, cook potatoes, covered, in a small amount of boiling water for 20 to 25 minutes or till tender. Drain. Mash potatoes with a potato masher or beat with an electric mixer on low speed. Add garlic, butter mix, chives, and salt-free seasoning. Gradually beat in enough of the milk to make light and fluffy. Makes 5 servings.

Nutritional facts per serving: 87 calories, 1 g total fat (0 g saturated fat), 0 mg cholesterol, 81 mg sodium, 18 g carbohydrate, 1 g fiber, 2 g protein. **Daily values:** 1% vitamin A, 12% vitamin C, 2% calcium, 2% iron.

Low-fat

Low-sodium

TWICE-BAKED POTATOES

Company coming? (See photo, right.) You can make these potoates ahead of time.
Just cover and refrigerate, adding 10 to 15 minutes to the baking time.

**4 medium baking potatoes or
    sweet potatoes**
¼ cup buttermilk or skim milk
¼ cup light dairy sour cream
**1 tablespoon snipped fresh
    chives or 1 teaspoon dried
    snipped chives**
  Paprika

1. Scrub potatoes and pierce several times with a fork. Wrap each in foil. Bake in a 425° oven for 40 to 60 minutes or till tender.

2. When potatoes are done, roll each one gently under your hand. Cut a lengthwise slice from the top of each potato. Discard skin from slice and place pulp in a bowl. Gently scoop out each potato, leaving a thin shell. Add pulp to the bowl.

3. With an electric mixer on low speed or a potato masher, beat or mash potato pulp. Add buttermilk or milk, sour cream, and chives. Beat till smooth. Pile mashed potato mixture into potato shells. Sprinkle with paprika. Place in a 2-quart square baking dish. Bake in a 425° oven for 20 to 25 minutes or till lightly browned. Makes 4 servings.

Nutritional facts per serving: 183 calories, 1 g total fat (1 g saturated fat), 3 mg cholesterol, 46 mg sodium, 39 g carbohydrate, 1 g fiber, 1 g protein. **Daily values:** 2% vitamin A, 38% vitamin C, 4% calcium, 12% iron.

Get Kids Involved in Good Nutrition

It's important to establish good eating habits early in a child's life. Here are a few ways to involve kids in good nutrition:

  Discuss what makes a healthful meal. Then set up guidelines for family meals to include a vegetable, fruit, whole grain, milk, and protein food. Let them help in menu planning.

  Allow your children to help prepare the food. Depending on their ages, let them stir together a yogurt fruit salad, toss a vegetable salad, or mash the potatoes.

  Put their green thumbs to work in a small garden. Carrots, green beans, lettuce, and spinach the kids grow themselves will have new appeal.

Low-fat

Low-calorie

HERBED POTATO-STUFFING PATTIES

Here's a low-fat alternative to traditional stuffing.

3 medium potatoes (1 pound), peeled and cubed

¼ to ⅓ cup skim milk

½ cup chopped red, yellow, or green sweet pepper

½ cup cornbread stuffing mix

¼ cup chopped green onions

2 tablespoons snipped parsley

1 egg white

½ teaspoon salt-free seasoning blend

⅛ teaspoon salt

Nonstick spray coating

1 tablespoon reduced-calorie margarine, melted

1. Cook potatoes, covered, in a small amount of boiling water for 20 to 25 minutes or till tender. Drain.

2. Mash potatoes with a potato masher or beat with an electric mixer on low speed, adding as much milk as needed. Stir in sweet pepper, stuffing mix, green onions, parsley, egg white, seasoning blend, and salt. Shape mixture into 6 patties.

3. Spray a baking sheet with nonstick coating. Place potato patties on baking sheet. Brush with margarine. Bake in a 425° oven for 7 to 10 minutes or till golden brown and heated through. Makes 6 servings.

Nutritional facts per serving: 122 calories, 2 g total fat (0 g saturated fat), 0 mg cholesterol, 167 mg sodium, 24 g carbohydrate, 1 g fiber, 4 g protein. **Daily values:** 10% vitamin A, 43% vitamin C, 2% calcium, 10% iron.

Low-fat

Low-calorie

Low-sodium

High-fiber

SWEET POTATOES CARIBBEAN-STYLE

Don't overlook the outstanding nutritional benefits of vitamin A-rich sweet potatoes.

3 medium sweet potatoes (about 1½ pounds)

1 cup chopped red, yellow, or green sweet pepper

½ cup chopped green onions

1 clove garlic, minced

1 teaspoon olive or cooking oil

1 tablespoon lime or lemon juice

2 tablespoons snipped cilantro or parsley

½ cup plain fat-free yogurt

⅓ cup mashed ripe banana

1 tablespoon finely shredded orange peel

1. Scrub sweet potatoes and prick several times with fork. Bake in a 425° oven for 40 to 60 minutes or till tender. Cool 10 minutes. Peel potatoes. Mash with a fork or a potato masher.

2. In a large nonstick skillet cook and stir sweet pepper, green onions, and garlic in oil for 3 minutes. Stir in lime or lemon juice and cilantro. Remove from heat. Add pepper mixture to potatoes. Stir in yogurt, mashed banana, and orange peel.

3. Spray a 2-quart square baking dish with *nonstick spray coating.* Turn potato mixture into dish. Cover and bake about 15 minutes or till heated through. Serves 6.

Nutritional facts per serving: 132 calories, 1 g total fat (0 g saturated fat), 0 mg cholesterol, 23 mg sodium, 29 g carbohydrate, 4 g fiber, 3 g protein. **Daily values:** 203% vitamin A, 80% vitamin C, 5% calcium, 4% iron.

Low-fat

Low-calorie

SPINACH AND BASIL SOUFFLÉ

For a light, airy soufflé, be sure none of the yolk gets into the egg whites. Just a little fat in the whites will inhibit proper beating.

1 10-ounce package frozen
    spinach, thawed
  Nonstick spray coating
3 tablespoons all-purpose flour
1 cup skim milk
½ cup nonfat ricotta cheese
2 tablespoons snipped fresh
    basil or 1 teaspoon dried
    basil, crushed
2 egg yolks, slightly beaten
6 egg whites
½ teaspoon cream of tartar

1. Drain spinach. Squeeze out excess moisture. Set aside.

2. Cut a piece of aluminum foil long enough to fit around the edge of a 1½-quart soufflé dish with 1-inch overlap. Fold lengthwise into thirds. Spray one side of foil and bottom of souffle dish with nonstick spray coating. Wrap foil around outside of dish, coated side in, allowing it to extend 3 inches above rim. Fasten the foil.

3. In a medium saucepan combine flour and milk. Cook and stir till mixture is thick and bubbly. Remove from heat. Stir in cheese, spinach, and basil till well combined. Stir spinach mixture into egg yolks.

4. Using electric mixer on high speed beat egg whites and cream of tartar till stiff peaks form (tips stand straight). Fold about one-third of the egg whites into spinach mixture to lighten it. Gradually pour spinach mixture over remaining egg whites, folding to combine. Turn mixture into prepared dish. Bake in a 350° oven about 50 minutes or till puffed and golden and a knife inserted near center comes out clean. Serve immediately. Makes 6 servings.

Nutritional facts per serving: 87 calories, 2 g total fat (1 g saturated fat), 74 mg cholesterol, 116 mg sodium, 8 g carbohydrate, 0 g fiber, 10 g protein. **Daily values:** 39% vitamin A, 7% vitamin C, 11% calcium, 5% iron.

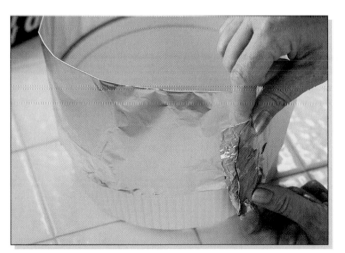

Fit a foil collar around the top of the soufflé dish to support the high soufflé during cooking. Secure the collar with a double fold.

Low-fat

Low-calorie

Low-sodium

SPAGHETTI SQUASH WITH TOMATOES

You'll find this stringy squash is a great substitute for pasta. (See photo, left.)

1 2½- to 3-pound spaghetti
    squash
2 tablespoons water
½ cup chopped red or green
    sweet pepper
½ cup sliced green onions
2 large tomatoes, chopped
2 tablespoons snipped parsley
2 teaspoons snipped fresh dill
    or ½ teaspoon dried
    dillweed
2 teaspoons snipped fresh basil
    or ½ teaspoon dried basil,
    crushed
1 tablespoon grated Parmesan
    cheese

1. Wash spaghetti squash; halve lengthwise. Scoop out seeds. Place squash halves, cut side down, in a baking dish. Bake in a 350° oven for 30 to 40 minutes or till tender.

2. Meanwhile, in a medium nonstick skillet heat water. Add sweet pepper and green onions and cook for 2 minutes. Stir in tomatoes, parsley, dill, and basil. Simmer, uncovered, for 5 minutes more or till of desired consistency.

3. Using two forks, remove stringy pulp from spaghetti squash and place on a serving platter. Spoon tomato mixture over spaghetti squash. Toss to combine. Sprinkle with Parmesan cheese. Makes 6 servings.

Nutritional facts per serving: 66 calories, 1 g total fat (0 g saturated fat), 1 mg cholesterol, 52 mg sodium, 13 g carbohydrate, 3 g fiber, 2 g protein. **Daily values:** 15% vitamin A, 59% vitamin C, 5% calcium, 8% iron.

Herb Basics

Whether you're watching fat, calories, sodium, or all three, good taste remains the most important element in any dish. Fresh and dried herbs are an easy way to boost the flavor in many dishes.

Fresh herbs are available in most supermarkets year-round. Use kitchen shears to quickly snip the amount you need. If you are substituting fresh herb for dried, use about three times more fresh than dried herb (1½ teaspoons fresh snipped herb instead of ½ teaspoon dried herb). A fresh herb sprig makes an easy garnish and brings new life to the most ordinary dish.

Store dried herbs in tightly covered containers in a dark place to protect them from air and light. Do not freeze dried herbs or store them near hot appliances. Replace dried herbs about once a year or whenever their aroma becomes weak.

To use a dried herb, first measure it, place it in the palm of your hand, and crush it with your other hand to release its flavor.

When cooking herbs, add dried herbs at the beginning of cooking to draw out their flavors and add fresh herbs at the end of cooking to retain their fresh flavors.

Low-fat

Low-calorie

Low-sodium

High-fiber

BAKED TOMATOES WITH FRESH HERBS AND PARMESAN

Baking tomatoes brings out their sweet, natural flavors.

4 medium tomatoes

1 tablespoon snipped fresh basil
   or 1 teaspoon dried basil,
   crushed

2 teaspoons snipped fresh
   rosemary or ½ teaspoon
   dried rosemary, crushed

⅛ teaspoon pepper

2 tablespoons grated Parmesan
   cheese

1. Remove stems and cores from tomatoes; halve tomatoes crosswise. Place tomato halves, cut side up, in a 2-quart rectangular baking dish. Sprinkle with basil, rosemary, and pepper.

2. Cover and bake in a 350° oven for 20 minutes. Uncover. Sprinkle with Parmesan. Bake, uncovered, for 5 minutes more. Makes 8 servings.

Nutritional facts per serving: 20 calories, 1 g total fat (0 g saturated fat), 1 mg cholesterol, 35 mg sodium, 3 g carbohydrate, 1 g fiber, 1 g protein. **Daily values:** 4% vitamin A, 19% vitamin C, 2% calcium, 2% iron.

To snip the fresh herbs, put the sprigs in a 1-cup glass measuring cup and snip them with kitchen shears.

Low-fat

High-fiber

SWEET POTATO-RUTABAGA PUREE

The sweet flavor of rutabagas is enhanced by the mild flavor of sweet potatoes.

4 medium sweet potatoes or
    yams (about 2 pounds),
    peeled and cut into ¾-inch
    cubes
1 medium rutabaga (about
    1 pound), peeled and cut
    into ¾-inch cubes
¼ cup chopped onion
⅓ cup skim milk
⅓ cup light dairy sour cream
¼ teaspoon ground nutmeg
⅛ teaspoon salt

1. Cook sweet potatoes or yams, covered, in boiling water for 5 minutes. Add rutabaga and onion; cook, covered, for 18 to 20 minutes more or till tender. Drain vegetables.

2. In a blender container or food processor bowl place about one-third of the vegetable mixture. Cover and process till smooth. Repeat with remaining vegetables. Stir together vegetable puree, milk, sour cream, nutmeg, and salt. Pour mixture into a 2-quart casserole. Bake in a 350° oven for 15 to 20 minutes or till heated through. Makes 6 servings.

Nutritional facts per serving: 160 calories, 1 g total fat (1 g saturated fat), 2 mg cholesterol, 91 mg sodium, 34 g carbohydrate, 4 g fiber, 4 g protein. **Daily values:** 231% vitamin A, 65% vitamin C, 7% calcium, 5% iron.

Low-calorie

HONEY-MUSTARD GLAZED TURNIPS

Look for medium-size turnips for this recipe because they're sweeter than the large ones.

3 medium turnips or rutabagas
    (1 pound), peeled and cut
    into julienne strips
1 tablespoon reduced-calorie
    margarine
2 tablespoons honey mustard
2 teaspoons lemon juice
½ teaspoon sugar
1 tablespoon snipped fresh
    chives or 1 teaspoon dried
    snipped chives

1. Cook turnips or rutabagas, covered, in a small amount of boiling water for 10 to 12 minutes or till tender. Drain. Cover and keep warm.

2. In the same saucepan melt margarine. Stir in mustard, lemon juice, and sugar. Heat through. Pour over turnips. Toss to coat with sauce. Sprinkle with chives. Makes 4 servings.

Nutritional facts per serving: 44 calories, 2 g total fat (0 g saturated fat), 0 mg cholesterol, 275 mg sodium, 7 g carbohydrate, 3 g fiber, 1 g protein. **Daily values:** 3% vitamin A, 23% vitamin C, 2% calcium, 1% iron.

Low-calorie

Low-sodium

PEA PODS, CARROTS, AND ONION MEDLEY

Serve this colorful combo (see photo, right) with grilled chops and wild rice.

1½ cups bias-sliced carrots

1 medium onion, cut into
    wedges

2 cups fresh pea pods, strings
    removed

2 tablespoons reduced-calorie
    margarine

1 tablespoon fresh snipped basil
    or thyme, or 1 teaspoon
    dried basil or thyme,
    crushed

2 teaspoons fresh snipped dill
    or ½ teaspoon dillweed

¼ teaspoon pepper

1. In a large saucepan cook carrots, covered, in enough boiling water to cover for 7 minutes. Add onion wedges and cook 5 minutes more. Add pea pods and simmer 2 minutes or till vegetables are crisp-tender. Drain vegetables. Return to saucepan.

2. Meanwhile, in a small saucepan melt margarine. Stir in basil or thyme, dill, and pepper. Spoon mixture over vegetables in saucepan. Toss well. Makes 5 to 6 servings.

Nutritional facts per serving: 68 calories, 3 g total fat (0 g saturated fat), 0 mg cholesterol, 74 mg sodium, 9 g carbohydrate, 1 g fiber, 2 g protein. **Daily values:** 19% vitamin A, 36% vitamin C, 2% calcium, 4% iron.

The Art of Writing a Grocery List

The beauty of a grocery list is that it allows you to cruise through a supermarket, buy what's necessary, and return home without feeling frazzled. These tips will help you write a complete list.

• Sit down at the same time every week to plan meals.

• Once your meals are planned, make a master grocery list. By doing this, you'll be assured of having the ingredients you'll need for the recipes you plan to prepare. Indicate on your grocery list whether you have coupons for any items.

• Keep your grocery list in a handy place. Remind family members to add to the list any item that they notice needs replenishing.

• Eliminate unnecessary backtracking at the store by grouping the foods on your list according to the supermarket's floor plan. Or, group the items on your list by categories, such as meats, dairy, produce, etc.

Low-fat

Low-calorie

Low-sodium

POTATO-CARROT LATKES

You fry these potato-carrot pancakes in just a bit of oil.

1 cup finely shredded peeled
   potatoes
½ cup finely shredded carrots
⅓ cup chopped green onions
1 beaten egg
2 egg whites
¼ cup fine dry bread crumbs
½ teaspoon salt-free seasoning
   blend
½ teaspoon dried thyme,
   crushed
1 tablespoon olive or
   cooking oil
1½ cups unsweetened applesauce

1. In a medium bowl stir together potatoes, carrots, green onions, egg, egg whites, bread crumbs, seasoning blend, and thyme.

2. Heat 1 teaspoon oil in a nonstick skillet or griddle. Drop potato mixture by tablespoonsful into hot skillet. With the back of a spoon press each latke to flatten slightly. Brown latkes on both sides, turning once. Cook remaining latkes adding remaining oil as needed. Serve with applesauce. Makes 18.

Nutritional facts per latke: 37 calories, 1 g total fat (0 g saturated fat), 12 mg cholesterol, 22 mg sodium, 6 g carbohydrate, 1 g fiber, 1 g protein. **Daily values:** 9% vitamin A, 2% vitamin C, 0% calcium, 1% iron.

MATCHSTICK CELERY AND CARROTS

Low-calorie

Many of your favorite vegetables can be prepared this way and topped with the spunky horseradish sauce.

2 cups celery cut in julienne
   strips
2 cups carrots cut in julienne
   strips
2 tablespoons reduced-calorie
   margarine
2 teaspoons lemon juice
½ to 1 teaspoon prepared
   horseradish
2 tablespoons snipped parsley

1. Place celery and carrots in a steamer basket over simmering water. Steam, covered, for 6 to 8 minutes or till crisp-tender. Drain. Cover and keep warm.

2. In the same pan melt margarine. Stir in lemon juice and horseradish. Pour over vegetables and toss to coat. Sprinkle with parsley. Makes 5 to 6 servings.

Nutritional facts per serving: 39 calories, 2 g total fat (0 g saturated fat), 0 mg cholesterol, 96 mg sodium, 4 g carbohydrate, 2 g fiber, 1 g protein. **Daily values:** 73% vitamin A, 8% vitamin C, 1% calcium, 2% iron.

Low-calorie

Low-sodium

VEGETABLE BUNDLES

Use these elegant vegetable bundles to enhance a serving platter of meat slices, roast turkey, or a pot roast.

4 medium carrots, peeled and
  quartered lengthwise
1 pound thin asparagus spears
  or broccoli spears
2 green onions
1 tablespoon reduced-calorie
  margarine
1 tablespoon lemon or lime
  juice
1 tablespoon snipped fresh
  chives or 1 teaspoon dried
  snipped chives

1. Cut each carrot strip in half. Snap off woody ends of asparagus. Trim green onions and cut off white portion and reserve for another use. Cut thin lengthwise strips from green portion of onions, about ¼ inch wide. Plunge strips in boiling water till limp. Drain on paper towels.

2. Tie 3 or 4 carrot strips and 3 or 4 asparagus or broccoli spears into bundles with green onion strips. Place bundles in a steamer basket over simmering water. Steam, covered, for 8 to 10 minutes or till vegetables are crisp-tender.

3. In a small saucepan melt margarine; stir in lemon juice and chives. Arrange vegetable bundles on a serving platter; drizzle with margarine mixture. Serves 8.

Nutritional facts per serving: 31 calories, 1 g total fat (0 g saturated fat), 0 mg cholesterol, 31 mg sodium, 5 g carbohydrate, 2 g fiber, 1 g protein. **Daily values:** 90% vitamin A, 18% vitamin C, 1% calcium, 3% iron.

Arrange carrot and asparagus spears in a small bundle. Tie the green onion strips around the bundles.

Low-fat

Low-calorie

Low-sodium

MEDITERRANEAN-STYLE VEGETABLES

Serve these flavorful stewed vegetables (photo, left) hot or at room temperature. Use leftovers stirred into hot cooked pasta.

2 cups sliced zucchini

2 cups sliced red, yellow, or
   green sweet peppers

2 cups broccoli flowerets

¼ cup reduced-sodium chicken
   broth

2 cloves garlic, minced

1 tablespoon snipped fresh basil
   or oregano, or 1 teaspoon
   dried basil or oregano,
   crushed

¼ teaspoon pepper

3 medium tomatoes, chopped

1. In a Dutch oven or large kettle combine zucchini, sweet peppers, broccoli, chicken broth, garlic, basil or oregano, and pepper. Bring to boiling; reduce heat.

2. Simmer, covered, for 6 to 8 minutes or till crisp-tender, stirring occasionally. Stir in tomatoes. Makes 6 to 8 servings.

Nutritional facts per serving: 40 calories, 0 g total fat (0 g saturated fat), 0 mg cholesterol, 44 mg sodium, 9 g carbohydrate, 3 g fiber, 2 g protein. **Daily values:** 28% vitamin A, 140% vitamin C, 2% calcium, 6% iron.

Shopping Tricks

Use the following tips to trim the time you spend in the grocery store:

Shop when others don't; try early morning or late evening. By avoiding the busy times, you'll steer clear of crowded aisles and a long wait in the check-out lanes.

Take the same in-store route every time you shop. The routine will make list-making easier and minimize shopping time.

Shop at the same store every week. You'll learn the layout of the store and be able to breeze through it.

Low-fat

Low-calorie

Low-sodium

BAKED PLANTAINS A L' ORANGE

Serve this dish in place of potatoes or rice with a roast or poultry.

2 plantains
  Nonstick spray coating
1 clove garlic, minced
1 teaspoon margarine
1 teaspoon cornstarch
½ cup orange juice
½ teaspoon finely shredded
    orange peel
⅛ teaspoon salt-free seasoning
    blend
⅛ teaspoon pepper
1 tablespoon snipped parsley or
    cilantro
  Orange slices (optional)

1. Peel plantains. Halve lengthwise, then crosswise into quarters. Spray a 2-quart square baking dish with nonstick spray coating. Arrange plantains, cut side up, in dish. Bake plantains, loosely covered, in a 400° oven for 20 minutes.

2. Meanwhile, in a small saucepan cook garlic in margarine for 1 minute. Stir cornstarch into orange juice. Add to saucepan. Cook and stir till mixture thickens and bubbles. Cook and stir for 1 minute more. Stir in orange peel, seasoning blend, and pepper. Spoon sauce atop plantains. Sprinkle with parsley or cilantro. Garnish with orange slices, if desired. Makes 4 servings.

Nutritional facts per serving: 120 calories, 2 g total fat (0 g saturated fat), 0 mg cholesterol, 16 mg sodium, 28 g carbohydrate, 2 g fiber, 1 g protein. **Daily values:** 9% vitamin A, 43% vitamin C, 0% calcium, 4% iron.

Low-fat

Low-calorie

Low-sodium

SOUTHERN VEGETABLE SAUTÉ

Quick-cooking is the best technique to help vegetables keep their color and retain their shape and texture.

8 ounces okra, sliced ¼ inch
    thick
1 chayote squash, peeled and
    chopped or 2 medium
    zucchini, sliced
1 clove garlic, minced
1 teaspoon olive or cooking oil
1 cup chopped tomatoes
½ cup loose-pack frozen whole
    kernel corn
½ teaspoon dried thyme,
    crushed
¼ teaspoon pepper
¼ teaspoon hot pepper sauce

1. In a large skillet cook okra, chayote, and garlic in oil for 5 minutes.

2. Stir in tomatoes, corn, thyme, pepper, and hot pepper sauce. Cook and stir for 5 minutes more or till vegetables are tender. Makes 6 servings.

Nutritional facts per serving: 48 calories, 1 g total fat (0 g saturated fat), 0 mg cholesterol, 8 mg sodium, 9 g carbohydrate, 2 g fiber, 2 g protein. **Daily values:** 6% vitamin A, 29% vitamin C, 3% calcium, 4% iron.

DILLED CORN AND PEA PODS

Frozen vegetables make this colorful accompaniment quick and easy to prepare.

1 cup frozen whole kernel corn
1 6-ounce package frozen pea
    pods
1 small sweet red or green
    pepper, cut into bite-size
    strips
2 teaspoons margarine
¼ teaspoon dried dillweed
⅛ teaspoon pepper

1. In a medium saucepan cook corn in a small amount of boiling water for 4 minutes. Add pea pods and sweet pepper. Cover and cook about 2 minutes or till vegetables are crisp-tender. Drain.

2. Add margarine, dillweed, and pepper. Toss till margarine melts and vegetables are coated. Makes 4 servings.

Nutrition facts per seving: 72 calories, 2 g total fat 0 g saturated fat), 0 mg cholesterol, 26 sodium, 12 g carbohydrate, 1 g fiber, 3 g protein. **Daily values:** 12% vitamin A, 51% vitamin C, 2% calcium, 8% iron.

TOMATO-APPLE CHUTNEY

This chutney is great with red meats, poultry, and even grilled fish.

2 large ripe tomatoes, finely
    chopped
2 large cooking apples, cored
    and finely chopped
1 medium onion, finely chopped
¾ cup apple cider or juice
½ cup red wine vinegar
½ cup packed brown sugar
¼ cup light raisins
⅛ teaspoon ground red pepper
2 teaspoons mixed pickling
    spice
1-inch stick cinnamon

1. In a 2-quart saucepan combine tomatoes, apples, onion, apple cider or juice, vinegar, brown sugar, raisins, and red pepper. Tie pickling spice and cinnamon in several thicknesses of cheesecloth to make a bag. Add to tomato mixture. Bring to boiling; reduce heat. Simmer about 45 minutes or till thickened, stirring frequently.

2. Remove spice bag. Transfer chutney to a bowl or storage container. Cover and chill up to 4 weeks. Mixture can be frozen. Makes 2½ cups (twenty 2-tablespoon servings).

Nutritional facts per serving: 47 calories, 0 g total fat (0 g saturated fat), 0 mg cholesterol, 5 mg sodium, 12 g carbohydrate, 0 g fiber, 0 g protein. **Daily values:** 1% vitamin A, 8% vitamin C, 0% calcium, 2% iron.

Low-fat

Low-calorie

Low-sodium

CURRIED VEGETABLE KABOBS

A spicy yogurt sauce glazes these colorful grilled vegetables (photo, right).

1 pound small new potatoes
2 medium yellow summer
   squash and/or zucchini, cut
   into ½-inch slices
6 medium fresh mushrooms
½ cup plain fat-free yogurt
1 tablespoon snipped fresh
   chives or 1 teaspoon dried
   snipped chives
1 teaspoon curry powder
¼ teaspoon salt-free seasoning
   blend
⅛ teaspoon ground cumin
6 cherry tomatoes
   Fresh chives (optional)

1. Cut potatoes into halves or quarters. Cook potatoes in enough boiling water to cover for 12 minutes. Add yellow squash or zucchini. Cook for 2 minutes more. Drain.

2. On 6 skewers alternately thread potatoes, squash, and mushrooms. In a small bowl stir together yogurt, chives, curry powder, seasoning blend, and cumin. Brush mixture liberally over vegetables.

3. Grill kabobs over medium coals for 5 to 8 minutes or till tender, turning once, and brushing frequently with curry mixture. Place a cherry tomato on the end of each skewer. Grill for 1 minute more. (Or, spray a broiler pan with *nonstick spray coating*. Place kabobs on broiler pan. Brush curry mixture liberally over vegetables. Broil 4 inches from the heat for 8 to 10 minutes or till tender, turning once, and brushing frequently with curry mixture. Add tomatoes to ends of skewers and broil for 1 minute more.) Garnish with fresh chives, if desired. Makes 6 servings.

Nutritional facts per serving: 98 calories, 0 g total fat (0 g saturated fat), 0 mg cholesterol, 22 mg sodium, 21 g carbohydrate, 2 g fiber, 4 g protein. **Daily values:** 2% vitamin A, 26% vitamin C, 5% calcium, 12% iron.

Mushroom Hunting

Choose mushrooms by their caps. Look for caps that are closed around the stem; wide-open caps are a sign of age. Color should be uniform, but depends upon the variety; white, off-white, and tan are most common.

Because mushrooms are highly perishable, they should be purchased only as needed. But, if necessary, store them loosely wrapped in the refrigerator for 1 or 2 days.

SESAME BROCCOLI AND EGGPLANT

Low-calorie

If you don't have sodium-reduced soy sauce, try substituting balsamic or red wine vinegar.

3 **Japanese eggplants or ½ of**
   a medium eggplant, peeled
2 **cups broccoli flowerets**
   Nonstick spray coating
2 **teaspoons sesame or**
   cooking oil
½ **cup sliced onion**
1 **teaspoon sesame seed**
1 **clove garlic, minced**
1 **tablespoon sodium-reduced**
   soy sauce
1 **tablespoon dry sherry**
⅛ **teaspoon crushed red pepper**

1. Cut eggplant into strips. Set aside.

2. Place broccoli in steamer basket over simmering water. Steam, covered, for 3 minutes. Drain.

3. Spray a large wok or nonstick skillet with nonstick spray coating. Heat oil in wok. Add eggplant and stir-fry for 3 minutes. Remove from wok. Add broccoli, onion, sesame seed, and garlic. Stir-fry for 3 minutes. Push vegetables to side of wok. Stir in soy sauce, sherry, and pepper. Return eggplant to wok. Toss vegetables to coat with sauce. Cover and cook 1 minute more. Makes 4 servings.

Nutritional facts per serving: 60 calories, 2 g total fat (0 g saturated fat), 0 mg cholesterol, 150 mg sodium, 8 g carbohydrate, 3 g fiber, 3 g protein. **Daily values:** 8% vitamin A, 73% vitamin C, 2% calcium, 5% iron.

Cut the eggplant into strips about 2 inches long and about ½ inch thick.

Low-fat

Low-calorie

Low-sodium

CORN AND ZUCCHINI RELISH

Serve this summertime relish with cold lean roast beef or pork, or try it sprinkled over a spinach salad.

1½ cups finely chopped zucchini
or yellow summer squash

1 cup loose-pack frozen whole
kernel corn, thawed

½ cup finely chopped red or
green sweet pepper

2 tablespoons sugar

1 tablespoon prepared mustard

¼ cup vinegar

¼ cup water

½ cup chopped onion

½ teaspoon salt-free seasoning
blend

⅛ teaspoon pepper

1. In a medium bowl combine zucchini, corn, and sweet pepper.

2. In a small saucepan stir together sugar, mustard, vinegar, water, onion, seasoning blend, and pepper. Bring to boiling; reduce heat. Cover and simmer for 2 minutes. Add to corn mixture and toss gently to mix. Cover and chill for 2 to 24 hours, stirring occasionally. Mixture can be frozen. Makes 3 cups (twenty-four 2-tablespoon servings).

Nutritional facts per serving: 11 calories, 0 g total fat (0 g saturated fat), 0 mg cholesterol, 5 mg sodium, 3 g carbohydrate, 0 g fiber, 0 g protein. **Daily values:** 2% vitamin A, 8% vitamin C, 0% calcium, 0% iron.

Low-fat

Low-calorie

POTATO AND CORN PUDDING

Here's a novel side dish to serve with an herb-roasted chicken or beef rump roast.

3 cups shredded peeled
potatoes

1 medium onion, chopped

1 cup frozen whole kernel corn

1 tablespoon reduced-caloric
margarine

1 tablespoon all-purpose flour

1 cup evaporated skim milk

1 egg, beaten

½ teaspoon dried thyme,
crushed

½ teaspoon chicken bouillon
granules

Dash paprika

1 tablespoon snipped parsley

1. In a large nonstick skillet cook potatoes, onion, and corn in margarine for 10 minutes.

2. Meanwhile, stir flour into skim milk and set aside. Add egg, thyme, bouillon granules, and ¼ teaspoon *pepper* to potato mixture. Remove skillet from heat. Stir milk mixture into skillet.

3. Spray a 9-inch pie plate with *nonstick spray coating*. Pour potato mixture into pie plate. Sprinkle with paprika. Bake in a 375° oven for 20 to 25 minutes or till set. Sprinkle with parsley. Makes 8 servings.

Nutritional facts per serving: 100 calories, 2 g total fat (0 g saturated fat), 28 mg cholesterol, 115 mg sodium, 18 g carbohydrate, 1 g fiber, 5 g protein. **Daily values:** 6% vitamin A, 9% vitamin C, 7% calcium, 3% iron.

Low-fat
Low-calorie

STIR-FRIED VEGETABLES

This vegetable dish (photo, left) can become the main course. Just add 4 boned chicken breast halves
or 1 pound of pork tenderloin cut into bite-size strips and stir-fry till no longer pink.

2 Japanese eggplants or
    ½ medium eggplant, peeled
1 teaspoon peanut or
    cooking oil
1 tablespoon grated gingerroot
2 cloves garlic, minced
2 tablespoons orange juice
1 cup red or green sweet
    pepper, cut into ½-inch
    pieces
3 green onions, cut into
    1-inch pieces
1 cup pea pods, strings
    removed
1 cup fresh bean sprouts
1 8-ounce can sliced water
    chestnuts, drained
2 tablespoons sodium-reduced
    soy sauce
2 tablespoons dry sherry, dry
    white wine, or orange juice
⅛ to ¼ teaspoon crushed red
    pepper

1. Cut eggplant into ½-inch pieces. In a large wok or nonstick skillet heat oil over medium-high heat. Add gingerroot and garlic. Stir-fry for 30 seconds.

2. Add 2 tablespoons orange juice, eggplant, sweet pepper, and green onions. Stir-fry for 1 minute. Add pea pods and bean sprouts. Stir-fry for 2 minutes more. Add water chestnuts, soy sauce, sherry, and crushed red pepper. Toss well to coat with sauce. Cook for 1 minute more or till heated through. Makes 5 to 6 servings.

Nutritional facts per serving: 70 calories, 1 g total fat (0 g saturated fat), 0 mg cholesterol, 218 mg sodium, 12 g carbohydrate, 2 g fiber, 3 g protein. **Daily values:** 13% vitamin A, 72% vitamin C, 1% calcium, 8% iron.

More About Eggplant

This large, typically pear-shaped fruit is used as a vegetable. It has a smooth, glossy, deep purple or white skin, and bright green cap. Eggplant has yellowish white flesh with tiny edible seeds. The mild flavor combines well with lots of seasonings. The flesh of the eggplant becomes soft and watery when cooked. Several varieties are available.

Western: Large with a smooth, glossy, purple or white skin. This is the most common eggplant in the United States. It can be round, but is usually pear-shaped.

White: Smaller and firmer than the Western eggplant, this variety has a tough, thick skin and requires peeling. The flesh is a little sweeter than the other varieties.

Japanese: This variety is long and slender with a mild flavor.

Baby: Smaller versions of the other types. Baby eggplants can be purple or white. These small eggplants are tender and sweet.

Fresh eggplant is available year-round. Look for plump, glossy, heavy eggplants. Skip any with scarred, bruised, or dull surfaces. The cap should be fresh-looking, tight, and free of mold.

Low-fat

Low-calorie

Low-sodium

SWEET AND SOUR CUKES

Here's a timeless classic that fits into today's lighter-eating style.

4 cups thinly sliced cucumbers

1 2¼-ounce jar diced pimiento, drained

⅓ cup vinegar

2 tablespoons sugar

1 teaspoon salt-free seasoning blend

½ teaspoon dillweed

⅛ teaspoon cracked black pepper

¼ cup light sour cream

1. In a medium nonmetal bowl place cucumbers and pimiento. In a measuring cup stir together vinegar, sugar, seasoning blend, dillweed, and pepper. Pour mixture over cucumbers. Toss to mix well. Cover and chill for 2 to 24 hours, stirring occasionally.

2. Drain off marinade and stir in sour cream before serving. Makes 6 servings.

Nutritional facts per serving: 45 calories, 1 g total fat (0 g saturated fat), 1 mg cholesterol, 18 mg sodium, 9 g carbohydrate, 2 g fiber, 2 g protein. **Daily values:** 3% vitamin A, 26% vitamin C, 2% calcium, 4% iron.

Low-fat

Low-calorie

Low-sodium

RHUBARB CHUTNEY RELISH

Perk up the flavor of roast pork or poultry with this spicy chutney.

8 ounces rhubarb, chopped (2 cups)

1 cup chopped onion

½ cup cranberry juice cocktail

⅓ cup vinegar

½ cup packed brown sugar

½ teaspoon ground allspice

1. In a medium saucepan combine all ingredients. Bring to boiling; reduce heat. Cover and simmer for 10 minutes.

2. Uncover and simmer for 30 to 40 minutes or till thickened, stirring occasionally. Remove from heat. Serve warm or chilled. Store up to 2 weeks in refrigerator. Makes 1½ cups (twelve 2-tablespoon servings).

Nutritional facts per serving: 51 calories, 0 g total fat (0 g saturated fat), 0 mg cholesterol, 5 mg sodium, 13 g carbohydrate, 1 g fiber, 0 g protein. **Daily values:** 0% vitamin A, 10% vitamin C, 2% calcium, 2% iron.

BOUNTIFUL BREADS

Few aromas are more enticing than the yeasty smell of home-baked bread. And fortunately for health-conscious eaters, most yeast breads fit quite nicely into low-fat and low-calorie diets. (Be sure to spread them with a low-fat spread instead of butter.) The Crusty French Bread perfectly accompanies almost any meal, while a slice of Whole Wheat Cinnamon-Raisin Bread makes a satisfying substitute for a gooey sweet roll. Those who like a heartier loaf should try Three-Grain Yeast Bread made with whole wheat flour, oats, and toasted wheat germ. In addition, you'll find fat-trimmed muffins and biscuits, a selection of pancakes, popovers that are virtually cholesterol-free, and an easy breakfast bread that begins with frozen bread dough.

Low-fat

Low-calorie

Low-sodium

CRUSTY FRENCH BREAD

This baking method will help ensure an authentic, crusty loaf. (See photo, right.)

5 to 5¼ cups all-purpose flour
1 package active dry yeast
2 cups warm water (115° to 120°)
¼ teaspoon salt
  Nonstick spray coating
  Cornmeal
  Water

1. In a mixing bowl mix *2 cups* of the flour and the yeast. Add warm water and salt. Beat with electric mixer on low speed for 30 seconds, scraping bowl constantly. Then beat on high speed for 3 minutes. Stir in as much remaining flour as you can.

2. Turn out onto a lightly floured surface. Knead in enough of the remaining flour to make a stiff dough that is smooth and elastic (8 to 10 minutes total). Shape into a ball. Spray a large bowl with nonstick spray coating. Place dough in bowl, turning once to coat surface. Cover; let rise in warm place till double in size (about 1 hour).

3. Punch dough down. Turn out onto lightly floured surface. Divide in half. Cover; let rest 10 minutes. Spray 2 baking sheets with nonstick spray coating; sprinkle with cornmeal. On a lightly floured surface, roll each half into a 15x12-inch rectangle. Tightly roll up, jelly-roll style, starting from one of the long sides. Seal with your fingertips as you roll; taper ends.

4. Place seam sides down on prepared baking sheets. Cover; let rise till nearly double in size (about 35 minutes). With a sharp knife, make 3 or 4 diagonal cuts about ¼ inch deep across tops. Fill a spritzer bottle with water; spray loaves lightly.

5. Bake in 400° oven for 5 minutes. Spray loaves again with water; bake 5 minutes more. Spray loaves with water a third time. Bake for 20 to 25 minutes more or till loaves sound hollow when you tap the tops with your fingers. Remove from baking sheets. Cool on wire racks. Makes 2 loaves (16 servings each).

Nutritional facts per serving: 68 calories, 0 g total fat (0 g saturated fat), 0 mg cholesterol, 17 mg sodium, 14 g carbohydrate, 1 g fiber, 2 g protein. **Daily values:** 0% vitamin A, 0% vitamin C, 0% calcium, 6% iron.

Hard Rolls: Prepare as directed above, except shape dough as follows. Cut each half of dough into eighths, making 16 pieces total. Shape each piece into a roll; place rolls 2 inches apart on prepared baking sheets. Cover and let rise till nearly double in size (about 45 minutes). Cut a shallow crisscross in tops. Bake as directed for loaves; except reduce final baking time to 15 to 20 minutes. Makes 16.

Nutritional facts per serving: 135 calories, 0 g total fat (0 g saturated fat), 0 mg cholesterol, 35 mg sodium, 28 g carbohydrate, 1 g fiber, 4 g protein. **Daily values:** 0% vitamin A, 0% vitamin C, 0% calcium, 12% iron.

PARMESAN BATTER ROLLS

 Low-calorie

There's no need for time-consuming rolling and shaping; just drop the batter into muffin cups.

Nonstick spray coating
3 cups all-purpose flour
1 package active dry yeast
1¼ cups evaporated skim milk
¼ cup margarine
2 tablespoons sugar
⅛ teaspoon salt
1 beaten egg
1 tablespoon skim milk
2 tablespoons grated Parmesan
    cheese

1. Spray eighteen 2½-inch muffin cups with nonstick stick coating; set aside.

2. In a large mixing bowl combine *1½ cups* of the flour and the yeast; set aside. In a medium saucepan heat and stir evaporated milk, margarine, sugar, and salt just till warm (120° to 130°) and margarine is almost melted. Add milk mixture to flour mixture. Then add egg. Beat with an electric mixer on low speed for 30 seconds, scraping the sides of the bowl constantly. Then beat on high speed for 3 minutes. Using a wooden spoon, stir in as much of the remaining flour as you can.

3. Spoon batter into prepared muffin cups, filling each half full. Cover and let rise till nearly double in size (about 45 minutes). Brush tops lightly with milk; sprinkle with Parmesan cheese. Bake in 375° oven for 15 to 18 minutes or till golden. Remove rolls from pans. Serve warm, or cool on wire racks. Makes 18.

Nutritional facts per roll: 122 calories, 4 g total fat (1 g saturated fat), 13 mg cholesterol, 82 mg sodium, 18 g carbohydrate, 1 g fiber, 4 g protein. **Daily values:** 5% vitamin A, 0% vitamin C, 5% calcium, 6% iron.

Low-fat
Low-calorie
Low-sodium

WHOLE WHEAT OAT TWIST

3½ to 4 cups whole wheat flour
1 package active dry yeast
1¾ cups skim milk
3 tablespoons dark molasses
2 tablespoons margarine
¼ teaspoon salt
1 cup rolled oats
    Nonstick spray coating
1 slightly beaten egg white
2 teaspoons rolled oats

1. Mix *2 cups* of the flour and the yeast. Heat and stir milk, molasses, margarine, and salt till warm (115° to 120°). Add to flour mixture. Beat with electric mixer on low speed for 30 seconds, scraping bowl. Beat on high speed 3 minutes. Stir in 1 cup oats and as much remaining flour as you can. Turn out onto lightly floured surface. Knead in enough flour to make moderately soft dough that is smooth and elastic (6 to 8 minutes). Shape into ball. Spray a bowl with nonstick coating. Place dough in bowl; turn once to coat surface. Cover; let rise in warm place till double (1 to 1½ hours).

2. Punch dough down. On lightly floured surface divide dough in half. Cover; let rest 10 minutes. Shape each half into a 12-inch log. Twist logs together; pinch ends. Place twist on a baking sheet sprayed with nonstick coating. Brush with egg white; sprinkle with 2 teaspoons oats. Cover; let rise till double (30 minutes). Bake in 375° oven 30 to 40 minutes. Remove from baking sheet; cool. Makes 1 loaf (20 servings).

Nutritional facts per serving: 114 calories, 2 g total fat (0 g saturated fat), 0 mg cholesterol, 58 mg sodium, 21 g carbohydrate, 3 g fiber, 5 g protein. **Daily values:** 2% vitamin A, 0% vitamin C, 4% calcium, 10% iron.

Low-fat

Low-calorie

Low-sodium

THREE-GRAIN YEAST BREAD

Serve these hearty loaves with a robust entrée such as Pork Stew with Squash (see recipe on page 262).

2¾ to 3¼ cups all-purpose flour
2 packages active dry yeast
1 cup water
1 cup skim milk
2 tablespoons brown sugar
2 tablespoons margarine
¼ teaspoon salt
1 beaten egg
2 cups whole wheat flour
1 cup rolled oats
½ cup toasted wheat germ
Nonstick spray coating

1. In a large mixing bowl stir together *2½ cups* of the all-purpose flour and the yeast; set aside. In a medium saucepan heat and stir water, milk, brown sugar, margarine, and salt just till warm (120° to 130°) and margarine almost melts. Add milk mixture to flour mixture. Then add egg. Beat with an electric mixer on low to medium speed for 30 seconds, scraping the sides of the bowl constantly. Then beat on high speed for 3 minutes. Using a wooden spoon, stir in the whole wheat flour, oats, wheat germ, and as much of the remaining all-purpose flour as you can.

2. Turn the dough out onto a lightly floured surface. Knead in enough of the remaining all-purpose flour to make a moderately soft dough that is smooth and elastic (6 to 8 minutes total). Shape the dough into a ball. Spray a large bowl with nonstick spray coating; place dough in bowl, turning once to coat the surface of the dough. Cover; let rise in a warm place till nearly double in size (about 50 to 60 minutes).

3. Punch dough down. Turn dough out onto lightly floured surface. Divide dough in half. Cover and let rest 10 minutes. Meanwhile, spray two 9x5x3-inch loaf pans with nonstick spray coating.

4. Shape each portion of the dough into a loaf by patting or rolling. To shape dough by patting, gently pull dough into a loaf shape, tucking edges underneath. To shape dough by rolling, on a lightly floured surface, roll each half into a 12x8-inch rectangle. Tightly roll up, jelly-roll style, starting from one of the short sides. Seal with your fingertips as you roll.

5. Place the shaped dough in the prepared loaf pans. Cover and let rise in a warm place till nearly double in size (25 to 35 minutes).

6. Bake in a 375° oven about 30 minutes or till bread sounds hollow when tapped with your fingers (if necessary, cover loosely with foil the last 10 minutes of baking to prevent overbrowning). Immediately remove bread from pans. Cool on wire racks. Makes 2 loaves (16 servings each).

Nutritional facts per serving: 93 calories, 2 g total fat (0 g saturated fat), 7 mg cholesterol, 32 mg sodium, 17 g carbohydrate, 2 g fiber, 4 g protein. **Daily values:** 1% vitamin A, 0% vitamin C, 1% calcium, 7% iron.

Is It Bread Yet?

You easily can check your bread for doneness by tapping the top of the loaf with your fingers. When you get a hollow sound, the bread is done. Rolls and coffee cakes don't need to be tapped. When their tops are golden brown, remove them from the oven.

Low-fat

Low-calorie

Low-sodium

WHOLE WHEAT CINNAMON-RAISIN BREAD

Toast this bread for breakfast and spread it with a fat-free cream cheese product or a low-calorie fruit spread. (See photo, left.)

2¼ to 2¾ cups all-purpose flour
1 package active dry yeast
1 cup apple cider or juice
½ cup skim milk
3 tablespoons brown sugar
1 tablespoon margarine
½ teaspoon salt
1 egg
2 cups whole wheat flour
Nonstick spray coating
¾ cup raisins
1 tablespoon margarine, melted
2 tablespoons sugar
1 teaspoon ground cinnamon
1 slightly beaten egg white
1 teaspoon water

1. In a large mixing bowl stir together *2 cups* of the all-purpose flour and the yeast; set aside. In a medium saucepan heat and stir apple cider or juice, milk, brown sugar, 1 tablespoon margarine, and salt till warm (115° to 120°), and margarine is almost melted (mixture will appear curdled). Add apple cider mixture to flour mixture. Then add egg. Beat with an electric mixer on low speed for 30 seconds, scraping sides of the bowl constantly. Then beat on high speed for 3 minutes. Using a wooden spoon, stir in whole wheat flour and as much of the remaining all-purpose flour as you can.

2. Turn the dough out onto a lightly floured surface. Knead in enough of the remaining all-purpose flour to make a moderately soft dough that is smooth and elastic (6 to 8 minutes total). Spray a large bowl with nonstick spray coating. Place dough in bowl, turning dough once to coat surface of the dough. Cover and let rise in a warm place till double in size (about 1 hour).

3. Punch dough down. Turn dough out onto a lightly floured surface. Divide dough in half. Cover and let rest 10 minutes. Meanwhile, pour enough boiling water over raisins to cover them. Let stand 10 minutes; drain. Spray 2 baking sheets with nonstick spray coating.

4. Roll each half of the dough into a 12x8-inch rectangle. Brush dough with 1 tablespoon melted margarine. In a small mixing bowl stir together raisins, sugar, and cinnamon; sprinkle half of the mixture evenly over each dough rectangle to within 1 inch of edges. Tightly roll up, jelly-roll style, starting from one of the long sides. Seal with your fingertips as you roll.

5. Place loaves on prepared baking sheets. With sharp knife, cut 4 diagonal slashes in top of each loaf. Combine egg white and water. Brush loaves with egg white mixture. Cover and let rise in a warm place till double in size (30 to 40 minutes).

6. Bake in a 375° oven for 25 to 30 minutes or till bread sounds hollow when you tap the top with your fingers (if necessary, cover loosely with foil the last 10 minutes of baking to prevent overbrowning). Immediately remove bread from pans. Cool on wire racks. Makes 2 loaves (16 servings each).

Nutritional facts per serving: 89 calories, 1 g total fat (0 g saturated fat), 7 mg cholesterol, 49 mg sodium, 18 g carbohydrate, 1 g fiber, 3 g protein. **Daily values:** 1% vitamin A, 5% vitamin C, 1% calcium, 5% iron.

Low-fat

Low-calorie

Low-sodium

HERBED PINWHEEL BREAD

Freeze one loaf to serve another time as an accompaniment to a soup, stew, or barbecue dinner.

1½ to 2 cups all-purpose flour
1 package active dry yeast
1 cup low-fat buttermilk
¼ cup water
2 tablespoons margarine
2 tablespoons sugar
¼ teaspoon salt
1½ cups whole wheat flour
   Nonstick spray coating
½ cup sliced green onion
1 tablespoon olive oil
2 tablespoons snipped fresh
   basil or 2 teaspoons dried
   basil, crushed
2 tablespoons snipped fresh
   rosemary, oregano, or
   thyme, or 2 teaspoons dried
   rosemary, oregano, or
   thyme, crushed
2 cloves garlic, minced

1. In a bowl mix *1¼ cups* of the all-purpose flour and the yeast; set aside. In a saucepan heat buttermilk, water, margarine, sugar, and salt till warm (120° to 130°). Add to flour mixture. Beat with an electric mixer on low speed for 30 seconds, scraping bowl constantly. Beat on high speed for 3 minutes more. Using a spoon, stir in whole wheat flour and as much of the remaining all-purpose flour as you can.

2. Turn dough out onto a lightly floured surface. Knead in enough of the remaining all-purpose flour to make a moderately soft dough that is smooth and elastic (6 to 8 minutes total). Shape into a ball. Spray a large mixing bowl with nonstick coating. Place dough in bowl, turning once to coat surface. Cover; let rise in a warm place till double (about 1 hour). Meanwhile, in a blender container or food processor combine green onion and olive oil. Blend or process till chopped. Add herbs and garlic. Blend or process till finely chopped, stopping and scraping sides as necessary. Spray a large baking sheet with nonstick spray coating.

3. Punch dough down. Turn out onto lightly floured surface. Cover and let rest 10 minutes. Roll into a 16x8-inch rectangle. Spread herb mixture over dough to within 1 inch of edges. Starting with a long side, roll up tightly, jelly-roll style; pinch edges and ends to seal. Place seam side down, on baking sheet. Cover; let rise in warm place till double (about 40 minutes). Bake in a 375° oven for 25 to 35 minutes or till bread sounds hollow when you tap the top. Remove from baking sheet. Cool. Makes 1 loaf (24 servings).

Nutritional facts per serving: 75 calories, 2 g total fat (0 g saturated fat), 0 mg cholesterol, 45 mg sodium, 13 g carbohydrate, 1 g fiber, 2 g protein. **Daily values:** 1% vitamin A, 0% vitamin C, 1% calcium, 4% iron.

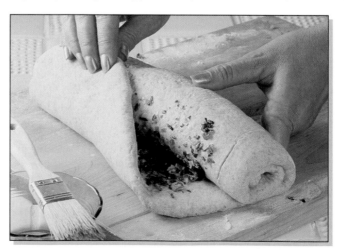

To ensure perfect pinwheel slices, pinch the seam of the loaf to seal it. If necessary, brush the edge of the dough with a little water. Then press down on the ends of the loaf to seal them.

Low-fat

Low-calorie

Low-sodium

BUTTERMILK YEAST BREAD

Low-fat buttermilk lends a rich texture to this tender white bread.

6 to 6½ cups all-purpose or unbleached flour

2 packages active dry yeast

2 cups low-fat buttermilk

¼ cup sugar

3 tablespoons margarine

½ teaspoon salt

1 egg

1 egg white

Nonstick spray coating

2 teaspoons reduced-calorie margarine, melted

2 teaspoons sesame seed or poppy seed

1. In a large mixing bowl stir together *3 cups* of the flour and the yeast; set aside. In a medium saucepan heat and stir buttermilk, sugar, margarine, and salt just till warm (115° to 120°) and margarine is almost melted. Add buttermilk mixture to flour mixture. Then add egg and egg white. Beat with an electric mixer on low speed for 30 seconds, scraping the sides of the bowl constantly. Then beat on high speed for 3 minutes. Using a wooden spoon, stir in as much remaining flour as you can.

2. Turn the dough out onto a lightly floured surface. Knead in enough of the remaining flour to make a moderately soft dough that is smooth and elastic (6 to 8 minutes total). Shape the dough into a ball. Spray a large bowl with nonstick spray coating. Place dough in bowl, turning once to coat surface of the dough. Cover and let rise in a warm place till double in size (45 to 60 minutes).

3. Punch dough down. Turn dough out onto a lightly floured surface. Divide dough in half. Cover and let rest 10 minutes. Spray two 9x5x3-inch loaf pans with nonstick spray coating.

4. Shape each portion of the dough into a loaf by patting or rolling. To shape dough by patting, gently pull dough into a loaf shape, tucking edges underneath. To shape dough by rolling, on a lightly floured surface, roll each half into a 12x8-inch rectangle. Tightly roll up, jelly-roll style, starting from one of the short sides. Seal with your fingertips as you roll.

5. Place the shaped dough in the prepared loaf pans. Cover and let rise till nearly double in size (35 to 45 minutes). Brush loaves with melted margarine and sprinkle with sesame seed or poppy seed.

6. Bake in a 375° oven for 35 to 40 minutes or till bread sounds hollow when you tap the top with your fingers (if necessary, loosely cover with foil the last 15 minutes of baking to prevent overbrowning). Immediately remove bread from pans. Cool on wire racks. Makes 2 loaves (16 servings each).

Nutritional facts per serving: 108 calories, 2 g total fat (0 g saturated fat), 7 mg cholesterol, 69 mg sodium, 19 g carbohydrate, 1 g fiber, 3 g protein. **Daily values:** 2% vitamin A, 0% vitamin C, 1% calcium, 7% iron.

Low-fat

Low-calorie

HEARTY DILL BATTER BREAD

Green onion, parsley, and dill flavor this round loaf. Cottage cheese adds a little zing.

2¼ cups all-purpose flour
 1 package active dry yeast
 1 tablespoon margarine
 ½ cup chopped green onion
 1 cup skim milk
 ¾ cup low-fat cottage cheese
 ⅛ teaspoon salt
 1 egg white
 1 cup whole wheat flour
 ¼ cup snipped fresh parsley
 2 teaspoons dried dillweed
 1 teaspoon poppy seed
   (optional)
   Nonstick spray coating

1. In a large mixing bowl stir together *2 cups* of the all-purpose flour and the yeast; set aside. In a medium saucepan melt margarine; add green onion and cook for 2 minutes. Stir in milk, cottage cheese, and salt; heat just till warm (115° to 120°). Add milk mixture to flour mixture. Then add egg white. Beat with an electric mixer on low speed for 30 seconds, scraping the sides of the bowl constantly. Then beat on high speed for 3 minutes. Using a wooden spoon stir in the remaining all-purpose flour, the whole wheat flour, parsley, and dillweed till batter is smooth.

2. Cover and let rise in a warm place till double in size (about 1 hour). Beat down with a wooden spoon. Spray a 1½-quart casserole with nonstick spray coating. Spoon dough into dish. Cover and let rise till nearly double in size (about 30 minutes). If desired, sprinkle with poppy seed.

3. Bake in a 375° oven for 45 to 55 minutes or till bread sounds hollow when you tap the top with your fingers. Remove from casserole. Cool about 15 minutes on a wire rack. Cut into wedges and serve warm. Makes 1 loaf (12 servings).

Nutritional facts per serving: 145 calories, 2 g total fat (0 g saturated fat), 2 mg cholesterol, 108 mg sodium, 26 g carbohydrate, 2 g fiber, 7 g protein. **Daily values:** 4% vitamin A, 4% vitamin C, 3% calcium, 11% iron.

Saving Time with Quick-Rising Yeast
The bread recipes in this chapter were tested with active dry yeast. You can, however, prepare these recipes using quick-rising active dry yeast. Just follow the same directions. The dough should rise in about a third less time, especially during the second rising step.

Low-fat

Low-calorie

Low-sodium

ROSEMARY POTATO BREAD

The potato and its cooking liquid give this bread a wonderful texture and also make it rise better.

1 medium potato, peeled
   and cubed
1½ cups water
   2 packages active dry yeast
   4 to 4½ cups all-purpose flour
   2 tablespoons brown sugar
   2 tablespoons olive oil or
      cooking oil
   1 teaspoon salt
   2 tablespoons snipped fresh
      rosemary or 1½ teaspoons
      dried rosemary, crushed
   2 cups whole wheat flour
   ¼ cup finely chopped onion
      Nonstick spray coating

1. In a medium saucepan cook potato in the water for 12 to 15 minutes or till tender; do not drain. Cool mixture to 105° to 115°. Pour off ½ cup of the cooking liquid; set aside. Mash potato in the remaining liquid; add enough of the reserved cooking liquid to make 2 cups of the potato mixture.

2. In a large mixing bowl stir together yeast and the reserved ½ cup potato liquid. Add mashed potato mixture, *2 cups* of the all-purpose flour, brown sugar, oil, salt, and rosemary. Beat with an electric mixer on low speed for 30 seconds, scraping the sides of the bowl constantly. Then beat on high speed for 3 minutes. Using a wooden spoon, stir in whole wheat flour, onion, and as much of the remaining all-purpose flour as you can.

3. Turn the dough out onto lightly floured surface. Knead in enough of the remaining flour to make a moderately soft dough that is smooth and elastic (6 to 8 minutes total). Shape the dough into a ball. Spray a large bowl with nonstick spray coating. Place dough in bowl, turning once to coat surface of the dough. Cover and let rise in warm place till double in size (about 1 hour).

4. Punch dough down. Turn dough out onto lightly floured surface. Divide dough in half. Cover and let rest 10 minutes.

5. Shape each half into a round or an 11-inch-long loaf. To shape dough, gently pat dough into a round or loaf shape, tucking edges underneath.

6. Spray 2 baking sheets with nonstick spray coating; place loaves on baking sheets. If loaves are round, flatten to 6 inches in diameter. If loaves are long, taper the ends and cut slashes in top. Cover and let rise till nearly double in size (about 30 to 40 minutes). Brush tops with a little water.

7. Bake in a 375° oven for 35 to 40 minutes or till bread sounds hollow when you tap the top with your fingers (if necessary, cover loosely with foil the last 10 minutes of baking to prevent overbrowning). Immediately remove bread from pans. Cool on wire racks. Makes 2 loaves (16 servings each).

Nutritional facts per serving: 95 calories, 1 g total fat (0 g saturated fat), 0 mg cholesterol, 68 mg sodium, 19 g carbohydrate, 2 g fiber, 3 g protein. **Daily values:** 0% vitamin A, 0% vitamin C, 0% calcium, 7% iron.

Low-fat

Low-calorie

Low-sodium

LEMON-BLUEBERRY MUFFINS

Mix a batch of these easy muffins for dinner tonight. They'll be ready in about half an hour. (See photo, right.)

Nonstick spray coating
2 cups all-purpose flour
3 tablespoons sugar
1½ teaspoons baking powder
½ teaspoon baking soda
⅔ cup plain nonfat yogurt
¼ cup frozen egg product, thawed
2 tablespoons cooking oil
1 teaspoon finely shredded lemon peel
1 cup fresh or frozen blueberries

1. Spray twelve 2½-inch muffin cups with nonstick spray coating; set aside.

2. In a large mixing bowl stir together flour, sugar, baking powder, and baking soda. Make a well in the center of dry mixture.

3. In a medium mixing bowl combine yogurt, egg product, oil, and lemon peel. Add yogurt mixture all at once to dry mixture. Stir just till moistened (batter should be lumpy). Fold in blueberries.

4. Spoon batter into the prepared muffin cups, filling each ⅔ full. Bake in 400° oven for 20 to 25 minutes or till a wooden toothpick inserted in center comes out clean. Cool in muffin cups on a wire rack for 5 minutes. Then remove muffins from muffin cups. Serve warm. Makes 12.

Nutritional facts per muffin: 119 calories, 3 g total fat (0 g saturated fat), 0 mg cholesterol, 68 mg sodium, 20 g carbohydrate, 1 g fiber, 3 g protein. **Daily values:** 2% vitamin A, 2% vitamin C, 2% calcium, 6% iron.

Reheating Muffins

Most muffins taste best when served hot from the oven, and this is especially true for reduced-fat muffins such as Lemon-Blueberry Muffins. If you want to enjoy muffins later, freeze them. Wrap the muffins tightly in heavy foil or place in freezer bags, and freeze for up to one month. To reheat, wrap frozen muffins in heavy foil. Heat in a 300° oven for 12 to 15 minutes for 1¾-inch muffins and 15 to 18 minutes for 2½-inch muffins.

Low-fat

Low-calorie

WHOLE WHEAT PUMPKIN MUFFINS

Serve these with light or non-fat cream cheese product or an apricot fruit spread.

Nonstick spray coating
1 cup all-purpose flour
¾ cup whole wheat flour
3 tablespoons sugar
2 teaspoons baking powder
1 teaspoon pumpkin pie spice
¼ teaspoon baking soda
⅛ teaspoon salt
1 beaten egg
¾ cup skim milk
2 tablespoons margarine, melted
½ cup canned pumpkin

1. Spray twelve 2½-inch muffin cups with nonstick spray coating; set aside.

2. In a large mixing bowl stir together the all-purpose flour, whole wheat flour, sugar, baking powder, pumpkin pie spice, baking soda, and salt. Make a well in the center of dry mixture. In a small mixing bowl stir together egg, milk, and margarine. Stir in the pumpkin. Add egg mixture all at once to dry mixture. Using a fork, stir just till moistened (batter should be lumpy).

3. Spoon batter into prepared muffin cups, filling ⅔ full. Bake in a 375° oven for 18 to 20 minutes or till toothpick inserted in center comes out clean. Cool in muffin cups on a wire rack for 5 minutes. Then remove muffins from muffin cups. Serve warm. Makes 12.

Nutritional facts per muffin: 106 calories, 3 g total fat (1 g saturated fat), 18 mg cholesterol, 146 mg sodium, 18 g carbohydrate, 1 g fiber, 3 g protein. **Daily values:** 26% vitamin A, 1% vitamin C, 7% calcium, 7% iron.

Low-fat

BERRY-ORANGE PANCAKE

This conversation-piece pancake bakes in one pan and holds any combination of fresh fruit you desire.

2 tablespoons margarine
1 cup frozen egg product, thawed
1 cup all-purpose flour
¾ cup skim milk
1 teaspoon finely shredded orange peel
¼ cup orange juice
2 cups fresh or frozen raspberries, strawberries, or blueberries, thawed (slice strawberries, if using)
1 orange, peeled and sectioned
2 tablespoons sifted powdered sugar

1. Place margarine in a 10-inch skillet with an ovenproof handle or a 10-inch round baking pan. Place skillet or pan in a 425° oven for 1 to 2 minutes or till margarine is melted. Meanwhile, in a medium mixing bowl combine egg product, flour, milk, orange peel, and orange juice. Beat with a wire whisk just till mixture is smooth (do not overbeat). Remove pan from oven; slowly pour batter into hot pan.

2. Bake for 25 to 30 minutes or till puffed and golden (do not open door during baking time). Meanwhile, combine berries, orange sections, and *1 tablespoon* of the powdered sugar. Remove pancake from oven; immediately cut into 6 wedges. For each serving, place a wedge on a plate; top with about ⅓ *cup* of the fruit mixture. Sprinkle with remaining powdered sugar. Makes 1 pancake (6 servings).

Nutritional facts per serving: 170 calories, 4 g total fat (1 g saturated fat), 1 mg cholesterol, 116 mg sodium, 26 g carbohydrate, 3 g fiber, 7 g protein. **Daily values:** 28% vitamin A, 35% vitamin C, 5% calcium, 12% iron.

Low-fat

Low-calorie

BUCKWHEAT PANCAKES

You'll find buckwheat flour in larger supermarkets or health food stores.

¾ cup whole wheat flour

¾ cup buckwheat flour

½ cup all-purpose flour

2 tablespoons brown sugar

½ teaspoon baking soda

½ teaspoon baking powder

1 beaten egg

1 egg white

2 cups low-fat buttermilk

2 tablespoons reduced-calorie margarine, melted

Nonstick spray coating

1. In a large mixing bowl stir together whole wheat flour, buckwheat flour, all-purpose flour, brown sugar, baking soda, and baking powder. In a medium mixing bowl combine egg, egg white, buttermilk, and margarine. Add egg mixture to flour mixture; stir just till moistened but still slightly lumpy (do not overbeat).

2. Spray a nonstick skillet or griddle with nonstick spray coating. Heat over medium heat. Pour about ¼ *cup* batter for each pancake onto the hot skillet. Cook till pancakes are golden brown, turning to cook second sides when pancakes have bubbly surfaces and slightly dry edges. Makes 12 to 14 pancakes.

Nutritional facts per pancake: 94 calories, 2 g total fat (1 g saturated fat), 17 mg cholesterol, 123 mg sodium, 16 g carbohydrate, 2 g fiber, 4 g protein. **Daily values:** 2% vitamin A, 0% vitamin C, 5% calcium, 5% iron.

Low-fat

Low-calorie

BANANA PANCAKES

Try stirring some ground cinnamon or nutmeg into light maple syrup, then heating it for a different pancake topping.

1½ cups all-purpose flour

1 tablespoon sugar

1½ teaspoons baking powder

½ teaspoon ground cinnamon

¼ teaspoon baking soda

¼ teaspoon ground nutmeg

2 medium bananas, mashed (½ cup)

1½ cups skim milk

2 tablespoons margarine, melted

2 egg whites

Nonstick spray coating

⅓ cup light pancake and waffle syrup, heated

1. In a large mixing bowl stir together flour, sugar, baking powder, cinnamon, baking soda, and nutmeg. In a medium mixing bowl combine the mashed banana, milk, and margarine. Add banana mixture to flour mixture; stir till nearly smooth but still slightly lumpy (do not overbeat). Beat egg whites with an electric mixer till stiff peaks form (tips stand straight). Fold egg whites into flour mixture.

2. Spray a nonstick skillet or griddle with nonstick spray coating. Heat over medium heat. Pour about ¼ *cup* batter for each pancake onto hot skillet. Cook till pancakes are golden brown, turning to cook second sides when pancakes have bubbly surfaces and slightly dry edges. Serve with light maple syrup. Makes about 16 pancakes.

Nutritional facts per pancake: 85 calories, 2 g total fat (0 g saturated fat), 0 mg cholesterol, 92 mg sodium, 15 g carbohydrate, 0 g fiber, 2 g protein. **Daily values:** 3% vitamin A, 1% vitamin C, 5% calcium, 4% iron.

SCONES WITH STRAWBERRY CREAM CHEESE

Low-fat

Scones are best eaten warm on the day they are made. (See photo, left.)

Nonstick spray coating
2½ cups all-purpose flour
¼ cup sugar
2 teaspoons baking powder
⅛ teaspoon ground nutmeg
2 tablespoons margarine, chilled
⅓ cup currants or raisins
⅔ cup skim milk
1 beaten egg
1 egg white
2 teaspoons skim milk
Strawberry Cream Cheese

1. Spray a baking sheet with nonstick coating; set aside. In a mixing bowl stir together flour, sugar, baking powder, and nutmeg. With a pastry blender, cut in margarine till mixture resembles coarse crumbs. Stir in currants. Make a well in the center of dry mixture. In a mixing bowl stir together ⅔ cup milk, egg, and egg white. Add milk mixture all at once to dry mixture. Using a fork, stir just till moistened.

2. Turn dough out onto a lightly floured surface. Quickly knead dough by folding and pressing dough gently for 10 to 12 strokes or till dough smooth. Pat into a 9-inch circle; cut into 10 wedges. Transfer wedges to the baking sheet. Brush tops of scones with 2 teaspoons milk. Bake in a 450° oven about 12 minutes, or till light golden brown. Serve warm with Strawberry Cream Cheese. Makes 10 scones.

Strawberry Cream Cheese: In a blender container or food processor bowl combine half of an 8-ounce container of *fat-free cream cheese product* and 3 tablespoons *reduced-calorie strawberry preserves.* Cover and blend or process till smooth. Makes ½ cup.

Nutritional facts per scone: 195 calories, 3 g total fat (1 g saturated fat), 24 mg cholesterol, 138 mg sodium, 34 g carbohydrate, 1 g fiber, 7 g protein. **Daily values:** 8% vitamin A, 1% vitamin C, 10% calcium, 10% iron.

SOUR CREAM-CHIVE DROP BISCUITS

Low-calorie

Chives, a member of the onion family, add a fresh taste to breads, sauces, and savory dishes.

Nonstick spray coating
2 cups all-purpose flour
1 tablespoon snipped fresh chives or 1 teaspoon snipped dried chives
2 teaspoons baking powder
2 teaspoons sugar
¼ teaspoon baking soda
Dash of salt
3 tablespoons margarine
⅔ cup skim milk
½ cup light dairy sour cream

1. Spray a baking sheet with nonstick spray coating; set aside. In a medium mixing bowl stir together flour, chives, baking powder, sugar, baking soda, and salt. Using a pastry blender, cut in margarine till mixture resembles coarse crumbs. Make a well in the center of dry mixture. In a small mixing bowl stir together milk and sour cream. Add milk mixture all at once to center of dry mixture. Using a fork, stir just till moistened.

2. Drop dough from a well-rounded tablespoon 1 inch apart onto prepared baking sheet. Bake in a 450° oven for 10 to 12 minutes or till golden. Remove biscuits from baking sheet and serve warm. Makes 12.

Nutritional facts per serving: 140 calories, 5 g total fat (1 g saturated fat), 2 mg cholesterol, 181 mg sodium, 21 g carbohydrate, 1 g fiber, 4 g protein. **Daily values:** 6% vitamin A, 0% vitamin C, 8% calcium, 7% iron.

Low-fat

Low-calorie

APPLESAUCE-BRAN WAFFLES

Egg whites help to lighten these waffles. Reheat any leftovers the next day in your toaster oven.

Nonstick spray coating
½ **cup whole bran cereal**
1¼ **cups skim milk**
1½ **cups all-purpose flour**
2 **teaspoons baking powder**
½ **teaspoon ground cardamom or ground cinnamon**
1 **beaten egg**
2 **tablespoons reduced-calorie margarine, melted**
1 **cup unsweetened applesauce**
2 **egg whites**

1. Liberally spray grids of waffle baker with nonstick spray coating; preheat. Place bran cereal in a small bowl; pour *¾ cup* of the milk over cereal. Let stand 5 minutes. Stir together flour, baking powder, and cardamom. Make a well in center of dry mixture. Whisk together remaining milk and egg; stir in margarine. Add milk mixture, bran mixture, and applesauce to center of dry mixture all at once. Stir till moistened but still slightly lumpy. Beat egg whites till stiff peaks form (tips stand straight). Gently fold beaten egg whites into batter till only a few streaks of white remain (do not overmix).

2. Pour *1 to 1¼ cups* batter over preheated waffle baker. Close lid quickly; do not open during baking. Bake according to manufacturer's directions. When done, use a fork to lift waffle off grid. Repeat with remaining batter. To keep baked waffles hot for serving, place in single layer on a wire rack placed atop a baking sheet in 300° oven. Makes 16 (4½-inch) square waffles.

Nutritional facts per waffle: 73 calories, 1 g total fat (0 g saturated fat), 14 mg cholesterol, 113 mg sodium, 13 g carbohydrate, 1 g fiber, 3 g protein. **Daily values:** 6% vitamin A, 2% vitamin C, 6% calcium, 7% iron.

Low-calorie

POPOVERS

Traditionally popovers are made with whole eggs. This adapted recipe uses egg whites only.

Nonstick spray coating
2 **tablespoons sesame seed**
4 **egg whites**
1 **cup skim milk**
1 **tablespoon cooking oil**
1 **cup all-purpose flour**
¼ **teaspoon salt**

1. Generously spray nonstick spray coating on the bottoms and sides of six 6-ounce custard cups. Sprinkle each with *1 teaspoon* sesame seed. Place prepared custard cups in a 15x10x1-inch baking pan; set aside.

2. In a medium mixing bowl combine egg whites, milk, and cooking oil. Add flour and salt. Beat with a rotary beater or wire whisk till smooth. Pour batter into prepared cups, filling each half full.

3. Bake in a 400° oven for 40 minutes or till very firm. Turn off oven. Remove popovers from the oven and immediately prick each popover with a fork to let steam escape. Return to the oven for 5 minutes more. Serve immediately. Makes 6 popovers.

Nutritional facts per serving: 133 calories, 5 g total fat (1 g saturated fat), 1 mg cholesterol, 148 mg sodium, 17 g carbohydrate, 1 g fiber, 6 g protein. **Daily values:** 2% vitamin A, 0% vitamin C, 4% calcium, 7% iron.

Low-fat

Low-calorie

Low-sodium

EASY APRICOT BREAD

Putting this breakfast bread together is a snap if you thaw the dough overnight in the refrigerator.

Nonstick spray coating

1 16-ounce loaf frozen white or whole wheat bread dough, thawed

½ cup low-calorie apricot, strawberry, or raspberry spread

½ cup chopped apricots; chopped, peeled peaches; blueberries; or raspberries

Powdered Sugar Icing

1. Spray 2 baking sheets with nonstick spray coating. Turn the dough out onto a lightly floured surface. Divide dough in half. Roll each half of the dough into a 12x7-inch rectangle. Carefully transfer each rectangle to a prepared baking sheet.

2. Cut up any large pieces of fruit in preserves. Spread *half* of the preserves over the center third of a dough rectangle. Sprinkle half of the fresh fruit over preserves. On the long sides, make 2-inch-long cuts from the edges toward center at 1-inch intervals. Starting at one end, alternately fold opposite strips of dough at an angle across fruit filling. Repeat with remaining dough rectangle, preserves, and fruit. Cover and let rise till nearly double in size (about 40 minutes).

3. Bake in a 350° oven about 20 minutes or till golden brown. Remove from baking sheet; cool slightly on a wire rack. Drizzle with Powdered Sugar Icing. Serve warm. Makes 2 loaves (12 servings each).

Powdered Sugar Icing: In a small bowl stir together ½ cup sifted *powdered sugar,* 1 teaspoon *lemon juice,* and 1 to 2 teaspoons *skim milk.* Stir in additional *skim milk,* 1 teaspoon at a time, till icing is smooth and of drizzling consistency.

Nutritional facts per serving: 61 calories, 0 g total fat (0 g saturated fat), 0 mg cholesterol, 5 mg sodium, 13 g carbohydrate, 0 g fiber, 1 g protein. **Daily values:** 0% vitamin A, 0% vitamin C, 1% calcium, 0% iron.

To shape the loaf, bring the opposite strips of dough to the center. Overlap the strips slightly at an angle to give the loaf a braided look.

Low-fat

Low-calorie

QUICK HERBED PITA ROUNDS

This quick, easy bread is a perfect complement for a main-dish salad, soup, or for grilled meats or fish entrées.

4 (8-inch) pita bread rounds
  Nonstick spray coating
1 tablespoon olive oil or
    vegetable oil
2 tablespoons snipped fresh
    basil or 2 teaspoons dried
    basil, crushed
1 tablespoon snipped fresh
    chives or 1 teaspoon dried
    chives, crushed
1 tablespoon snipped fresh sage
    or 1 teaspoon dried sage,
    crushed
1 clove garlic, minced
⅛ teaspoon pepper

1. Place bread rounds on a large baking sheet. Spray surface of rounds with nonstick spray coating. Combine oil, basil, chives, sage, garlic, and pepper. Spread *one-fourth* of the herb mixture over each bread round.

2. Bake in a 350° oven about 10 minutes or till crisp. Cut into wedges; serve warm. Makes 8 servings.

Nutritional facts per serving: 99 calories, 2 g total fat (0 g saturated fat), 0 mg cholesterol, 161 mg sodium, 17 g carbohydrate, 0 g fiber, 3 g protein. **Daily values:** 0% vitamin A, 0% vitamin C, 2% calcium, 5% iron.

Low-fat

Low-calorie

CORN BREAD

Our corn bread has fewer calories than the classic because it uses less oil and sugar, and skim milk replaces 2 percent milk.

  Nonstick spray coating
1 cup all-purpose flour
1 cup yellow, white, or blue
    cornmeal
2 tablespoons sugar
1 tablespoon baking powder
¼ teaspoon salt
2 slightly beaten egg whites
1 beaten egg
1 cup skim milk
2 tablespoons cooking oil

1. Spray a 9x9x2-inch baking pan with nonstick spray coating; set aside.

2. In a medium bowl stir together flour, cornmeal, sugar, baking powder, and salt. In a small bowl stir together egg whites, egg, milk, and cooking oil. Add to flour mixture; stir just till batter is smooth (do not overbeat). Spoon batter into the pan. Bake in a 425° oven for 20 to 25 minutes or till golden brown. Makes 12 servings.

Nutritional facts per serving: 122 calories, 3 g total fat (1 g saturated fat), 18 mg cholesterol, 161 mg sodium, 20 g carbohydrate, 1 g fiber, 4 g protein. **Daily values:** 2% vitamin A, 0% vitamin C, 9% calcium, 7% iron.

Corn Muffins: Prepare as above, except spray twelve 2½-inch muffin cups with nonstick spray coating. Spoon batter into muffin cups, filling each ⅔ full. Bake for 12 to 15 minutes or till golden brown. Makes 12.

DELIGHTFUL DESSERTS

If you thought desserts were off-limits in a healthy lifestyle, you'll be amazed with the wide array of taste-tempting sweets on the following pages. For family celebrations, try Frozen-Yogurt Brownie Sundaes, fat-slashed brownies topped with frozen yogurt and chocolate sauce. Do you crave old-fashioned flavor that's low in calories? Sample either crisp Brown Sugar 'n' Spice Cookies or creamy Rice Pudding Parfaits. If your family asks for something sweet when you're short on time, turn to Gingered Peach-and-Pear Crisp—canned fruit makes it easy. These delectable treats are just a few of the many healthful desserts you'll find here, ready to become favorites in your home.

Low-fat

Low-calorie

PUMPKIN CHEESECAKE

A food processor or blender makes quick work of mixing this slimmed-down cheesecake. (See photo, right.)

¾ cup graham cracker crumbs

2 tablespoons reduced-calorie
margarine, melted

1 15-ounce carton light ricotta
cheese

1 8-ounce container fat-free
cream cheese product

1 cup canned pumpkin

½ cup skim milk

1 envelope unflavored gelatin

½ cup orange juice

2 teaspoons finely shredded
orange peel

⅓ cup granulated sugar

⅓ cup packed brown sugar

2 teaspoons vanilla

1 teaspoon pumpkin pie spice

1. For crust, in a medium mixing bowl stir together graham cracker crumbs and margarine till moistened. Press mixture onto the bottom of a 9-inch springform pan. Chill while preparing filling.

2. For filling, in a food processor bowl or blender container combine ½ of the ricotta cheese, cream cheese, pumpkin, and milk. Cover and process or blend till smooth. Transfer to a large mixing bowl. Repeat with remaining ricotta, cream cheese, pumpkin, and milk.

3. In a small saucepan sprinkle gelatin over orange juice; let stand 5 minutes. Heat gelatin till dissolved. Stir into pumpkin mixture with orange peel, granulated sugar, brown sugar, vanilla, and pumpkin pie spice. Pour mixture into chilled crust. Cover and chill several hours or till firm. Makes 12 servings.

Nutritional facts per serving: 142 calories, 2 g total fat (0 g saturated fat), 7 mg cholesterol, 214 mg sodium, 23 g carbohydrate, 1 g fiber, 11 g protein. **Daily values:** 58% vitamin A, 11% vitamin C, 18% calcium, 4% iron.

Simply Citrus

Citrus fruits are wonderfully low in calories and sodium, virtually fat-free, and packed with vitamin C. They have a fresh flavor and natural sweetness that can be used in endless ways. Citrus fruits, such as lemons, limes, oranges, grapefruit, tangerines, and tangelos, are available year-round but more abundant December to March.

The next time a recipe calls for shredded citrus peel, go ahead and shred more than you need. Place any extra shredded peel in a small airtight container, then label and freeze. It's ready when you need it and as fresh-tasting as the minute you shredded it. You can store shredded citrus peel in the freezer for up to 6 months.

PEACH UPSIDE-DOWN CAKE

◢ *Low-fat*

Top wedges of this family-style dessert with a dollop of our Whipped Milk Topping (see tip, below).

Nonstick spray coating
2 cups frozen unsweetened
   peach slices, thawed
3 tablespoons light pancake and
   waffle syrup
1⅓ cups all-purpose flour
2 teaspoons baking powder
½ teaspoon ground cinnamon
⅛ teaspoon ground nutmeg
¼ cup margarine, softened
¾ cup sugar
1 teaspoon vanilla
⅔ cup skim milk
2 egg whites

1. Spray a 9x1½-inch round baking pan with nonstick coating. Arrange peach slices in a decorative pattern on bottom of baking pan. Pour syrup over peaches; set aside.

2. In a medium mixing bowl stir together flour, baking powder, cinnamon, and nutmeg; set aside. In a large mixing bowl beat margarine with an electric mixer on medium speed for 30 seconds. Add ½ cup of the sugar and the vanilla. Beat till well combined. Alternately add the flour mixture and milk to the sugar mixture, beating on low to medium speed after each addition just till combined.

3. Wash and dry beaters. In a small mixing bowl beat egg whites till soft peaks form (tips curl). Gradually add remaining sugar, beating till stiff peaks form (tips stand straight). Gently fold egg white mixture into batter. Spoon batter over peaches in prepared pan. Bake in a 350° oven for 30 to 35 minutes or till a toothpick inserted near the center comes out clean. Cool cake in pan on a wire rack for 5 minutes. Invert a serving plate over cake pan. Invert cake onto serving plate. Serve warm; cut into wedges. Makes 8 servings.

Nutritional facts per serving: 233 calories, 6 g total fat (1 g saturated fat), 0 mg cholesterol, 99 mg sodium, 41 g carbohydrate, 1 g fiber, 4 g protein. **Daily values:** 9% vitamin A, 3% vitamin C, 3% calcium, 6% iron.

Better Than Cream

For a light, sweet topping that adds a rich touch to your favorite desserts, try this one that starts with evaporated milk. It contains only 8 calories a tablespoon and less than 1 gram of fat.

Whipped Milk Topping: Pour ½ cup *evaporated milk* or *evaporated skim milk* into an 8x8x2- or 9x9x2-inch baking pan. Freeze milk for 20 to 30 minutes or till soft ice crystals form throughout milk. Pour milk into a chilled mixing bowl. Beat with an electric mixer on high speed for 2 to 3 minutes or till soft peaks form (tips curl). Add 2 teaspoons *lemon juice*, ½ teaspoon *vanilla*, and ⅓ cup sifted *powdered sugar*. Serve immediately. Makes 2½ cups.

Low-fat

Low-calorie

Low-sodium

GINGERED PEACH-AND-PEAR CRISP

Fresh gingerroot perks up the taste of this baked crisp. In a pinch you can substitute ¼ teaspoon ground ginger.

1 16-ounce can peach slices
    (juice pack), drained
1 16-ounce can pear halves
    (juice pack), drained and
    cut up
1 teaspoon grated gingerroot
6 gingersnaps, crushed (½ cup)
½ cup quick-cooking rolled oats
2 tablespoons packed brown
    sugar

1. In a 2-quart square baking dish place peaches, pears, and grated gingerroot. Toss to mix.

2. In a small mixing bowl stir together gingersnaps, oats, and brown sugar. Sprinkle evenly over fruit. Bake in a 425° oven for 15 to 20 minutes or till heated through. Makes 6 servings.

Nutritional facts per serving: 138 calories, 1 g total fat (1 g saturated fat), 0 mg cholesterol, 48 mg sodium, 32 g carbohydrate, 2 g fiber, 2 g protein. **Daily values:** 2% vitamin A, 4% vitamin C, 1% calcium, 7% iron.

Low-calorie

Low-sodium

CHOCOLATE ZUCCHINI CAKE

Zucchini makes this chocolate cake so moist that you even skip frosting it!

  Nonstick spray coating
⅔ cup granulated sugar
½ cup packed brown sugar
¼ cup cooking oil
3 egg whites
1 cup all-purpose flour
¾ cup whole wheat flour
⅓ cup unsweetened cocoa
    powder
1½ teaspoons baking powder
¾ teaspoon pumpkin pie spice
¼ teaspoon baking soda
2 cups finely shredded zucchini
2 teaspoons powdered sugar
½ teaspoon unsweetened cocoa
    powder

1. Spray a 6-cup fluted tube pan or a 9x9x2-inch baking pan with nonstick coating. (If using a fluted pan, dust with all-purpose flour.) Set aside.

2. In a large mixing bowl stir together the granulated sugar, brown sugar, oil, and egg whites till well blended. Add the all-purpose flour, whole wheat flour, the ⅓ cup cocoa powder, baking powder, pumpkin pie spice, and baking soda. Stir mixture just till moistened. (Batter will be thick.) Stir in zucchini.

3. Spoon batter into prepared pan. Bake in a 350° oven for 45 to 50 minutes or till a wooden toothpick inserted near center comes out clean. Cool in pan on wire rack. (For tube pan, cool on wire rack 15 minutes; remove cake from pan.)

4. Combine the powdered sugar and ½ teaspoon cocoa powder. Sift cocoa mixture on cake. Makes 16 servings.

Nutritional facts per serving: 148 calories, 4 g total fat (1 g saturated fat), 0 mg cholesterol, 68 mg sodium, 26 g carbohydrate, 1 g fiber, 3 g protein. **Daily values:** 0% vitamin A, 2% vitamin C, 5% calcium, 7% iron.

Low-fat
Low-sodium

COFFEE AND CREAM DESSERT

This elegant dessert can be made the night before. (See photo, left.)

1½ teaspoons instant coffee
    granules
⅓ cup hot water
1 8-ounce container fat-free
    cream cheese product
⅓ cup sugar
2 tablespoons almond or coffee
    liqueur, or orange juice
1 teaspoon vanilla
1½ cups frozen, light, whipped
    dessert topping, thawed
12 ladyfingers, split
    Fresh raspberries or
    strawberries (optional)
    Fresh mint leaves (optional)

1. Dissolve coffee in hot water. Set aside.

2. In a food processor bowl or blender container combine cream cheese product, sugar, liqueur or orange juice, and vanilla. Cover, and process or blend till mixture is smooth. Transfer to a medium mixing bowl. Fold in whipped topping.

3. Brush cut side of ladyfingers with coffee mixture. In each of 6 dessert dishes arrange 4 ladyfinger halves, cut side up. Spoon the cheese mixture into each glass. Cover and chill for 2 to 24 hours before serving. Garnish with fresh berries and mint leaves, if desired. Makes 6 servings.

Nutritional facts per serving: 171 calories, 2 g total fat (0 g saturated fat), 22 mg cholesterol, 46 mg sodium, 28 g carbohydrate, 0 g fiber, 9 g protein. **Daily values:** 10% vitamin A, 0% vitamin C, 28% calcium, 2% iron.

Meal-Ending Beverages

Instead of something sweet for dessert, try a steaming cup of coffee or tea to end the meal.

For a special treat, brew one of the flavored dessert coffee blends. Check the selection of dessert coffees available in specialty coffee shops or your grocery store. You'll find they range from flavored regular coffees to decaffeinated blends. Some coffees are flavored with nuts or chocolate. Dress up the coffee with a dollop of thawed, frozen whipped dessert topping and a sprinkling of ground cinnamon or nutmeg. (A tablespoon of the whipped dessert topping adds about 15 calories.)

Flavored teas are another possible finale. Look for spice- and fruit-flavored varieties at a supermarket or specialty shop.

Low-calorie

Low-sodium

BROWN SUGAR 'N' SPICE COOKIES

Enjoy these cookies with an ice-cold glass of skim milk.

⅓ cup margarine, softened
⅓ cup granulated sugar
⅓ cup packed brown sugar
¾ teaspoon baking powder
½ teaspoon ground cinnamon
½ teaspoon ground ginger
¼ teaspoon ground nutmeg
1 egg
1 teaspoon vanilla
1¼ cups all-purpose flour
⅓ cup whole wheat flour
1 tablespoon granulated sugar
⅛ teaspoon ground cinnamon

1. In a large mixing bowl beat margarine with an electric mixer on medium to high speed for 30 seconds. Add the ⅓ cup granulated sugar, brown sugar, baking powder, ½ teaspoon cinnamon, ginger, and nutmeg. Beat till combined. Beat in egg and vanilla. Beat in as much of the all-purpose flour and whole wheat flour as you can. Stir in any remaining flour with a wooden spoon.

2. Shape dough into 1-inch balls. Place 2 inches apart on ungreased baking sheets. Slightly flatten each with the bottom of a drinking glass dipped in a mixture of the 1 tablespoon granulated sugar and ⅛ teaspoon cinnamon. Bake in a 350° oven for 7 to 9 minutes or till cookies are firm. Cool on cookie sheet for 1 minute. Then remove cookies from cookie sheet and cool on a wire rack. Makes 3 dozen cookies.

Nutritional facts per cookie: 52 calories, 2 g total fat (0 g saturated fat), 6 mg cholesterol, 23 mg sodium, 8 g carbohydrate, 0 g fiber, 1 g protein. **Daily values:** 2% vitamin A, 0% vitamin C, 0% calcium, 2% iron.

Low-fat

Low-calorie

Low-sodium

APRICOT-CARDAMOM BARS

Because the applesauce adds moistness, we were able to cut the oil to just 2 tablespoons in these flavorful bars.

1 cup all-purpose flour
½ cup packed brown sugar
½ teaspoon baking powder
¼ teaspoon baking soda
¼ teaspoon ground cardamom
   or ⅛ teaspoon ground
   cloves
½ cup apricot nectar or orange
   juice
¼ cup unsweetened applesauce
2 tablespoons cooking oil
1 slightly beaten egg
½ cup finely snipped dried
   apricots
Apricot Icing

1. In a medium mixing bowl stir together flour, brown sugar, baking powder, baking soda, and cardamom or cloves; set aside. In another mixing bowl stir together apricot nectar or orange juice, applesauce, oil, and egg till combined. Add to dry ingredients, stirring till just combined. Stir in snipped apricots.

2. Spread batter in an ungreased 11x7x1½-inch baking pan. Bake in a 350° oven about 25 minutes or till a wooden toothpick inserted near the center comes out clean. Cool in pan on a wire rack. Drizzle with Apricot Icing. Cut into bars. Makes 24 bars.

Apricot Icing: In a small mixing bowl stir together ½ cup *powdered sugar* and 2 to 3 teaspoons *apricot nectar* or *orange juice*.

Nutritional facts per serving: 67 calories, 1 g total fat (0 g saturated fat), 9 mg cholesterol, 17 mg sodium, 13 g carbohydrate, 0 g fiber, 1 g protein. **Daily values:** 3% vitamin A, 3% vitamin C, 0% calcium, 3% iron.

Low-fat

Low-calorie

Low-sodium

LADYFINGER SANDWICHES

Although these dainty cakes require a bit of time to prepare, they are well worth the effort.

Nonstick spray coating
4 egg whites
½ cup sugar
2 egg yolks
½ teaspoon finely shredded
  lemon peel
2 teaspoons lemon juice
1 teaspoon vanilla
¾ cup sifted cake or all-purpose
  flour
4 teaspoons powdered sugar
¼ cup low-calorie raspberry
  or strawberry spread

1. Line a cookie sheet with parchment or plain brown paper. Spray very lightly with nonstick coating. Set aside.

2. In a large mixing bowl beat egg whites with an electric mixer till soft peaks form (tips curl). Gradually add ¼ cup of the sugar, beating till stiff peaks form (tips stand straight). In a small mixing bowl beat egg yolks on medium speed for 1 minute. Gradually add remaining sugar, beating till thick and lemon-colored. Beat in lemon peel, lemon juice, and vanilla. Fold egg yolk mixture into egg whites. Fold in flour.

3. Spoon batter into a decorating bag fitted with a large round tip (about ½ inch in diameter). Pipe 3½x¾-inch strips of batter 1 inch apart on the prepared cookie sheet. Sift powdered sugar over batter.

4. Bake in a 350° oven for 8 to 10 minutes or till lightly browned. Cool on cookie sheet on a wire rack for 15 minutes. Remove ladyfingers and completely cool on the wire rack. If desired, wrap and freeze unfilled ladyfingers. Just before serving, spread about ¾ teaspoon of the raspberry or strawberry spread on the flat side of 15 ladyfingers. Top with the remaining ladyfingers. Makes 15 cakes.

Nutritional facts per cake: 67 calories, 1 g total fat (0 g saturated fat), 28 mg cholesterol, 20 mg sodium, 13 g carbohydrate, 0 g fiber, 2 g protein. **Daily values:** 4% vitamin A, 0% vitamin C, 0% calcium, 2% iron.

Using a decorating bag and a large round tip, pipe the batter into 3½-inch-long strips onto a cookie sheet lined with parchment paper. Leave about 1 inch between the strips.

Low-sodium

High-fiber

APPLE CRUMBLE

Sliced, peeled pears make an equally delicious stand-in for the apples used in recipe photo (right).

Nonstick spray coating
8 cups sliced, peeled cooking
  apples
1 tablespoon lemon juice
½ cup rolled oats
¼ cup all-purpose flour
¼ cup packed brown sugar
1 teaspoon ground cinnamon
¼ teaspoon ground nutmeg
3 tablespoons margarine,
  chilled
Vanilla low-fat yogurt
  (optional)
Honey (optional)

1. Spray a 2-quart square baking dish with nonstick coating. Place apples in dish. Sprinkle with lemon juice.

2. In a medium bowl stir together rolled oats, flour, brown sugar, cinnamon, and nutmeg. With a pastry blender cut in margarine till mixture resembles coarse crumbs. Sprinkle mixture evenly over apples.

3. Bake in a 350° oven for 40 to 45 minutes or till apples are tender. Serve warm topped with combined yogurt and honey, if desired. Makes 6 servings.

Nutritional facts per serving: 211 calories, 7 g total fat (1 g saturated fat), 0 mg cholesterol, 70 mg sodium, 38 g carbohydrate, 4 g fiber, 2 g protein. **Daily values:** 7% vitamin A, 16% vitamin C, 2% calcium, 7% iron.

Selecting Fresh Fruit

There's no better low-fat choice for dessert than fresh fruit. Choose the best quality you can find for the most after-dinner satisfaction.

Fruits should be plump, brightly colored, and heavy for their size (this indicates moistness). Avoid fruits with mold, mildew, bruises, cuts, or other blemishes.

To ripen apricots, plums, peaches, nectarines, pears, or tomatoes, place fruit in a paper bag and let it stand at room temperature for a few days or till desired ripeness. Once the fruit is ripe, store in the refrigerator.

FROZEN CRANBERRY PIE

Low-fat

Try this frosty pie with peach or strawberry low-fat ice cream, too.

Nonstick spray coating
6 chocolate wafer cookies,
    crushed (about ½ cup)
1 quart vanilla low-fat or light
    ice cream
1 cup whole-berry cranberry
    sauce
1 teaspoon finely shredded
    orange peel
  Orange slices or twists
    (optional)

1. Spray a 9-inch pie plate with nonstick coating. Coat with cookie crumbs. Set aside.

2. In a chilled medium mixing bowl stir the ice cream with a wooden spoon just till softened. Fold in cranberry sauce and orange peel till nearly blended. Spoon mixture into prepared pie plate. Cover and freeze several hours or till firm. Cut into wedges and garnish with orange slices or twists, if desired. Makes 8 servings.

Nutritional facts per serving: 176 calories, 3 g total fat (1 g saturated fat), 11 mg cholesterol, 83 mg sodium, 36 g carbohydrate, 1 g fiber, 2 g protein. **Daily values:** 9% vitamin A, 7% vitamin C, 2% calcium, 1% iron.

Place the ice cream in a chilled bowl, then stir with a wooden spoon until it is soft enough to stir in the remaining ingredients.

GRAPE CREAM TART

Low-fat

Use a combination of red and green grapes for a dazzling topping.

1½ cups graham cracker crumbs
5 tablespoons reduced-calorie
    margarine, melted
2 4-serving-size packages
    sugar-free instant vanilla
    pudding mix
2 cups skim milk
1 8-ounce carton vanilla
    low-fat yogurt
1½ cups halved seedless red or
    green grapes
2 tablespoons apple or
    currant jelly
¾ cup frozen, light, whipped
    dessert topping, thawed

1. In a medium mixing bowl stir together graham cracker crumbs and melted margarine till moistened. Pat mixture in a 9-inch tart pan with removable bottom. Chill while preparing filling.

2. In a large mixing bowl whisk together pudding mix, milk, and yogurt till well-blended. Pour mixture into prepared crust. Cover and chill several hours or till set.

3. Arrange grapes, cut side down, over pudding layer just before serving. In a small saucepan heat jelly till melted. Brush grapes with jelly. Pipe or spoon whipped topping around edge. Makes 10 servings.

Nutritional facts per serving: 183 calories, 5 g total fat (1 g saturated fat), 2 mg cholesterol, 182 mg sodium, 30 g carbohydrate, 1 g fiber, 4 g protein. **Daily values:** 10% vitamin A, 5% vitamin C, 9% calcium, 4% iron.

Low-fat
Low-sodium

VANILLA-CHOCOLATE DESSERT WITH CHOCOLATE SAUCE

Both kids and adults will love this simple, yet dramatic, frozen dessert—and they'll never guess it's low in fat.

¼ cup chocolate wafer crumbs
1 teaspoon reduced-calorie
    margarine, melted
1 pint vanilla flavored low-fat
    ice cream
1 pint chocolate or coffee-
    flavored low-fat ice cream
½ cup sugar
3 tablespoons unsweetened
    cocoa powder
2 teaspoons cornstarch
½ cup skim milk
1 tablespoon reduced-calorie
    margarine
1 teaspoon vanilla

1. Line an 8x4x2-inch loaf pan with plastic wrap. In a bowl combine crumbs and the 1 teaspoon margarine; press into bottom of pan. Freeze for 30 minutes. In a mixing bowl stir vanilla ice cream with a spoon just till softened. Spread over wafer crust. Cover and freeze 1 hour. Soften chocolate ice cream as above and spread over vanilla ice cream. Cover and freeze several hours.

2. For chocolate sauce, in a saucepan combine sugar, cocoa, and cornstarch. Stir in skim milk. Cook and stir over medium heat till thickened and bubbly. Cook and stir for 2 minutes more. Remove from heat. Stir in the 1 tablespoon margarine and vanilla till margarine is melted and mixture is smooth. Cover surface with plastic wrap and refrigerate until serving time. To serve, remove from loaf pan and cut into 10 slices. Serve with chocolate sauce. Makes 10 servings.

Nutritional facts per serving: 157 calories, 3 g total fat (1 g saturated fat), 8 mg cholesterol, 67 mg sodium, 30 g carbohydrate, 0 g fiber, 3 g protein. **Daily values:** 7% vitamin A, 0% vitamin C, 7% calcium, 3% iron.

FROZEN-YOGURT BROWNIE SUNDAES

Low-fat

If you wish, bake the brownie batter in a 9x9x2-inch baking pan for 20 minutes, instead of muffin cups as shown in photo (left).

Nonstick spray coating
1 cup all-purpose flour
¼ cup unsweetened cocoa
   powder
1 teaspoon baking powder
¼ teaspoon baking soda
¼ cup margarine
⅔ cup sugar
½ teaspoon vanilla
⅔ cup cold water
2 egg whites
1 quart frozen yogurt, any
   flavor
½ cup chocolate-flavored syrup

1. Spray 12 muffin cups with nonstick coating. Set aside.

2. In a medium mixing bowl stir together flour, cocoa powder, baking powder, and baking soda; set aside. In a large mixing bowl beat margarine with an electric mixer on medium speed about 30 seconds. Add the sugar and vanilla; beat till well combined. Add flour mixture and cold water alternately, beating on low speed after each addition.

3. Thoroughly wash beaters. In a small mixing bowl beat egg whites till stiff peaks form (tips stand straight). Gently fold egg whites into batter.

4. Gently spoon into prepared muffin cups, filling ¾ full. Bake in a 375° oven for 13 to 15 minutes or till brownies spring back and leave no imprint when lightly touched. Cool for 2 minutes in pan on rack. Remove from pan and cool on racks.

5. To serve, cut each brownie into fourths and place into a dessert dish. Top with a scoop of frozen yogurt and 2 teaspoons chocolate syrup. Makes 12 servings.

Nutritional facts per serving: 224 calories, 5 g total fat (1 g saturated fat), 0 mg cholesterol, 118 mg sodium, 41 g carbohydrate, 0 g fiber, 5 g protein. **Daily values:** 4% vitamin A, 0% vitamin C, 10% calcium, 6% iron.

The Scoop on Frozen Desserts

The freezer section is brimming with a variety of ice-cream-like treats in a multitude of tempting flavors. Which one is best for a healthy diet? Here's the scoop to help you decide:

Ice cream: This silky smooth dessert is made by law with at least 10 percent milk fat. Watch out, however, because some of the premium ice creams go well beyond the 10 percent mark.

Ice milk: It's a kissing cousin to ice cream in flavor and texture, but contains a lower fat content (2 to 7 percent milk fat).

Frozen yogurt: Currently there are no federal standards for this product, which means you'd better read the label to find out its nutrition profile. Some brands are similar to ice cream; others are more like ice milk.

Sherbet: This fruity dessert must contain between 1 and 2 percent milk fat by weight. To offset the tanginess from the fruits used, more sweetening is often added to sherbets.

FRUIT SUNDAE CREPES

Low-fat

To make this dessert really simple, look for ready-made crepes in the produce section of your grocery store.

4 Crepes (see recipe, page 168)
1 pint low-fat or light ice cream
   or frozen yogurt, any flavor
2 cups fresh fruit such as cut-up
   peaches, bananas, or kiwi
   fruit; sliced strawberries; or
   raspberries or blueberries

1. Place crepes on 4 dessert plates. Top each crepe with one-fourth of the ice cream or yogurt. Fold crepes over filling.

2. Spoon mixed fruit over filled crepes. Serve immediately. Makes 4 servings.

Nutritional facts per serving: 213 calories, 5 g total fat (2 g saturated fat), 35 mg cholesterol, 88 mg sodium, 40 g carbohydrate, 1 g fiber, 5 g protein. **Daily values:** 8% vitamin A, 45% vitamin C, 11% calcium, 4% iron.

Low-fat

Low-calorie

Low-sodium

CITRUS ANGEL CAKE

Angel cake adds a sweet, guilt-free indulgence to healthy eating. This one's drizzled with an orange-scented glaze.

1½ cups egg whites (10 to
      12 large)
1½ cups sifted powdered sugar
   1 cup sifted cake flour or all-
      purpose flour
1½ teaspoons cream of tartar
   1 cup granulated sugar
   1 teaspoon finely shredded
      orange or lemon peel
   Citrus Glaze

1. In a large mixing bowl allow egg whites to stand at room temperature for 30 minutes. Meanwhile, sift powdered sugar and flour together 3 times. Set flour mixture aside.

2. Beat egg whites and cream of tartar with an electric mixer on medium to high speed till soft peaks form (tips curl). Gradually add granulated sugar, about 2 tablespoons at a time, beating till stiff peaks form (tips stand straight).

3. Sift about ¼ of the flour mixture over beaten egg whites, gently fold in. Repeat folding in ¼ of the flour mixture at a time, then fold in orange or lemon peel.

4. Spoon batter evenly into an ungreased 10-inch tube pan. Gently cut through batter with a knife or narrow metal spatula. Bake on the lowest oven rack in a 350° oven for 40 to 45 minutes or till top springs back when lightly touched. Immediately invert cake in pan. Cool completely. Remove cake from pan. Drizzle with Citrus Glaze. Makes 16 servings.

Citrus Glaze: Mix 1 cup sifted *powdered sugar* and 1 teaspoon finely *shredded orange* or *lemon peel*. Stir in 1 to 2 tablespoons *orange juice,* 1 teaspoon at a time, till of drizzling consistency.

Nutritional facts per serving: 120 calories, 0 g total fat (0 g saturated fat), 0 mg cholesterol, 35 mg sodium, 27 g carbohydrate, 0 g fiber, 3 g protein. **Daily values:** 0% vitamin A, 0% vitamin C, 0% calcium, 3% iron.

Low-fat

Low-sodium

High-fiber

POACHED PEARS WITH GINGER CREAM

Serve these spiced pears with thin gingersnap cookies.

¾ cup apple cider or juice

1 tablespoon brown sugar

1 teaspoon finely shredded
   lemon peel

3 inches stick cinnamon
   Thin slice of gingerroot
   (optional)

4 medium pears, peeled and
   cored

¼ cup frozen, light, whipped
   dessert topping, thawed

¼ cup fat-free dairy sour cream

2 teaspoons finely chopped
   candied ginger

1. In skillet combine apple cider or juice, brown sugar, lemon peel, cinnamon, and if desired, gingerroot. Bring to boiling. Add pears. Simmer, covered, for 5 minutes. Turn pears over. Simmer, covered, for 7 to 10 minutes more or till tender. Remove cinnamon and gingerroot.

2. In each of 4 dessert dishes, place one pear. Spoon some poaching liquid over each. Combine whipped topping and sour cream; top each pear with a dollop of the whipped topping-sour cream mixture. Sprinkle with candied ginger. Makes 4 servings.

Nutritional facts per serving: 159 calories, 2 g total fat (1 g saturated fat), 2 mg cholesterol, 23 mg sodium, 36 g carbohydrate, 5 g fiber, 2 g protein. **Daily values:** 2% vitamin A, 12% vitamin C, 3% calcium, 4% iron.

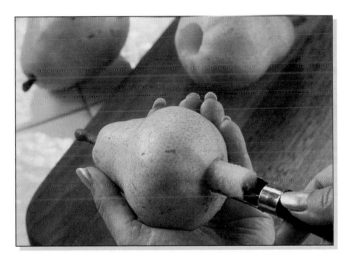

Use an apple corer to remove the cores from the pears and leave tops intact.

Low-calorie

Low-sodium

MANGO MOUSSE

Look for mangoes that have a healthy red blush and feel soft to the touch like a ripe tomato for this recipe. (See photo, right.)

2 ripe mangoes, pitted, peeled and chopped
1 envelope unflavored gelatin
2 tablespoons sugar
2 teaspoons lemon juice
1 8-ounce container frozen, light, whipped dessert topping, thawed
Mango or kiwi fruit slices (optional)

1. In a food processor bowl or blender container place mangoes. Cover and process or blend till smooth. Add water to make 2 cups puree. Transfer mango puree to a medium saucepan and bring to boiling.

2. In a large mixing bowl stir together the gelatin and sugar. Pour mango mixture over gelatin mixture and stir till gelatin dissolves. Stir in lemon juice. Cover and freeze for 45 to 60 minutes or till mixture mounds when dropped from a spoon, stirring occasionally. Beat the chilled mango mixture with an electric mixer for 2 to 3 minutes, or till thick and light. Fold whipped topping into mango mixture.

3. In each of 6 dessert dishes or parfait glasses spoon or pipe mango mousse. Cover and chill till set. Garnish with mango or kiwi fruit slices, if desired. Makes 6 servings.

Nutritional facts per serving: 149 calories, 5 g total fat (0 g saturated fat), 1 mg cholesterol, 31 mg sodium, 25 g carbohydrate, 2 g fiber, 1 g protein. **Daily values:** 31% vitamin A, 34% vitamin C, 2% calcium, 1% iron.

Thawing Ahead

Be prepared to top off a dessert! Get in the habit of placing frozen whipped dessert topping in your refrigerator as soon as you buy it. Or, put the topping in your refrigerator the night before you plan to use it so it will thaw overnight. If you don't need it, refreeze the topping.

Low-fat

Low-calorie

Low-sodium

WARM FRUIT COMPOTE

For a change of pace, you can substitute other dried fruits for the apricots and prunes.

12 dried apricot halves
1 cup pitted prunes
1 apple, chopped
1 cup halved seedless grapes
1 cup orange juice
1 inch cinnamon stick
1 tablespoon chopped
  crystallized ginger
1 tablespoon orange liqueur
  (optional)

1. In a medium saucepan combine apricots, prunes, apple, grapes, orange juice, cinnamon, and ginger. Bring to boiling; reduce heat. Simmer, covered, for 5 minutes.

2. Stir in liqueur, if desired. Serve warm or chilled. Makes 6 servings.

Nutritional facts per serving: 133 calories, 0 g total fat (0 g saturated fat), 0 mg cholesterol, 2 mg sodium, 34 g carbohydrate, 3 g fiber, 1 g protein. **Daily values:** 5% vitamin A, 41% vitamin C, 2% calcium, 6% iron.

Low-fat

Low-calorie

Low-sodium

STRAWBERRY-RHUBARB ICE

Layer in parfait glasses with sliced fruit for an especially refreshing dessert.

2 cups sliced rhubarb
¼ cup orange juice or water
¾ cup sugar
2 cups strawberries
2 teaspoons lemon juice

1. In a small saucepan combine rhubarb, orange juice, and sugar. Bring to boiling; reduce heat. Simmer, covered, for 5 minutes or till rhubarb is tender.

2. Meanwhile, in a food processor bowl or blender container place strawberries. Cover, and process or blend till smooth. Add rhubarb mixture and lemon juice. Cover, and process or blend till smooth. Turn mixture into a 9x9x2-inch baking pan. Freeze at least 4 hours or till slushy. Scrape mixture with a spoon into serving dishes. Makes 6 servings.

Nutritional facts per serving: 124 calories, 0 g total fat (0 g saturated fat), 0 mg cholesterol, 3 mg sodium, 31 g carbohydrate, 2 g fiber, 1 g protein. **Daily values:** 0% vitamin A, 62% vitamin C, 3% calcium, 2% iron.

FRUIT AND GRANOLA PARFAITS

Low-fat

Kids will enjoy helping arrange the layers of this dessert.

½ cup vanilla low-fat yogurt
¼ cup fat-free cream cheese
    product
1 tablespoon honey
¼ teaspoon ground cinnamon
2 kiwi fruit, peeled, halved
    lengthwise, and sliced
1 medium banana, sliced
1 medium orange, peeled, cut
    into fourths lengthwise, and
    sliced
1½ cups frozen red raspberries,
    thawed and drained
1 cup low-fat granola cereal

1. In a small mixing bowl beat yogurt, cream cheese, honey, and cinnamon with an electric mixer on medium speed till combined. Chill.

2. To assemble, stir together fruit in another small mixing bowl. Divide ⅓ of the fruit mixture among 4 parfait glasses or wine goblets. Spoon about 2 tablespoons each of cream cheese mixture and granola atop fruit. Repeat. Top with remaining ⅓ of fruit mixture. Serve immediately. Makes 4 servings.

Nutritional facts per serving: 243 calories, 3 g total fat (0 g saturated fat), 4 mg cholesterol, 164 mg sodium, 51 g carbohydrate, 3 g fiber, 8 g protein. **Daily values:** 14% vitamin A, 122% vitamin C, 16% calcium, 12% iron.

Low-fat

Low-calorie

Low-sodium

RICE PUDDING PARFAITS

A ribbon of fresh fruit brightens this fat-slashed rice pudding.

1⅓ cups water
⅔ cup skim milk
⅓ cup long grain rice
2 tablespoons sugar
1 beaten egg yolk
1 teaspoon vanilla
1 teaspoon finely shredded
    lemon peel
1 tablespoon lemon juice
1½ cups frozen, light, whipped
    dessert topping, thawed
2 cups chopped fresh fruit or
    one 16-ounce can fruit
    cocktail (juice-pack),
    drained
Cut-up fresh fruit (optional)

1. In a medium saucepan combine water, milk, and rice. Bring to boiling; reduce heat. Simmer, covered, for 20 minutes or till rice is tender, stirring frequently. Stir in sugar. Add 1 cup of the rice mixture to the egg yolk; stir to blend. Return all to saucepan. Cook and stir over low heat for 2 minutes. Remove from heat. Stir in vanilla, lemon peel, and lemon juice. Cool mixture thoroughly.

2. Fold whipped topping into cooled pudding. In 8 parfait glasses or dessert dishes, alternately layer pudding and fruit. Cover and chill for 2 to 6 hours. Garnish with additional fruit, if desired. Makes 8 servings.

Nutritional facts per serving: 108 calories, 3 g total fat (0 g saturated fat), 27 mg cholesterol, 22 mg sodium, 20 g carbohydrate, 1 g fiber, 2 g protein. **Daily values:** 7% vitamin A, 5% vitamin C, 3% calcium, 3% iron.

Low-fat

Low-calorie

AMBROSIA TERRINE

Perfect for a buffet or potluck (photo, left), this glistening dessert could be embellished with fresh fruit and whipped topping.

1 8-ounce can pineapple chunks
(juice-pack)
2 4-serving-size packages sugar-
free orange-flavored gelatin
2 cups boiling water
1½ cups cold water
1 banana, thinly sliced
1 11-ounce can mandarin
orange segments, drained
½ cup halved, seedless red
grapes
1 cup orange or lemon-flavored
fat-free yogurt
½ cup frozen, light, whipped
dessert topping, thawed
2 tablespoons toasted coconut
Fresh mint leaves (optional)

1. Drain pineapple, reserving juice. Set pineapple and juice aside.

2. In a large mixing bowl dissolve gelatin in boiling water. Stir in cold water and reserved pineapple juice. Measure 1 cup of gelatin and keep at room temperature. Chill remaining gelatin mixture till partially set (consistency of unbeaten egg whites).

3. Fold pineapple, banana, mandarin oranges, and grapes into partially set gelatin mixture. Pour ½ of the fruit mixture (about 2¼ cups) into a 9x5x3-inch loaf dish. Chill for 30 to 45 minutes or till almost firm (gelatin will appear firm, but be slightly sticky to the touch). Keep remaining fruit mixture at room temperature.

4. In a medium mixing bowl stir together yogurt and whipped topping. Stir in the 1 cup gelatin mixture. Carefully spoon yogurt mixture over first fruit layer. Cover and chill 30 minutes or till almost firm. Carefully spoon remaining fruit mixture over yogurt layer. Cover and chill for 4 to 24 hours or till firm. Unmold onto serving plate. Sprinkle with coconut and garnish with fresh mint leaves, if desired. Makes 10 servings.

Nutritional facts per serving: 83 calories, 1 g total fat (0 g saturated fat), 1 mg cholesterol, 85 mg sodium, 17 g carbohydrate, 0 g fiber, 2 g protein. **Daily values:** 0% vitamin A, 7% vitamin C, 3% calcium, 1% iron.

Low-fat

Low-calorie

Low-sodium

LIME MOUSSE AND BERRY PARFAITS

Fresh strawberries or raspberries are layered with a light yet creamy mousse for a delightful finale to almost any meal.

1 envelope unflavored gelatin
¼ cup sugar
1⅔ cup white grape juice
½ teaspoon finely shredded lime peel
¼ cup lime juice
½ teaspoon vanilla
1 cup frozen, light, whipped dessert topping, thawed
Green food coloring (optional)
2½ cups sliced strawberries and/or whole raspberries
Lime twists (optional)

1. In a medium saucepan combine gelatin and sugar. Stir in grape juice. Heat and stir till gelatin dissolves. Remove from heat and stir in lime peel, lime juice, and vanilla. Chill till mixture is the consistency of unbeaten egg whites.

2. Fold in whipped topping. Tint with green food coloring, if desired. In each of 8 parfait glasses or dessert dishes alternately spoon mousse with berries. Cover and chill for 2 or 3 hours or till set. Garnish with lime twists, if desired. Makes 8 servings.

Nutritional facts per serving: 102 calories, 2 g total fat (0 g saturated fat), 0 mg cholesterol, 12 mg sodium, 20 g carbohydrate, 1 g fiber, 1 g protein. **Daily values:** 2% vitamin A, 62% vitamin C, 1% calcium, 1% iron.

Spoon a little of the mousse into the bottom of a parfait glass. Add a layer of berries, then top with additional mousse to fill the glass.

Low-fat

Low-calorie

Low-sodium

MOCHA FLOATS

Try making these floats with flavored coffees, such as hazelnut, almond, or raspberry.

3 cups strong hot coffee

1⅓ cups vanilla-, chocolate-,
    or coffee-flavored light or
    low-fat ice cream

1 teaspoon grated semi-sweet
    chocolate

1. Pour coffee into 4 mugs.

2. Add ⅓ cup ice cream to each. Sprinkle chocolate over floats. Serve immediately. Makes 4 servings.

Nutritional facts per serving: 78 calories, 2 g total fat (1 g saturated fat), 7 mg cholesterol, 34 mg sodium, 14 g carbohydrate, 0 g fiber, 2 g protein. **Daily values:** 6% vitamin A, 0% vitamin C, 2% calcium, 1% iron.

Low-fat

Low-sodium

BANANA–PEACH YOGURT SHAKE

This fruity drink also tastes great as an eye-opening breakfast on the run.

2 large bananas, cut into
    chunks

2 cups frozen unsweetened
    peach slices

1 8-ounce carton plain fat-free
    yogurt

2 teaspoons sugar

1 teaspoon vanilla

½ to ¾ cup skim milk

1. In a blender container combine bananas, frozen peach slices, yogurt, sugar, vanilla, and ½ cup milk. Cover and blend till smooth.

2. Add additional milk if a thinner consistency is desired. Serve immediately. Makes four 6-ounce servings.

Nutritional facts per serving: 152 calories, 1 g total fat (0 g saturated fat), 1 mg cholesterol, 60 mg sodium, 33 g carbohydrate, 2 g fiber, 6 g protein. **Daily values:** 7% vitamin A, 20% vitamin C, 13% calcium, 2% iron.

**How We Figure Nutrition
Information**
With each recipe, we give important
nutrition information. The calorie count
of each serving and the amount, in
grams, of fat, saturated fat, cholesterol,
sodium, carbohydrate, fiber, and protein
will help you keep tabs on what you eat.
    You can check the levels of each
recipe serving for vitamin A, vitamin C,
calcium, and iron. These are noted in
percentages of the Daily Value. The
Daily Values are dietary standards
determined by the Food and Drug
Administration (FDA).

How We Analyze
• We omit optional ingredients from the
nutrition analysis.
• When ingredient choices appear in a
recipe (such as raspberries or
strawberries), we use the first one
mentioned for analysis.
• We use the first serving size listed
when a range is given.

What You Need
• Calories: about 2,000 • Cholesterol:
less than 300 milligrams • Total Fat: less
than 65 grams • Saturated Fat: less than
20 grams • Carbohydrates: about 300
grams • Dietary Fiber: 20 to 30 grams
• Sodium: less than 2,400 milligrams

METRIC COOKING HINTS

By making a few conversions, cooks in Australia, Canada, and the United Kingdom can use the recipes in Better Homes and Gardens® *Healthy Family Cookbook* with confidence. The charts on this page provide a guide for converting measurements from the U.S. customary system, which is used throughout this book, to the imperial and metric systems. There also is a conversion table for oven temperatures to accommodate the differences in oven calibrations.

Volume and Weight: Americans traditionally use cup measures for liquid and solid ingredients. The chart (top right) shows the approximate imperial and metric equivalents. If you are accustomed to weighing solid ingredients, here are some helpful approximate equivalents.
- 1 cup butter, caster sugar, or rice = 8 ounces = about 250 grams
- 1 cup flour = 4 ounces = about 125 grams
- 1 cup icing sugar = 5 ounces = about 150 grams

   Spoon measures are used for smaller amounts of ingredients. Although the size of the tablespoon varies slightly among countries, for practical purposes and for recipes in this book, a straight substitution is all that's necessary.

   Measurements made using cups or spoons should always be level, unless stated otherwise.

Product Differences: Most of the ingredients called for in the recipes in this book are available in English-speaking countries. However, some are known by different names. Here are some common American ingredients and their possible counterparts:
- Sugar is granulated or caster sugar.
- Powdered sugar is icing sugar.
- All-purpose flour is plain household flour or white flour. When self-rising flour is used in place of all-purpose flour in a recipe that calls for leavening, omit the leavening agent (baking soda or baking powder) and salt.
- Light corn syrup is golden syrup.
- Cornstarch is cornflour.
- Baking soda is bicarbonate of soda.
- Vanilla is vanilla essence.
- Green, red, or yellow sweet peppers are capsicums.
- Sultanas are golden raisins.

USEFUL EQUIVALENTS: U.S = AUST./BR.

⅛ teaspoon = 0.5 ml	⅔ cup = ½ cup = 5 fluid ounces = 150 ml
¼ teaspoon = 1 ml	¾ cup = ⅔ cup = 6 fluid ounces = 180 ml
½ teaspoon = 2 ml	1 cup = ¾ cup = 8 fluid ounces = 240 ml
1 teaspoon = 5 ml	1¼ cups = 1 cup
1 tablespoon = 1 tablespoon	2 cups = 1 pint
¼ cup = 2 tablespoons = 2 fluid ounces = 60 ml	1 quart = 1 litre
⅓ cup = ¼ cup = 3 fluid ounces = 90 ml	½ inch = 1.27 centimetres
½ cup = ⅓ cup = 4 fluid ounces = 120 ml	1 inch = 2.54 centimetres

BAKING PAN SIZES

American	Metric
8 x 1½-inch round baking pan	20 x 4-centimetre cake tin
9 x 1½-inch round baking pan	23 x 3.5-centimetre cake tin
11 x 7 x 1½-inch baking pan	28 x 18 x 4-centimetre baking tin
13 x 9 x 2-inch baking pan	30 x 20 x 3-centimetre baking tin
2-quart rectangular baking dish	30 x 20 x 3-centimetre baking tin
15 x 10 x 2-inch baking pan	30 x 25 x 2-centimetre baking tin (Swiss roll tin)
9-inch pie plate	22 x 4- or 23 x 4-centimetre pie plate
7- or 8-inch springform pan	18- or 20-centimetre springform or loose-bottom cake tin
9 x 5 x 3-inch loaf pan	23 x 13 x 7-centimetre or 2-pound narrow loaf tin or paté tin
1½-quart casserole	1.5-litre casserole
2-quart casserole	2-litre casserole

OVEN TEMPERATURE EQUIVALENTS

Fahrenheit Setting	Celsius Setting*	Gas Setting
300°F	150°C	Gas Mark 2 (slow)
325°F	160°C	Gas Mark 3 (moderately slow)
350°F	180°C	Gas Mark 4 (moderate)
375°F	190°C	Gas Mark 5 (moderately hot)
400°F	200°C	Gas Mark 6 (hot)
425°F	220°C	Gas Mark 7
450°F	230°C	Gas Mark 8 (very hot)
Broil		Grill

Electric and gas ovens may be calibrated using Celsius. However, increase the Celsius setting 10 to 20 degrees when cooking above 160°C with an electric oven. For convection or forced-air ovens (gas or electric), lower the temperature setting 10°C when cooking at all heat levels.